STRATEGIC PLANNING FOR
INFORMATION SYSTEMS

John Wiley
INFORMATION SYSTEMS SERIES

Editors

Richard Boland
Case Western Reserve University

Rudy Hirschheim
University of Houston

STRATEGIC PLANNING FOR INFORMATION SYSTEMS

John Ward

Cranfield School of Management

Pat Griffiths

DCE Information Management Consultancy

Paul Whitmore

Hong Kong Bank

John Wiley
INFORMATION SYSTEMS SERIES

JOHN WILEY & SONS
Chichester · New York · Brisbane · Toronto · Singapore

Reprinted September 1990
Reprinted August 1991
Reprinted March 1992
All rights reserved.

Other Wiley Editorial Offices

John Wiley & Sons, Inc., 605 Third Avenue,
New York, NY 10158-0012, USA

Jacaranda Wiley Ltd, G.P.O. Box 859, Brisbane,
Queensland 4001, Australia

John Wiley & Sons (Canada) Ltd, 22 Worcester Road,
Rexdale, Ontario M9W 1L1, Canada

John Wiley & Sons (SEA) Pte Ltd, 3 Jalan Pemimpin #05-04,
Block B, Union Industrial Building, Singapore 2057

Library of Congress Cataloging-in-Publication Data:

Ward, John
    Strategic planning for information systems / John Ward, Pat
Griffiths, Paul Whitmore.
        p.   cm.—(John Wiley information systems series)
    Includes bibliographical references.
    ISBN 0 471 92002 9
    1. Business—Data processing.   2. Management information systems.
3. Business—Communication systems.   4. Strategic planning.
I. Griffiths, P. M. (Pat M.)   II. Whitmore, Paul.   III. Title.
IV. Series.
HF5548.2.W319   1990   89-29726
658.4'038'011—dc20   CIP

British Library Cataloguing in Publication Data:

Ward, John
    Strategic planning for information systems.
    1. Business firms. Information systems. Management
    I. Title   II. Griffiths, Pat   III. Whitmore, Paul.
    658.4'038

    ISBN 0 471 92002 9

Phototypeset by Dobbie Typesetting Limited, Plymouth, Devon
Printed and Bound by Courier International Limited, East Kilbride

CONTENTS

SERIES FOREWORD

In order for all types of organisations to succeed, they need to be able to process data and use information effectively. This has become especially true in today's rapidly changing environment. In conducting their day-to-day operations, organisations use information for functions such as planning, controlling, organising, and decision making. Information, therefore, is unquestionably a critical resource in the operation of all organisations. Any means, mechanical or otherwise, which can help organisations process and manage information presents an opportunity they can ill afford to ignore.

The arrival of the computer and its use in data processing has been one of the most important organisational innovations in the past thirty years. The advent of computer-based data processing and information systems has led to organisations being able to cope with the vast quantities of information which they need to process and manage to survive. The field which has emerged to study this development is *information systems* (IS). It is a combination of two primary fields, computer science and management, with a host of supporting disciplines, e.g. psychology, sociology, statistics, political science, economics, philosophy, and mathematics. IS is concerned not only with the development of new information technologies but also with questions such as: how they can best be applied, how they should be managed, and what their wider implications are.

Partly because of the dynamic world in which we live (and the concomitant need to process more information), and partly because of the dramatic recent developments in information technology, e.g. personal computers, fourth-generation languages, relational databases, knowledge-based systems, and office automation, the relevance and importance of the field of information systems, and office automation, the relevance and importance of the field of information systems has become apparent. End users, who previously had little potential of becoming seriously involved and knowledgeable in information technology and systems, are now much more aware of and interested in the new technology. Individuals working in today's and tomorrow's organisations will be expected to have some understanding of and the ability to use the rapidly developing information technologies and systems. The dramatic increase in the availability and use of information technology, however, raises fundamental questions on the guiding of technological innovation, measuring organisational and managerial productivity, augmenting human intelligence, ensuring data integrity, and establishing strategic advantage. The expanded use of information systems also raises major challenges to the traditional forms of administration and authority, the right to privacy, the nature and form of work, and the limits of calculative rationality in modern organisations and society.

The Wiley Series on Information Systems has emerged to address these questions and challenges. It hopes to stimulate thought and discussion on the key role information systems play in the functioning of organisations and society, and how their role is likely to change in the future. This historical or evolutionary theme of the Series is important because considerable insight can be gained by attempting to understand the past. The Series will attempt to integrate both description—what has been done—with prescription—how best to develop and implement information systems.

The descriptive and historical aspect is considered vital because information systems of the past have not necessarily met with the success that was envisaged. Numerous writers postulate that a high proportion of systems are failures in one sense or another. Given their high cost of development and their importance to the day-to-day running of organisations, this situation must surely be unacceptable. Research into IS failure has concluded that the primary cause of failure is the lack of consideration given to the social and behavioural dimensions of IS. Far too much emphasis has been placed on their technical side. The result has been something of a shift in emphasis from a strictly technical conception of IS to one where it is recognised that information systems have behavioural consequences. But even this misses the mark. A growing number of researchers suggest that information systems are more appropriately conceived as social systems which rely, to a greater and greater extent, on new technology for their operation. It is this social orientation which is lacking in much of what is written about IS. The current volume, *Strategic Planning for Information Systems*, tackles a particularly thorny area of IS that of its planning. The authors attempt to integrate theory with practice, and in doing so, provide a thoughtful and practical treatment of the strategic nature of IS.

The Series seeks to promote a forum for the serious discussion of IS. Although the primary perspective is a more social and behavioural one, alternative perspectives will also be included. This is based on the belief that no one perspective can be totally complete; added insight is possible through the adoption of multiple views. Relevant areas to be addressed in the Series include (but are not limited to): the theoretical development of information systems, their practical application, the foundations and evolution of information systems, and IS innovation. Subjects such as systems design, systems analysis methodologies, information systems planning and management, office automation, project management, decision support systems, end-user computing, and information systems and society are key concerns of the Series.

Rudy Hirschheim
Richard Boland

PREFACE

During the 1980s much was said and written about the need for organisations to take a strategic approach to managing investments in information systems and technology (IS/IT). There appear to be two main reasons for this.

First, many of the investments in the past failed to deliver anticipated business benefits, and many organisations became concerned that IS/IT expenditure did not produce 'value for money', or any direct contribution to achieving business objectives. Second, the use of IS/IT by a number of innovative organisations to gain a significant competitive advantage has shown that the use of IS/IT can be of strategic importance. In both cases IS/IT has become a critical business issue—to ensure it is being deployed to gain maximum benefit for the organisation.

A lack of a coherent strategy for IS investment can produce a number of problems; for example:

- Business opportunities are missed, the business may even be disadvantaged by the IS/IT developments of others. Systems and technology investments do not support the business objectives and may even become a constraint to business development.
- Lack of integration of systems and ineffective data management produces duplication of effort, inaccuracy, delay and inadequate information for managing the business.
- Priorities are not based on business needs, resource levels are not optimal, project plans are constantly changed. Business performance is not improved, costs are high, solutions are of poor quality and IS/IT productivity is low.
- Technology strategy is incoherent, incompatible options are selected and large sums of money are wasted attempting to fit things together retrospectively.
- Lack of understanding and agreed direction between users, senior management and the IS/IT specialists leads to conflict, inappropriate solutions and a misuse of resources.

Some, or all of these can occur when the organisation does not develop the means to plan IS/IT strategically, i.e. driven by the business needs for the long-term benefit of the organisation.

Much of the failure of IS/IT to deliver consistent benefits is due to the short-term business focus and the delegation of planning to the IS/IT specialists. Over the long term any organisation will get the system it deserves, according to the approach adopted to the use and management of IS/IT.

Historically most planning approaches have been bottom-up, piecemeal, driven by IS/IT issues rather than the business demand for information and systems.

Whilst it is easy to state that IS/IT must be managed more strategically, it is not obvious how that can be achieved, given the rapidly changing nature of business and the available technology. Many organisations have spent large sums, usually with consultants, to obtain a 'strategy', only to find it has marginal, short-term value, and can be out of date before the ink is dry. Others try to develop their own strategic plans but find that nothing in practice changes, often because the IS/IT professionals, by default, dominate the process.

Clearly a strategic IS/IT plan is merely one component of the business plan and as such must be integrated with that plan. That implies that strategic IS/IT planning must become an integral part of the business planning process. The IS/IT strategy must be understood by the business management and owned by them if it is to be implemented effectively.

It is against that background that this book considers how Strategic Planning for Information Systems can be brought about and then sustained. The means proposed are intended to provide a practical approach, expressed in primarily business language. It can be adopted jointly by senior management, line managers and IS/IT professionals to apply their various knowledge and skills most effectively to identifying what needs to be done and how best to do it.

How to develop IS/IT strategic plans cannot be prescribed, but a structured approach or framework can be developed within which a variety of tools and techniques can be used to devise the strategy and then update and monitor progress. Developing a strategy is not a once off exercise, nor can its need for review be predicted—it must be constantly improved and reviewed as achievements are made, options alter or business issues change. Defining a strategy for any organisation is a creative process, which can be assisted by the use of tools, techniques and models to identify and select the most appropriate options.

Any strategy must clearly identify 'where the organisation wants to be' in the future, and also assess accurately 'where it is now' in order to decide 'how best to get there' given the alternative routes and resources available. The first part of the book considers how the organisation can assess where it is with regard to IS/IT, in the context of the current business environment, and what the business wants to achieve in the future. In most organisations IS/IT has a history which, for better or worse, will influence its potential for the future. That often chequered history has to be viewed from a strategic perspective—how does it constrain or facilitate further development? One key aspect of any strategy is to obtain the maximum benefit from past investments, build on existing strengths and overcome current weaknesses. This implies achieving an objective, consensus view of the current situation before defining new requirements, which given the current capability may not be achievable.

At the same time the business situation, the environment in which the organisation exists, the competitive pressures and the future strategy must be understood and perhaps clarified to enable the strategic planning process to be focused on areas of criticality for the future.

The short-term business objectives and organisational issues must be interpreted and analysed and supplemented by creative thinking, so that the IS/IT strategy not only supports the business strategy but also enhances it where that is possible. The resulting demands established become a 'portfolio of systems requirements' which will evolve over time. A core concept of the book is the use of a portfolio management approach, derived from business ideas, to enable the management to ensure that each investment is managed according to its expected contribution.

The second half of the book considers how this portfolio of requirements and demands can be best satisfied in terms of 'supply' management strategies which can bring together the means by which the plans are to be achieved. It considers the various ways in which the IS/IT assets, resources and skills can be developed most appropriately to satisfy the variety of demands. This must take account of the business and organisation structure in order to establish the appropriate balance between centralised and decentralised roles and responsibilities. The aim is to produce a relevant set of policies and a partnership between business people and IS/IT specialists cooperating to achieve common goals.

Whilst the book concentrates on the development of strategic planning mechanisms to meet the needs of most organisations today, the last chapter looks to the future implications for IS/IT strategic planning. The potential and effects of IS/IT on any business, its strategy and even its organisation have been steadily increasing over the last 20 years and this is not likely to abate in the future. It has been suggested that organisations will be designed round their information systems, that industry structures will be radically altered and managers will fulfil quite different roles in the future. The implications of these ideas for IS/IT strategy are considered.

The overall purpose of the book is to demonstrate that Strategic Planning for Information Systems is both essential and feasible. It is not a once off process—the organisation must establish a way of continuing to manage IS/IT strategically as a part of the business development process. The approaches described in this book are intended to enable that to be done.

ACKNOWLEDGEMENTS

This book could not have been written without the help and support of a number of people.

At DCE, the encouragement and time made available to Pat by Mike Broddle enabled the writing to be completed. Others at DCE, who have shared their experience and ideas on strategic IS/IT planning, contributed to the richness of the content; in particular Rosemary Rock-Evans, Brian Watson, Danesh Omrani and Simon Holloway have allowed their recent work to be quoted.

The many people who have attended Developing Information Systems Strategies courses and workshops at Cranfield have indirectly contributed a wealth of practical experience to the contents. By using the ideas and techniques they have demonstrated the relevance and value of the approaches described. In particular David Lambert and John Kwok have provided valued insights over an extended period, which have proved that the strategic planning of IS is both advantageous and feasible.

The book could not have been produced without the expert preparation of the original text and diagrams, most of which was done by Brigitte Edwards.

At a personal level, without the support, patience and understanding of our families this book would not have been completed. So finally a special thank you to: Rachel, Jeremy and David Griffiths, and Carol, Ellen, Anna and John Ward.

Chapter 1

THE EVOLVING ROLE OF INFORMATION SYSTEMS AND TECHNOLOGY IN ORGANISATIONS — A STRATEGIC PERSPECTIVE

INTRODUCTION

It is important to understand how the role of technology based information systems has evolved, in order to be able to manage information systems and information technology (IS/IT) more effectively in the future.

Whilst most organisations want to develop a more 'strategic' approach to managing IS/IT in the future, they have probably achieved their current situation through what can politely be described as various short-term 'tactics'. Many organisations would no doubt like to rethink their strategy without having to cope with the results of a less than strategic approach to IS/IT in the past. This is rarely possible, neither is it necessarily advisable—there is no real reason to expect more success in the future than the past unless ability and knowledge have increased in the meantime! Learning from experience—the successes and failures of the past—is one of the most important aspects of strategic management.

However, no one organisation is likely to have been exposed to the whole gamut of IS/IT experiences and neither is it likely that what has been experienced can always be evaluated objectively as a basis for future management.

This chapter provides such an appraisal of the general evolution of IS/IT in major organisations, against which any organisation can chart its progress and from which valuable lessons can be learned for future management. The appraisal examines IS/IT evolution from a number of viewpoints, using a number of models, some of which are used later in the book, when considering the particular approaches required in strategic planning for information systems and technology.

A number of strategically important forces affect the pace and effectiveness of progress in using IS/IT. The importance or weighting of each factor varies over time and also will vary from one organisation to another. These factors include:

- the capabilities of the technology,
- the economics of using the technology,
- the applications which are feasible,

1

- the skills and abilities available to develop the applications,
- the pressures on the particular organisation or its industry to improve performance,
- the ability of the organisation to make appropriate judgements about the deployment of IS/IT and the associated resources.

This list is not meant to be exhaustive and could be expressed in other terms—but it is in a deliberate sequence of increasing 'stress', as the complexity and criticality of the management decision-making process becomes more strategic.

Most assessments of IS/IT evolution tend to focus on one or two aspects of its development—organisational, applications, management of technology, planning, etc.—but here these various views will be brought together, as far as possible.

EARLY VIEWS AND MODELS OF IS/IT IN ORGANISATIONS

The use of computers in business started in the early 1950s but really only became significant in the mid to late 1960s with the development of multi-purpose 'mainframe computers'. Major increases in processing speed, cheaper memory and more useful magnetic disc and tape storage, plus better programming languages made 'batch' data processing a viable option for many applications in many organisations.

During the 1970s mini-computers of increasing power and sophistication were used for a variety of applications, often not feasible or economic in a mainframe environment. However, the views developed of the role of information systems and their past and expected future evolution were based strongly on a centralised, integrated concept derived from the mainframe origins.

The most well known of these evolutionary models was developed by Gibson and Nolan (1974) and Nolan (1979) during the 1970s. This model in turn used a hierarchical application portfolio model described by Anthony (1965). Anthony's model defined a structure for information systems in an organisation based on a stratification of management activity into:

- strategic planning,
- management control,
- operational control.

Typical systems developed to support this model are shown in Figure 1.1.

Based on analyses of the actual use of IS/IT in a number of large US organisations Nolan and Gibson proposed an evolutionary model containing initially four 'stages of growth'. Later two further stages were added by Nolan. This six-stage model is summarised in Box 1.1

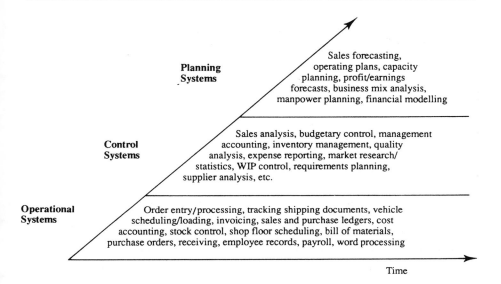

FIGURE 1.1 Typical planning, control and operational systems. A traditional hierarchical application portfolio model based on Anthony's structuring of management activities

The analysis involved considered six aspects or benchmarks of IS/IT and its management in the organisations studied. These were:

(a) the rate of expenditure,
(b) the technological configuration, e.g. batch/on-line/database,
(c) the applications portfolio (as per Anthony's model),
(d) the DP organisation,
(e) DP planning and control approaches,
(f) user awareness characteristics.

The validity and usefulness of the six-stage model has been explored by a number of researchers since 1979 when it was published.

Drury (1983) found that in practice the benchmarks did not map consistently on to the stages as suggested by the original model—in particular in the later stages the complexity of the real world is not reflected in the simplicity of the model. He concluded that—'Categorising of DP from initiation to maturity may no longer be feasible with the diffusion of new technologies and functions being introduced'.

However, he accepts that individual benchmarks can be usefully adopted in assessing how effectively an organisation is coping with the increasing importance of IS/IT.

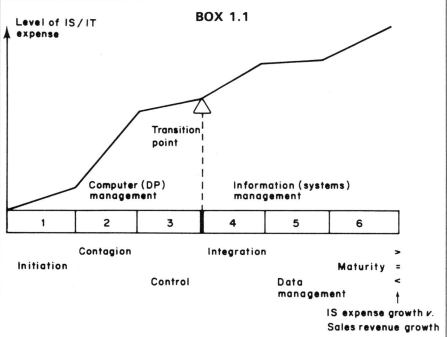

Stages of evolution of IS/IT in relation to expenditure (reprinted by permission of *Harvard Business Review*. An exhibit from 'Managing the crises in data processing', by R. Nolan (March–April 1979). Copyright © 1979 by the President and Fellows of Harvard College; all rights reserved)

1. *Initiation*—batch processing to automate clerical operations to achieve cost reduction —purely operational systems focus—lack of management interest.
2. *Contagion*—rapid growth as users demand more applications based on high expectations of benefits—move to on-line systems—high rate of expense as DP tries to satisfy all user demands. Little control if any, except a drive to centralise in order to control.
3. *Control*—in response to management concern about cost, systems projects are expected to show a return, plans are produced and methodologies/ standards enforced. Often produces a backlog of applications and dissatisfied users.
4. *Integration*—considerable expenditure on integrating (via database) existing systems. User accountability for systems established and DP provides a service to users not just solutions to problems.
5. *Data administration*—information requirements rather than processing drive the applications portfolio and information is shared within the organisation. Database capability is exploited as users understand the value of the information.
6. *Maturity*—the planning and development of IS/IT in the organisation is closely co-ordinated with business development.

King and Kraemer (1984) believe that the model has several weaknesses. In particular, the empirical evidence for the stages is inconsistent and many of the assumptions of the model are too simplistic to be useful. But they equally point out that many aspects of the model ring true to practitioners and researchers and it has had a considerable influence on IS management thinking since the 1970s. Its weakness—its simplicity—may be the key to its popularity! It does suggest an evolutionary approach during which different forces control the destiny of IS/IT in an organisation and during which it is possible to succeed and fail with IS/IT for understandable reasons.

More significantly perhaps, Wiseman in his book *Strategy and Computers* (1985) suggests that the influential combination of the Anthony three-tier structural approach to defining organisational systems and the 'Nolan' stage model inhibited the strategic use of IS/IT until relatively recently. He states that 'up to 1983 at least, Nolan's general purpose approach to information systems (based in part on the Anthony model) is clearly incomplete, for it offers no guidelines for identifying or explaining strategic information systems opportunities'.

In summary, a model of the evolving role of IS/IT in organisations is of value. The 'Nolan' model is a useful starting point but is not altogether satisfactory. Equally, it only really described events up to the mid-seventies, since when much has changed.

One problem perhaps with the 'Nolan' model is its details of four or six stages, and the undue emphasis, placed by others since, on the 'rate of expenditure' associated with each stage—should it be more or less? increasing or decreasing? etc. Focusing attention on the trees, often loses sight of the wood! Viewed from a more distant perspective, the six stages of the model divide into two larger 'eras' separated by a transition point between three and four (Control and Integration). It can be summarised as a transition from *Computer (DP) Management* to *Information (Systems) Management* during which major changes in who manages what for whom and how, occur. In essence it is a fundamental change in how IS/IT resources are to be managed, and how the role of IS/IT in the organisation is to be evaluated.

This major transition—change of organisational attitude and behaviour with regard to 'computing'—is often the biggest step forward since the first computer was installed. The relationships involved and the transition required are depicted in Figure 1.2.

During the early stages of computerisation the preoccupation is with managing the activities—operations, programming, data collection, etc. Later an organisation is established which can cope with a variety of types of application, over an extended life cycle during which the technology will change significantly. The 'department' is managed as a co-ordinated set of resources which are planned to meet expected future requirements.

While this was evolving, relationships with users will have developed: the effectiveness of any relationship being determined by success to date and the users' awareness of the role computers could play—not because of business priorities,

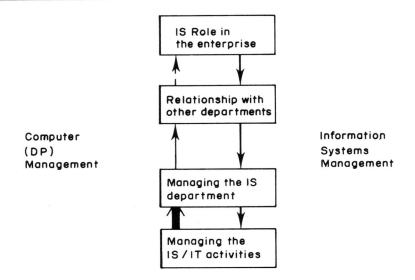

Computer
(DP)
Management

Information
Systems
Management

FIGURE 1.2 Transition between computer and information management: relationships and emphases. (Source: Partly derived from EDP Analyser, 'How the management job is changing', June 1984, Vol. 22, No 6)

but due to the ease with which computers can be applied. Accounting is likely to be far more advanced in computer use than marketing and if DP reports to Finance then that relationship is likely to be very effective—but possibly at the expense of relationships with more business critical parts of the enterprise. Occasionally the role of IS/IT in the organisation may be reviewed but the focus on current issues and problems will prevent an overall picture being seen.

Up to this point the main driving force has been managing computer resources and activities with the effort applied in proportion to the technical and application difficulties, without much regard for the value to the business of the applications.

To achieve effective information management a new top down approach is required—a 'strategy' for the management of IS/IT, associated activities and resources throughout the organisation. This should be based on a defined role for IS in the enterprise—but that in turn will depend on the role of IS in relation to the outside world, as will be discussed later.

Research by Hirschheim *et al.* (1988) supports the rationale of this transition, based on studying the evolving issues associated with IS/IT management in organisations. They describe it in terms of a three-stage model. The stages are described as:

Delivery IS issues are mainly internal—improving the ability to deliver and support the systems and technology. Achieving top management credibility as a valuable function is a prime objective. This means improving delivery performance not necessarily providing users with what they really need.

Re-orientation Establishing good relationships with the main business functions, supporting business demands through the provision of a variety of services as computing capability spreads through the business. The issues focus is extended to the 'department' and a key objective is to provide a valued service to all business functional management. Different areas will benefit differently without regard to business importance.

Re-organisation The high level of awareness created both 'locally' in the business area and 'centrally' in senior management creates the need for a reorganisation of responsibilities designed to achieve integration of the IS investment with business strategy and across business functions. A key objective becomes the best way of satisfying each of the differing business needs through a coalition of responsibilities for managing information and systems.

The last stage equates to the top down, strategic view whilst the first two describe the 'climb' to the position of considering the 'role in the enterprise'.

Application Portfolio Models—up to 1980

The concept of the 'Anthony' hierarchical application portfolio was introduced above (see Figure 1.1). The evolutionary models used so far have considered the management of DP during the 1960s and 1970s and essentially from the inside—the development of DP/IS management rather than exploitation of DP/IS in the enterprise. During the 1970s the types of application and how they could be developed changed and made the application model used as the basis of evolutionary analysis potentially obsolete.

Starting from the Anthony model of planning, control and operational systems, Nolan and Gibson showed how the applications developed, during the evolution of DP, spread up the hierarchy slowly. Perhaps more importantly, it spread at different rates in different parts of the organisation, accounting functions were often in the vanguard of progress! These differential rates of evolution in different areas constrained the potential for integration of control and planning systems which by their nature are cross-functional. However, the general progress was upward from the operational base of the company.

Normally a firm foundation of operational systems is built first, function by function. On this foundation, control systems are introduced by accumulating operational information and analysing it to improve cross-functional co-ordination and control. Finally the portfolio is completed by transforming the information so that planning systems can be developed to help senior management define the future of the business. The control and planning systems may force improvements to be made lower down the portfolio structure, in order to realign information and its processing for planning and control purposes.

By the mid-1970s ways of developing successful operational systems, either centrally or on distributed minis were well established. Control systems, usually centralised, were generally well understood and especially in financial areas could be linked to the required operational data if only in a 'read only' mode. However, little progress had been made on planning systems beyond crude forecasting.

Traditional, mainly operational and control, systems were essentially of two types:

● monitoring—transaction handling and control,
● exception—triggered reporting and/or action.

Although these provide management with information they are primarily process based depending for success on pre-definition and consistency of requirement— i.e. data-processing systems which are primarily operational in nature, but may enable some control and planning.

In the early 1980s, the micro-computer and a new set of software tools enabled 'end-user computing' to take off. At about the same time 'office automation' systems provided new means of processing and communicating information.

These new extensions of IS/IT enabled two new functions to be added to the repertoire:

● enquiry—flexible access initiated by user request,
● analysis—decision support, flexible processing.

Here the application needs are not pre-definable, and often the applications are rapidly changed during a short useful life. They therefore tend to be characteristic of some control and planning systems, rather than operational systems. These applications essentially provide information to managers and professionals who require it and the ability to process/transform it to satisfy their information requirements.

The main differences between these types of applications, named Data Processing and Management Information Systems after their primary objectives, are detailed in Table 1.1.

Although these have different characteristics they do to a large extent share a common information base and need to communicate—there is an obvious danger of total separation. Therefore, in addition to managing two different types of application it became critical that the organisation effectively organised its overall information resource.

It can be concluded that from the 1960s to the early 1980s IS/IT and its deployment in organisations passed through a major transition which linked two eras.

TABLE 1.1

	Operational and control systems (Data Processing)	Control and planning systems (Management Information Systems)
Objectives	Efficient transaction handling and effective resource control	Effective problem resolution and support for decision making
Life-cycles	3–12 years depending on rate of change	From hours to months and occasionally recurring
Information time frame	Recent history, current and short-term future	Consolidated history, current and extended future
Information sources	Internal plus external transactions	Internal plus external 'research' data
Logical processes	Strictly algorithmic	Probabilistic and 'fuzzy'
Users	Operators, clerical staff and first line supervisors	Professionals and middle to senior managers
Technologies	Mainframe/mini controlled processing at work stations	Local processing linked to information resources

These first two eras can be summarised as

1. Data processing from the 1960s onwards—*the DP era* and
2. Management information systems from the 1970s onwards—*the MIS era.*

Obviously from this definition the two eras overlap—DP continuing to mature as MIS emerges and grows. As will be discussed later, the 1980s has seen the beginning of a third era which can be called the 'strategic information systems' era. This book will focus considerable attention on the applications and implications of the third era, but it also must be remembered that

(a) Many organisations have yet to emerge successfully from the problems of the first two eras.
(b) A considerable part of future investment will be in data processing and management information systems and these investments must be part of any strategic plan.
(c) Much can be learned from the experiences gained in the first two eras to improve the chances of success in the third era, when the potential prizes are greater, but the penalties for failure more severe!
(d) Everyone has to live with the legacy—asset or liability—of the applications previously developed, and often developed for reasons and using methods relevant to the past.

The implications for the organisation are that a complex inheritance must be appropriately supported, improved and replaced, while current opportunities are exploited and future possibilities explored.

THE THREE-ERA MODEL

Although it is tempting to simplify thirty years of often haphazard, uncertain progress with the benefit of hindsight into three, albeit overlapping eras, it must be remembered that it is never that simple. A 'three-era model' is being proposed from which a number of insights can be drawn which help in planning or developing strategies for the future. In fact, how the planning of IS/IT has evolved over that time will be considered at the end of the chapter.

Whilst a simple three-era model is easy to criticise as being over-simplistic it has proved popular with a number of IS/IT theorists and researchers and hence many useful analyses are available from which a pattern of conclusions can be drawn.

Before assessing the legacy from the first two eras and identifying the key emerging issues of the third era it is worth just clarifying the fundamental differences and interdependencies of the three eras.

The prime objective of using IS/IT in the eras differs.

1. *Data processing* to improve operational efficiency by automating information based processes.
2. *Management information systems* to increase management effectiveness by satisfying their information requirements.
3. *Strategic information systems* to improve competitiveness by changing the nature or conduct of business.

The objectives of DP and MIS are strictly speaking a subset of the SIS objective—to improve competitiveness. But this tends to be achieved indirectly by using IS/IT to improve current business practices. Whilst the SIS objective is more immediately related to the business, success in achieving the DP and MIS objectives can contribute considerably to business success. Much remains to be achieved against the first two objectives and further improvements are always possible as IT capabilities are enhanced and the cost reduces.

Wiseman (1985) has perhaps most succinctly represented both the relationship of the three eras and the evolving application portfolio and the application objectives. Figure 1.3 demonstrates those relationships in the terms used above.

The key points are that:

(a) Just as good MIS systems rely on good operational DP systems for accurate, timely information, strategic information systems (such as those linking the

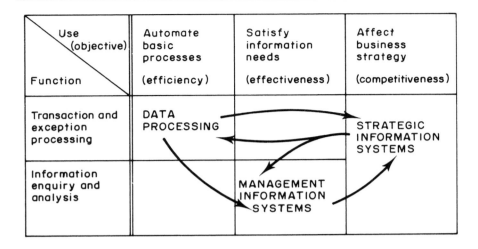

Use (objective) / Function	Automate basic processes (efficiency)	Satisfy information needs (effectiveness)	Affect business strategy (competitiveness)
Transaction and exception processing	DATA PROCESSING		STRATEGIC INFORMATION SYSTEMS
Information enquiry and analysis		MANAGEMENT INFORMATION SYSTEMS	

FIGURE 1.3 Extended application portfolio model (after C. Wiseman, Strategy and Computers (Dow Jones–Irwin, 1985) and reproduced with permission). Note: the Wiseman nomenclature for the 'eras' is different. He uses: 1. Management information systems = data processing (DP); 2. Management support systems = management information systems (MIS); 3. Strategic information systems—same. The reason this book has used DP and MIS is to emphasise the prime objective—process improvement—information provision, of the different types of system

company to its customers) rely on good DP or MIS systems for appropriate information provisioning or dependent processing. It is similar to the need for good foundations for a skyscraper—built on a base of sand it may not last long!

(b) Strategic information systems (SIS) are not intrinsically different applications—the functions are the same as for DP or MIS applications—it is their impact on the business that is different.

(c) The strategic applications may put considerable stress on the DP and MIS applications which were developed for a less stressful environment—they may need to be redeveloped not because of intrinsic shortcomings but because they inhibit the benefits to be gained from the SIS.

It is perhaps worth commenting on two facets of this analysis briefly. Firstly, the 'functions' have not been extended as yet, but with the arrival of knowledge-based systems, plus the potential offered by image processing, further functions may prove possible. Those functions in essence would rely on the 'machine' to make informed judgements and use its 'intelligence' to identify situations requiring attention. Expert systems already do this in a large number of specialised fields

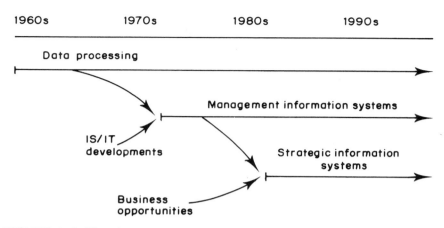

FIGURE 1.4 *The three-era model: relationships over time*

and are entering the business IS domain steadily—mainly from specialist areas. But perhaps 'expertise' in the systems controlling stock market transactions in October 1987 might have prevented the helter-skelter spiral of Black Monday!

Second, it must be emphasised that 'eras' is not perhaps the ideal word—suggesting as it does a sequential relationship. The DP era is still with us, the ever improving economics enabling the technology to be applied to extend the automation of processes. So too with MIS. A combination of improved economics and extended facilities (such as graphics) enabling the analysis and presentation of information to be made more effective.

One reason why 'strategy' has become such a popular term in the 1980s is the need to manage a complex situation—a situation which did not exist until the 1980s in most organisations. Figure 1.4 shows in simple terms this increasing requirement for better, more strategic planning.

THE DP AND MIS ERAS—THE LESSONS FOR THE FUTURE

There have been essentially three parallel threads of evolution which have enabled more extensive, and better DP systems to be developed:

1. *Hardware*—reducing cost and size, improving reliability and connectability, enabling the system to be installed closer to the business problem.
2. *Software*—more comprehensive and flexible operating software and improved languages enabling more to be produced, more quickly, with greater correctness, with less experience. Plus the extended availability of application packages.
3. *Methodology*—ways of organising and carrying out the multiplicity of tasks, in a more co-ordinated, better synchronised and more efficient way to enable ever more complex systems to be implemented and large projects managed successfully.

But inevitably, 'the data processing' approach is problem/task/process focused to ensure that the 'automation' through IS/IT of those tasks achieves the required benefits—the required return on investment. The relationship to business strategic planning is similar to that of installing a new widget-making machine which produces twice as many in half the time, uses half the energy, needs less operators and produces a better yield from the material—i.e. enabling performance improvements. Similarly, automation of a warehouse improves efficiency and can improve inventory management—but does not fundamentally alter the business process, it is a more effective 'implementation' to support the achievement of strategic aims.

Automation through DP can, however, produce a competitive advantage. For example, the Aalsmeer Flower Auction (*Verenigde Bloemenveilingen Aalsmeer*) in Holland, computerised the auction clocks in the 1970s and linked the auction transactions to the time critical administration and distribution systems. The speed and integrity of the systems enabled the auction to handle ever increasing volumes to the satisfaction of both the flower growers and buyers—increasing the auction's market and market share.

The problems of producing data-processing systems are generally well known, if not fully resolved, in most organisations. Consequently, they have been addressed most comprehensively. Even in the future perhaps more than 50% of all IS/IT investments will be about improving efficiency—'data processing' in their philosophy. Wiseman (1985) refers to the 'hybrid nature' of many major systems investments. He says that even so-called competitive/strategic systems such as American Airlines' SABRE system have a very large 'data-processing' component as well as a strategic importance to the organisation. A 'point of sale' system in retailing includes a large data-processing component—data capture, verification, storage, processing, transmission—as well as providing important information which may be employed to improve competitiveness.

As more 'data' became stored in computer systems, managers realised that using the information could increase the effectiveness of control and planning, and decision making in their departments. Database software seemed to provide the means to give the necessary flexible access to information via on-line enquiry and analysis systems. This required managers to think about the information they used and how they used it. However, managers do not use data in predefinable, structured ways. Neither do managers rely solely on 'hard facts' in their decision making. The methods used successfully to construct large volume, structured DP systems did not work given the vagueness of the requirements. Neither could the cost involved be easily justified given the intangible nature of the benefits and the potentially short life of the systems. Return on investment calculations did not look as attractive for MIS as they did for DP—even though both could be based on ever-reducing hardware costs.

The legacy of process based DP applications, each optimised in its construction to maximise project return on investment, was at best a fragmented data resource, at worst a chaotic mess of data with little or no integrity. Database disciplines required a heavy user involvement in data definition—a tedious and difficult task. Frustration developed as large restructuring projects were undertaken to reorganise data and applications into integrated data based systems to enable MIS to be developed. Even when this was complete the data bases often proved inflexible—the users did not get the information in the way they needed it. IS specialists spent inordinate amounts of time on data analysis and design and then still had to write mundane retrieval systems. The 'response' to the problem by IS/IT suppliers was to introduce new languages—4GLs—which were easy to use on well defined data, relational databases to overcome the constraint of rigid structures and also personal computers to free the user from the tangled web of IS development. In particular, the personal computer brought with it the 'spreadsheet' which enabled considerable analytical scope without the need for programming.

Most IS departments eventually identified the need for new user support services. A manifestation of this was the 'information centre', by whatever name— a new service whose prime purpose was to support and encourage, but minimise the risks of, end-user computing. New relationships were established with users who had previously been on the verge of total rebellion. Many IS departments took on board the new software and used it to improve the responsiveness and productivity of more conventional IS development. Agreement was reached on user and IS roles—which 'systems' aspects were to be entrusted to users and which needed the disciplines already developed. Appropriate organisational policies, rather than DP methodologies could be established.

In some organisations, however, rifts between users and IT professionals developed, causing active antagonism and consequent failure to resolve the issues of the MIS era. Often the corporate information resource instead of being integrated via the database approach became fragmented as separate users regained control of their data. Frequently the MIS applications became divorced from the data processing systems—often resulting in, at best, unsynchronised and, at worst, totally different data being used to operate the business and manage it!

Into this arena in the early 1980s was thrust the newly christened concept of 'office automation'—an unfortunate misnomer which sent shivers of apprehension through those whose world was apparently about to be automated and offered a new opportunity for conflict between the IT professionals and user management!

The net result was that more forms of information, not just data but certainly text and potentially images and voice could be channelled through the same technology. In some cases this would enable more efficient information processing and in others provide better ways of communicating and presenting management information—providing a more comprehensive matching of technology to a greater proportion of typical managers' tasks.

Unfortunately, two factors served to confuse the progress in evolutionary terms even the best managed companies were achieving.

1. How was the large new investment required in hardware and software—many hundreds of workstations, networking costs and multiple copies of software packages—to be justified? This refocused management's attention on *technology* rather than its use—the much quoted word 'convergence' distracted management from a need to ensure their systems and information were appropriate and effective before throwing technology at the problem. Those organisations who can claim success from 'office automation' are those who applied the lessons learned in successful DP and MIS investments to the extension of the technology use. The rationale for investment had reverted in many cases from 'business pull' to 'technology push' and the management style often regressed accordingly.
2. How should the new applications and supporting technology be managed and even more critically who should be responsible? Should the role of the IS departments be extended or should such systems be the responsibility of users? Were the new office systems an extension to a department level of personal computing or an integral part of the organisation's information processing ability and resources? How did the management of personal computing and office systems relate?

At a point when many organisations were resolving the MIS issues, success was delayed by the complication of office systems—but seeing them as an extended role of technology based on already established principles of processing and information management offered the greatest chance of success.

As the new 'strategic' potential of IS/IT began to be appreciated in the early 1980s most organisations were still wrestling with the problems of rapidly developing and concurrent DP and MIS applications based on a fast evolving technology. Policies, planning, organisation structures and processes were established to control and co-ordinate the increasingly diverse and complex requirements.

Good practice in the planning and management of DP and MIS was hard won after a long fight! The extended business role now envisaged did not undo that requirement—much of the future investment would be of a 'traditional' nature and would produce more benefits if well planned and managed. DP and MIS applications might be less 'glamorous' but management should equally expect them to be more certain of success. Table 1.2 summarises a number of the key lessons from the first two eras.

Paul Strassman in his book *The Information Payoff* (1985) assesses the contribution of IS/IT to businesses from a very careful examination of the two essential premises of the first two eras

Data Processing—increasing efficiency,
Management Information Systems—improving effectiveness.

From his many observations and conclusions the following are particularly important:

TABLE 1.2 Summary of lessons from DP and MIS eras

DP lessons
- Need to understand the process of developing complete information systems, not just the programs to process data;
- more thorough requirements and data analysis to improve systems linkages and a more engineered approach to designing system components;
- more appropriate justification of investments by assessing the economics of efficiency gains and converting these to a return on investment;
- less creative, more structured approaches to programming, testing and documentation to reduce the problems of future amendments. More discipline was introduced with 'change control procedures' and sign off on specifications and tests;
- extended project management which recognised the need for co-ordination of both user and DP functions and the particular need to establish user management in a decisive role in the systems development—the user had to live with the consequences;
- the need for planning the interrelated set of systems required by the organisation. Better planning produced overall improvements in systems relevance and productivity.

MIS lessons
- justification of IS investments is not entirely a matter of return on investment/financial analysis;
- data bases require large restructuring projects and a heavy user involvement in data definition—data integration had been weak based on the project by project DP approach;
- the IS resource needs to move from a production to a service orientation to enable users to obtain their own information from the data resource—the information centre concept;
- need for organisational policies not just DP methodologies;
- personal computers and office systems enable better MIS to be developed provided that users and IS people both focus on the information needs rather than the technology.

(a) IS/IT deployment has generally improved the *efficiency* of information based functions in organisations when technology is used to automate discrete, structured, repetitive, stable information intensive tasks (e.g. invoicing, accounting, order handling, word processing, etc.). However, the return on investment is lower than the often quoted figures such as 25–30%—a net 5–10% return is more likely, although some isolated spectacular gains are possible.

   Efficiency gains can and should be measured wherever possible, although this can be difficult if tasks are rationalised or integrated when computerised.

(b) The results with regard to management effectiveness are less consistent. First, measuring effectiveness improvements—'value added' of managers—is difficult. Strassman's 'measurements' consider managements' contribution in terms of profitability or those aspects of profit which managers can influence against the costs incurred by management. When IS/IT is added to this cost 'burden' how does it affect the value added side of the equation?

   According to Strassman's research and analysis the expected happens: good managers get even better, bad managers get worse!

This is explained as follows: good management, with a high and improving value/cost ratio will use new resources to increase their effectiveness further by focusing on adding more value still—getting better at their job or they will discard the technology. Poor management will focus on improving the value/cost ratio by reducing the cost component and will be looking for IS/IT to produce efficiency savings—implying automation, but of tasks which do not lend themselves to automation. This piecemeal automation approach misses the opportunity to improve personal and collective effectiveness. It could be argued that IS/IT in these circumstances speeds up the mess! It is important to deal with the basic reasons for low management productivity and effectiveness before employing the technology.

Another way of assessing *effectiveness* is based on its dictionary definition: *achieving the required result* (or objective). Again, this is not easy to measure directly but it should be feasible, as will be considered later, to relate the application of IS/IT to the achievement or otherwise of business objectives to determine whether managerial and organisational effectiveness is improving from IS/IT investments.

As mentioned earlier, others have classified IS/IT into three types or eras in a similar way to the above discussion. Galliers and Somogyi (1987) in the introductory article to the book *Towards Strategic Information Systems* plot the erratic progress of IS/IT, its use and its management through two eras

Data Processing (= DP)
Management Services (= MIS)

and into the emerging third era of *strategic information systems*.
They summarised that progress under eight headings:

- nature of the technology,
- nature of systems operations,
- focus of systems effort,
- characteristics of systems development,
- reason for using the technology,
- characteristics of information systems,
- type of applications,
- way of applying the technology.

They recognise a number of trends that have occurred during that evolution, including the move into the third era. These trends are summarised in Figure 1.5, in the terms used above. The only problem with such a 'sequential' view is that it suggests that 'DP' has finished and cannot benefit from future developments. Ignoring that limitation the points made reflect the rapid changes over 25 years.

| Aspects | 'Era' | | |
	DP	MIS	SIS
Nature of the technology	'Computers' ──────→ 'Distributed process'──→ 'Networks' fragmented ──────→ interconnected ──────→ integrated (hardware limitation ──→ software limitation ──→ people/vision limitation)		
Nature of operations	Remote from users controlled by DP ──→	Regulated by management ──────→ services	Available and supportive to users?
Issues in systems development	Technical issues (programming/ ──────→ project management)	Support business users' needs ──────→ (information management)	Relate to business strategy?
Reason for using the technology	Reducing costs (especially ──────→ administrative) –technology driven	Supporting the business (manager)──→ –user driven	Enabling the business? –business driven
Characteristics of systems	Regimented/ operational ──────→ (internal)	Accommodating/ control ──────→	Flexible/ strategic? (external?)

FIGURE 1.5 Trends in the evolution of business IS/IT (adapted with permission, from R. D. Galliers and S. K. Somogyi, 'From data processing to strategic information systems—a historical perspective', Towards Strategic Information Systems (Abacus Press, 1987) pp. 5–25)

THE NEW ERA—STRATEGIC INFORMATION SYSTEMS

During the 1970s a number of organisations began to use IS/IT in ways which fundamentally changed the way their business was conducted, and changed the balance of power in their industry with respect to competitors, customers or suppliers. The use of IS/IT was directly influencing their competitive position and had become a strategic weapon. Historically, of course, improvements in efficiency through DP or increased management effectiveness through MIS should have translated into improved business performance—competitiveness—but the relationship between IS/IT success and strategic development was normally indirect.

Among the earliest examples of competitive advantage from IS/IT were the SABRE system of American Airlines and the direct terminal based ordering system of American Hospital Supplies. Both involved putting technology into the

customers initially and in the process precluded similar competitive responses—
'who wants two terminals on their desks?'—but also caused fundamental changes
in the 'systems' operating in their industries to their advantage. These two
particular cases are extensively documented, along with a number of others—
United Airlines, Merrill Lynch, Thomson's Holidays, ICI, McKesson, Dun &
Bradstreet, etc. Charles Wiseman in his 1985 book *Strategy and Computers* investigates
a number of them in some detail, and shows how business strategic development
became largely focused around how IS/IT could produce long-term competitive
leverage for the organisations.

Initially these concepts of successful strategic use of IS/IT were 'sold' to the
less adventurous via anecdotes, the success stories, given legitimacy by business
journals—a new IS/IT 'hype' had begun.

During the early 1980s an endless stream of examples were quoted in many
journals and books on Strategic Information Systems (SIS) under the generic title
of '*How* IS/IT Provides Competitive Advantages'. These articles did more than
describe what had been done; they considered how the advantage had been
achieved and proceeded to propose how any organisation might analyse its business
to identify similar opportunities. In each case a tool or technique was described
and substantiated by selected examples. Although these various approaches will
be considered in detail later it is important to note at this stage that they are all
fundamentally different from the IS/IT analysis approaches traditionally employed.
They are therefore additional tools and techniques that need to be included
in the IS/IT planning toolkit. However, they need to be considered in the
overall context of both business planning and IS/IT planning as will be
demonstrated later.

It is worth noting at this stage that although some of the 'classic' competitive
advantage examples resulted from strategic planning, most were the product of
excellent exploitation of situations which arose in the course of business. The
various tools and techniques that have been subsequently developed should enable
organisations to succeed more by judgement than luck!

In Box 1.2 a selected few of these well known examples are briefly outlined.*
They are a small subset of many hundreds of examples. More will be considered
later. From this large directory of examples a number of patterns can be identified.
These are considered below from two main viewpoints at this stage:

● to identify the differences between the SIS era and the previous DP/MIS eras
  and the implications;
● to consider the effects on IS/IT planning and the development of IS/IT
  strategies in an organisation.

---

*These short extracts are based on the examples as contained in the following articles: 'Information's
Market Force' by John Large (1986), 'Technological Myopia' by John Wyman (1985).

BOX 1.2   *Examples of competitive IS/IT advantages*

THOMSON'S HOLIDAYS

On the night of 3 November 1985, Britain's bargain hunters camped in the streets to be the first in line for the cut-price holidays on offer in the tour operators' price war. The next morning, when the travel agents' doors opened, the computers of Thomson Holidays handled 3,291 bookings in the first frantic hours of business—almost a customer a second. Some of their competitors fared less well, as their systems ground to a halt under an avalanche of enquiries, leaving frustrated customers out in the cold.

Small wonder that Colin Palmer, Thomson Holidays' deputy Managing Director, says that 'technology has become the basis of our business'. The firm's market leadership is actually founded on technological supremacy. It was the first tour operator to offer on-screen bookings to high street agents via TOP, its on-line viewdata system, which has earned a reputation as the most efficient in the business.

In the summer of 1986 Thomson carried a million extra passengers, one in four package holiday goers, and 85% will have booked via TOP. It is this ability to handle mass bookings that has enabled Thomson to pursue its fiercely aggressive marketing strategy, and to stimulate huge demand.

In October 1986 Thomsons announced it would only take bookings via the system in future.

MERRILL LYNCH

In the US, Merrill Lynch launched its cash management account back in 1978. This combines traditionally separate banking products such as line of credit, cheque, investment and equity accounts into a single monthly statement, with idle funds being swept automatically into a high interest account. The new account attracted $1 billion of assets in the first year. Today, Merrill Lynch manages $85 billion, and still has almost 70% of the market. Merrill Lynch set out to permanently change the shape of the financial marketplace by taking several existing but separate services and tying them together through information technology to create a new service that shattered the traditional boundaries between the banking and securities industries.

AMERICAN AIRLINES

American Airlines gained a lead over the competition as the first US carrier to offer an on-line reservation system to travel agents. This system, Sabre, has captured 10,000 of the 24,000 automated travel agents in the US, 40% more than any other. Sabre lists the flight schedules of over 400 airlines, but, when launched, it gave American a crucial edge by displaying its own flights first. So effective was this tactic that other US carriers persuaded the Government to intervene. American still benefits, however, by charging them $1.75 for every booking made, bringing in an estimated $170 million last year. The technological window of opportunity for on-line travel systems proved to be small: only five US carriers now offer an on-line reservation service.

continued on next page

McKESSON

The company provided pharmacists and druggists with hand-held data entry terminals to record replacement stock details, and the information is downloaded over telephone lines direct to McKesson's computers. McKesson fills the order overnight and delivers it the next day in boxes arranged to match the shelf divisions of the retailers' store. Druggists who signed up with the service, called Economost, typically doubled or tripled their order volumes. In many cases, they began to rely exclusively on McKesson. The total service helps retailers' stock, price-label rotate and display merchandise according to Marketing reports generated.

In another area of its business McKesson provides a service via pharmacists to process the insurance claims for 23 million medical insurance customers' prescriptions. The system processes the claims via prescriptions completed and sends them to 150 Healthcare insurers for reimbursing.

GENERAL TIRE

General Tire arranged to have a telemarketing centre take over the service support functions that had been previously performed by the field sales force. Telemarketing specialists handle questions like: 'Have you got it?', 'Did it ship?', and 'There's something wrong with my bill.' This lowered General Tire's unit costs by freeing the field sales force to devote more of their time to selling. General Tire then decided to let the telemarketing centre take over the selling and account management role for some of the company's marginally profitable accounts—accounts that could not be profitably serviced by the sales team. In the first month of operation, General Tire's telemarketing people sold more to these accounts than the field sales force had sold to them over the entire previous year.

PITNEY-BOWES

Pitney-Bowes has found a strategic application of information technology in the way it dispatches its service people. Currently, they dispatch over 3,500 customer engineers from each of their 99 branch locations throughout the US. Drawing upon a central database in Danbury, Connecticut, and 20 dispatch centres that feed into it, Pitney-Bowes has found a very efficient way to send out its customer engineers. The customer calls in on an 800 number and identifies his problem, and someone at Pitney-Bowes puts it into a diagnostic system to see if it can be solved over the telephone—thereby saving the cost of dispatching a customer engineer. If not, he checks the database to find not only the service engineer who is in nearest proximity to the customer but also the engineer who can handle it at the least possible cost. Before the new system was put in place, every customer engineer had to be trained to service every kind of machinery in his area: now the company can assign someone who has a skill that matches the problem, so that the high end of their product line does not suffer because of problems at the low end. The customer benefits from this arrangement

continued on next page

continued

not only by having a specialist work on his problem, but by having a 30% improvement in response time.

AMERICAN HOSPITAL SUPPLY

American Hospital Supply, as its name suggests, has selected the health care industry as its niche in the wholesale business. To gain an important edge over its rivals, American Hospital Supply pioneered an order entry distribution system that links most of the firm's customers to its computers. In addition to ordering merchandise, the system also allows customers to control their inventories, increasing the likelihood of their coming to rely upon American Hospital Supply as a key supplier. The fact that the company's initial move to electronic ordering was spearheaded by a regional manager seeking to meet the needs of a single customer suggests that starting small may be a key to success.

STRATEGIC USES OF IS/IT—A CLASSIFICATION AND FACTORS FOR SUCCESS

From a research base of over 150 such examples the following classification can be shown to be helpful in considering the implications of strategic IS/IT use. In general the examples can be classified into one of four types, although some of the examples clearly include more than one type.

The four main types of strategic systems appear to be:

(a) those that link the organisation via technology based systems to its customer/consumers and/or suppliers;
(b) those that produce more effective integration of the use of information in the organisation's value adding process;
(c) those that enable the organisation to develop, produce, market and deliver new or enhanced products or services based on information;
(d) those that provide Executive Management with information to support the development and implementation of strategy.

These are in descending order of commonness of occurrence in the analysis. This classification immediately enables the organisation to consider four areas of opportunity, one or more of which may prove important.

Other classifications are similar.

Benjamin *et al.* (1984) divide the types of potential opportunities between those that focus on the *competitive marketplace* or *internal operations*. Within each IS/IT can be used to improve traditional ways of doing business or to cause 'significant structural changes' in the way the company does business.

Notowidigdo (1984) divides strategic information systems into

(a) internal systems that have direct benefit to the company,
(b) external systems that have direct benefits to the company's customers.

Both are reduced subsets of the overall classification above.

Hence, the four categories suggested above seem to cover most of the possibilities. Each of these types of strategic IS/IT application has different implications in terms of identification, planning and implementation.

(a) *Links to customers, suppliers, etc.* For example, the key people involved in the consideration of external linkage systems will be sales/marketing and distribution management at the customer end, or purchasing/receiving/quality control managers at the supplier end. The initiator of American Hospital Supplies' strategic IS developments was a depot manager who provided a disorganised customer with a terminal through which he could place emergency orders. These applications require a strong drive from the sharp end line management. Also they are not entirely in the organisation's power to control—since suppliers, customers and competitors may take the initiative at any stage.

(b) *Improved integration of internal processes.* To produce effective internal integration of information requires the organisation to overcome some of the traditional barriers to successful IS/IT application in the DP/MIS eras: sharing information, reorganisation of roles, etc. For instance, 'Telemarketing' as exemplified by General Tire for routine selling can dramatically reduce the cost of generating orders. But, imagine the reaction of a good customer to the telephone ringing suggesting a re-order when he has just received a final demand letter from Accounts for payments for goods he did not receive to use on a machine that is idle due to a service engineer calling without the right parts! All the relevant information about the customer and the organisation's ability to 'deliver' is required at the point of selling to make it effective.

Senior management need to understand the organisational implications of this new information based approach to the roles of people and departments since reorganisation may be required if significant benefits are to be obtained and any relative advantages sustained.

(c) *Information based products and services.* The classical example of enhancing the product/service based on information is the Merrill Lynch Cash Management Account, a consumer service which combines cheque, credit, savings and investment facilities. Unlike many of the examples, this concept resulted from strategic planning in the corporate planning department where it was realised that a whole range of Financial Services were converging. They realised that providing an information service to customers about what are information based products could be very lucrative.

To achieve advantages in this type of application requires a thorough knowledge of the products of the industry, their relative merits and in particular what the customer uses them for, how the customer obtains value from them. Obviously, an understanding of the organisation's products and services and the economics of providing them is also required. Relating customer need and product possibility is critically important.

For example, a company who provides scaffolding to the construction industry developed a system to calculate a customer's detailed 'bill of materials' requirements from a basic description of the size and type of job. If a customer buys a lot of poles, joints, planks, etc. they can have a copy of the system for their own use. This is an information based service which provides a competitive edge. Interestingly, the whole system was developed by a 'user'— in terms of DP and MIS the organisation could be said to be unsophisticated, being polite, but the company has developed a sophisticated IT based marketing tool.

(d) *Executive information systems.* The final type of strategic IS/IT application—to provide executive management with strategic information—is dependent on other factors for success.

Management information systems have, historically at least, rarely affected top management in the organisation directly. There are two main reasons for this: (i) the lack of external information included in the systems; and (ii) the simplicity of the systems, the rawness of the data, the lack of context, i.e. they require knowledge not just information.

Recent developments in external business databases which are readily tapped into plus the potential offered by knowledge based (or expert type) systems to process the raw information based on experience have made this use of IS/IT more practicable. This aspect of competitive advantage is explored through a number of examples in Meyer and Boone's book *The Information Edge* (1987). For instance, organisations can link into the PIMS (Profit Impact of Market Share) database run by the Strategic Planning Institute in Boston— to obtain information about customers' and suppliers' industries and business performance.

Although, to date, this type of application provides the smallest number of examples, it is likely to become much more significant in the future.

A second aspect of the analyses of the 150 or so examples identifies some of the key factors that seem to recur frequently. Few strategic information systems show all of the factors but many show a number. Again, these factors are often at odds with traditional IS/IT approaches and show more commonality with business innovation.

1. *External not internal focus*—looking at customers, competitors, suppliers, even other industries and the business's relationships and similarities with the

outside business world. Traditionally IS/IT has been focused on internal processes and issues.

2. *Adding value not cost reduction*—although cost reductions may accrue due to business expansion at reduced marginal costs. 'Doing it better, not cheaper' seems to be the maxim. This is consistent with the requirements of companies to differentiate themselves from competitors—better products, better services—to succeed. Historically, IS/IT was seen as a way of increasing efficiency—doing it cheaper—and whilst this is obviously important in any business environment it is not the only way to succeed.

3. *Sharing the benefits*—within the organisation, with suppliers, customers, consumers and even competitors on occasion! In many cases in the past systems benefits have not been shared even within an organisation, but used instead to give departments or functions leverage over each other. This reduces the benefits and does not allow the benefits to be sustained. Sharing benefits implies a 'buy in', a commitment to success, a switching cost. Almost all the examples involve a sharing of the benefits, with suppliers, customers, consumers, even competitors to provide barriers to entry to the industry. For instance, the introduction of 'debit cards' to replace cheque books depends for its success on sharing some of the reduced processing costs with the retailers and consumers, since the benefits the bank can gain depend on the commitment of retailers and consumers.

4. *Understanding the customer* and what he does with the product or service—how he obtains value from it, and the problems he may encounter in gaining that value. McKesson followed this principle very closely in providing a range of information based services to drugstores, starting from a simple problem of stock control—solved by delivering products in shelf-sized batches. Black and Decker, a low-cost producer, supplied a value added service to retailers to enable them to 'swap' goods they had over or under stocked for the season. They did not want returns—but the retailer could not be expected to predict precisely how many lawnmowers, for instance, he would sell. It helped solve a customer's problem.

5. *Business-driven innovation*, not technology driven. The pressures of the market place, often interpreted by IS/IT users caused the developments in most cases.

    This tends to cast doubt on the idea of 'competitive advantage from IT'—but in practice it means that IT, often well established, provides or enables a business opportunity or idea to be converted to reality. The lead or the driving force is to come from the business, not necessarily a traditional route to using IS/IT, which has often been supply driven, pushed by the IS/IT professionals not pulled through by the users to whom the latest technology is probably of little interest. It makes business sense—why take two risks at the same time, i.e. new business process based on new technology—it is a recipe for failure!

    Considering the last two factors together, Peter Keen summed it up well by saying: 'Major failures in using IT are often based on much better technology and bad business vision. Successes come from good enough technology and a clear understanding of the customer'.

6. *Incremental development*, not the total application vision turned into reality. Many examples show a stepped approach—doing one thing and building on and extending the success by a further development. To some extent developing applications by trial and error but also not stopping when a success is achieved but considering what could be done next. This again is against the traditional notion of clarifying all requirements, defining all boundaries, agreeing the total deliverables of the system before embarking on the expensive, structured process of design and construction, freezing the requirements at each stage. Prototyping of systems obviously has a key role to play here.

7. *Using the information gained* from the systems to develop the business. Many mail-order and retailing firms are segmenting their customers according to the purchasing patterns shown by transactions and then providing different, focused, catalogues. Product and market analyses plus external market research information can be merged and then recut in any number of ways to identify more appropriate marketing segmentation and product mix.

As discussed above, these factors in general imply different attitudes to the use of IS/IT than have prevailed in the past. Again, this implies we need new tools and techniques to uncover such opportunities and then new approaches to managing these applications to ensure success. These points will need in-depth consideration in developing strategies.

Another general observation can be made from these examples, by considering what actually produces the success—information technology, information systems or information.

Technology itself is the 'enabler'—that provides short-term advantage and the opportunity to develop new systems and capture potentially valuable information. But, normally, competitors will be able to purchase the same technology, and any advantages could soon be negated.

However, new information systems developed, utilising the technology, could provide advantages which can be less vulnerable to erosion by competitive copying. The potential gain will depend on how conclusively and exclusively the systems alter business relationships.

In time, however, the existing competition or new entrants enticed into the profitable parts of industry could redefine the relationships by introducing alternative information systems. If the firm wishes to sustain its competitive advantage it must use the information gleaned from its systems to improve its products or services—to match the requirements of the market place.

THE STRATEGIC INFORMATION SYSTEMS ERA — THE PLANNING IMPLICATIONS

By viewing IS/IT evolution another way the management implications have ascended from the basement of the business to the penthouse executive suite, from where strategic vision is possible!

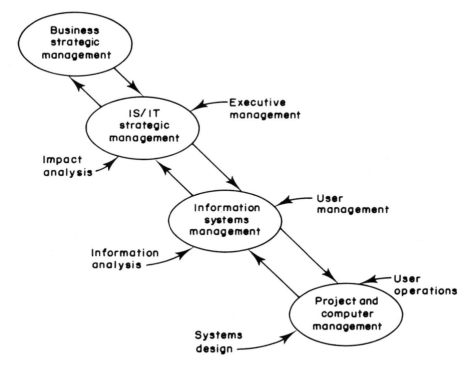

FIGURE 1.6 The relationship between the business, SIS, MIS and DP

The focus of data processing was, and still is, on the effective application of systems and technology to automating operations and thereby increasing efficiency. The planning focus is therefore on the project, the application and its successful design and implementation! The main prerequisite for success is a design for the system that carries out the operation to improve efficiency.

Management information systems involved user management in considering the information they used and how they used it. The IS professionals had to find new techniques of 'information analysis' (entity analysis, etc.) to devise ways of arranging information for effective use by management. Since managers rarely rely on a single source for information, the focus of planning has moved to the integration of individual systems into coherent sources of management information.

Up to this stage the view of IS/IT in the business was an internal resource over which the management has total discretion as to its use. The portfolio models mentioned earlier described the overall structure and logic to the process of IS/IT application to the business. It was very much an internally driven choice as to whether, and how much, to invest in IS/IT.

IS/IT strategic management which is a reflection obviously of the SIS era is different for two main reasons. Firstly, the outside world, competitors, customers and suppliers may be the instigators of IS/IT uses which affect the organisation's own need for applications or types of applications—external as much as internal factors will drive the needs.

Second, executive management will have to make judgements about such investments in terms of how they will effect the business strategy of the organisation—in some cases how IS/IT can be used to formulate that strategy. Management will need some way of assessing the importance of IS/IT in business terms and the opportunities will need to be elicited via business based techniques to enable that management judgement to be applied. These two needs have been grouped together under the term *impact analysis*—ways of understanding the potential IS/IT has in the business from a business strategic perspective.

In summary, the contribution and performance of IS/IT in the business has become more significant and hence the level of management involvement required has been elevated to executive level—no longer is their task to sign the cheque, they now have to understand and often decide what is being purchased. In essence, what has happened is that the SIS era has completed the links between computer systems and the business strategy—but all the aspects need to be managed coherently and successfully to gain all the potential benefits available.

However, it is worth reiterating that the strategic use of IS/IT is not a replacement for sound data processing or delivering valuable management information—it is supplementary and must be developed in a complementary way. Probably 50% of an organisation's future IS/IT investment will be in data processing functions, perhaps 30% in MIS and only 20% in what are seen as strategic information systems. However, the business leverage obtained may be in reverse proportion—although it will not be quantifiable in traditional 'savings' terms. Understanding these differences and relationships is vital if a rational, balanced management approach to IS/IT is to be sustained over periods of dramatic change and uncertainty.

Professor William King in a letter to *Datamation* in 1987 expressed concern that he saw 'evidence that the competitive advantage argument is beginning to be used excessively—primarily to rationalise projects that cannot otherwise be justified'. This causes the idea to lose management credibility. He says that we must manage IS/IT and its various applications in accord with the type of contribution it is making—improving efficiency, effectiveness and/or competitiveness—not elevate all aspects to a new and artificial plane of importance. However, he does make the point that an organisation cannot afford to ignore the potential strategic opportunities IS/IT may offer and therefore 'the potential of information as a strategic resource should be incorporated as a routine element of the business planning process, so that all managers become used to thinking in these new terms'—i.e. understand the potential impact.

In fact what can be concluded from a number of different directions is that we should treat IS/IT like any other normal part of the business, which, like marketing or production or purchasing for example, must be carried out efficiently

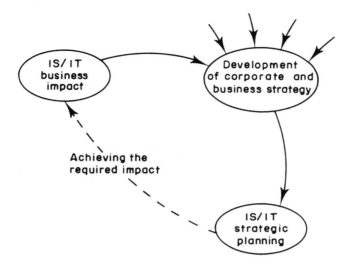

FIGURE 1.7 IS/IT strategic planning in context

and effectively for the business to survive, but which can also provide competitive/strategic leverage for the organisation if astutely managed. This implies an approach to developing strategies and plans for IS/IT and its application as portrayed in Figure 1.7.

If the organisation were developing the marketing part of its business strategy then it would first analyse its position in the market place, i.e. have a marketing input to the process. After evaluating marketing requirements and options in conjunction with other needs, opportunities and constraints, a marketing strategy would result which would be aimed at achieving the appropriate effects in the market place. That is all the diagram shows—that we should do the same with IS/IT—identify the potential impact first—then evaluate IS/IT implications in the overall business context before defining the strategy—to achieve the desired effects. After all, that is effectively what the successful strategic IS/IT stories tell us—change the competitive capability of the organisation through developing business strategies based on IS/IT.

An Application Portfolio for the 'Combined Era'

The applications in the overall DP and MIS and SIS portfolio need to be planned and managed according to their existing and future contribution to the business. Traditional portfolio models consider the relationship of systems to each other and the tasks being performed rather than the relationship with business success. Such a portfolio model can be derived from a matrix concept developed by

STRATEGIC	TURNAROUND (or high potential)
● Applications which are critical for future success	● Applications which may be of future strategic importance
FACTORY	SUPPORT
● Applications which are critical to sustaining existing business	● Applications which improve management and performance but not critical to the business

FIGURE 1.8 IS business contribution—application portfolio

McFarlan (1984), which considered the contribution of IS/IT to the business now and in the future, based on its industry impact.

This variation on the matrix is represented in Figure 1.8.

Each application of IS/IT in the business, e.g. payroll or sales analysis or capacity planning, etc. can be positioned in one segment of the matrix according to its existing and anticipated contribution to the business. Then each application can be managed in accordance with that contribution. Whilst some applications may straddle the boundaries, most can be assessed by the business managers in terms of their contribution to the business and the future strategy. It is important to allocate the systems by the main *functions* they perform, e.g. sales forecasting, rather than just the system title, which may incorporate many different functions. The system acronym should not be used, neither should generic IT descriptions like 'office automation' which are employed in many applications. All applications, including user PC systems should be included.

Figure 1.9 shows a possible portfolio for a manufacturing company.

The matrix, as described here, shows some obvious similarities to other portfolio management matrices, such as the 'Boston Matrix' for product portfolio management. Those similarities, concerning balancing the portfolio, life cycles and management approaches, etc. will be examined in detail later when the value of the matrix in IS/IT strategic management will be explored. At this stage it is perhaps sufficient to point out that the four segments will require quite different strategies to achieve successful planning, development, implementation and operation of the applications—because they fulfil a different role in the business.

IS/IT PLANNING—YESTERDAY, TODAY AND TOMORROW?

The final objective of this introductory chapter is to provide a view of how IS/IT

STRATEGIC	TURNAROUND
● Computer-integrated manufacturing ● MRP II (manufacturing resource planning) ● Links to suppliers ● Quality control ● Sales forecasting ● Product profitability analysis	● Electronic data interchange (EDI) with wholesalers ● Manpower planning ● Electronic mail ● Decision support ● Expert diagnostic systems ● Image processing
● Employee database ● Maintenance scheduling ● Inventory management ● Shopfloor control ● Computer-aided design of products ● Product (bill of material) database ● Accounts receivable/payable	● Time recording ● Budgeting ● Expense reporting ● Cost accounting ● General accounting ● Payroll ● Word processing
FACTORY	SUPPORT

FIGURE 1.9 A possible application portfolio for a manufacturing company—examples of typical applications

planning has evolved, to what stage it has developed in organisations and the implications of this on the future requirements.

Earl (1987) has studied the changing focus and increasing maturity of the IS/IT planning process in a number of organisations and has identified five major steps in the process. The chief characteristics of these five stages are defined in Figure 1.10, adapted from Earl's more detailed analysis.

The analysis considers the main task which is carried out, the main objectives, who drives the planning forward and the approaches adopted. By looking at each of these aspects, the effectiveness of the linkage between IS/IT planning and business strategy can be determined, and consequently how likely the organisation is to be gaining strategic advantage from IS/IT. The stages can also be mapped on to the portfolio model described above. This implies that although the organisation needs to develop more 'mature' planning approaches in order to achieve a full and relevant portfolio, some earlier stage planning approaches need to be maintained in order to manage the total matrix of applications. Not every application of IT needs all the complexity implied in stage 5.

Increasing organisational maturity with respect to IS/IT planning →

	1	2	3	4	5
MAIN TASK	IS/IT application mapping	Defining business needs	Detailed IS planning	Strategic/ competitive advantage	Linkage to business strategy
KEY OBJECTIVE	Management under-standing	Agreeing priorities	Balancing the portfolio	Pursuing opportunities	Integrating IS and business strategies
DIRECTION FROM	DP/IS led	Senior management initiative	Users and IS together	Executives/ senior management and Users	Coalition of users/ management and IS
MAIN APPROACH	Bottom-up development	Top down analysis	Balanced top down and bottom-up	Entre-preneurial (user innovation)	Multiple method at same time

FIGURE 1.10 (Reproduced with permission, from M. J. Earl (1989) Management Strategies for Information Technology, *Prentice Hall)*

When considering this evolution in the context of the three-era model previously described it seems reasonable to equate stages 1 to 3 to data processing and management information systems, with the transition point from 'computer' to 'information system' management in stage 2—when management perceive the need for integration of systems. The strategic information systems era begins to dawn in stage 4 to be consolidated in stage 5.

But even at this stage DP, MIS and SIS are being simultaneously developed and provided there is an overall strategic IS/IT planning framework, different, relevant planning approaches can be adopted and should be adopted for different types of applications. These requirements will be considered in more detail later.

An organisation can identify from the types of planning approaches in place (a) where it is in relation to the eventual need for integration of IS/IT and business planning, and (b) which approaches it needs to adopt in the short term to move it towards that eventual goal.

Figure 1.11 shows how the stages of planning evolution map on to the portfolio model and this can be explained as follows (note: the 'process' does not always occur sequentially, and there will always be overlap across the stages. In large

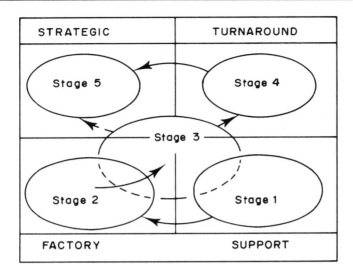

FIGURE 1.11 Mapping the evolution of IS/IT planning on to the application portfolio model

organisations different businesses or functions will be at different stages. What is surprising, in some ways, is how often the stages are followed quite sequentially):

Stage 1   Typical early DP planning—the IS/IT department need to plan the interfaces between applications developed separately, project by project, in order to make them work effectively. Obtaining management understanding of the increasing dependence of the business on its systems is the key objective—to enable a more coherent approach to be adopted. Essentially SUPPORT applications are being built and management perceives IS/IT in that limited role—but the dependence is steadily increasing.

Stage 2   Management, now aware, initiate a top down review of IS/IT applications in the light of business dependence—priorities are to be agreed based on the relative importance of business needs. Should the order processing development take precedence over the new sales analysis system? etc. The approaches used are very methodological, normally based on derivatives of IBM's 'Business Systems Planning' and involve gaining a management consensus of criticalities and priorities. An extended, prioritised shopping list of FACTORY type applications for both operational (DP) and management support (MIS) needs will have been established.

Stage 3   The next task is detailed IS/IT planning—to determine the best way of implementing the applications or in some cases reimplementing existing systems in more appropriate integrated ways, often databased. The portfolio needs to be better balanced—greater attention is paid to the now (perceived to be critical) FACTORY systems and less resource is dedicated to SUPPORT applications—each having been 'prioritised' in stage 2. The 'information centre' concept may be implemented for SUPPORT type systems, or application packages introduced, etc. Stage 3 can take considerable time to plan and implement effectively and while this is going on, nothing else can really happen! Unless . . .

Through stages 1 to 3 the evolution from isolated 'efficiency' driven applications to integrated 'effectiveness' systems has been happening—but the objective has not yet been overt use of IS/IT for competitive advantage.

Stage 4   The users take the reins, not necessarily encouraged by senior management, but not discouraged either, because they do not wish to prevent business initiative—entrepreneurial use of IS/IT by users seeing new opportunities, using information primarily in new ways to provide business leverage/competitive advantage. This may start during stage 3 as frustration builds up in the 'jam tomorrow' stage of detailed planning and implementation. It is important that users, unfettered in any way by IS/IT procedure or control, exercise this freedom to innovate, even if 90% of the ideas are of little strategic potential. It is the source of ideas, tested ideas which with later IS/IT support can be turned to advantage—literally TURNAROUND opportunities driven by the business (remember, many strategic applications originate this way).

Stage 5   This is the difficult stage to achieve, particularly if stage 3 is delayed and stage 4 is more user rebellion than business stimulated innovation. It requires bringing it all back together—not just IS/IT based planning as in stage 2, but also business planning. In essence, the innovation ideas of stage 4 need to be evaluated, focused in the business context along with the opportunities now made available from the factory, support infrastructure—i.e. the knowledge of what to do and the ability to deliver it effectively. Linking IS/IT potential to the business strategy is the main task, and this requires the simultaneous attention of senior executives, line management and IS specialists—the first time in this process they have all acted as a coalition together. There is no 'methodology' available—multiple methods implies business planning methods plus IS/IT top down and bottom up approaches. Truly STRATEGIC applications of IS/IT can be determined and delivered.

All these variations on IS/IT planning will be discussed in more detail later, with special focus on the later, less well known stages.

A final question in this introduction. In practice, where in this planning evolution are most organisations? It is often difficult to assess:

- it depends who you ask. IS management generally think the situation is more advanced than it actually is—probably because of the amount of planning they do!
- in large organisations the pattern will not be simple. In some business or functional areas, such as distribution or finance, IS and business strategy may be closely linked. Elsewhere, say in marketing, little or no linkage may exist.

The most comprehensive and perhaps perceptive survey of the maturity of IS/IT planning in major organisations was carried out by Bob Galliers in 1985/86. The results and conclusions of the survey, conducted in the UK and Australia have been thoroughly documented (Galliers, 1987a,b). The survey obtained the views of senior management, user and IS managers and also consultants actively involved in systems planning for major companies. A number of aspects of the analysis will be drawn on later in this book, but some initial observations are worth recording.

1. *Focus of IS Planning:* in terms of seeking improved efficiency or effectiveness or competitiveness

   Competitiveness focus 6% of organisations (sample size 101 organisations)
   Effectiveness focus   78%
   Efficiency focus   59%

   Obviously, the focus can cover all three as the percentages show. Interestingly, 23% were *exclusively* focused on efficiency.

   This suggests that in 1985/6 the priority for IS/IT planning has an 'MIS' bias—improving effectiveness—although 'DP' type planning for efficiency is still very important and planning for competitive advantage through IS/IT is still only emerging. He concludes that 'improved competitiveness is a byproduct of such (planning) endeavours but it is clear that the focus of current IS planning practice in the UK tends not to be on matters of competitiveness'.

2. *Objectives of IS planning:* those objectives which are agreed upon by everyone. Two out of the 'top three' objectives in the opinion of everyone, i.e. users, IS management, senior management and consultants, were:

   1. prioritised application portfolio
   2. align IS to corporate objectives

   This tends to suggest that most organisations saw IS/IT planning as having objectives in stages 2 and 3 in the Earl model above and this ties in with the focus.

3. *Linkage of IS/IT planning to business planning*—how integrated are the two processes? This showed that the need for integrated planning is well understood—by at least 69% of respondents, but in practice the linkage is very weak. Galliers figures are (percentage of organisations):

10% 'inextricably linked' (integrated)
32% 'somewhat linked'
42% 'only tenuously linked'
16% 'totally isolated'

This tends to confirm the assessment based on the first two points. In general, the need for more strategic planning of IS is beginning to be understood, but the practice is still essentially lower level, systems and data planning, more appropriate to DP and MIS eras.

Only one survey has been quoted but its findings seem to reflect the observed state of IS/IT planning in many organisations in the latter half of the 1980s. Many people have observed that the IS/IT planning process in many, perhaps the majority of organisations, does not reflect the potential role IS/IT can play in business success, and a less than optimal contribution is the predictable result.

SUMMARY

Information systems evolution in a business and organisational context has been erratic, but IS/IT has inexorably increased its importance as the economics and capability have enabled more to be achieved. Increasingly competitive business environments have provided a motivation to invest in more efficient and effective ways of carrying out business processes and managing the business. Although the progress has been fitful and unsynchronised, patterns of IS development can be observed.

Two major 'eras' are well established and much can be learnt from them—in particular that the best ways of planning for the applications, given the contribution they can make to the business, were only discovered well into the eras, from painful experience in many cases.

Often the secret of better IS/IT planning was only discovered after initial enthusiasm had turned to frustration—just before disillusion was about to occur?—necessity perhaps being the mother of invention of better approaches.

We are now entering a third era, with higher prizes and reciprocally greater risks, when the business could become critically dependent on its investment in systems for its success—information systems planning has become strategic for many companies. That does not mean that previously developed good IS planning practice is obsolete, merely inadequate for the new era. Can companies in this new era of IS afford to wait to find the appropriate planning approaches until the enthusiasm has faded into frustration? It may be too late. The third era implies winners and losers with IS/IT, not just relative success and failure, which may not reflect directly in the overall business performance.

The last obvious conclusion about IS/IT planning evolution is that it has crept unerringly away from the computer room, through the IS department and is now clearly a process that depends on users and senior management involvement for success. It has become difficult to separate aspects of IS/IT planning from business planning. Hence, it is important to use the tools and techniques of business strategic analysis and planning to cement that relationship. More specific IS/IT planning approaches have to be knitted into this pattern of business strategic management.

REFERENCES

Anthony, R. N. (1965) 'Planning and control: a framework for analysis', Harvard University Press.

Benjamin, R. I., Rockart, J. F., Scott Morton, M. S., and Wyman, J. (1984) 'Information technology: a strategic opportunity', *Sloan Management Review* (Spring).

Drury, D. H. (1983) 'An empirical assessment of the stages of DP growth', *MIS Quarterly* (June).

Earl, M. J. (1989) *Management Strategies for Information Technology*, Prentice Hall.

Galliers, R. D. (1987a) 'Information technology planning within the corporate planning process', published in Pergamon Infotech State of the Art Report (Duling and Berry (eds), *Controlling Projects within an Integrated Management Framework*).

Galliers, R. D. (1987b) 'Information systems and technology planning within a competitive strategy framework', published in Pergamon Infotech State of the Art Report (Griffiths (ed.), *The Role of Information Management in Competitive Success*).

Galliers, R. D., and Somogyi, S. K. (1987) 'From data processing to strategic information systems—a historical perspective', *Towards Strategic Information Systems* (pp. 5–25), Abacus Press.

Gibson, C. F., and Nolan, R. L. (1974) 'Managing the four stages of EDP growth', *Harvard Business Review* (Jan.–Feb.).

Hirschheim, R., Earl, M. J., Feeny, D., and Lockett, M. (1988) 'An exploration into the management of the IS function: key issues and an evolving model', *Proceedings of the Joint International Symposium on IS* (March).

King, W. R. (1987) 'It's time to get out of the dark', Letter to Datamation (July).

King, J. L., and Kraemer, K. L. (1984) 'Evolution and organisational information systems: an assessment of Nolan's stage model', *Communications of ACM*, **27**, 5 (May).

Large, J. (1986) 'Information's market force', *Management Today* (Aug.).

McFarlan, F. W. (1984) 'Information technology changes the way you compete', *Harvard Business Review* (May–June).

Meyer, N. D., and Boone, M. E. (1987) *The Information Edge*, McGraw-Hill.

Notowidigdo, M. H. (1984) 'Information systems: weapons to gain the competitive edge', *Financial Executive*, **52**, 3, 20–25.

Nolan, R. L. (1979) 'Managing the crises in data processing', *Harvard Business Review* (Mar.–Apr.)

Strassman, P. A. (1985) *Information Payoff*, Free Press.

Wiseman, C. (1985) *Strategy and Computers*, Dow Jones–Irwin.

Wyman, J. (1985) 'Technological myopia', *Sloan Management Review* (Winter).

Chapter 2

THE LINK BETWEEN BUSINESS STRATEGY AND IS/IT STRATEGIC PLANNING — AN OVERVIEW OF BUSINESS STRATEGY CONCEPTS

INTRODUCTION

In Chapter 1 the evolution of IS/IT in organisations was discussed and it should now be clear that information systems strategies must be developed within the context of the wider corporate and business strategic planning processes. In this way the expenditure on information processing within an organisation, consisting of central information systems departments, distributed departmental computing, and end-user computing environments, can be directed towards the achievement of corporate and business unit objectives and goals. It was also shown in Chapter 1 that often in the past, the money spent on information processing within the organisations has failed to support the main objectives of the organisation and there are many reasons and excuses as to why the promises of DP have not been realised. However, today the most important measure of success is the maximising of return on investment on the money invested in information processing within an organisation as a whole coupled with the strategic use of information to either gain competitive advantage or to repel competitive threat.

Once this argument is accepted then it is vital that managers of the business are involved in the process of information and systems planning and this means that the process must be clearly understood by those managers. It must be conducted using tools which are familiar to them and in a language that they understand, i.e. in business terms, completely avoiding the jargon of computing, and be related to their everyday issues, divorced from concerns about developments in computing technology.

The more formal approaches to business planning started in the 1950s, and have evolved since then in order to take account of technical, economic, social and political changes and will continue to evolve in response to the dynamics of the business environment. In this chapter some of these well established business planning concepts and processes are outlined. As will be explained later in the book, many of these can be effectively used within the information systems planning area.

THE STRATEGIC FRAMEWORK

Many business planning techniques are used to focus on a particular area, such as the analysis of competitors, the strength of the existing portfolio of products, or the relative merits of different courses of action. However, there exists a far broader perspective for strategic planning which we shall call the 'strategic framework'*.

The framework considers the factors involved in business strategic management in three layers:

- the external environment,
- pressure groups and stakeholders,
- internal business planning.

Each of these is considered in more detail below before outlining some of the approaches which can be adopted to analyse their impact and formulate appropriate strategies.

THE EXTERNAL ENVIRONMENT

Businesses or enterprises operate within a broadly defined external environment as represented in Figure 2.1. There are many aspects of the external environment which need to be analysed and understood as part of the business planning process but probably the most important factors today are:

1. the economy,
2. society,
3. politics,
4. law,
5. ecology,
6. technology.

These are important because of the speed with which they are changing and the effect they have on an increasingly 'global' business market place. Careful monitoring of these factors may lead to significant business opportunities. Conversely changes in these factors could pose considerable threat. Some examples will serve to illustrate the need for analysis.

Economy

The swing in emphasis to monetarism and the economics of free markets could not have been predicted before the end of the the 1970s. However, by the end of the 1980s this is a feature not only of the Western world but also of the Soviet Union and China and, increasingly, other communist countries. The opportunities for increased trade are undeniable.

A further aspect to consider is the extreme fluctuations of the US dollar and the impacts of Third World debt on the Western financial system. To offset this

Acknowledgement: the strategic framework is based on a structure first described to the authors by John Constable—Visiting Professor of Business Policy at Cranfield School of Management.

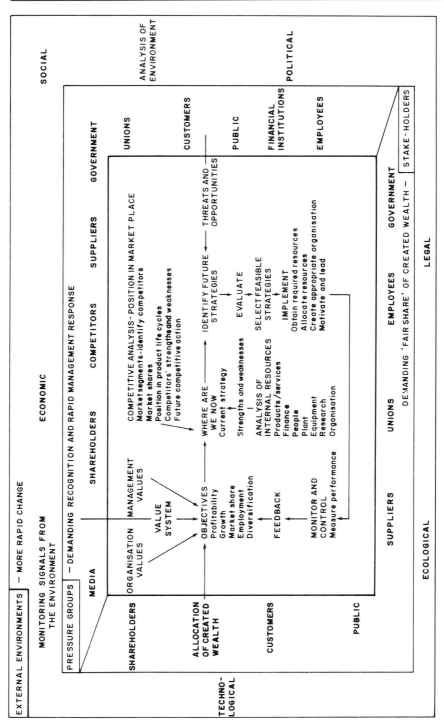

FIGURE 2.1 A strategic framework

there is the vigorous performance of the newly industrialised countries with their strong trading surpluses. This has led to Western countries focusing their attention on the Far East and away from Africa and South America.

The effects of

- relative strengths of different currencies,
- inflation rates,
- money market rates,
- tax legislation,

impose increasingly complex challenges on global business. It affects decisions on where to invest, where to take profits, transfer pricing and management of customer and product profitability.

Society

Within the social environment there is a growing awareness of the problems and opportunities afforded to organisations by the increasing numbers of retired people and their relative affluence. As the general population is living longer there is a consequent demand on pensions and geriatric health-care services. On the other hand this part of the population has a high level of disposable income, with few commitments. It is anticipated that a large proportion of children born in Western Europe in 1988 will live to be 100. The impact of this is going to be enormous. Governments will have to contend with supporting a large number of retired people on a shrinking taxable labour force. On the other hand there is ample scope for changing the face of the leisure and consumer retailing industries to cater for the tastes of the older population.

Politics

1987 marked the twenty-fifth anniversary of the founding of the European Economic Community. Whilst this loose arrangement between countries has largely been noted for its policies on agriculture and subsidies to farmers, many other activities have gone largely unnoticed but could well have a profound long-term effect. One of the most significant changes to take place is the formation of a true common market by 1992 with the dismantling of trade barriers between member states and the removal of restrictive legislation. This will be accompanied by a synchronisation of taxes on purchases and elimination of tariffs. When this is seen in the context of the legislation which already exists which provides for free movement of labour within the community then, for the first time, there will be a market of sufficient buying power and size to be able to offer a real competitive threat to the US domestic market.

It is very important, clearly, that enterprises should take note of these developments and bring this into their planning. On the wider front there will be, inevitably, a strengthening of ties between America and Japan and, indeed, a changing role for Japan itself. This may well manifest itself in increasing aid for Third World countries and an increase in its own military expenditure. The emergence of Japan as a world political as well as economic power is going to have a profound effect not only in the Pacific Basin, but worldwide.

Law

In the legal environment it is quite evident that there is significant change underway in nearly all of the statute books of the Western countries. In the UK the Financial Services Act of 1987 was a most complex piece of legislation, and, coupled with the changes in financial markets around the world, has altered business in that particular industry out of all recognition. Further domestic changes are the introduction of data protection legislation in most Western countries and, in the UK, the Community Charge or 'Poll Tax' which fundamentally changes the way that local government is financed. All of these acts offer opportunities to those organisations which are prepared, for example, to invest in developing software packages and service based products.

Ecology

The ecological lobby is becoming increasingly vocal throughout the world. The emergence of the 'Green Peace' movement and the Greens' political parties in Western Europe is clearly a sign of an increasing awareness of the need to protect the environment. This has had substantial effects on such diverse activities as commercial whaling and the generation of power with a swing away from nuclear power generation back to coal, with the consequent problems of acid rain and an increasing emphasis on the search for alternative sources of power. A further example of the wide-ranging nature of the ecological lobby concerns the water industry where at least one organisation has an ecologist reporting to the chief executive to ensure that whatever engineering works are undertaken by the water authority, measures will be taken to properly preserve the natural habitat of all wildlife, particularly the otter.

Far from imposing limitations on companies, these pressures lead to increasing activity in research and development, for example in chemical scrubbers for pollution control at power stations.

Technology

The technological environment is, in common with the other environments, changing increasingly quickly. Consider the major changes in the information processing technologies in the last eight to ten years. These have included:

- the advent of the personal computer with its dramatic impact on business worldwide;
- the changes in telecommunications including fibre optics, networking, international protocols and the widespread use of facsimile machines now enable companies to respond so much quicker to political, economic and industrial changes elsewhere;
- the increasing use of computers and technology within the financial services sector which, it has been argued, was a major feature in the stock market crash of 1987. The effects of the crash were probably made much worse by programmed trading and the inability of systems to cope with the large volumes of transactions;
- it is also within the last ten to fifteen years that the use of technology in its wider sense has been used by organisations in order to gain competitive advantage. For example, the integration of manufacturing processes so that custom-made items can be manufactured at production line costs has significantly enhanced the competitiveness of many manufacturing organisations. These advances include developments in CAD/CAM, Computer Integrated Manufacturing (CIM), and just-in-time (JIT) inventory management. Toyota of Japan now say that they can make a car to the exact customer specification within four days of taking the order. The costs involved in achieving this level of flexibility are enormous. But this is easily offset by the working capital released by the reduction in finished goods and component inventories;
- further major advances have occurred in the areas of image processing and Artificial Intelligence. In both of these areas we are only just beginning to see the potential applications.

Summary

These elements of the external environment have to be understood in order to identify problems which may have to be resolved and, just as importantly, to identify opportunities which may be presented to the organisation for exploitation. Signals from the external environment must be monitored constantly in order to be able to position the enterprise both offensively and defensively for the future.

To assist management in obtaining and understanding the implications of such signals, many public databases are now available providing hard data and commentary on many of the factors described. These can be interrogated from computer terminals. The main problem is finding the appropriate sources for relevant, up to date, reliable information.

Whilst an individual enterprise can react to its environment, unless it is a very big company, it cannot, by itself, have influence over the environment. However, by grouping together with others in the same industry, it is possible for the combined group to exert influence over its external environment. This may be achieved through the sharing of information via trade associations, and can be a major factor in the search for advantage. Trade associations through effective lobbying can change, or modify laws; and can enforce standards. It will be shown later, though, that in a mature enterprise, well used to planning, it is possible for an individual enterprise to shape the external environment to its particular requirements, thus creating significant, sustainable, long-term competitive advantage.

PRESSURE GROUPS AND STAKEHOLDERS

The enterprise functions within the context of the external environment, and also under the direct influence of two sets of forces. These two groups are represented in Figure 2.1 and are categorised as Pressure Groups and Stakeholders. Some of the forces are to be found in both 'camps', implying they can influence the organisation in more than one way. The two categories are considered separately below.

Pressure Groups

Pressure groups are characterised by their making demands on the enterprise. They require that the enterprise acknowledges the pressure being exerted on it and they expect rapid response from management to that particular pressure.

Pressure groups comprise the following:

1. *Media*—one of the characteristics of the media in the past decade or so has been the increasing power and influence which they can exert over organisations. In particular, in so far as business planning is concerned, the influence of the financial press is very strong indeed. This is possibly strongest in the United Kingdom where the standard of investigative and analytical journalism within the financial media is probably the highest in the world. It is very common for companies to report substantial increases in turnover and profit but still fall short of the expectations of the financial journalists. This immediately marks down the stock market valuation of that company's shares.

    One particular example of the power of the financial journalists concerns a company in the retail sector which, every time that it was mentioned in the press, was compared unfavourably with its major competitor on the basis of turnover per square foot, and gross margins. This gradual but constant pressure from the financial press stimulated the company into a number of courses of action, focusing on improving performance. These included upgrading stores, better advertising, streamlining distribution and the commissioning of a strategic information systems planning exercise!

Another example of the power of the media concerns a group of companies in the food industry. This group had, for many years, been promoting the use of powdered milk as a suitable means of providing baby formula in Third World countries, in particular in Africa. The environmentalist lobby was concerned that the impression being given to these Third World mothers was that powdered milk was preferable to breast milk and that it was more sophisticated to feed babies this way. There is a major problem with this approach as non-caucasian children frequently do not have the enzyme which enables them to digest cows milk and therefore the cows milk substitute was a positive disadvantage to them. This biological fact had been known for years but it was the pressure exerted on the company by the press that really caused it to change its approach and to modify the advertising and promotion of this type of baby formula in Third World countries.

2. *Shareholders*—can also exert considerable pressure on companies in terms of how they conduct the business as well as what they do with shareholders' funds. In the USA annual general meetings have frequently been an opportunity for individual shareholders and shareholder groups to demonstrate their power by the voting down of proposals, the rejection of nominated directors and the severe and strong questioning of company policies and objectives. In the past, in Britain, little attention has been given to shareholders in this regard and this is characterised by many annual general meetings of large companies with many individual shareholders taking place in small boardrooms rather than in the large concert halls which is commonplace in North America. However, this is changing, and many examples are now available where shareholders have exerted considerable pressure on companies during AGMs, for example in the case of recently privatised UK companies, such as British Telecom. In addition, the minority shareholders which have representation on the Board of Directors of companies are by no means as quiet and undemanding as they used to be. Minority shareholders are frequently insisting on changes of policy, changes in objectives and changes in management.

   Some shareholder groups, such as pension funds, control significant votes and will only invest if they are assured of long-term prospects, and frequently look for properly developed long-term plans.

3. *Competitors, suppliers, customers*—are obvious pressure groups each exerting direct business pressure in its own particular way due to their mutual interdependence; each of them being part of the 'value chain' involved in bringing a product or service into the market. These pressures are dealt with in more detail later in this chapter.

4. *Governments*—exert pressure in a number of different ways by framing legislation and then monitoring performance against the various laws. This includes monopolies and mergers; health and safety legislation; taxation levels and laws; product liability; deregulation.

    This does not only apply to national governments; pressure may be exerted by other groupings such as United Nations or the European Parliament and Commission particularly in respect of international standards, trade embargoes and tariffs.

5. *Unions*—these exert pressure particularly when it comes to grievances and working practices. This type of pressure was historically very high during the 1970s but has diminished, in the UK particularly, with the advent of much higher unemployment in the 1980s; and this type of pressure waxes and wanes according to the political party in government at the time.

6. *Public*—the general public can exert pressure, for example, through the boycotting of certain consumer items, and through the unpredictable nature of fashion. The impact of fashion goes beyond clothes to toys and foods as well. The Cabbage Patch dolls of the mid 1980s soon went out of fashion —but the move to healthy eating and 'real' food has been sustained.

7. *Financial institutions*—exert pressure through the increasingly wide range of financial instruments available for the lending of money and the increased level of analytical ability within the institutions themselves. It is of vital importance for enterprises to continually lobby these financial analysts in order to keep a reasonable stock market valuation and debt rating. This can be self defeating: these enterprises must perform according to their own, and the financial analyst's, expectations, or risk losing their valuation and rating, putting more strain on them for ever-increasing performance.

8. *Employees*—the pressure which employees can exert can take many forms including the needs for comparability across job functions, job enrichment, personnel appraisals and evaluations.

The interfaces with each of these pressure groups must be constantly monitored as they pose considerable threat to the enterprise. It has to defend against these threats but, on the other hand, these pressure groups also offer opportunities which can be exploited to the advantage of the enterprise. It is the careful balance of the threats against the risks and the searching out of the opportunities that separates the successful from the unsuccessful companies.

Stakeholders

On the other side there are those groups, the stakeholders, who have a share in the enterprise, and who demand a fair share of the wealth created.

1. *Shareholders*—first and foremost amongst these stakeholders are the group called 'shareholders' who are, of course, expecting increased dividends year on year and an increased stock market valuation, i.e. revenue, income and capital growth, the latter having become more important over the last few years. There has also been a change in the type of shareholder. Institutional investors and pension funds still control significant blocks of shares but with privatisation of nationalised industries taking place on a worldwide basis there are now millions of private individuals who are shareholders.

Other stakeholders include:

2. *Customers*—who are constantly requiring higher quality in the products or services provided by the enterprises at the same or lower cost, in order to improve their own financial performance.
3. *Suppliers*—who are always looking for an increase in the volume and price of the goods that they sell to the enterprise.
4. *Unions*—who negotiate for better conditions of service, a better quality of working environment, including investments for safety of employees, more sick pay, more holidays, and, of course, higher wages.
5. *Employees*—who would share in the improvements negotiated organised by unions but probably, in addition, would want to look forward to other demonstrations of success of the company, such as performance-related bonuses, additional holidays, and so on. Their personal future depends on the success of the company.
6. *Government*—would expect to benefit from the success of the enterprise by way of increased taxation, overall economic growth, provision of more jobs, training for employees, etc.
7. *Public*—the general public would expect to see some sort of benefit from the success of an enterprise. For example, a successful company in a small town might feel obliged to donate a community centre to the town for the benefit of the people living there.

These stakeholders are all expecting some form of material and financial benefit from the success of the enterprise and it is a characteristic of those companies which have been most successful in the past that the fruits of their labours have indeed been passed through, not just to the shareholders by way of increased dividends, but also through to the community at large and their customers, suppliers and employees.

Summary

It is very important to note that some members can be from both the pressure groups and stakeholders: for example, shareholders, customers, employees. The most sophisticated planning mechanisms take account of each group and recognise that the signals can be those of divergent needs, depending on the circumstances prevailing at the time. In a competitive environment the company that understands the needs of external pressure groups and reacts to them or exploits them most effectively will succeed in the longer term. As 'privatisation' has proceeded rapidly during the 1980s, many public sector organisations now have to accommodate these external factors as well as internal preferences in their strategies.

BUSINESS PLANNING PROCESSES

As mentioned above, the enterprise exists within the context of the external environment and the pressure groups and stakeholders. The enterprise must consider the signals coming in from the external environment and the threats and opportunities posed by the pressure groups and then consider what strategies it, as an enterprise, is going to undertake. It then has to establish the means of incorporating these into its business planning along with the need to achieve its chosen mission by effective development and use of resources. The key components of that business planning process are considered below in the context of the framework (see Figure 2.2).

Objectives

The first task in the business planning process is to set objectives. These are usually described by reference to profitability, growth, market share, diversification, employment, social responsibility, and so on.

Objectives are not simply plucked out of thin air but reflect the values held by the organisation, by management and by major shareholders. These values are often expressed in terms of the 'mission' of the organisation which is usually a 'philosophical' statement of purpose. Examples of mission statements and objectives are considered in more detail in Chapter 5, as part of the process of identifying how IS/IT can contribute to the business strategy.

Typically these objectives do not change dramatically year-to-year, but may evolve quite significantly over a period of time.

For example, assume that a company is in the transportation business. It started out in shipping then evolved into rail, road haulage and airfreight. As part of this business it developed expertise in freight forwarding and handling and so took on agencies for other, complementary transportation companies and began operating warehouses and container terminals. Company objectives in the early days focused on high volume/low margin business to utilise the ships in the fleet. However, as time went by in the later 1970s and early 1980s the objectives were slowly modified to reduce the dependence on shipping, which was in a decline, to focus instead on low volume/high margin business of air cargo, and high value-added services such as cargo handling and forwarding. Their objectives evolved

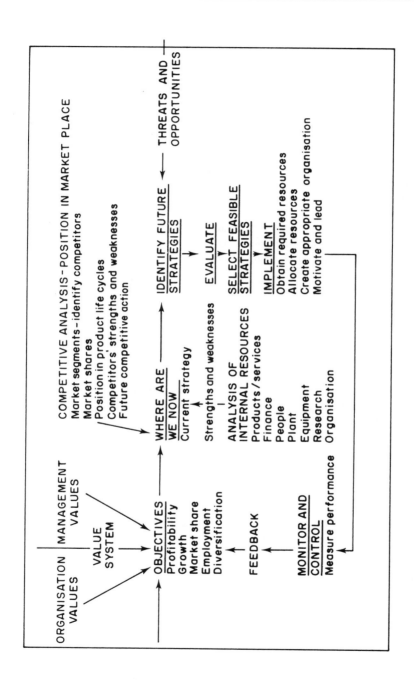

FIGURE 2.2

over time; they did not change dramatically overnight. Their objectives continued to be consistent with the established mission, namely to continue to operate in the transportation industry. If the values enshrined in the mission had not been so strong, then the company could have increased profit significantly by selling all the assets, terminating all the staff and investing in property. But this would have been quite contrary to the values held by the organisation and so stability, and steady growth were the result.

Situation Analysis

In order to determine strategy it is not sufficient simply to determine a set of objectives (see Mintzberg, 1987). This is rather like looking at a map. It is not good enough simply to know that one wants to get to point B because one can get to point B from any one of the 360 degrees on the compass. In order to get to point B it is first necessary to understand very clearly where you are now, point A.

'Where we are now' consists of two essential elements; one looking inside the organisation and one looking outside.

The first concerns current strategy and an understanding of the enterprise's strengths and weaknesses. This involves a thorough analysis of:

● the resources available within the organisation by way of the products and services being offered by the organisation;
● the financial health of the organisation in respect of its debt, liquidity, assets;
● the people, their level of education, training, experience, motivation;
● the plant and equipment, its age, the technology employed, its usefulness;
● research and development, the proportion of turnover reinvested into researching new products and markets, the number of new products awaiting development, the quality of the past history of the R&D function;
● the organisation, its rigidities, flexibility, attitudes, level of bureaucracy.

The second element in understanding 'where we are now' involves an analysis of competitors so that the enterprise can quite clearly identify its position in the market place. This will involve looking at:

● market segments and within those market segments identifying competitors both current and potential;
● market shares to see if there is opportunity for increasing the share of the market or for increasing the total size of the market;
● the enterprise's position in the product life-cycles by considering products which are nearing obsolescence, products which are mature, products which are of strategic importance and products coming into the strategic importance arena

from the research and development area, and looking at the length of the product life-cycles themselves to see if there are ways in which they can be shortened or extended;

- an examination of all current and potential competitors for their strengths and weaknesses, in their entirety, concerning products, engineering, marketing, finance, people;
- future competitive action which may take place concerning potential substitute products and thrusts into new markets.

This type of analysis is often called SWOT—Strengths, Weaknesses, Opportunities and Threats. Once the analysis has been completed, then using creative thinking and brainstorming sessions the enterprise searches for ways it can use its strengths to exploit opportunities, whilst addressing its weaknesses and defending against the threats.

Future Strategies

Once the enterprise has a good understanding of what it is trying to achieve by way of objectives, and understands exactly where it is by reference to its current strengths, weaknesses and analyses of the competition, then it still has to identify future strategies. These must provide both a defensive mechanism against possible future threats and the capability to exploit the opportunities identified by analysing the pressure groups and stakeholders.

These future possible strategies are evaluated against a number of criteria, including:

- the risk, both financial and managerial;
- the degree to which the enterprise is going to be offensive or defensive;
- the ability of the organisation to implement the strategy in terms of people, finance, plant, culture.

Implementation

Once the feasible strategies have been selected then they need to be implemented and this requires that an adequate level of resourcing be obtained, that these resources are allocated sensibly, that the appropriate organisation is created and that people are motivated properly to achieve the objectives inherent in those strategies.

As these strategies are being implemented it is obviously important to both monitor and control these strategies by reference to the way in which they are assisting the organisation in achieving longer-term objectives. The results of this performance measurement will be used in a feedback loop to refine the objectives of the organisation.

Summary

In the ideal world this strategic planning framework would be the basis of planning in the enterprise and would cater for all elements of planning that is corporate, business, strategic, financial, organisation and information systems. However, it is not yet evident that such planning frameworks are widely used perhaps due to the implicit high degree of formality in this approach. It need not be prescriptive, but each of the elements should be addressed.

Instead it would appear that many organisations use a number of different planning tools, often without the benefit of a coherent framework and with no apparent sequence to their use.

To quote from Michael Porter (1987) 'Criticism of strategic planning was well deserved. Strategic planning in most companies has not contributed to strategic thinking. The answer, however, is not to abandon planning. The need for strategic thinking has never been greater . . . few have transferred strategic planning into the vital management discipline it needs to be.'

This implies that 'strategy' is not the result of strategic planning but the product of a number of processes. Strategy can be defined as:

An integrated set of actions aimed at increasing the long-term well-being and strength of the enterprise relative to competitors.

There are essentially three processes that can contribute to the establishment of such a 'strategy'.

(a) Strategic planning—systematic, comprehensive analysis to develop a plan of action.
(b) Strategic thinking—creative, entrepreneurial insight into the ways the company could develop.
(c) Opportunistic decision making—effective reaction to unexpected threats and opportunities.

To achieve any or all of these a thorough understanding of the environment, pressure groups and the business's capability is required. The combination of all three means of achieving the best strategy are probably best described as 'strategic management' which includes not only setting the strategy but also implementing it. As discussed both formal and informal approaches are required with the outcome of planning being refined and improved as the implementation proceeds. This relationship is shown in Figure 2.3. Similar relationships are inherent in the strategic management of IS/IT and the balance of formal and informal approaches should reflect the 'strategic culture' of the organisation.

FORMAL STRATEGIC PLANNING

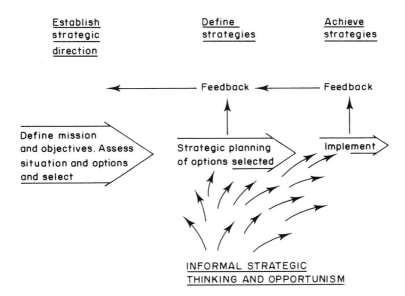

FIGURE 2.3 Strategic management process

BUSINESS PLANNING TOOLS AND TECHNIQUES

There are many different business planning tools and techniques in use. In this section a few of the more common tools and techniques are briefly described, under the main headings: quantitative and qualitative.

Quantitative Techniques

There are a number of quantitative approaches, which have been developed over the last sixty years mainly from management science, operational research and accountancy origins.

(a) *Forecasting techniques*—which use one or more mathematical approaches for trying to predict the future based on what has happened in the past. For a brief review of these techniques and their associated strengths and weaknesses see Georgoff and Murdick (1986).

These can be broken down into several different approaches:

1. Judgemental—including simple extrapolation; sales force predictions; consensus of experts; scenarios; Delphi; historical analogy.

2. Counting methods—market testing; consumer market surveys; industrial market surveys.
3. Time series—moving averages; exponential smoothing; time series extrapolation; time series decomposition; Box-Jenkins.
4. Causal—correlation; regression models; leading indicators; econometric models.

(b) *Financial evaluation processes*—involving the use of discounted cash flow; net present value; return on capital employed; return on investment.
(c) *Risk analysis*—which uses a number of different techniques to assess the risk of certain courses of action. These risk analyses often involve the use of mathematical modelling techniques to assist in assessing those risks.
(d) *Optimisation and simulation*—where the use of mathematical techniques such as linear programming, Monte Carlo and queuing theory are used to model situations so that predictions can be made.

All of these, and many other quantitative approaches, are useful when applied to appropriate planning problems with a clear understanding of the quality of the data used. But they can cause misjudgement if misunderstood because they tend to result in simplistic answers usually expressed as single figures implying black and white, yes/no, type decisions. The real world is not like this and so further techniques must also be used.

Qualitative Techniques

In the 1960s a number of business planning models emerged, which initially focused on managing portfolios of products. These then evolved by taking other factors into account in order to assess the strengths and weaknesses of particular courses of action.

The Boston Consulting Group Business Matrix

The Boston Matrix (or Boston Square) is one of the earliest examples of a qualitative technique. It is essentially based on two precepts—a product life-cycle and the coincidence of high market share and high profitability. The latter relies on the rationale of the 'experience curve'—whereby the more times something is made the lower the cost will become due to continuing improvements in the process and the achievement of economies of scale.

The basic parameters apply to many types of products and many industries but the model does not work in certain circumstances. For instance, in some commodity markets there is a high degree of government intervention which distorts the market by artificial control.

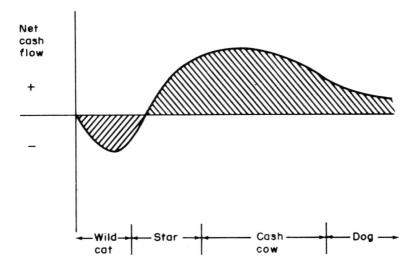

FIGURE 2.4 Product life-cycles

The product life-cycle shows how a product over time develops from concept via acceptance through high demand to eventual decline according to market demand (see Figure 2.4). Not all products follow the same cycle—some never get off the drawing-board, others never gain market acceptance. Life-cycles can be very different in duration. Some products, such as Guinness, are still going, if declining, after 100 years. Others, such as skateboards, go through the whole cycle in a year or two. Whole industries also go through life-cycles of emergence, growth, maturity and decline. The changing role of information systems during these cycles is discussed in detail in Chapter 6.

Relating the product life-cycle to the market position produces the 2 × 2 matrix which plots market growth against relative market share (see Figure 2.5).

The four cells produced by the matrix reflect the stages in the life-cycle and the success of the product *vis-à-vis* competitive products. One reason perhaps that the technique was so successfully adopted was the simple names given to the different cells—'wild cats', 'stars', 'cash cows' and 'dogs'. By superimposing these on Figure 2.4 the relationship between the matrix and cash generation and use can be seen.

The position of a product, or a whole business, on the matrix gives indications as to appropriate future strategies.

The 'Stars' represent products with the best profit and growth potential. They are in the sector of the matrix with both high market growth potential and high market share. These 'star' products will generate a lot of cash, but may also require substantial cash injections in order to establish themselves in the markets. Take, for example, the car industry. Products in the star category will require significant

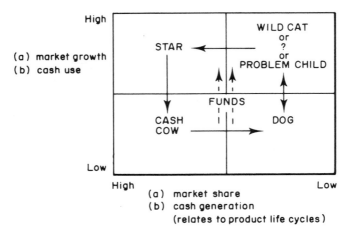

FIGURE 2.5 Product portfolios (BCG)

cash injected by way of advertising and dealer commissions to establish the car. Once established, new variations of the product can be introduced with, say, different engine capacities, braking systems and high value-added extras.

There will come a time, almost inevitably, when the growth of the market has slowed down considerably. At this point, the previous 'star' products, being well established, no longer require cash to be injected; rather they now generate cash. These are called 'cash cows'. In the example of the car industry, products in this category are characterised by 'cosmetic' improvements rather than the introduction of new models. For example, new colour combinations, redesigned lights and more refined instrumentation will appear, often as a reaction to innovation from a competitor. During this period, the firm endeavours to maintain a level of quality of these products so as to preserve its share of the market and to continue the cash generation for as long as possible.

However, after a further period of time, market share is gradually eroded by the introduction of new products or by the effects of fashion or gradual reduction in value as perceived by the customer. At this point the product is nearing obsolescence and the company must be wary of putting more money into the product with consequent reduced rate of return. These products are called 'dogs' and ideally should be disinvested. In our car industry example, the production line may be kept going for a period, but no new enhancements are announced. The manufacture and supply of spare parts is left to third parties. Eventually the manufacture of the car quietly stops.

Products in the last quadrant, where market growth is high, but market share is low, are called 'problem children' or 'wild cats'. These products require a lot of cash and give back little in return. The cash is sourced from the cash cows and is used to promote some of these 'problem children' for it is hoped that these will turn into tomorrow's stars and next year's cash cows. Other problem children should be disinvested as they will never turn into stars. In the car industry these 'problem children' are represented by products in the R&D environment. They may be new bodyshapes, engines, suspension systems, etc, sometimes brought together for exhibitions as 'concept cars'. Typically, they bear no relationship to existing models, but without the investment in R&D the new 'stars' will not arrive.

The whole model emphasises a couple of key issues in strategy:

● the need to manage the product according to market pressures not internal factors
● the need to reinvest net cash inflows into future products to ensure long-term sources of revenue.

One variation of the BCG Business Matrix to be mentioned briefly is the Portfolio Model which considers the total enterprise and values the different parts of the business separately to identify under-valued assets. This enables the company to dispose of those parts of the business which are under-performing so as to maximise the total company stock market valuation. The company can then leverage more borrowing to acquire new businesses and then repeat the cycle. A prime example of a company thriving on this planning approach is the Hanson Trust.

However, whilst the BCG matrix is an important planning model because it focuses on key issues such as cash flow, market share and industry growth it may over simplify many of the factors involved in achieving business success. For example, the high and low positions on the two axes are simplistic. In addition, the dimensions of growth rate and market share are only two aspects of industry attractiveness and competitive position respectively. It became clear that more variables needed to be considered. A number of such matrices, their pros and cons and the detailed business and management issues implied by the various segmentations are described in detail by Higgins (1985). Some are summarised here to give an overview of the different variables considered.

Other Planning/Policy Matrices

These all extend the number of variables considered and hence the options available. This usually results in a 3 × 3 or 3 × 5 matrix as shown, for example, in Figure 2.6. Some matrices are similar to the Boston Square in considering an extended version of the industry life cycle. The BCG matrix only really allows for growth and mature stages in the four-stage cycle of emergence, growth, maturity, decline during which strategies must change. Obviously high growth markets are inherently more attractive but other factors which make industries more or less attractive are: size, diversity, existing competitive

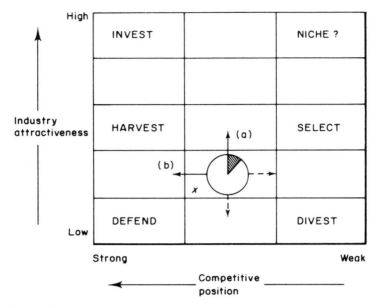

FIGURE 2.6 Policy/portfolios matrices

structure, prices, profitability, technology development effects, legal and social and environmental factors. Equally, market share obviously is a reflection of a company's strength but other factors are important: technology position, people, brand image, financial structure, capacity, strengths in related industries, etc.

The first stage in using any of the matrices is to understand the current position of the business unit or product—say *x* in Figure 2.6. Then two options exist for positive growth, by (a) developing the industry, perhaps to the benefit of others, by product or service innovation by attracting new types of customer, or (b) gaining market share from competitors. Equally, strategies need to be considered to defend the existing position against industry decline or competitive pressure. In general any strategy must be incremental through the matrix—new options open up as the business migrates over time. But it is not realistic to jump dramatically across the matrix unless some major innovation is achieved which others cannot copy.

All the matrices are useful in identifying the current position of a business and its products in relation to the market and the position of competitors, as well as the desired strategy for the business. They then enable the management to select feasible options from those potentially available, both to improve the position and to counter threats from competitors. They also enable changing positions to be monitored and the implications and reasons to be understood. The main objective is to ensure the organisation's resources are allocated to achieve the maximum benefit.

Profit Impact on Market Strategies (PIMS)

All of the models offer some relevant and valuable approaches to assessing why businesses succeed or fail within competitive environments, but they lack the rigour of valid research so it is often difficult to associate cause and effect. In order to identify what other variables ought to be taken into account a project called PIMS was organised in 1972 by the Market Science Institute which is affiliated to the Harvard Business School.

The purpose of the program was to determine the profit impact of market strategy. By analysing many organisations in many industries they found that some of the more significant contributory variables included the following:

1. market share,
2. product or service quality,
3. marketing expenditure,
4. research and development expenditures,
5. intensity of investment (the ratio of total investment to sales),
6. corporate diversity,
7. other company factors—for example, organisational size.

These variables are fed into a database and the resulting position of an enterprise is compared with that of other organisations across industries to examine, for example, how it can improve the allocation of resources to enable it to respond more effectively to changes in the market place. Once the ways in which an enterprise is profitable are understood then appropriate courses of action can be proposed (Kirchhoff, 1975).

Competitive Strategy

Based on the PIMS database, and other research at Harvard, Michael Porter (1980) developed some new approaches to considering strategic choices in competitive environments.

The basis of this model is that an enterprise exists within an industry and to succeed, it must effectively deal with the competitive forces which exist within the particular industry. For example, the forces in an emerging industry such as biotechnology and genetic engineering are considerably different from those of a growth industry, say leisure or financial services, or the more mature or declining industries such as steel manufacturing, or super-tanker oil carriers. In addition, the pressures of operating globally as in the international money markets are very different from those in localised industries such as DIY retailing where international competition is very limited.

The enterprise interacts with its customers, suppliers and competitors, but in addition to these interactions, there are potential new entrants into the particular

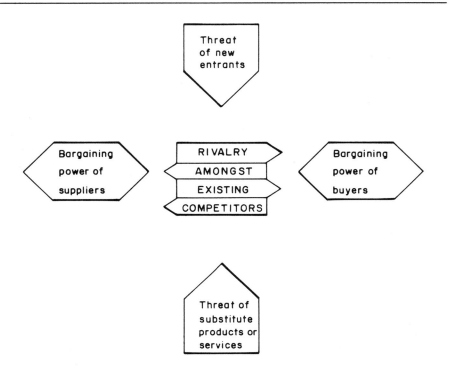

FIGURE 2.7 Competitive forces in an industry (adapted with permission of The Free Press, a Division of Macmillan, Inc. from COMPETITIVE ADVANTAGE: Creating and Sustaining Superior Performance *by Michael E. Porter. Copyright © 1985 by Michael E. Porter)*

competitive market place and potential substitute products and services. To survive and thrive in this environment, it is obviously vital to understand these interactions and the implications in terms of opportunities for competitive advantage can occur (see Figure 2.7).

At any one time one or more of the forces may be exerting particular pressure on the competing firms. The existing rivals may be competing viciously via a price war and/or aggressive advertising campaigns. Alternatively, competitors may be 'cooperating' to ward off an external threat.

The buyers or suppliers may be powerful enough to bargain away much of the profitability available to the firm and its immediate competitors. Increasing buyer and supplier switching costs, making a change of relationship expensive, can reduce that power.

New companies may be a threat in terms of new entrants to the industry because of low entry barriers or weak competitive rivals. Substitute products are always possible, not just in terms of replacement products or services but also as alternative ways for buyers to spend their money (e.g. holidays *v.* luxury goods).

TABLE 2.1 Factors affecting the impact of competitive forces

New entrants
Capital requirements
Patents and specialist skills required
Distribution channels available
Achieved/required economies of scale and resultant cost advantages
Number and size of existing rivals and intensity of competition
Differentiation and brand establishment/loyalty
Access to raw materials/critical resources, etc.

Substitute products/services
(implies achieving a higher priority for customer spend)
Customer awareness of needs and means of satisfaction
Customer sensitivity to value for money and ability to compare
Existing loyalty of customers—impact of 'industry' promotion
Ability to differentiate products, etc.

Competitive rivalry
will be intensified by:
Market growth is slow (or in decline)
Small number of similar sized competitors dominate
High fixed costs and/or high exit barriers for all rivals
Over-capacity and/or capacity increments are large units
Commodity like, undifferentiated products, etc.

Buyers power
will be increased by:
Concentrated/few buyers making high volume and/or high value of purchases
Low switching costs across suppliers
Price sensitive and many alternative sources of supply
Weak brand identities, products not differentiated
Buyers capable of backward integration due to low 'entry' costs, etc.

Suppliers power
will be increased by:
Few suppliers—high switching costs for rivals, and suppliers deal with many small
    customers
Potential substitute supplier/resources not easily available
Supplied goods make up large part of firms costs
Suppliers capable of forward integration or bypass to customers, etc.

If all the forces are exerting intense pressure at the same time, the company faces serious problems! But if it addresses the competitive forces according to their potential impact now and in the future it can establish a better business position than its rivals. How the impact of these forces can be affected by IS/IT is reviewed in depth later in the book. Table 2.1 briefly outlines the types of factors which determine whether the forces will have a major influence on a business.

Another precept of the model is that in the long term successful performance results from being the lowest cost producer of that good or service or by differentiating the product or service from that of competitors. Lowest cost is normally

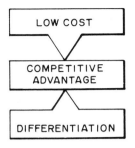

TYPE OF ADVANTAGE SOUGHT

Low cost	Differentiation	
Overall cost leadership	Differentiation (value added)	Broad - industrywide **Competitive scope**
Cost based focus (niche)	Differentiation based focus	Narrow - selected market

FIGURE 2.8 Competitive strategy and competitive scope (adapted with permission of The Free Press, a Division of Macmillan, Inc. from COMPETITIVE ADVANTAGE: Creating and Sustaining Superior Performance *by Michael E. Porter. Copyright © 1985 by Michael E. Porter)*

associated with volume production, i.e. high market share, or by flexible manufacturing systems. These two strategies can either be followed overall or by focusing on particular narrow markets—'niches' (see Figure 2.8).

An example of these generic strategies can be seen by reference to Mercedes-Benz. The Mercedes-Benz limousine is regarded in most parts of the world as being the type of car that a successful businessman should be driving. The Mercedes-Benz company has consistently advertised its cars in that way. The products are very cleverly promoted and the emphasis is always on high quality, high reliability, high price. So in this particular regard Mercedes-Benz is differentiating from its competitors in the executive car market. However, within Europe the Mercedes-Benz is probably the most common car to be seen in taxi fleets. Taxi operators are not known for their profligate expenditure on executive cars but are usually very careful to assess the long-term costs of running their taxi fleets and in this regard Mercedes-Benz comes out extremely well due to the emphasis of the company on high reliability, low maintenance costs and high resale value, thereby making their cars the most attractive, on average, for a taxi fleet

TABLE 2.2

Generic strategy	*Commonly required skills and resources*	*Common organisational requirements*
Overall cost leadership	Sustained capital invest-ment and access to capital	Tight cost control, frequent, detailed control reports
	Process engineering skills	Structured organisation and responsibilities
	Intense supervision of labour	Incentives based on meeting strict quantitative targets
Differentiation	Strong marketing abilities and creative flair	Strong co-ordination among functions in R&D, product development, and marketing
	Product engineering skills	Subjective measurement and incentives instead of quantitative measures (market based incentives)
		Amenities to attract highly skilled labour or creative people
	Strong capability in basic research	Looser, more trusting organisational relationships
	Corporate reputation for quality or technological leadership	
	Strong co-operation from distribution channels	
Focus	Combination of the above policies directed at the particular strategic target	Combination of the above policies directed at the particular strategic target

The generic strategies may also require different styles of leadership and can translate into very different corporate cultures and atmospheres. Different sorts of people will be attracted.

operator. In this way Mercedes-Benz is operating in the niche market of the taxi fleet operator by being the market leader using a low cost strategy.

Some of the major requirements for an enterprise to be able to adopt these 'generic strategies' are shown in Table 2.2. The key aspects of each are quite different and would imply different organisational structures and management styles. The most common error organisations make is to get stuck between strategies by not deciding on their market scope and basic advantage—low cost or differentiation. Consequently costs are too high and prices cannot be sustained leading to low margins.

ORGANISATIONAL UNITS AND APPROACHES TO DEFINING STRATEGY

A key issue of any planning process is to determine the scope. Should it cover the organisation as a whole or should the organisation be broken down into smaller, discrete parts where it may be easier to apply the tools and techniques, and develop coherent strategies and plans? These organisational components are often called 'strategic business units' or SBUs.

A business unit can be defined as '*a unit that sells a distinct set of products or services, serves a specific set of customers and competes with a well-defined set of competitors*'. A business unit, though, may also contain Product Development, Research and Development, Engineering and Manufacturing. Generic models for both centralised (or functional) and decentralised (or business unit) organisational structures is shown in Figure 2.9. Most major organisations have moved more towards business units and away from functional structures over the last 10–15 years. An advantage of the SBU approach as far as planning is concerned is that it encourages creativity and innovation, both being important aspects of entrepreneurship. This usually results in better responsiveness to markets, greater operational flexibility and clear accountability for results.

Clearly, in the derivation and development of strategies, and the application of these tools it is important to consider both the enterprise as a whole, and the individual business units. This can be reconciled by considering the enterprise strategy as the combination of achievement of corporate objectives via the contribution of the SBUs.

Shortcomings of Planning Approaches

It is a feature, however, of these planning methods that few of them take any recognition of: (a) people as a long-term resource, or (b) technology as a major strategic weapon.

These shortcomings would seem to be a major problem in the business world of the 1980s and 1990s as the availability of skilled people is one of the major factors limiting growth. Organisations are experiencing substantial increases in the amount of time and money invested in training their existing staff. It is not unusual to find companies allocating 30 days training per year on employees at all levels. It is now widely recognised that staff need to be continually trained, and often retrained, during their working lives. Naisbitt (1984), points out that it is quite possible that individuals may go through two or three distinct careers before retirement. This is extremely expensive and, obviously, planning techniques must take account of this.

The second major concern is that none of the models recognise the dramatic impact that technology, in all its forms, has had on industries. None of these models specifically reviews the organisation to examine how its capability in these technological areas might be used for competitive advantage. For example, there are now, literally, hundreds of organisations which have gained competitive advantage through the use of information systems and technology. Yet in the majority of cases it is almost impossible to state that the competitive advantage actually arose through the application of traditional planning approaches. It would

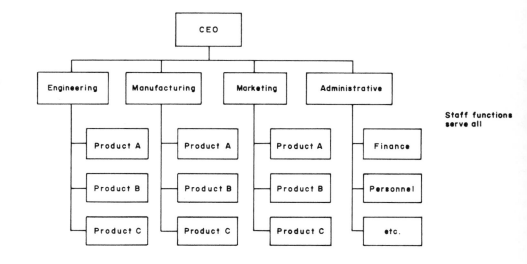

(a)

(b)

FIGURE 2.9 Alternative organisation structure, (a) Functional organisation (centralised). (b) Divisional/business unit organisation (decentralised)

appear that usually these competitive advantage opportunities came about through serendipity, chance or good luck.

We must accept that good fortune is often an ingredient in success but we must not overlook that there are a number of planning mechanisms currently available which enable technological opportunities to be discovered. This is the focus of the second part of this book. It must be said, though, that the identification of technological opportunities by themselves is by no means sufficient. There has to be a culture and a value system in place in the organisation which will spot innovative ideas and exploit them. Typically, the organisations which have such a culture encourage entrepreneurship through having simple structures with a concentration on the basic business of the enterprise.

New Planning Approaches for the 1990s

These new planning methodologies must address a number of key issues, which the previously considered techniques fail to address overtly:

(a) *A strategy for technology*—to exploit the opportunities afforded by the dramatically changing technologies in order to gain competitive advantage or repel competitive threat.
(b) *A people strategy*—to enable organisations to maximise their return on investment in the people, the scarcest and often most valuable of all resources. This has implications on the structure of organisations and the roles that people adopt within the organisations and how people and activities are controlled.
(c) *An information strategy*—to manage information as an asset and resource which can be exploited to gain direct advantages. Consider a relatively trivial example from Sears-Roebuck, which has tens of millions of credit card customers within the US. When a woman buys maternity clothes from a Sears-Roebuck retail outlet, she typically pays by credit card. The information is kept and six to nine months later that same person is sent a catalogue of baby clothes, nursery furniture and items for the newborn baby. This shows how Sears-Roebuck is clearly targeting its marketing effort and leveraging off the information which it has at its disposal.
(d) *Entrepreneurship*—enterprises which prosper are generally characterised by having a relatively high number of entrepreneurs (or intrapreneurs) within the organisations, who are innovative not only in the development of products and markets but also in the way in which they conduct and manage the business. Many of these innovators have deployed IS/IT to create new products and services, attack new markets and streamline the operation and control of the business.

Some Concerns about the Use of Planning Tools

It was stated earlier in the chapter that these planning methods have evolved since the 1950s and are continuing to evolve. However, the question must be raised about why it is that the Western world, which has typically been in the forefront in developing these methods, has underperformed the Far East since the 1950s and yet those companies in the Far East do not adopt the same planning methods. Is it that the traditional 'ends–ways–means' approach, which forms the basis of these Western planning methods, does not work? Is there value in the concept of looking at means, then ways, then ends, i.e. defining what resources are available to the enterprise and letting that determine how the resources could be used and then using that to define what can be achieved by the enterprise? Is this the way in which planning will go in the future? (Hayes, 1985).

Of course there is no simple answer to this conundrum, but it could be argued that the reason why the planning methods do not appear to have worked successfully to date is that the time period for the planning exercise is often far too short, considerably less than five years, and typically, planning has a very strong financial emphasis rather than a focus on business or strategic issues. In Japan, for instance, the types of models described here are apparently used to consider the long-term development of 'Japan Incorporated' to ensure the economy as a whole is 'planned'.

It must also be stated that the concept of the 'annual strategic planning cycle' must be regarded with a degree of scepticism. Rarely do organisations go through major change in direction and therefore the idea of repeating the same exercise every year to some extent devalues the exercise. Indeed, it has been shown that many organisations only go through major change once in a generation and strategy is as much a function of understanding, not only where you are, but where you have come from, as well as understanding where you want to go. In this context strategic planning is adding incrementally to the existing body of understanding and knowledge of what the organisation is capable of doing. This is probably where organisations in the Far East have benefited, as they seem to have a very clear understanding of where they have come from and what they are capable of achieving (see Mintzberg, 1987).

Each of these planning methods has a role to play. Each of these planning methods, including the more radical views of means-ways-ends rather than ends-ways-means, are employed not only in strategic planning but also in the area of information systems planning. The particular approaches and methods in relation to IS planning will be explained in more detail in succeeding chapters.

IS/IT INFLUENCE ON CORPORATE STRATEGY

Until recently IS/IT was seen as an instrument of implementation of strategy— where informal strategic thinking could improve on the general direction by deploying IS/IT to enhance the strategy in some way, as depicted in Figure 2.3. However, as described in Chapter 1 and shown in Figure 1.7, IS/IT can and should be considered as an input to strategy in terms of its potential to change the strategy or open up new potential strategies. It must be remembered that the same potential opportunities may exist for competitors! and, therefore, IS/IT can constitute a threat, just like a new competitive product.

It should also be borne in mind that IS strategy can modify corporate and business unit strategies, in both positive and negative ways. For example, a worldwide conglomerate wanted to increase its business presence in the US. This was to be achieved via a number of different business units but largely through the expansion of its aviation business into the US. This business unit went through its own planning processes, including information systems planning, and it became apparent that the expansion of aviation activities into the US would be thwarted through the inability of the communications network to sustain an increase in VDU terminal population in the US. The new communications hardware and software would not be in place for eighteen months. This resulted not only in the airline having to scale down its ambitions in that direction, but also, at corporate level, the holding company had to modify its objectives. In this case the IS strategy had a detrimental impact on the corporate objectives.

To give an example of the opposite effect, an agency operation was seriously considering the application of computing technology to increase its business. The nature of the agency, with a very high level of fixed costs represented by highly trained staff, meant that an increase in business volumes of 15% would double profit. The decision was taken to invest heavily in a computer system in order to increase market share, with a target of 15% more business. It was assumed that the business volume would increase by 7½% in the first year and 15% in the second year, but when the system was commissioned, business volume increased by 15% within the first year and by 25% in the second year. This enabled the business objectives to be revised upwards rather than downwards and so enabled the enterprise to broaden its horizons considerably, such that it went out into the acquisition market which had previously not been an option open to it. This shows how strategic information systems planning affected objectives in a positive fashion.

These examples serve to reiterate the changing nature of the role IS/IT is playing within the strategic framework (Figure 2.1). Traditionally, the major part of IS/IT spend has been in the area of implementation of agreed strategy, and in capturing information to monitor and control progress, as shown on the diagram. In the future, the more significant role of information systems may be as part of the formulation of strategy, not merely its implementation. As shown above, and discussed in Chapter 1, IS/IT has a role to play not only in formulating that strategy but also will affect relationships with the pressure groups and stakeholders and may enable the organisation to collect signals from the environment and use them to advantage. IS/IT can therefore be considered as something which could affect any aspect of the framework in the future.

MATURITY IN STRATEGIC PLANNING

Whilst it has been stated that planning methods are evolving, it must also be recognised that organisations go through phases of maturity in their approach

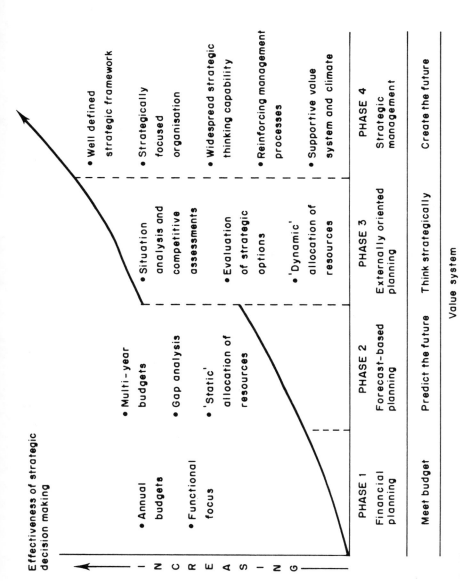

FIGURE 2.10

to strategic planning. Figure 2.10 shows four main phases and is derived from a model described in Gluck *et al.* (1980).

In *Phase 1* the focus is on cash flow and annual financial planning and uses relatively simple techniques to develop medium-term budgets. These exercises are usually carried out internally, department by department, and consolidated. The focus of management is to reduce everything to a financial problem— meeting the budget. Planners' attention is mainly directed at factors within the company.

In *Phase 2* the focus is on trying to predict, or forecast, what is likely to happen within, say, a five-year planning horizon, usually by reference to historical performance analysed and projected into the future using internal trends and external parameters such as exchange rates and inflation rates. It forecasts sales and market growth and predicts the effect on income and expenses and changes to the balance sheet. Plans, though, are still quantitative and internally orientated, focusing on the gap between what is targeted and the resources that are available.

In *Phase 3* the organisation starts to look outside itself and concentrate on understanding the nature of competition in its industry and positions itself to gain advantage. The planners might seek to shift the company's product portfolio to more attractive market sectors. This implies identification of product and market resourcing options and evaluation to find the one that not only suits the organisation, but will have the required implications for the other competitive forces.

In *Phase 4* the organisation is driven by innovation and becomes capable of creating its own business environment. Its values, culture and organisation structure will reinforce the processes required to develop and sustain a leading role in the industry and enable the company to have significant control over its own destiny. Obviously sustaining this leadership will require continuing innovation.

Whilst some organisations such as 3M and Disneyland, and others, are capable of a truly creative strategy, at least for significant parts of the business, they also have to monitor the competitive environment, forecast effectively and deliver an annual profit. Developing to stages 3 and 4 implies that 1 and 2 are handled effectively and the strategic thinking can be converted to results. The major gain implied in the move from stage 2 to 3 is because of the external perspective taken to consider the organisation, what it does and how well it does it in the context of its competitive environment.

It is interesting to note that the various tools and techniques of strategic analysis and formulation described earlier in the chapter show this evolution to some extent. The early quantitative and financial tools and forecasting techniques are only relevant to stages 1 and 2. The various models and matrices, such as the Boston Square were a way of moving from stage 2 to 3 and Michael Porter's competitive analysis approaches are clearly tools to the externally orientated planning of stage 3 and may lead to the development of creative strategy—although stage 4 is perhaps too creative for the strict use of tools and techniques. The overall move is from hard tools—quantitative—to soft tools—people-based strategy.

SUMMARY AND CONCLUSION

As discussed in Chapter 1, it is vital that the IS/IT plans and strategies be linked directly to the objectives and strategies of the business unit and of the corporation. There are now a number of examples where IS/IT planning takes place within the same process as corporate, strategic, and financial planning, and indeed the entire planning process is now fully integrated with a number of specialists taking information from the planning function to develop plans for their own particular areas. However, the evidence, as quoted in Chapter 1, is that this applies to a minority of organisations as yet.

Each of the tools and techniques described above have been shown to have value in the various planning processes. If there are going to be links between IS/IT planning and business planning then these same tools and techniques should have value in IS/IT planning, if only because they enable business managers to become positively involved in IS/IT planning. It will be demonstrated in later chapters that the tools and techniques used for business strategic planning can be transferred from one type of planning to another, in particular to IS/IT strategic planning.

This chapter has considered in overview a number of aspects of business strategic planning and management. Many of the ideas introduced, albeit briefly, in this chapter are developed more extensively and in more depth in subsequent chapters in the context of IS/IT strategy, rather than business strategy. This will perhaps demonstrate the value and use of the ideas more thoroughly than has been possible in this chapter.

The next task is to establish that context for IS/IT strategy more coherently. Chapter 3 will develop models and approaches to IS/IT strategic planning— but all of those models and approaches recognise the need to link effectively to the business strategy, its determination and management as considered in this chapter.

REFERENCES

Georgoff, D. M. and Murdick, R. G. (1986) 'Managers guide to forecasting', *Harvard Business Review* (Jan./Feb.).

Gluck, F. W., Kaufmann, S. P. and Walleck, A. S. (1980) 'Strategic management for competitive advantage', *Harvard Business Review* (July/Aug.).

Hayes, R. H. (1985) 'Strategic planning—forward in reverse?' *Harvard Business Review* (Nov./Dec.).

Higgins, J. M. (1985) *Strategy—Formulation, Implementation and Control*, The Dryden Press.

Kirchhoff, B. A. (1975) 'Empirical analysis of strategic factors contributing to return on investment, *Proceedings of the Academy of Management*.

Mintzberg, H. (1987) 'Crafting strategy', *Harvard Business Review* (July/Aug.).
Naisbitt, J. (1984) *Megatrends—Ten New Directions Transforming Our Lives*, MacDonald and Co.
Porter, M. E. (1980) *Competitive Strategy*, The Free Press.
Porter, M. E. (1987) 'The state of strategic thinking', *The Economist* (23 May 1987).

Chapter 3

STRATEGIC INFORMATION SYSTEMS PLANNING — WHAT IS INVOLVED?

INTRODUCTION

To plan for the effective application of IS/IT in business is not a new objective, nor is the concept that systems and technology contribute to the competitive success of organisations, if only indirectly. Over the last few years, the belief that it is possible to substantially increase this contribution has gained growing acceptance, and is now widely acknowledged in both business and IS/IT communities. As a direct result of this, strategic planning for IS/IT has become a key activity in pursuit of delivering increased value to the business, both in terms of exploiting opportunities and in countering threats.

The necessity to improve return on investments, coupled with the high risk potential of investing very substantial sums unwisely, have been key stimuli in arousing interest in IS/IT planning. The ever-increasing number of good examples of improved competitive success resulting from implementing computer and telecommunications systems has also boosted awareness and interest. American Airlines, Merrill Lynch, American Hospital Supplies, Thomson Travel (all briefly described in Box 1.2), and several others have been reported so extensively that they have been elevated almost to legend status. There are many other examples which have so far received less widespread coverage, but are equally significant as sources of ideas for other organisations. Many of these are referenced later.

It is frequently suggested that these often reported successful implementations were not derived from formalised and comprehensive planning. This is probably true but it has in no way dampened enthusiasm for strategic IS/IT planning. Indeed, new planning approaches are steadily gaining momentum, especially those that aim to pinpoint ways of delivering improved competitive advantage.

But what is good information planning? And how can success be ensured and measured? Assuredly its impact is not instantaneous, and it may, in fact, take some time—two or more years—between embarking on strategic IS/IT planning for the first time and demonstrating any consequent impact on business practices and results. The outcome of planning varies widely with

- the starting point (how sound a systems infrastructure has been built),
- the opportunities (whether to search for some 'early winners'—easily achieved, high impact applications),
- the degree to which top management are involved in the impetus.

These and other issues such as defining and implementing an appropriate relationship between IS/IT and the business, and setting objectives for IS/IT have to be addressed.

At the outset, it is important to distinguish between IS/IT objectives and implementation issues. IS/IT objectives have nothing to do with relational or conventional database technology; with distributed or centralised IS/IT functions and hardware; or with end-user or central DP development. These are prominent implementation issues. Objectives for IS/IT are the same as those for the business. They focus on, for example, customers' perceived quality based on service parameters, or product differentiation. Decentralisation and extensive investment in corporate communications may be important implementation issues as a result of a change in business strategy to reorientate operating units into distributed strategic business units. The introduction of selectively focused knowledge based systems may be a factor in providing high quality, information intensive service support to customers.

The role of IS/IT through the DP, MIS and SIS eras was examined in Chapter 1 which highlighted the transition from computer management to information management and from a technology focus to a business orientation. IS/IT planning approaches also have their own evolutionary history, and their focus and objectives have likewise advanced through each era. DP planning has traditionally concentrated on cost reduction, improved efficiency, and at its best, solving users' pressing problems in an environment of partnership between users and IS/IT professionals. MIS planning reflects the growing need for integration and for making pertinent information readily accessible to non-IT specialists. It focuses on improving the effectiveness of managers and teams, and of the business itself in an increasingly complex and integrated environment.

Strategic information systems planning in today's competitive era is not easy to achieve. By definition it must be deeply embedded in business issues, since it promotes IS/IT into prominence as direct tools of competitive strategy. At the same time it must continue to meet DP and MIS needs, but its primary orientation has turned a full 180 degrees, from cost cutting to direct value adding; from administrative efficiency and organisational fluency to delivering aggressive competitive impact, or sometimes equally ferocious defence. Its objectives and priorities are derived from business imperatives. Long-term benefits are sought from the strategic exploitation of information and it has a formulative part to play in advancing business strategy.

Once it has been acknowledged that the objectives for IS/IT are far more than just improving the efficiency of individual operations, then it becomes abundantly evident that in order to develop strategy for IS/IT, and for it to make a significant impact on the business, it is essential to have a clear understanding of the business strategy, its objectives and potential, its immediate competitive environment and of the external forces influencing the industry. Increasingly this means acquiring a global perspective as world-wide competition increases, and communications technology overcomes time and distance barriers.

The business environment and business planning approaches were examined in Chapter 2, which laid out in some detail the elements that make up the wider business environment, and the more specific aspects of business planning.

If the contribution from IS/IT is to be maximised, it is necessary not only for IS/IT people to understand business issues, but also for business people to have an awareness of the potential offered by technology. Once this two-way awareness and cooperation is achieved, then IS/IT can take its place as a significant contributor to creating and supporting business strategy.

THE STRATEGIC IS/IT PLANNING PROCESS

For the organisation which has not undertaken strategic IS/IT planning before, there is often a problem in knowing how to go about it. It is a far from trivial change to go from planning to develop information systems based on catalogued users' demands—usually referred to as 'shopping lists'—to business strategy-based IS/IT planning, especially since the outcome of such planning is very likely to have far-reaching impacts on the future role of the IS/IT function in the business. It is even more difficult to tackle this type of strategic planning if no IS/IT planning has been done before. In such a business, investment on IS/IT may still tend towards building only absolutely necessary systems. In this case, the organisation is hardly moving out of the 'support' quadrant of the Applications Portfolio matrix, repeated here in Figure 3.1 from Chapter 1, where the various categories of systems were set out. Support systems are those said to be not critical to the business.

When the move is from traditional planning to strategic IS/IT planning (SISP), where the portfolio is more balanced across all quadrants and where the new

STRATEGIC	TURNAROUND (or high potential)
● Applications which are critical for future success	● Applications which may be of future strategic importance
FACTORY	SUPPORT
● Applications which are critical to sustaining existing business	● Applications which improve management and performance but are not critical to the business

FIGURE 3.1 Business IS contribution—application portfolio

emphasis is on future strategic importance, in offensive or defensive terms, then several characteristics need to change. Timescales for the planning horizon move out from typically one to three or more years. Development plans are driven by current and future business needs rather than being incremental extensions from earlier developments or recorded backlog lists.*

Before embarking on SISP, there are many questions to be considered.

- What should be the scope of the planning study?
- Where should planning be focused—on the corporate organisation as a whole, or at strategic business unit level?
- How many studies should be undertaken, in what sequence, and with what linkage?
- Should the approach employed be totally prescriptive, or tailored, or a mixture of both?
- What are the most effective approaches, and which techniques achieve the best results—for example, determining the critical success factors associated with top level business functions or employing business analysis down to a very detailed level?
- What resources should ideally be assembled for the project and are they available? How long will it take?
- What is the ultimate target, and what deliverables are required?

These and other issues are introduced here and examined in more detail in later chapters. It should be emphasised that there is no one best way to tackle strategic planning for IS/IT. It is vital to assess the situation and the needs carefully, and then to employ the most appropriate methods and techniques to suit. The prime requirement is undoubtedly for experienced, highly skilled and well motivated people to be involved, and for them to be committed to the work. Each organisation merits a different approach, which will vary according to the current circumstances, and the stimuli prompting the need for planning.

Whilst much of the emphasis in this and succeeding chapters is on the planning process, it should be stressed that a strategic planning study is only one part of a continuous and evolving operation.

- Plans need to be updated regularly, the frequency determined by the underlying pace of business-driven change.
- Development of applications, and the supporting infrastructure take place as a result of prioritised demands, refreshed at appropriate intervals.

Note: The term 'SISP' is an abbreviation for 'strategic IS/IT planning', and is widely used by a number of organisations who promote and use their own planning methodologies (DCE, 1987). It is used in this book for brevity, and as a generic term, not related to any specific applied methodology.

- Mechanisms for monitoring internal and external business and IS/IT perspectives move into gear.

Then if all goes well, the culture of partnership between business and IS/IT reorientates itself to treat information, systems and technology as core resources in the day-to-day life of the business and its continuing development.

Planning for Planning

For each organisation, the decision about how to initiate planning depends on a number of factors and it is crucial that it spends an adequate amount of time and effort in the process of planning for planning. How to go forward depends on the starting point, the purpose of planning and the targets being sought, if they can be defined. It is also markedly affected by the stimuli prompting the activity. It is necessary to determine very carefully:

1. The current situation

   - The current role of IS/IT in the organisation, its effectiveness and maturity, and the role IS/IT is playing in comparable external organisations, in the same industry or field of business.
   - The triggers and underlying causes which are stimulating the need for planning

2. Expectations and objectives

   - The scope and boundaries within the business to be considered
   - The purpose for which the strategy is being devised, its precise objectives and what should be delivered as a result

3. How to proceed

   - The approach to be adopted, and the techniques and tools to be used to identify the required information
   - The resources and skills required to ensure that the best results are obtained within the constraints at the time
   - The 'marketing' approach to adopt to ensure that optimal support and cooperation is obtained from the organisation.

It is unlikely that a business about to embark on strategic IS/IT planning for the first time is not also engaged in the reorientation of the role of IS/IT in that enterprise. If this reorientation from technology-led to business-led is not already underway then the expectation is that the planning process itself will be the stimulus to set it off.

The approach chosen and its objectives and focus is, in effect, an indication of the stage of reorientation reached. They exemplify the maturity of the IS/IT organisation, and the levels of awareness and commitment within the business as a whole to extending the contribution offered by IS/IT.

Current Situation

It is essential to obtain an objective view of the current role of IS/IT in the business, and of the perception of the function from the rest of the business. An objective and largely qualitative perspective can be drawn by considering a number of different aspects. For example an analysis of the current application portfolio gives a great deal of information. By categorising the portfolio into strategic, high potential, factory or support systems, as in Figure 3.1, it can indicate how well current and future business strategy is supported. Further classification shows whether systems are primarily supporting efficiency or effectiveness, or adding value to the business.

Consideration of how many of the business functions are underpinned by systems, and of the size of the backlog, gives an indication of the level of support to the operational needs of the enterprise. This is illustrated in Figure 3.2, which is based on a chemical manufacturing company in the UK.

A more generalised picture of the coverage of the business can be obtained by assessing the levels of infusion and diffusion, and plotting them on a model. Sullivan (1985) describes infusion as the degree to which technology has been employed in the basic operational activities of the organisation. Diffusion gives a measure of how far technology has extended out into the user community. As the model shows (Figure 3.3), the lower left quadrant indicates a centralised IS/IT function, and little or no departmental or personal computing, with the emphasis on legally and operationally necessary functions computerised. Movement out along the horizontal axis indicates an increasing number of operational systems, covering a wider span of business functions. Movement up the vertical axis indicates increased use of end-user computing facilities and departmental systems. The scenario illustrated by the top right quadrant is one of considerable organisational experience of computing and usually increasing awareness about the potential of technology. Organisations moving into this quadrant are clearly ready for strategic IS/IT planning, and probably already have 'strategic' applications.

Assessment of levels of user satisfaction (Figure 3.4), taken from the same chemical company mentioned earlier, illustrating the use they make of technology and the support it gives to their business needs, gives a preliminary view of the partnership achieved between IS/IT and the business. Further analysis of the role and the structure of the IS/IT function in relation to the structure of the organisation, indicates whether IS/IT is already well integrated with the business. Similarly user involvement in managing projects and in developing business cases together with the IS/IT group gives a measure of cooperation. If the IS/IT group acknowledge the need to market their role, then that is also a clear indication of change from a reactive to a proactive stance.

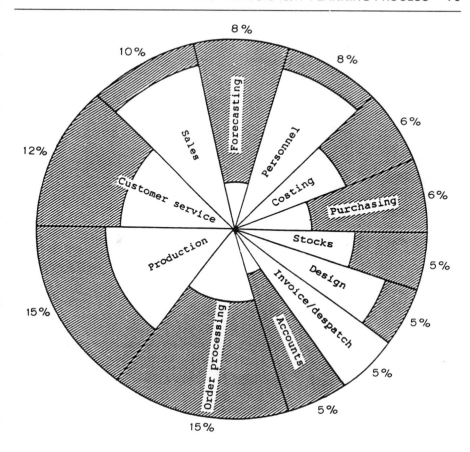

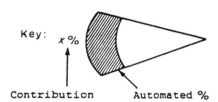

FIGURE 3.2 Relative importance of business activities, and the degree to which they are backed by systems

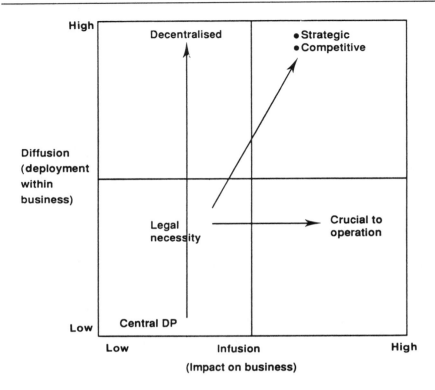

FIGURE 3.3 IS profile based on the Sullivan matrix (Sullivan, 1985)

The level of integration achieved between systems and across different technologies, and the status of data management in the business gives a good measure of the degree to which information is considered a key corporate resource.

One last example of an indicator of the current role and value of IS/IT comes from the level in the management hierarchy where overall responsibility for IS/IT resides. This is increasingly a board level appointment in businesses where IS/IT is considered a major function and contributor.

The other aspect of the current situation which needs assessing at a very early stage is the business perspective itself. During strategic planning a great deal of effort will be expended in analysing and understanding the business environment, its objectives, strategy and structure, its values, culture and management style, and of course derived information needs and technological opportunities. At this stage of planning it is necessary to have a broad overview of all of this and to ascertain how the business strategy is determined and progress monitored towards its targets.

Levels of satisfaction

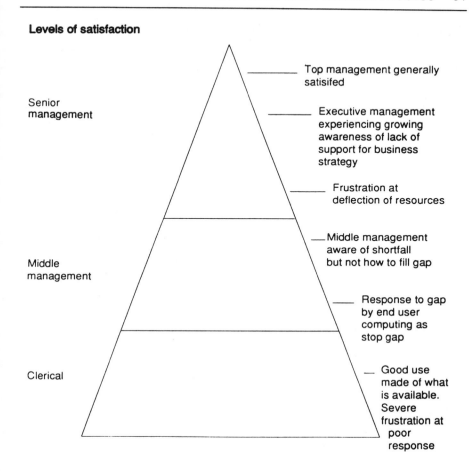

FIGURE 3.4 *Assessment of user levels of satisfaction*

Triggers and Causes

Insight into the current situation will be invaluable in deciding how to proceed. It is also necessary to have a good understanding of the triggers and underlying causes which have prompted the need for planning. The majority of initiatives stem from the IS/IT department and aim to address those issues it perceives to be important. Consideration of those that give most concern to IS managers, and how they have changed over the years, lends supporting evidence to the view that technology issues were considered less critical in the late 1980s than in the first half of the decade and that the management issues relating to the role of IS/IT in the business are much more important in the emerging SIS era than in earlier eras. Table 3.1 (Brancheau and Wetherbe, 1987) shows an analysis of the prioritised

TABLE 3.1 Issues analysis (position in ranking—IS management opinion)

(a) *Management and business issues*	(b) *Technology and IS application issues*
1. (1) Strategic planning (ν)	
2. (2) *Competitive advantage* (*)	
3. (3) *Organisational learning* (*)	
4. (5) *IS role and contribution* (*)	
5. (7) *Alignment to organisation* (*)	
6. (6) End-user computing (ν)	
7. (8) Data as a corporate resource (ν)	
8. (9) *Information architecture* (*)	
9. (4) Measuring effectiveness ($\downarrow$)	
	10. (10) Integrating DP, OP, Factory automation, TC ($\downarrow$)
	11. Telecoms management (ν)
12. Human resources ($\downarrow$)	
	13. Software development (ν)
	14. *Multi-vendor integration* (*)
	15. *Artificial intelligence* (*)
	16. Applications portfolio (existing) ($\downarrow$)
	17. *Factory automation* (*)
	18. Security and control ($\downarrow$)
	19. Packaged software ($\downarrow$)
20. IS funding level ($\downarrow$)	
	21. Office automation ($\downarrow$)
22. Data integrity/quality ($\downarrow$)	
	23. Decision support systems ($\downarrow$)
	24. Data and document storage (ν) (image)

Key: * Increasing importance 1980–83–86, ν Equal importance 1980–83–86, $\downarrow$ Decreasing importance 1980–83–86, ( ) General management ranking.

issues of some 70 IS directors and managers studied in 1980, 1983 and then again in 1986. These are the consensus views of the group on the top issues which they considered would remain critical into the 1990s. The surveys also sought general management opinion of the issues which overall shows an accord on the major, higher priority issues.

Some of the main reasons for embarking on strategic planning, taken from a cross-section of businesses with whom the authors worked in the UK in 1988 are listed in Table 3.2.

Several hypotheses about planning for IS/IT can be drawn from examination of these tables.

(a) The need to plan has always been a top issue (the fact that it does not appear in Table 3.2 is because the organisations who contributed these views were all intending to undertake strategic IS/IT planning, or had already begun).

TABLE 3.2 Common IS/IT issues in 1988

1. Budgeting and resourcing
   - to improve utilisation of scarce resources, especially human resources.
   - to prioritise tasks that provide greatest contribution.
2. Use of information as a competitive weapon
   - How to go about planning for this.
3. Integrating information to serve the business as a whole and to satisfy growth in user demand for access to information,
   - Horizontally across operational functions
   - Vertically throughout the business.
4. Aligning the business and IS/IT strategies, following change in the business environment, or to improve effectiveness of service.
5. How to undertake cost–benefit analysis, especially of infrastructural investments.
6. Security and protection of the information resource.
7. Setting up an IS/IT infrastructure including an information architecture and methods and tools to support the architecture and systems development life-cycle.

(b) Competitive use of IS/IT was and still is a very key issue. However, documented evidence in the form of case studies or examples of sound practice suggests that even after several years as a stated top priority issue, few organisations know how to go about exploiting IS/IT for competitive advantage.

(c) Technology issues have moved down in priority, probably because they are now better understood and do not threaten IS managers so much. This does not necessarily mean that they have been satisfactorily incorporated into the IS/IT repertoire. Fourth generation environments, distributed systems and databases, telecommunications and networks are examples of technology far from satisfactorily harnessed in many cases. This is partly because the available products do not meet the expectations of their users, and partly because of lack of expertise or investment to employ them effectively.

Whilst not reflected in these tables, the technology issues that are coming to the fore in the late 1980s and into the 1990s revolve around the successful implementation of an integrated or interfaced set of computer-assisted systems engineering (CASE) tools, ranging from those that capture output from the strategic planning process, to automatic code generators, comprehensive data dictionaries, and aids for reverse engineering.

(d) Most of the top issues listed in Table 3.1 relate to reorientating IS/IT more centrally in the business—providing a greater contribution to business success, understood by the business as a whole, and making information and its supporting technologies widely accessible to the user community.

(e) Information architecture and information as a corporate resource now figure much more significantly, presumably with the recognition that aligning strategies is not sufficient without making sure that information can be effectively integrated, horizontally and vertically, and then accessed and exploited by the whole organisation.

Any of these may be brought into sharper focus as a result of significant change within the business, IS/IT, or the external environment.

If the thrust comes from change in the business environment, this will mean that senior management commitment is already given for clarifying and probably changing the role of IS/IT. However, whilst the strategy may achieve a *new* definition of this role, it may be more difficult to determine its *appropriate* role and applications' priorities while the business itself is in a state of flux. For this reason any strategy produced under organisational stress may not be particularly appropriate when the business settles down once more, and it will need early revision.

Sometimes external events pose threats or opportunities that directly stimulate IS/IT planning. For example,

● competitive threats (real or potential) based on IS/IT,
● new products or markets created by IS/IT,
● major cost factor changes producing an urgent need to improve productivity via technology or risk losing business,
● legislative demands or pressure from stakeholders, shareholders or other bodies which call for IS/IT response.

The association of business and IS/IT in a competitive alignment means that the emphasis in the strategy will be exploitative and entrepreneurial. This implies new attitudes to the use of IS/IT and probably the need for new skills, and for different people to become involved with new types of technology.

If the scope is limited and focused on one area of the business, senior general management may not get involved, although senior line management in the area concerned may become very involved. In this case it may be inappropriate to consider the whole of the IS/IT strategy, but rather to concentrate on identifying particular business imperatives.

Any of these stimuli are bound to have an effect on the aims and objectives, even if they are not the outright reason for undertaking planning.

IS and IT Strategies

Whilst most IS/IT practitioners understand that their objectives have shifted, there is still a tendency to consider technology issues alongside business needs in such a way that confuses the *supply* (technology as a means of delivery), and *demand* (business needs expressed as information systems requirements).

A model, created by Earl (1987), neatly expresses the distinction between IS strategy and IT strategy (Figure 3.5). They are both essential elements of overall IS/IT strategy, but it is important at the outset to acknowledge a clear distinction between them.

IS strategy deals with **what** to do with Information, Systems and Technology, and how to manage the applications from a business point of view. It thus focuses

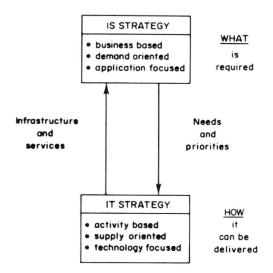

FIGURE 3.5 IS and IT strategies delineated (reproduced with permission, from M. J. Earl (1989) Management Strategies for Information Technology, *Prentice Hall)*

on the close alignment of information in support of business needs and on identifying and exploiting competitive opportunities for IS/IT.

IT strategy designates **how** technology is to be applied in delivering information and systems and ultimately competitive advantage into the business. These meanings will be used throughout the rest of the book.

Determining the Scope/Structure for IS/IT Planning

One of the most vital decisions to make when undertaking strategic planning, is to define the scope of planning. In a large organisation, where there are likely to be a number of distinct business units, it is probable that each should have its own IS strategy, tightly coupled to its business strategy. The evidence available suggests that organisations who have done this achieve and recognise a more direct contribution from IS/IT to business performance. It does not necessarily follow that there should be IT strategies one for one with IS strategies in that organisation. A single IT strategy may be appropriate for the whole organisation, especially if there is centralisation of other corporate functions. On the other hand, it may be more effective to focus IT support at divisional, regional, or even unit level in a diverse and highly distributed enterprise.

The PIMS/MPIT study (Strategic Planning Institute, 1984) shows that IS/IT is generally more effectively deployed in organisations where vertical integration

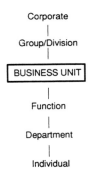

Corporate
|
Group/Division
|
BUSINESS UNIT
|
Function
|
Department
|
Individual

FIGURE 3.6 Relating IS/IT strategy to the business

is between 50–75%, i.e. 50–75% of total business costs are under the control of the business unit, enabling management to control the degree of systems integration across functions. Secondly the study shows it is more feasible to develop a coherent IS/IT strategy for a strategic business unit than for any other organisational grouping (see Figure 3.6). Given the arguments above this would seem to follow.

Integration of management focus and business purpose—a coherent business strategy—enables a coordinated approach to the management of resources, including information. The re-orientation of many major organisations towards market based SBU structures has often meant a distribution of secondary/support functions, reallocating them within the primary activity chains of the business units. These functions (accounting, market research, forecasting, planning, etc.) are heavily information based. Previously, systems in functional organisations were less satisfactory—the result of compromises between the service functions' needs and the diverse primary activity needs. Less compromise is required when both line unit and specialist functional management focus their information requirements on SBU related needs. Vertical rather than horizontal co-ordination is more focused on achieving business results and enables IS/IT to be employed more coherently.

Having said all that there may be a simpler reason! In practice, information flows vertically through the business—to/from customers, about logistics and product processes, to and from suppliers—to enable supply and demand and other business parameters to be reconciled. The primary systems requirements depend on effective vertical linkages. The secondary/supportive control and planning systems can be overlaid on that structure, but in the past these types of systems have often driven the primary systems requirements. This aspect will be considered in more detail when the value chain analysis techniques are discussed later.

Considering the implications of the PIMS/MPIT findings, as reflected in Figure 3.6 briefly once more, some conclusions can be drawn. Historically, 'strategies' were essentially the cumulative total of functional and/or departmental systems 'strategies' which often lacked integration with the business and each other. Personal computing in the 1980s has often caused an even lower set of 'individual' strategies to develop, as discussed in Chapter 1. The senior management and IS management reaction is often to develop a '*Corporate* IS/IT strategy'. There is little evidence that this can be achieved. Most case histories of the attempts of companies such as Union Carbide and ICI in the early 1980s to develop even limited areas of 'Corporate IS/IT' strategy show lengthy planning blights descend on the units and then nothing results! In both companies strategies were subsequently developed more effectively at a business unit level. Unless the corporation is essentially a single business unit company the task is almost impossible. Developing IS/IT strategies at 'Group level' is equally unlikely to be successful unless it is a group of very similar businesses. Part of the ICI 'failure' to develop common accounting systems was due to the several regroupings of companies that occurred while the strategy was being formulated. Often dramatic 'group' reorganisation can occur, such as the restructuring of Thorn EMI in the 1980s from a manufacturing based group structure to a market based structure. Many business units were reallocated in the change, making a nonsense of any previous group systems synergy. In conglomerates where the buying and selling of businesses is a key part of the corporate strategy it obviously makes most sense to align the strategy to each business unit and it is probably impossible in reality to do much else.

The 'Corporation' in many cases is best seen as a business unit in its own right—it will have information systems needs based on the way it chooses to manage the component businesses, whatever at any one time they are.

Focus and Objectives of Strategic IS/IT Planning

It is also very important to clarify the focus and objectives before embarking on planning. It is necessary to ensure that the objectives are sensible and achievable given the current situation and available resources. A general set of objectives may be set, as in Table 3.3. These could form the bulk of a blueprint set of objectives for introducing strategic planning for IS/IT into an organisation, but they hardly meet the real world conditions normally encountered.

Usually there are pressing stimuli, and obvious problems to be resolved. These in turn predetermine the focus and critical requirements. Clearly every case is different and must be examined on its merits, balancing needs, starting position, resources, etc. A number of examples are given in Chapter 4.

Even when the primary objectives are the alignment of business and IS/IT, and the pursuit of competitive advantage, it is most probable that the recommendations will include the development of an integrated architecture, coupled with the stabilising of the information resource and minimising maintenance, amongst other things.

TABLE 3.3 General set of objectives for strategic IS/IT planning

To build a robust information management framework for the long-term management of information and its supporting technologies, and to:

● Identify current and future information needs for the organisation that reflect close alignment of business and IS/IT strategies, objectives and functions.
● Determine policies for the management, creation, maintenance, control and accessibility of the corporate information resource.
● Reposition IS/IT function more centrally in the business, with representation at top management level.
● Ensure that a sound information systems architecture is created so that high quality systems can be built and maintained.
● Identify a portfolio of skills that will be required over the lifetime of the plans.
● Determine an effective and achievable organisation structure for the IS/IT function.
● Ensure that the IS/IT function is outward looking and not focused internally on technology issues, also that the aims of the function are not only clearly linked to business needs but also widely communicated.
● Ensure that there is an acceptance of shared responsibility between IS/IT and business people for the successful exploitation of information and technology.

TABLE 3.4 Motivation for IS/IT planning as undertaken in UK organisations (Galliers, 1987)

Motivation	Percentage
1. Matching IS to business	20
● competitive advantage	
● strategic impact	
2. Resource considerations	18
● accountability	
● IS justification	
● ROI	
3. Coordination	16
● consistent corporate approach to IS	
4. 'Sound management practice'	10
5. Need for effective IS	10
● past failures	
6. Need to prioritise IS developments	8
● increased demand for IS services	
7. External advice or other requirement	7
● consultancy advice	
● HQ policy	

A number of other motivations for undertaking SISP are cited by Galliers (1987), already referred to in Chapter 1. From a survey of 130 UK organisations into aspects of IS planning in UK organisations, he cites seven motivations, see Table 3.4. The percentages refer to the proportion of the organisations surveyed who gave these as their primary motivations for commencing strategic IS/IT planning.

How to Proceed

As has been argued it is probably most effective to concentrate on determining IS/IT strategy at the strategic business unit level, rather than to develop IS/IT strategy at the overall corporate level. Unless the whole organisation is very similar in terms of its products, operational strategies and markets, then each unit is likely to have very different business needs. In this case an IS strategy that meets one unit's needs is not likely to be optimal for another's. Even when the individual business units are very similar, they are still likely to have different IS priorities. For example their market penetrations may be different, or their customer base has a different profile, or because of scale factors, their unit costs are very different.

There may be a need for an IS strategy to meet the corporate information requirements, which are entirely different from those of the business units, whose interests are in supporting their own particular business strategies. Corporate information needs, on the other hand, support long-term planning and allocation of resources, and draw on consolidated information from the business units. Frequently, common policies for IT across the whole organisation are implemented to achieve economy of supply, and consistency across internal interfaces. The focus of strategies at the corporate, business and IS/IT levels, and the relationships between these levels is illustrated in Figure 3.7.

As far as recommending an approach to planning, this book supports a mixture of the formal and informal. Formal techniques are employed to ensure that all appropriate elements of the business are explored in a structured manner, and that the same parameters are applied to achieve effective prioritisation. Consistency and integrity must be preserved in all the findings, and in choosing and implementing the strategy. But informal approaches are also included to capture innovative ideas where they arise in the business, both during the initial planning process, and thereafter. The overall approach put forward in the book consists of a composite model in which business planning, business analysis, information analysis and innovative thinking all have a part to play.

Chapter 4 concentrates on the initial stage of planning for planning, and covers resourcing and skill requirements, marketing the case to top management, and developing the terms of reference for the planning project.

MODELS FOR STRATEGIC IS/IT PLANNING

Strategic IS/IT planning is taken to mean planning for the effective long-term management and optimal impact of information, information systems (IS), and information technology (IT), incorporating all forms of manual systems, computers and telecommunications. It also includes organisational aspects of the management of IS/IT throughout the business. The main purpose of this chapter is to build up a multidimensional picture covering the many facets of SISP, as it can exist in a variety of environments.

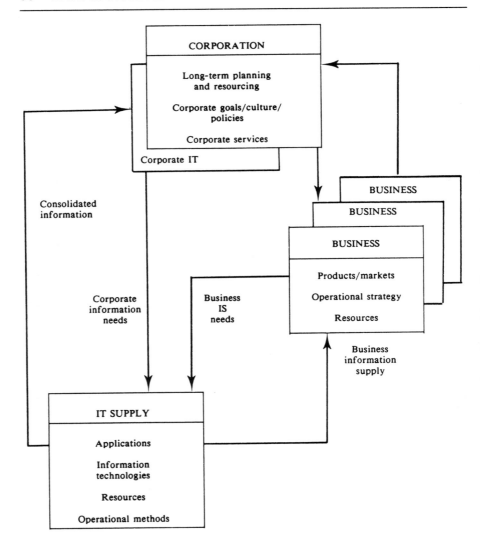

FIGURE 3.7 Relationships and information demand/supply

It is insufficient and somewhat confusing to try to represent in a single model all the different components and aspects involved in strategic planning for IS/IT. It is preferable to build up a rich picture through several models, each of which highlights a particular facet. These include the essential elements of the process; where it sits within the business; the dynamics of the interfaces between IS/IT planning and the rest of business planning.

One model has already been introduced, which splits the planning process up into two parts.

- IS planning, which determines demand,
- IT planning, which responds with a supply strategy.

Three other models are now introduced.

Information Flows and Feedback Routes

Though it is necessary to distinguish between IS planning and IT planning in the way described in the earlier model, it is far from adequate to envisage the planning process as a simple discreet closed loop, and even worse, one which is the sole province of IS planners. It is vital to bring into the picture a number of feedback processes and the collecting and feeding of intelligence and information to and from the external environment. These include a technological perspective covering developments in opportunities for applying technology, and what competitive organisations are doing. It is also useful to envisage SISP as a continuous process with periodic discreet activities such as application portfolio reviews, searches for innovative thrusts, budgeting, and planning activities, all of which involve top management, IS/IT management, and business users.

Figure 3.8 illustrates directive and feedback flows, and the gathering of external intelligence. Clearly these are not all equally and continuously active information

FIGURE 3.8 Information flows and feedback

routes, but at one time or another all are important. These are a parallel set of activities to those shown in Figure 1.6, which focuses on management relationships. The activities shown here are mainly planning activities, dropping down into an operational level in the IS/IT function. Similarly the information flows are those that prompt, feed and support planning.

At the top level, corporate and individual business unit planning take into account all the elements in the strategic framework, both internally and in the external environment, in particular the pressure groups and stakeholders exerting direct forces on the organisation, described in Chapter 2. Ways of identifying innovative opportunities to impact the competitive environment are considered in Chapter 6.

Coming out of the corporate and business planning processes are strategic plans setting out how the business will meet its objectives. These then become primary inputs into the business IS planning process. In an organisation where the role of IS/IT is already closely aligned to the business, then it is likely that IS/IT opportunities and threats have already been considered when determining business strategy. Then, a characteristic of the continuous nature of the process would be for innovative ideas for application of information and technology to flow back up into the strategy formulation process.

A detailed perspective of IS/IT both internally and externally is also input into the business IS strategy development process.

A number of business IS planning processes may be underway concurrently, for each SBU. Coming out of each of these are prioritised information needs and management policies for the development of applications, infrastructure and services. Also stated here are resourcing needs and organisational change requirements.

The next level down is where the demand stated in the business IS strategy is converted into supply plans—IS tactical development plans, and plans for the provision of IT facilities and services. Feeding in also are more detailed views on users' requirements and an analysis of skills, resources, capacities, etc. to match against the newly stated demands.

At the lowest level are the development and implementation activities, and the provision of IT facilities and services in response to detailed development plans and allocated resources. In any well ordered and dynamic organisation, to ensure that each level of planning has the clearest perspective, it is essential to put into place mechanisms for collecting information from appropriate sources, and feeding it back through the planning nodes ahead of the next planning activity. Thus at the implementation and provision of services level, it is necessary to be fully aware of users' levels of satisfaction, and to comb the external environment for potential ways of improving the services. This in turn feeds back into the tactical planning level in the form of effectiveness reviews, and impact analyses, together with potentially innovative ideas.

Not all aspects of the model are equally relevant in all organisations, but consideration needs to be given to them all in the first instance, so that their relevance can be determined.

There are also organisational implications on the mainstream of the business that emerge from the planning process. Recommendations need to be fed back through normal mechanisms into corporate planning, and also across into the relevant business planning functions. Unless IS/IT is already acknowledged as contributing value to the business, it is unlikely that far-reaching impacts on the business will be identified within strategic planning, let alone accepted. For that reason it is advantageous to implement a promotional campaign to realign the image of the role of IS/IT in the business and to monitor the resultant cultural acknowledgement of an increasing contribution from the function. Clearly the most effective promotion is achieved through delivering systems of strategic importance. Unless this happens by chance, it is the responsibility of IS/IT management to convince business management that their own IS/IT department can deliver such systems. A somewhat unpalatable (and perhaps risky!) way of doing this may be to show them what the competition have achieved. Vigorous promotion is one of the most important factors in changing from reactive to proactive contribution and without it that change is proportionately more difficult to effect.

STRATEGIC IS/IT PLANNING WITHIN THE BUSINESS FRAMEWORK

Another view of SISP within an overall business framework is shown in Figure 3.9. This model aims to illustrate that there are several dimensions to the overall IS/IT arena, and that there are many interdependencies to be collated, in pursuit of supporting the business. The model illustrates many of the issues that need to be addressed under its overall planning umbrella, and then translated into policies, plans and management strategies.

The model represents a cycle which starts in the business with the corporate and business planning processes. Then following IS/IT strategic planning are a series of linked processes that terminate in the delivery of required information into the business at the desk of the end user. Also stemming from planning are the aims and objectives of IS/IT, that is, its role and purpose in the business, and a set of policies for the management of the function.

More complex variations could occur when IS/IT itself forms part or all of the products or services of the business, or when information is delivered to users in the business' external environment—say, suppliers or customers.

The processes in the linked information thread after IS/IT planning are:

- creating tactical plans for development of the application portfolio and the ongoing management of the strategy.
- business analysis of the prioritised application areas, continuing the activity and information analysis begun in SISP.

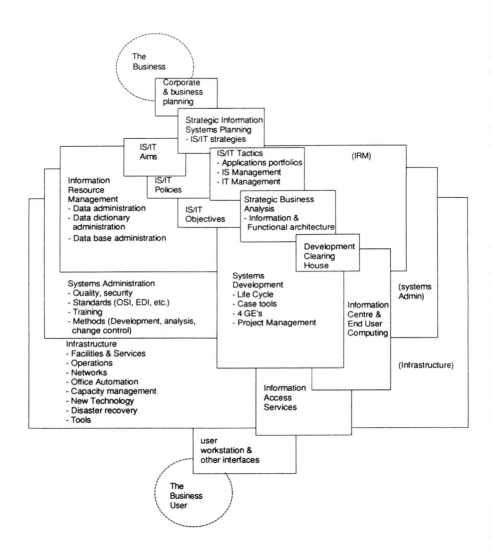

FIGURE 3.9 SISP within the business framework

- a 'clearing house' function as described by Tozer (1987) to vet all requests and allocate an appropriate development approach.
- end user development, perhaps in conjunction with an IS/IT supported information centre, or traditional systems development by the IS group.
- the resulting system's output may be made widely accessible via information access services.

- information is ultimately delivered to the users in the business via a workstation—perhaps through a common user interface, or perhaps through a variety of access mechanisms.

Underlying the thread that traverses the business through from planning to delivery of relevant information to the end users are a number of other factors.

- An infrastructure supplying technical facilities and services in the form of hardware, software, tools, communications, networks, capacity management, disaster recovery, operations and first line support to production systems.
- Systems administration, ensuring that policies are effectively managed on quality, security, and adherence to standards, and that effective methods are installed and used.
- Information Resource Management (IRM) covering the management, protection, consistency, integrity, and accessibility of the corporate information resource using the tools of data administration, data dictionary administration, and data base administration.

AN INPUT–OUTPUT–PROCESS MODEL

The last model in this chapter is directed at the core of SISP itself. It introduces and describes the building blocks of the planning process—the inputs, outputs and processing activities, as shown in Figure 3.10.

Inputs

1. The internal business environment—current strategy, objectives, resources, and activities and the culture and values of the business.
2. The external business environment—the economic, industrial, and competitive climate in which the organisation operates.
3. The internal IS/IT environment—the current IS/IT perspective in the business, its maturity, business coverage and contribution, skills, resources and the technological infrastructure.

    The current application portfolio of existing systems and systems under development, or budgeted but not yet underway is also part of the internal IS/IT environment.
4. The external IS/IT environment—technology trends and opportunities and the use made of IS/IT by external bodies.

Outputs

1. IS management strategy—the common elements of the strategy which apply throughout the organisation ensuring consistent policies where needed.

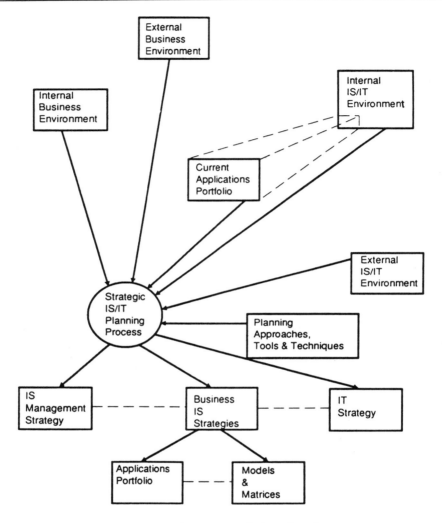

FIGURE 3.10 The inputs and outputs of the planning process

2. Business IS strategies—how each unit or function will deploy IS/IT in achieving its business objectives. Alongside each are applications portfolios to be developed for the business unit and sets of business models, describing the information architectures of each unit. The portfolios may include how IS/IT will be used at some future date, to help the units achieve their objectives.

3. IT strategy—policies and strategies for the management of technology and specialist resources.

Processes

These are a mixture of analytical and creative approaches using a selection of tools and techniques in order to provide the necessary deliverables for the process.

Analytical techniques are used to examine and decompose the business requirements into their constituent parts and to derive resultant information needs. A high level model of business activities and information elements is also produced. A second route takes the business analysis products and extends them, to determine a conceptual model of the enterprise, comprising its principal information entities, functions, and information flows.

The creative element provides additions to the portfolio, since it looks for opportunities (or threats) within the business, and especially at the boundaries with the external environment, where innovative information systems, or use of technology may be possible. Searches for innovative opportunities are not appropriate in all circumstances, and probably not at all if the culture of the organisation is not sympathetic to innovation, and when support is not available to back potentially high impact, high risk schemes. However, it may be that one or more creative ideas can be brought to fruition very quickly, and it may be one of the aims of strategic planning to find and implement such ideas in order to demonstrate a more positive contributory role from IS/IT, and thus to accelerate the re-orientation process.

Each of the inputs, outputs and processes is now explained in more detail.

INPUTS

The principal inputs and their constituent parts are described below. They are considered again in more detail in Chapters 5 and 6, which deal with understanding and interpreting the business needs and opportunities.

Internal Business Environment

Independent of the aims of the planning process, it is absolutely necessary to obtain a very thorough understanding of the internal business environment, as a prerequisite to determining the business IS needs.

Business Objectives, Strategies and Plans

These exist in a variety of forms. They may be available through formally recorded corporate, business unit or functional area strategy documents, or less formally in other documents. In the latter case they can usually be confirmed and expanded through discussions with senior management.

In many instances, business strategies and objectives are not recorded formally, and are not well constructed. Then they can only be identified through interview, analysis and creative prompting. In this case the main achievement of the planning process may be to focus attention (subtly, if necessary!), on the inadequacies, and at best formulate a business strategy which considers technological opportunities as significant elements.

There may be no business strategy at all, and objectives that point only at the bottom line. In this case all that can be achieved is to analyse and record current activities, tactics and operational needs, from a top down viewpoint. The analysis of the business and of its critical components will provide invaluable input into any future formulation of business strategy, and in the interim, short-term IS planning can focus on supporting current high priority business needs.

In the event that no planning documents are available, there is normally an annual report which describes the business, its results and short-term plans, and it is often a surprisingly useful document, in its ability to point to the issues to investigate at the outset of the process.

Business Activities and Key Entities

The activities are those that the organisation undertakes to produce, promote and distribute its products or services, and to develop, support and administer its infrastructure. The key entities within an activity are those 'things' that are of particular importance to the activity, and for which there will be associated information.

Analysis of these activities and major entities may be called 'strategic information analysis', since its aim is to develop an overall blueprint for the business's information needs—the existing 'information architecture' of the business. The outputs of strategic information analysis are hierarchical activity models, data models showing the relationships of the key entities or entity groups relevant to the business, and data flow diagrams indicating the movement of information around, into and out of the business.

Alongside the information architecture which represents the existing situation, are other conceptual models. One represents the 'ideal' architecture of information and activities of the business, achieving its objectives and a second represents the evolving architecture at any time, as it migrates from the present to the ideal.

Organisational Environment

When considering the information needs of a dynamic organisation, and when attempting to uncover IS/IT opportunities, it is essential to have a clear understanding of the organisations' structure, relationships and the people of which it is composed. These organisational dynamics form an important input into the planning process. It is necessary to understand the environment and its skills, resources, values, culture, social interactions, as well as its management style and relationship with the external environment.

Information Needs

The whole process of IS/IT planning exposes, expands and converts raw information needs into an architecture which is the basis for application planning.

The relationship between objectives, activities and information needs is clearly of great significance. It can be illustrated by considering a framework inside the business which links these and other items together.

Mission—the long-term, overall aim of the organisation. Its primary role is to set a direction.

Objectives—statements of the targets of an organisation, at its global or strategic business unit level. They are normally quantified, with associated values and deadlines.

Strategies—define the way in which objectives will be met.

Operational activities—the proposed activities that would most effectively meet the objectives via the selected strategies. They are quite likely to be different from the current activities.

Performance measurement activities—other activities, required to measure performance against objectives and strategy.

Information needs—associated with both types of activities. The majority are internal, generated in the operational activities, and in the communications passing between activities. Others relate to external factors, and are of particular significance in areas concerned with competitive activity.

Critical success factors (CSFs)—part of the business strategy framework. They are the few key areas where 'things must go right' for the business to flourish. It is very important to identify them when aiming to obtain a profound understanding of the business. The very act of determining CSFs may help to crystallise objectives and strategies, and certainly to emphasise priority activities.

External Business Environment

This is the environment described in Chapter 2, within an overall strategic framework. It incorporates the forces and pressure groups acting on the organisation, and is one of the strongest influences on the scope of the business strategy to be adopted. For the purposes of information strategic planning, it is essential to understand and analyse the environment, so that opportunities for contributing to the business strategy are identified and explored.

Internal IS/IT Environment

The most significant aspect to analyse here is the current applications portfolio, since it represents the starting point from which future developments will begin. It is also a key determinent to how IS/IT is perceived by the business people.

Current Applications Portfolio

This is the portfolio of current systems that supports the business. It includes centralised, distributed and end user systems which support various aspects of the business—administrative, operational, control, planning, strategic. They may be categorised and assessed in a number of ways that represent their value to the organisation and their impact on the business and objectives being pursued. These categorisations were discussed earlier in the chapter with reference to assessing the current situation prior to commencing planning.

Gaining a thorough understanding of the portfolio enables measurement of its value to the business, and the contribution systems make towards satisfying business objectives.

The current portfolio includes not only existing systems but also systems under development, and systems planned but not yet underway. Clearly any of these could be revised as a result of the planning process. The current portfolio does not include the backlog, whose contents will be re-identified during the planning process, if they reflect genuine information systems requirements.

Current IS/IT Environment

There are several other aspects of the IS/IT environment that are influential in creating business IS strategies. There are a mixture of hard and soft aspects to consider, for example:

1. The IS organisation, its size, structure and relationship with the business, at a departmental and individual level. How it is managed, and the level at which it reports into the corporate level and individual businesses.
2. The decision-making processes and any steering committee structure in place. How business cases are prepared and by whom, and how they are authorised.
3. The assets of the organisation in terms of hardware, software, communications capability, and any other technology employed, together with the human assets and skills of IS/IT people and users.
4. The investment in capital in IS/IT and the expenditure in relation to turnover or overall organisational budget.
5. The methods in use for business and systems analysis, systems development, data management, project management and control, quality assurance and control, and estimating. This includes any structured methodologies, systems

development life cycle standards, use of CASE or IPSE tools, fourth generation environment products, prototyping, decision support, expert systems or any other specialised tools.

6. End user computing activities and the role and status of an information centre, if present.

7. Training and education methods employed, and any particular awareness programmes directed at the business to raise understanding of IS/IT. Similarly any awareness or other training available for technical people on business matters.

8. A view of the prevailing attitudes in the department and the business about the role and contribution of IS/IT, and the degree of cooperation achieved. The level of loyalty and pride in the department.

External IS/IT Environment

This final input into the planning process relates to the external IS/IT environment where the purpose is to gain a perspective on technical trends and opportunities for using IS/IT in fresh and innovative ways. It does not necessarily mean seeking ideas for implementing leading edge technology, although these are not precluded. The aim may be to find ways of using existing technology at lower cost, or in previously unconsidered ways.

Part of this is looking at what competitors or other comparable organisations are doing. This outward view is useful, not only to pick up ideas, but also to obtain a measure of the relative maturity of the business' own IS/IT contribution. It may be a deliberate policy of the company not to be pioneers of any new technology in their own business sector, or indeed leaders in innovative use of IT at all, but to follow at a measured pace behind the leaders.

Another aspect of this external survey may be to categorise elements of technology that may be worth examining in more detail later, when implementation issues are addressed. Clearly any organisation which makes a point of following external trends and opportunities through an established mechanism, will have all the required information available as input to the planning process.

OUTPUTS

The products stemming from the planning process are a mixture of hard and soft deliverables. The hard outputs are documents defining strategies and plans, and frequently include computer-based material in the form of dictionaries and information analysis models. Soft outputs relate to human factors, such as skills, awareness and motivation.

There are many ways in which an IS/IT strategy can be structured. The objective is to ensure that users, management and IS professionals all understand the key elements of the strategy and each thoroughly appreciate those parts of the strategy they have to carry through. It should contain the following components.

1. IS/IT management strategy
2. Business IS strategy including:
   - IS strategy and policies
   - Applications portfolio—existing
     - —required
     - —potential
   - Models, matrices and tables
3. IT strategy

The statements of demand in terms of requirements for information, systems and technology are contained in the business IS strategy, and the accompanying applications portfolio. The supply elements are contained in the IT strategy, whilst the IS management strategy contains the overall policies for satisfying and balancing the demand and supply.

There should be one IS/IT management strategy for any organisation where consistent policies for IS/IT are applied throughout the corporate body. However there may be several business IS strategies, one for each strategic business unit, or even separate strategies for defined functional or geographic units. For the purposes of the remainder of this section, the abbreviation SBU will be used to indicate whatever units have been used in the determination of IS strategies. There may be only one IT strategy for the whole organisation, though there could be separate hardware and IT services dedicated to certain business units.

Information analysis models may be created for the whole corporate body or at SBU or even major business function level. In the latter case, there may need to be a rationalisation process to identify common entities, cross functional entity relationships, and common logical activities. Policy and implementation issues relating to rationalisation would then follow in the management of corporate information and development of application systems. There may also be organisational implications if there is merit in rationalising operational activities.

The vital result of the strategy is a future applications portfolio which meets corporate and business needs and can be sustained in terms of technologies and resources. Given that principal strategic objective of IS/IT for the business, the main objectives and issues addressed by each component are considered next.

Business IS Strategy—Management of Demand

The business IS strategy is considered first, since it contains a statement of the business demand. It states how the business will deploy IS/IT in achieving its objectives, and it will remain the responsibility of the executive management of the SBU. Its purpose is to link IS/IT firmly to the business strategy. The strategy, defined by the business management and users, states the applications and service requirements for the SBU, with reference to the business plans and activities, and any associated priorities for development of infrastructural or application systems. It should contain:

- a business perspective describing the business strategy, in the context of its internal and external environment,
- the key figures in the external environment, the customers, suppliers and competitors, and any other influential external bodies,
- the information needs and thus information systems requirements derived from the analysis of the business environment and its competitive framework,
- a description of the use of IS/IT in the business area; its assets, strengths and weaknesses, relative maturity, adopted methods and current portfolio.

The unit's management style, corporate values and cultural factors, as well as skills, resources and business practices are also recorded here. Such information may already be documented in the corporate or business unit strategies, but if not this is an appropriate time to determine and record these details. In the context of defining IS and IT strategies that have considerable impacts on the business, organisational dynamics play a significant role, since it is necessary to be able to assess the effect of a strategy which runs counter to the culture of the business. In this case, it is necessary to assess with great care whether to implement the recommendations or whether it may be better first to focus on changing the underlying contrary culture. If it cannot change then the likelihood that the recommendations will deliver their potential benefits is remote, and it may be better to revise the strategy, taking a more incremental approach to change.

One engineering business, managed jointly by two managing directors, commissioned a SISP exercise, using external consultants. The sponsor—one of the two managing directors—was taken ill during the course of the planning process, and was forced to retire. Having lost his very vigorous commitment, the positive attitude hitherto displayed by the directors and senior managers collapsed, prompted by the second MD, who had not shared his former colleague's optimism and active leadership.

Not all of the requirements will be for new application developments. Some will need extensions to existing operational systems which will improve their effectiveness on behalf of the business.

Application Portfolio

Brief details of application systems requirements are recorded within the business IS strategy, but a further more detailed report is required. It describes the applications and how they will be developed and managed.

The portfolio is categorised in terms of the components and their role in supporting current and future business strategy, as illustrated in Figure 3.1. Most portfolios are likely to contain elements in the four categories already described—strategic, high potential, factory and support.

The portfolio not only contains analysed requirements but may also include potential applications and propositions for enhancing the business strategy in the future. These proposals are most likely to address competitive activities, and may well be described in outline only at this point, since significant research may need to be undertaken before they are introduced. It may conclude that the way to proceed is to develop a small pilot idea, with the intention of adding increments to it as the idea proves itself.

Wiseman (1985), describes a case where a company followed this course. Metpath Inc., a clinical laboratory, began to use IS/IT to bolster its competitive performance in a small way at first. The clinical laboratory industry was typified by fierce competition, price cutting, and low customer loyalty. Its customers, medical practitioners, were accustomed to sending samples for analysis to the laboratories and receiving the analysis back by post. Metpath decided to improve its customer service by providing the doctors with a terminal linked to the laboratory computer. A simple system enabled them to send the results back to the doctors as soon as they were determined. This timely service was very important to the doctors, and the initial step differentiated Metpath's services and gained them an edge over their competitors—simply, but very effectively. They then honed this edge by building customer loyalty through add-on services. They offered:

- Analysis reports from the historical records they had built up.
- Basic business systems such as billing and accounts payable to help the doctors run their own businesses more efficiently.
- Access to stock market quotations on Dow Jones.

They thereby demonstrated that they understood their customers' needs, and peripheral interests!

The systems so far had tied in a healthy customer base, leaving Metpath confident enough to announce their future plans for expanding their services into new and more specialised areas—drug interaction testing and diagnosis, using expert systems technology. Figure 3.11 illustrates the steps.

There are numerous examples of sustained competitive advantage which began in a small way with the introduction of simple technology in the first instance. The risk of this is that once exposed in the competitive market place, the instigator must keep ahead of any rivals who may try to leapfrog into a leading position. The battle that ensued between Carrier and Trane in the OEM air-conditioner market place is an example of leapfrogging.

There was a great boom in the 1970s when Carrier was the main supplier of air-conditioner units in the USA. They offered to their customers, architects,

METPATH - CLINICAL LABORATORY

- Industry-fragmented
- low differentiation
- price cutting

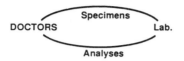

Action	Result
Terminals - Doctors Direct results	(1) Systems edge (2) Differentiated services
Add on Services (1) Historical records (2) Billing and A/P Services (3) Access to Dow Jones	Tie in customers
Planned (1) Diagnosis (AI) (2) Drug interaction testing	Springboard

FIGURE 3.11

a postal based service whereby they calculated the air-conditioning requirements of a building based on architects plans. Their main rivals in this business, Trane, took over the leading position by offering a far better service, based on on-line connections. Carrier had to respond to this in order to regain its lost market share. To do so they were forced to invest heavily in better systems that would tempt back their lost customers. They succeeded, but the cost had been very substantial. It has been suggested that the cost of catching up in this kind of situation may be up to seven times the cost incurred by the market leader.

This is the most creative part of defining IS/IT strategy, and it requires a very deep understanding of the business, its competitive environment, and a sound knowledge of how IS/IT may be applied innovatively to changing the business. Methods of coming up with creative proposals, and assessing their likely influence, and ongoing resilience and development potential are explored in Chapter 6.

The various styles of management appropriate for each category in an applications portfolio are described in Chapter 8.

IT Strategy—Management of Supply

This should not only cover the strategy of the 'Central' IT function, but also the responsibilities of users, where appropriate.

Its prime purpose is to define how resources and technologies will be managed and developed to satisfy business IS strategies within the management strategy framework. In addition, it should reflect current trends and developments in IT which could cause future opportunities or constraints.

Many of the elements of the IT strategy may have already been defined separately, in which case there are also likely to be procedures for reviewing and updating the strategy. Nevertheless a review of the IT policies, methods and standards in place, and adherence to them is needed. The IT strategy will then focus on the areas where change is necessary due to business requirements, or where new options are available due to changes in technology, experience, or capability, which may not have been recognised and pursued.

Whether they are defined during IS/IT planning or separately, an IT strategy should normally at least address the following, preferably in business terms (not obscure 'techie' jargon, using manufacturers' acronyms and numbers!).

Information Resource Management (IRM)

The activities concerned with the management and effective application of the corporate information resource in all its forms, together with the provision of facilities to enable those entitled to gain easy access to use and manipulate this information. Information may exist as data, text, image and voice, and include all the business's information, whether maintained in central or distributed computer databases, personal databases, accessible external databases, or manual records. The likelihood is that only some of the information resource will be actively managed at any one time, and that the boundary separating the managed from the unmanaged will be constantly changing. It is also rare to find data management policies covering manual records.

Information resource management can be classified under four main headings: data administration, data dictionary administration, database administration and information access services. These are all described, together with the implementation issues associated with introducing information resource management in Chapter 10.

A strategy for provision of an information centre can also be covered within the subject of information resource management, although there are several views about the ideal organisational placing and management reporting lines for information centres, and they frequently are not directly associated with IRM.

Communications Systems and Networks

These are normally centrally planned and controlled. Within the IS/IT strategy will be a statement of communications and network requirements for all forms of information, as appropriate, and the likely growth of activity and service needs over the life of the IS strategies. These will then need to be consolidated for all SBUs, and projections made for the future. Communications issues are addressed in Chapter 12 on technology.

Capacity Policy

Capacity requirements, including the need for back-up capability can be spelled out in the planning process. The policies for meeting capacity requirements differ according to whether services are resourced for a group of business units, or dedicated to one unit. In the former case, some prioritising may be necessary, and limits on consumption imposed. Policies may vary by service type—on-line transactions, batch, user retrieval, timesharing, development, etc. Different policies will be required for the different segments of the application portfolio—strategic, high potential, factory, support, because contribution and risks are different.

It should be noted that the main driving force for capacity on mainframe and networked systems comes from the growth of terminals and PCs, and that as a result of determining an IS/IT strategy for a complete business, there is likely to be a surge in demand from the business users. Also as the demands for integration and information sharing increase, so does the probability that the networking requirements for an organisation will become more complex, and capacity demands grow.

This particular strategy should be closely linked with the hardware and network strategies.

Hardware and Software

The strategy should differentiate

> *core* system architecture hardware and software fundamental to the established systems base,
> *optional* hardware and software to enhance the core architecture—not application specific,
> *application driven* hardware and software required to satisfy certain types of requirement.

Policies for vendor 'management', including the aspect of balancing avoidance of proliferation against the opportunities offered by innovation need to be included here, as do guiding policies for retiring and replacing obsolescent hardware and software. As with many of the policies in the IT strategy, there is a good chance that they have been established in previous IT strategies, but they need continuous review to ensure that they remain compatible with business needs.

Application Management

The application management strategy should reflect the mix of application types in the matrix (Figure 3.1), which require different types of approach.

For each category, an overall strategy is required which guides the use of techniques and standards with the objective of limiting risks and ensuring eventual integration can be achieved when required.

Systems administration issues such as those indicated in Figure 3.9 are needed separately from the strategy. These address such matters as project management methods, development standards, project planning and budgeting, system development lifecycle standards, etc. In the IT strategy, any absolute requirements relating to any of these should be defined explicitly. For example, the 'pilot' of a high potential system, say an office automation pilot, may only be affected by a few of the system's administration guidelines, whereas an operational database rewrite will be subject to a much stricter interpretation of the standards.

Operations

This strategy should address the key issues in managing existing systems and in-place technology and cover:

- Service level objectives, i.e. the uptime and response requirements.
- Maintenance service objectives and allocation of responsibility for diagnostics and resolution.
- Channels of communication on operational issues.
- Change management procedures.
- Security procedures.
- Priorities in case of system failure.

Whilst many of these will be particular to applications, some general strategies should be in place to minimise peculiarities of different applications and clarify basic responsibilities.

Organisation and Resourcing

There are two key elements:

- The organisation of the IS/IT functions, and how responsibilities are allocated. The functions should include—operations, systems programming, technical services, systems development, IRM, business analysis, information centre, etc. How the functions interrelate and also relate to the business functions they serve.

• A 'people' strategy covering recruitment, training, career development, use of external resources. This also needs to cover the exchange of personnel between the business and IT areas.

These and other important organisational and 'people' issues are addressed in Chapter 9.

IS Management Strategy—Balancing Supply and Demand

The management strategy covers the common elements of the strategy which apply throughout the organisation, ensuring consistent policies where needed. It is necessary where several SBUs develop their own business IS strategy, and may or may not operate their own IT supply function.

Where there is a high degree of centralisation in the organisation, then the number of issues addressed in the management strategy, and the degree to which common policies are imposed will be considerably higher than in an organisation where the central corporate body is small, and each unit operates virtually autonomously. Even then it is quite likely that the autonomous units will share centralised support functions, of which, IT services are quite likely to be one.

Any information system's needs of the corporate body can be addressed in a business IS strategy treating the corporate body as if it were an SBU. Clearly some of its information needs will be closely linked to the other SBUs, and frequently derived by consolidation of output from applications run in the SBUs.

Aside from its information needs, the management strategy should state known corporate objectives, and CSFs relating to corporate activities and needs. The strategy should also contain a concise summary of the individual business IS strategies, and any IT strategies derived for the organisation. It should also relate these to its own stated corporate aims and CSFs.

A minimum number of common issues are addressed in the management strategy.

Organisation

Resources and the allocation of responsibility and authority for IS/IT decisions. This implies both formal and informal structures and steering group overlay structures. The allocation of responsibility and authority is an indication of how much control is retained in the corporate body and how much is dispersed into the business and functional units.

Investment Policies

Implementation of the strategies will require many separate decisions on investments to be made. Management cannot consider each one in detail and certainly not continuously allocate priorities. Rules must be defined—pertinent to each of the elements of the portfolio (strategic, factory, etc.) stating how investments should be appraised—the need for financial evaluation and acceptance of business judgement of line and IS managers and the balance and discretion expected. It should state how the budgeting for expense and capital items and later project or capital expenditure allocation processes tie together.

It also needs to define a mechanism, which reflects the investment decision-making process, for 'day-to-day' priority setting for resource allocation to ensure the best return on investments is obtained from the actual resource available. Some measurement of results, and any control and audit procedures should be incorporated here.

Vendor Policies

These may state specific vendors, or the parameters which must guide choice of vendors, such as interconnectability, financial soundness, service provision, etc. It should also cover differences in policies where central approval is needed or where local decisions can be taken.

Human Impact Policies Including Education

It is only too easy to jeopardise IS/IT strategies due to mismanagement of the people issues—new job content, re-organisation, even redundancy. Some organisations have 'technology agreements'—with unions or staff groups.

Where organisational issues are seen as critical to success, this must be adequately addressed at a corporate level. A common set of policies and guidelines must be laid down to avoid evolution by precedent and a negative reactive stance by those affected. Each project, in each area, with each new technology should not need separate negotiation—progress will be slow and inconsistent—the strategy will undoubtedly be continuously disrupted.

IS Accounting Policies

In many organisations, strategies fail due to insensitive accounting policies for the charging of IS resources. The objectives of such policies should be clearly stated and understood. Whilst they initially appear to be management accounting systems for cost allocation, once implemented they become 'transfer pricing' systems on which users will make decisions. The policies will depend on, amongst other things:

● Other cost accounting/transfer pricing policies for other services.
● Profit/cost centre management of organisational units (including IS units).
● The cost of administering the charging system itself which when the budgeting complexity is added may prove very expensive to carry out.

Chapter 9 goes into more detail on accounting policies in relation to IS/IT.

For each of these, and any other elements of the IS management strategy considered at a corporate level, there should be a clear statement of:

- Rationale,
- Objectives,
- Policy,
- Procedure for review and exception handling.

It is quite likely that the IS management strategy has been determined in a separate phase before any individual SBU conducts its own strategic IS/IT planning. In this case it has to ensure that the policies laid down in the management strategy are consistent with the business needs being addressed, and that there is a mechanism for feeding back into the IS strategy management process any anomalies or troublesome constraints uncovered during the planning process.

Models

It is advantageous when undertaking IS/IT planning to have some automated tools available—preferably integrated with one another and with the tools used within information resource management and systems development. A basic diagramming tool and matrix manipulator simplify the creation and manipulation of models, matrices and tables. Integrated computer-assisted systems engineering tools (I-CASE) which are discussed in Chapter 11, may be available although the discussion that follows makes no assumption about the vehicle for recording and updating the outputs.

The main models which are produced during planning are entity models, activity decomposition diagrams and data flow diagrams plus a set of matrices representing the information architecture. Naturally they are all high level models, obtained from top down analysis of the business. Nevertheless whenever possible these models are built and recorded in such a form that they can become input to successive stages of feasibility and systems development. Each of these models is discussed in more detail in Chapter 5, but is defined below to clarify the differences and role of each.

Entity Models

Very high level entity models are developed when analysing the business's activities. Their main purpose is to define the underlying information architecture, independent of any functional considerations. They also provide a means of clarifying company wide business language, and are the source of the initial entries into the business unit's data dictionary. They may also provide a means of identifying some high level redundancies of data, and at the same time indicate areas where further investigation will be necessary.

The entities comprise the elements of fundamental importance to the business, about which information is almost certain to be kept, although it is not necessary for this to be held in computerised systems. They may include people (customers, suppliers), objects (products, invoices), places (workshop, laboratory), or abstractions such as events (sale, order). The models also indicate relationships between the entities (optional or mandatory, one-to-one, etc.).

They are purposely retained at a high level, and tend to be somewhat imprecise, since so much of the detail is absent, but clearly are capable of successive decomposition so that they become increasingly more precise, and thus effective at the systems development level. The entities themselves are likely to become the focus of the subject databases subsequently developed and maintained.

In a large organisation with several business units it is most probable that separate models will be created for each unit, and that there will be no attempt to create a global model for the whole organisation. However, where there is a good deal of similarity between the units, or business synergy, then reconciliation between common entities becomes important, when the interfaces are explored. Similarly when consolidation of information from various units up to corporate level is considered, reconciliation may also be desirable.

Activity Decomposition Diagrams

Activity models or functional decomposition diagrams describe the business units' activities. The models, which are usually expressed in hierarchical form are produced by activity analysis. This breaks down the business into broad activity categories (sell and produce products etc.), defining what it does or wants to do, and then into successively more detailed categories. In strategic planning, activity decomposition diagrams are usually created at the global level, and at each major functional level, but only decomposing activities down to two or at most three levels below the broad grouping level.

Once all the activity diagrams have been built, it is usual to rationalise them, and create what is the fundamental activity set for the future that would meet the business objectives. After rationalisation this may bear little resemblance to the organisational layout of the business, and its current activities.

Its purpose then, is having clarified the essential activities of an organisation, it can point to the likely set of information requirements and thus the basis for identifying future conceptual information systems.

Data Flow Diagrams

Data flow diagrams are used to indicate movements of information between entities and activities. Activites shown on DFDs indicate something the business does or wants to do in order to achieve its objectives. For example, it produces articles, or sells to customers. In a DFD an activity is usually expressed as a verb followed by an object. At the strategy level, data flow diagrams are very broad approximations of information flows, since it is not possible to describe simply the complexity of information moving around the area being modelled.

Their purpose in SISP is firstly as a vehicle for understanding what is happening in an organisation, and then to present current activities in a manner easy to comprehend. Thereafter the set of DFDs can be used as a lever for defining conceptual activities and the basis for proposing change.

Matrices and Tables

There are several matrices that can be produced during the planning process, once all the fact finding, and analysis of information systems needs has taken place. Collectively the matrices and models represent the total corporate or business unit architecture, conceived to satisfy business requirements.

The matrices provide a tabular representation of the business, and illustrate the relationship between information entities, conceptual business activities, and conceptual application areas. These are supported by other tables of objectives, activities, critical success factors and derived information needs.

Since the architectural representation of the business is maintained at a high level, it necessarily lacks the analytical precision possible at lower levels of detail. Nevertheless it enables a first pass attempt at matching application areas to the important business needs of the business, and showing how information will be shared across applications. This step represents the beginning of the business-wide information architecture, which when completed, should enable optimal distribution of systems and information across the business's computing infrastructure.

The most useful matrix which can be built, is the activity–entity matrix. This plots the usage of information entities against the business activities. It also records whether the particular activities create, use, or modify the entities. Other matrices can be created, for example one linking activities and application areas, or an entity–location matrix which is useful if distribution of information around a number of sites is an issue to be considered.

Soft Outputs

As well as the hard deliverables, there are a number of other delivered benefits from a well conducted and well received planning process.

The people that have been heavily involved are likely to be well motivated and well versed, not only in the planning process, but also with a very broad understanding of the business, its people, direction and environment. They should continue to motivate the organisation towards maximum exploitation of IS/IT from wherever they are based, be it managing the IS/IT strategy, in business planning or from a user location.

The other 'soft' output should be an enthusiastic and committed senior management. This is most likely to be gained if the enthusiasm and commitment was earned before the process began, and has been courted throughout.

Both of these are endorsed by widespread and appropriately packaged presentation of the process, findings, conclusions and recommendations. If the strategy is not effectively promulgated to all of those who are involved in its implementation, then there is a real danger of a consequent reduction in expected benefits.

It is not possible to generalise about who should be kept informed, and at what stage or to what depth, since this depends on so many factors in each situation. But it is likely that the audience should include:

- top management,
- the whole of the IS/IT functional group,
- all participants in the planning process,
- user area representatives,
- any other focal points within the organisation. These could be, for example, corporate planning groups, organisation and methods groups, union committees etc.

It may also be useful to include certain external bodies, such as suppliers of systems and technology, or selected suppliers or customers of the business, particularly if proposed systems emphasise communication between them and the firm.

There are substantial benefits to be derived from effectively communicating the strategy. First and foremost among these is the necessity of obtaining demonstrable commitment from the organisation to implementing the recommendations and to providing resources to do so. It is also important to obtain prior agreement from all concerned on how the impacts on the organisation will be absorbed. A good example of how this prior agreement was not obtained is from the printing industry, where modern technology, which was to cause profound changes to the structure of that industry, was not 'sold' to the print unions ahead of its attempted introduction, with long term and extremely serious consequences.

Other benefits from communication can be obtained by asking for feedback from people who did not participate directly in the planning process (usually for straightforward practical reasons). They may be able to identify problems which were not exposed during the process, and perhaps introduce potentially better options than those proposed.

APPROACHES, TOOLS AND TECHNIQUES

The process of strategic planning for effective exploitation of IS/IT is complex, if tackled comprehensively. It needs to address several dimensions within its overall scope, and thus a combination of approaches and tools are required.

It seeks to satisfy efficiency, effectiveness and competitive or value adding objectives. Its implementation timescales encompass the immediate future and a horizon in keeping with the business strategy planning horizon. Whilst the critical future applications are probably 'strategic quadrant' systems, it is probable that the planned development portfolio will include entries in all quadrants. In addition, there is a high probability of there being an information and systems architectural infrastructure to be constructed. Also, the planning process could well be diverted into some business strategy formulation, organisational change management or even into product development with an emphasis on delivery of the product through IS/IT, or because information or technology are an essential element in the product.

These dimensions are encompassed within two basic approaches—one analytical and one creative. The former takes a structured analysis route through the upper levels of the organisation, systematically probing and decomposing the business requirements into their constituent parts, and delivering a structured view of the business objectives, strategy, activities and information needs. The latter, while having at its disposal several powerful techniques, focuses on points of likely high potential, and relies more on creative thinking. There is a good deal of crossing over—since in the initial analysis of the business environment, it is likely that embryonic ideas for future winners may emerge. Figure 3.12 illustrates the approaches, and their common roots.

The analytical approach can be sub-divided into a top-down analysis of the business and its internal and external environment, and a bi-directional analysis of information and processes. The first of these derives from continuing the top-down analysis of the business, with the emphasis on information needs and activities that are already in place, or need to be implemented to support objectives and strategy. The other is a bottom-up examination of the information and processes reflected in the existing application systems portfolio.

The creative approach is used to identify business opportunities that can be sustained, strengthened or even created by application of IS/IT. Increasingly, innovative proposals are based on the systems and technology themselves where the product or service has an intrinsic IS/IT element, or is delivered via the technology.

These ideas can be conceived anywhere in the business, and are frequently directly associated with competitive activity. In Chapter 1 the four main types of strategic systems and commonly observed characteristics of such systems were described.

A multidimensional approach similar to the combined analytical and creative one suggested here, is put forward by Earl (1987). His dimensions are

● top-down, business led, and analytic,

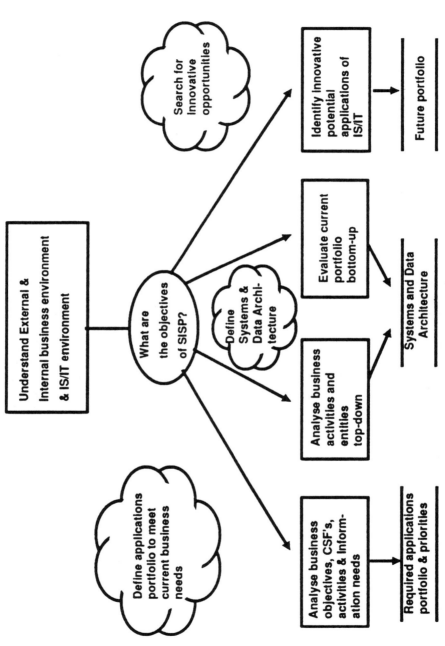

FIGURE 3.12 Analytical and creative approaches to interpret business strategy

- bottom-up, technology led, evaluative,
- inside-out, opportunistic, creative.

He suggests that as an organisation matures in IS/IT planning terms, it graduates from bottom-up only (to gain credibility and evaluate the current value of IS/IT), to eventually using all three approaches when an effective partnership has been forged between business users, executives and IS/IT.

His view differs from the analytical/creative approach above in that it does not advocate use of information analysis techniques to model the conceptual activities of the business and its future visualisation.

Associated with the analytical and creative approaches are a collection of techniques, which can be applied depending on the circumstances in the individual study. They are described later in the book, as they become appropriate for the processes being described.

It is invariably necessary to perform a fact-finding process, to gain a comprehensive understanding of all of the elements defined as inputs. Methods for fact finding include:

- Reviewing all suitable original material; annual reports, business plans, job descriptions, market intelligence material, etc.
- Interviewing, with careful preparation, and a mixture of skilful and structured questioning, discussion, and using recording methods that minimise narrative while maximising useful documentation.
- Group discussions, varying from the open brainstorming type to structured sessions designed to identify options for development, or those set up to gain complete or partial consensus of findings.
- Intelligence gathering about the external business and technology environment.
- Prioritising based on any appropriate techniques to arrive at objective and demonstrably just results.
- Analysis of the current IS portfolio documents, IS/IT standards etc.

Consolidation across Business Units

When there are several business units in an organisation, then there may well be common factors emerging from the outputs for each unit.

If more than one unit is conducting IS/IT planning, and especially if the units are similar in their business profile, then cross-referencing during the planning process is a good idea. Alternatively planning activities can be staggered to take advantage of common elements.

Opportunities for mutual support can be as diverse as:

- Acting as sounding-boards during analysis, perhaps holding some joint opportunity identification workshop sessions.

- Sharing tools, or at least using common tools for capturing planning output.
- Sharing applications portfolios or individual applications. Similar portfolios do not necessarily emerge from what at first sight are similar businesses. Synergy is most likely to occur when the product/industry profiles are in comparable stages of maturity, when their generic strategies are similar, and when there are sufficient common features in their business competitive strategies.
- Sharing software developments if appropriate. When environments and implementation policies differ, this may be down to the end of the analysis process only.
- Building common conceptual models for selected parts of the business. This may occur even when the applications portfolios differ considerably. There may still be substantial overlap in the conceptual information architecture, and much to be said for sharing high level models, common naming standards and data dictionary definitions. This is covered further in Chapter 10, which considers information management. Some rationalisation may be needed between models for different units.
- Allowing for effective intercommunications, by using consistent information definitions. This could facilitate sharing databases, or pave the way for sharing systems, implemented in different environments, but worth reverse engineering effort to make them available to other businesses in the organisation.

Some large businesses have well defined, comprehensive corporate IS/IT management strategies which impact all the business units. Such strategies can include policies for consolidation, for example to combine business data models across the corporation.

However if corporate headquarters are only interested in, say, financial considerations, then the potentially massive task of rationalising models across a large enterprise would not be sensible or justifiable, except for the finance functions.

SUMMARY

Strategic planning for the role of IS/IT in the SIS era is accepted as a major issue, and despite a plethora of methodologies, automated planning tools and brigades of consultants willing to propel organisations into strategic systems developments, is still relatively in its infancy!

Those who follow a planning process, do so with various aims in view. The most commonly sought after are expressed as:

1. Alignment of IS/IT with the business, and the impartial determination of priorities for development.
2. Competitive advantage through IS/IT, by exploiting opportunities and combating threats in the external business environment, using the strengths of the organisation.
3. Building a rationalised and flexible platform for the future.
4. Improved budgeting and resourcing and an ability to develop cost/benefit cases for long-term or infrastructure developments, or those where a payback is difficult to define.

They share as a characteristic the basis that information is a key resource, and that information and technology must be managed as such, and not as an overhead.

This chapter has focused on the planning process, and emphasised the continuous nature of that process (for example ensuring that practical and cultural mechanisms are put in place to capture and communicate intelligence throughout the business and IS/IT environments), thus facilitating genuine lasting and productive partnerships between business and IT.

Experience has shown that the most effective strategic IS/IT planning takes place at the strategic business unit level, with appropriate rationalisation and consolidation across the whole organisation.

There is no 'ideal' approach to SISP but there are a number of factors which aid effectiveness of the process.

1. Using the 'best' people available—from the business, IS function, external advisers—they provide the invaluable knowledge of the industry and the business, the IS/IT relevance and above all the creativity, none of which can be derived from a methodology.
2. Gaining the enthusiasm, commitment and involvement of top management.
3. Getting a thorough understanding of the internal and external business and IS/IT environments, the business imperatives and culture and the real stimuli driving planning.
4. Setting objectives consistent with experience and maturity, and tailoring the approach to meet these, employing a mixture of analytical and creative techniques.
5. Ensuring that the business believes its own recommendations and backs them, meeting the business demand by gearing all the demand elements—applications, priorities etc., and supply—portfolio management, organisation, information, development, service, and infrastructure, to the purpose.

To refer to one of the principal techniques used in strategic IS/IT planning—Critical Success Factor Analysis, these points could be put forward as generic CSFs for IS/IT planning.

The next chapters go into more detail about the various analytical and creative approaches, and how different techniques are applied to extract high priority, and high impact systems and what infrastructural activities are needed in a short and longer time frame. Key implementation issues are then addressed one by one, linking them to the objectives, stimuli and conclusions of the planning process.

REFERENCES

Brancheau, J. C. and Wetherbe, J. C. (1987) 'Key issues in information systems management', *MIS Quarterly*, March.

(DCE, 1987) DCE Information Management Consultancy registered SISP as a service mark in 1987.

Earl, M. J. (1989) *Management Strategies for Information Technology*, Prentice Hall.

Galliers, R. D. (1987) 'Information systems and technology planning within a competitive strategy framework. Published by Pergamon Infotech in Griffiths (ed.), *The Role of Information Management in Competitive Success*.

Strategic Planning Institute (1984) *Management Productivity and Information Technology*. Overview Report.

Sullivan, C. H. (1985) 'Systems planning in the information age', *Sloan Management Review*. Winter.

Tozer, E. (1987) 'The information factory'. Published by Pergamon Infotech in Griffiths (ed.), *The Role of Information Management in Competitive Success*.

Wiseman, C. (1985) *Strategy and Computers*, Dow Jones–Irwin.

Chapter 4

PLANNING FOR PLANNING—
ESTABLISHING THE STRATEGIC INFORMATION
SYSTEMS PLANNING PROCESS

INTRODUCTION

Earlier chapters have provided a retrospective on the evolving role of IS/IT in organisations and an appreciation, at a high level, of strategic business planning and strategic information systems planning. An obvious problem is how to start the process, ensuring old methods are stopped and better, more comprehensive approaches are adopted. Although strategic IS/IT planning should be an on-going process, to achieve the transition in an acceptable timescale a planning project or study is often needed to bring about change which can then be perpetuated. The planning study should introduce the required disciplines, tools and techniques, establish relationships and identify tasks and responsibilities and hence planning resource requirements. Control can be maintained and a future practical approach defined. This chapter will address this initial issue of how a process can be established for the successful strategic planning of information systems via an initial strategic planning study.

The first step may be seen as a scoping study in which the terms of reference for the following planning study are determined. This scoping study can often be difficult to perform satisfactorily. It is quite common for there to be differences of opinion between the key users and the IS community. There can be political issues at stake. There can be well entrenched positions to be overcome. For these reasons it is often advisable if it is conducted by someone outside of the mainstream activities of the business and MIS. For example, in a conglomerate operation where the exercise is to be conducted in a particular subsidiary, the appraiser could come from another subsidiary, or maybe from Head Office. A different approach would be to use an external consultant; someone who is independent and has good experience of developing IS strategies.

Whoever is chosen, that person will have, as part of the appraisal, to 'sell' the concept to senior management of the organisation under review because, ultimately, it is that senior management who will have to pay for the development of the strategy, and, more importantly, to manage its implementation.

The main tasks in the scoping study are to:

1. Conduct a situation appraisal in which the current role of IS/IT in the business and the stimuli and problems prompting planning, are identified.

2. Determine the expectations of the study and define its objectives, scope, any constraints, critical success factors and measures, and the deliverables of the process.
3. Determine the planning approach and techniques to be used, that suit the organisation's requirements and complements its former experience of planning.
4. Determine the team composition roles and responsibilities, and other required resources.
5. Create the mechanism for steering and controlling the process.
6. Identify the participants from the business who will be involved in discussions, interviews or workshops.
7. Lay out a plan for the work, identifying phases, timescales and checkpoints.

Each of these tasks is considered later in the chapter.

Before the planning process can begin in earnest, these terms of reference have to be documented and presented to the management sponsor, and possibly the executive board of the business for endorsement and approval to proceed.

It may also be necessary to provide education for the team in the approach and techniques to be adopted. At the least, all team members need to spend some time in order to:

● understand the principles behind strategic IS planning,
● review the terms of reference (if they do not participate from the start) and the study plan,
● agree on individual tasks and review the analytical tools and techniques available,
● understand deliverables and take responsibility for specific report topics,
● see how these deliverables are used in subsequent development projects (e.g. in a feasibility study),
● learn how to use the techniques of IS planning such as determining critical success factors, information analysis, value chain analysis, organisational modelling, interviewing.

One of the major differences between strategic information systems planning and a more conventional IS project is that some of the team members will have absolutely no knowledge of any information analysis methods or procedures. Conversely some of the more technical people will have little or no knowledge of the business world of the organisation. This means that education will be a continuous on-the-job process for all team members.

The aim is *successful* strategic planning. Here, success means implementing recommendations that meet the needs of the business and that are understood and committed to by its key managers.

Planning for planning is an essential step which sets the scene, and in so doing determines whether 'success' is achievable. There is no standard approach, that can guarantee success, each situation is unique and warrants careful consideration.

SITUATION APPRAISAL

It is necessary at the outset to understand why the strategy is required and what are the issues prompting planning. This is needed within the broader context of the business strategy and its internal and external environment.

There are two factors that need to be examined in this appraisal:

1. *Current role of IS/IT* It is necessary to understand what the current role of IS/IT is in the business, and how it is perceived by the business. Several ways of assessing the current situation were described in Chapter 3. One of these is evaluating the current applications portfolio to assess the balance between strategic, high potential, factory and support systems, to derive the main focus of systems in relation to current and future business strategy. Other indicators include organisational location; reporting lines; levels of user awareness of IT and satisfaction with current support; size and composition of backlog; and comparisons with other comparable businesses.
2. *Stimuli and problems* The stimulus for a strategic study can come from the need to restructure or integrate IS/IT as a result of changes in the business environment, such as:

   - New owner or manager—this may simply mean a new attitude to technology, or may herald more drastic change as a result of merger or takeover;
   - Major rationalisation—caused by, for example, downturn in the economy, necessitating a severe trimming of IS/IT budgets;
   - Restructuring—often resulting from corporate strategic planning, for example, changing a business from a production-led to a marketing-led orientation;
   - New products or markets—where there is a recognition that the present infrastructure is incapable of adapting to new requirements;
   - Recognition of the importance of strategic planning for IS/IT—based on the need to establish its precise role in the business.

It is also important to look at the key problems facing the IS manager, since finding solutions to these need to be included in the planning objectives, unless they are specifically excluded from the scope of the study.

The survey shown earlier in Table 3.1 of key issues in information systems management indicates a remarkable degree of consistency between the information systems manager's key issues and the general manager of the business. The top ten issues are the same. The major difference is that the general managers view measuring effectiveness as being significantly more important than do the IS managers.

EXPECTATIONS OF THE STUDY

Having ascertained why the strategy is required, and broadly understood the current situation, it is then possible to clearly lay out the expectations of the study.

This requires definition of the objectives, scope, constraints and deliverables, and for extra clarity, critical success factors and measures for the process.

Objectives

It is possible to state a generalised set of objectives, namely:

- To produce short-term and long-term plans for the development of information systems which support the corporate business strategy.
- To identify ways in which information may be used to gain a competitive business advantage.
- To specify the technological and organisational resources necessary to support the plans produced.

Whilst these objectives can serve as guidelines, they are normally not detailed enough to give accurate direction to the study.

However, no two strategic planning studies have precisely the same objectives. The variations arise because of factors such as:

- the size of the business unit under consideration,
- the sophistication of the current applications portfolio,
- the stage of development of the organisation,
- the immediate problems facing the management team.

Depending on the reasons which prompt the study, different emphasis may be placed on certain activities and deliverables.

For example a set of common scenarios which may be encountered are given below. They illustrate how the focus of planning may vary from business to business.

- *Gradual evolution of IS/IT planning*   Strategic planning may be initiated as one in a series of regular IS/IT planning events where there is a gradual reorientation from a technology-based to a business-based focus.
- *Gaining management understanding*   In an environment where there is a low level of awareness of the potential of IS/IT amongst the business community, and

a history of disappointed expectations from the business viewpoint, the planning process may be initiated by the IS/IT group with the express purpose of determining objectively the value of the contribution made by existing systems to the current and future needs (where known) of the business.

- *Determining priorities for allocation of budget and resources*   Frequently the main objectives of planning are to develop prioritised plans for provision of information and systems. These could stem from new systems, enhanced existing systems, and more accessible integrated information. Invariably this is coupled with the need to budget and resource from an apparently insufficient supply of funds and skills.

- *Gaining a competitive edge*   Seeking out opportunities for using IS/IT as a competitive weapon, directly or indirectly in offensive or defensive competitive activity is often quoted as an objective. It is almost treated as an obligatory objective by commercially oriented organisations, although few, including it for the first time in their planning, know how to go about finding the most promising opportunities.

- *Finding an early winner*   A high risk objective for strategic planning may be taken up by the IS/IT group to find one or two 'prizewinner' ideas, that can be implemented quickly—bringing significant benefit to the enterprise. The underlying reason may be to win over reluctant supporters within the executive controlling body to commit to IS/IT taking a more central role in the business.

- *Defining a global information architecture*   The focus is often the creation of a global architecture for each business unit, where the purpose is to instil consistency and integrity throughout the information resource, and to provide a springboard for comprehensive and flexible provision of information from an integrated resource. Alongside the development of the conceptual global architecture, it is frequently associated with the introduction or upgrading of structured methods suitable for modelling at business strategy level, and closely linked to systems development methods, and possibly the introduction of computer-assisted systems engineering (CASE) tools.

There are others which are rather more 'tactical' in nature—for instance:

- Justification of the MIS budget—it is quite common for MIS management to be under attack from senior management for the seemingly endless rapid increases in MIS budgets—if the budget can be directly related to the business strategy these attacks can be avoided.
- How to select new technological environments for the future.
- How to distribute data and systems development capabilities to end-users.

It should always be remembered that vague project objectives can result not only in the loss of a few months of valuable top executive time, but can have disastrous consequences for the long-term management of information in the company, e.g. user disillusionment, development of unwanted systems, selection of limited hardware and software, creation of an infrastructure which inhibits future business growth.

This argues that the setting of objectives is an area of vital importance both to the planning team and to the organisation as a whole, and why it is important to understand very clearly the major business and IS management issues, and the particular stimuli.

Scope of Study

There are many factors to be considered when defining the scope of strategic planning. These factors include:

- Size of the organisation.
- Culture and history.
- Time and resource.

Size of the Organisation

The strategic plan may be required for

- the whole organisation,
- one business area or a group of business areas,
- a geographical region.

Typically, there are two common problems:

- The study is too limited because only one system is really at issue and everybody knows this. In this case, a feasibility study and not a strategy study is required. This situation can be recognised on asking what the business objectives are, and getting the reply that it is irrelevant because everybody knows them (and, what is more, could not change anything even if they disagreed with them).
- An attempt is made to do the strategic plan for the whole organisation starting at the level of the holding company, or its equivalent for a group of companies in extremely diversified industries. The problem here is that the holding company is really only concerned with a very limited number of objectives and, as such, only needs a few elementary enquiry and modelling systems. For example, in the commercial world, a holding company may only be interested in profit and revenue figures.

    In this case a strategic planning study is probably relevant at the level of the operating companies but not at corporate headquarters level.

    In general strategic planning is most effective when the scope covers a complete strategic business unit, as argued in Chapter 3.

It is sometimes necessary to change the scope during the planning process, especially if the original boundary cuts across a natural business unit. In the process of identifying essential business activities, it frequently emerges that certain integral activities are carried out in other parts of the business, outside the defined scope. The reasons for such a spread of activities may not be rational, but the scope of study may have to be extended.

It is worth noting that although the scope must be defined as clearly as possible, it should not be 'drawn in blood', because it may well be modified by subsequent events.

Culture and History

Whilst the scope may be obvious when there is only one SBU under consideration, it may be more difficult when there are several.

A few pointers may be worth considering in making a choice of starting point, for example, choosing an SBU where:

- strong management commitment and involvement are assured;
- clear business plans and direction are known and available;
- the role of IS/IT is already respected;
- strategic business planning is well established.

In cases where strategic planning is not well established it might be more appropriate to scale down the scope of the exercise so that the learning curve can be contained and the new techniques and processes of strategic IS planning can be exercised on a small scale to demonstrate their validity before being applied to a larger organisational unit.

Time and Resource

Most planning studies should take between three and six months to complete. Ideally the planning team should include business and IS/IT members both being drawn from senior levels. This criterion itself tends to limit the team size, since it is always difficult to free up busy senior managers for any significant period. Both of these factors, discussed later in the chapter, have a bearing on the scope of the study.

Constraints

Theoretically, constraints should be defined as a by-product of objectives and scope. However, it is often wise to state clearly the reverse of objectives and scope, i.e. what the study will not do, for example:

- No recommendations will be made concerning specific hardware and software products.
- Overseas and branch companies are outside the scope of the study.

It is very difficult to define a completely generalised theoretical list of areas in which constraints should be specified. However, in practice, there are always one or two very clear areas of doubt concerning the problems or areas which are to be analysed. If what will be done about these areas is not clearly spelt out at the start, the whole study could fail. It often seems so obvious to the study sponsor, or the board of directors, that certain items of major concern to them will be covered, but which the planning team have never heard of. Normally such complications would be resolved at the first project checkpoint. Even so, it is much wiser to have the debates about what will or will not be done as early as possible. This could, and has, resulted in immediate cancellation of embryonic projects. This may be drastic, but it is infinitely preferable to an end-of-project bloodletting.

An example will illustrate the problem.

An American company in the entertainment industry had a major operation in Europe. A strategic planning study was initiated following a request from headquarters in the USA. A team of ten people was set up and they began fact finding in Scandinavia in early summer and as the year went on they migrated south so that by October they were finishing the fact finding in Italy and Spain. They then went to Madeira, a Portuguese island off the coast of Africa for four weeks to complete the analysis and write the report. The final report, as presented to senior management was 1500 pages long. After much discussion, and severe editing, a 30-page summary was sent to headquarters. The reply came back that this was a long reply to what they thought was a simple question requiring a YES/NO answer. The original request was 'Would the IBM 4300 be an appropriate machine for the European operations?' The study which resulted was obviously far too big, visiting 14 countries and costing $2 million. The team should have clearly defined the objectives and scope at the outset!

Deliverables

In Chapter 3 the outputs from the planning process were described and categorised as 'hard' and 'soft'; 'hard' being the reports and documentation, 'soft' being the human factors. This step should focus attention on the 'hard' outputs and describe what the final reports, and appendices will contain.

Reports

There are likely to be a number of reports which will address the following items as described in Chapter 3:

(1) IS/IT management strategy,
(2) Business IS strategy,

(3) Applications portfolio,
(4) IT strategy.

The benefit of having separate reports is that many issues will only concern a subset of the organisation. If all of the detail is given to everyone, there will be difficulty in assessing relative priorities and important aspects may be submerged in a mass of detail.

It is useful to draft out the report layouts at this stage, and to allocate reponsibility for sections of these to members of the planning team.

A suggested checklist of key topics is given in Table 4.1. Clearly this should not be taken as a table of contents, since these will be dictated by the focus of the particular study and the organisation's 'house style'. There are a few general points relating to the reports:

1. Management Summary. This should be short, maximum 10–12 pages. If the report is to be presented to the Board of Directors, then it should be in the form of a board paper, so that it can go directly into the minutes.

   A key item to remember at this point: the project team may comprise senior members of the user community and MIS and be working for up to six months on what they, and the rest of senior management, rightly believe to be a very important task. However, when it comes to discussing the report at a board meeting it will be one of a number of items on the agenda and may only receive 30 minutes or even less at that meeting. So if important decisions need to be made there it is necessary to prepare the case carefully, document it succinctly in the board papers and ensure that individual members have been lobbied successfully.

2. As discussed in Chapter 2, strategy is as much an understanding of where the organisation has come from as it is a statement of where the organisation is going in the future.

   The historical perspective is very important as this is the base on which the future is built and on which decisions have been taken. Strategy is living and breathing and evolving; it is not set in tablets of stone. As such there will be frequent questions asked as to why certain decisions were taken during the formulation of the various strategic options. During the first few months after publication of the report the issues will still be fresh in the minds of team members but after one or two years the background knowledge will be lost. So it has to be documented.

3. The IS perspective is equally important due to the pace of change in the industry in general. This pace of change must be contrasted with the innate conservatism of the typical MIS department which is usually resistant to change whilst expecting user departments to accept change willingly. This dichotomy is difficult to manage and the strategic planning team should document its findings carefully.

TABLE 4.1 Checklist of key topics for strategy report

IS/IT STRATEGY REPORT—SKELETON CONTENTS

Management Summary
Terms of reference
Summary of conclusions
Summary of recommendations
Acknowledgements

Introduction
Circumstances of study

Business environment
Business objectives, key issues, plans, critical success factors, critical problems
Business functions and processes
External and internal strategic framework
Competitive environment and competitive strategy
External and internal value chain
Information needs and conceptual information systems

IS/IT environment
Current portfolio of applications, current databases
Current IS/IT functions, strategy, policies
Current IS/IT organisation, values, style, SWOT
Information architecture
External IS/IT perspective

Business IS strategy
Business conclusions
Business recommendations
Applications portfolios
● Required development portfolio
● Existing portfolio upgrade
● Future potential portfolio
● Analysis of portfolios
● Priorities
● Costs and benefits
Business and information models

IT management strategy
IS/IT organisation
Investment and prioritisation policies
Vendor policies
Human impact policies
IT accounting policies

IT supply strategy
Application portfolio management
Information resource management
Application development management
Hardware, communications and networks
Capacity policy
Software and development tools
Operations management   *(continued)*

Appendices
1. Conduct of the study and the planning process
2. Current applications portfolio evaluation
3. Development portfolio—descriptions, justification, etc.
4. Information architecture and enterprise models
5. Tables of objectives, CSFs etc.
6. Value chain analysis
7. Workshop, interview, and discussion records
8. Glossary of terms

4. The overall report must be big enough to provide adequate reference to the rationale for choices made, and for documenting which options were considered and rejected, and why. This latter point will prevent a newcomer to the organisation reopening items for discussion unnecessarily as the reasons for rejection will be recorded and helps any future planners to avoid fruitless avenues.

Once the reports have been produced, the study findings, conclusions and recommendations will need disseminating to a wide audience. This will include, but not be limited to:

(a) Senior management.
(b) IS/IT management and staff.
(c) Business community participants.
(d) End-users, their representatives and focal points.
(e) Individual follow-on project teams.
(f) Other interested parties if appropriate, such as union representatives, suppliers, major customers.

The strategy needs to be communicated in a consistent fashion so that the right items are emphasised, and so that misunderstanding and false impression are avoided. It should reach audiences at different levels, with different interests and over a protracted period, possibly several months. It is therefore worthwhile developing well-structured presentations with properly prepared visual aids and handouts.

Critical Success Factors and Measures

At the same time as defining the objectives for the study, it is helpful to sharpen the perspective on these by setting out a few critical success factors and measures for how success will be measured at the end of the planning process. Clearly it is impossible to give a general set of success factors for any planning process as they will be dictated by the objectives, stimuli and perception of the business community, and other factors. However they are likely to reveal the 'hidden agenda' under the stated Terms of Reference and objectives, for example, understanding and meeting the sponsor's expectations, or 'achieving and maintaining credibility in the business environment'. They may also include one or two reminders to the planning team, for example, to avoid delving into too much detail at any point, or to keep the final product in mind.

Once success factors and measures are agreed, they can be reviewed regularly; at least at every progress meeting, to ensure that they are being satisfied.

PLANNING APPROACH AND METHODOLOGY

Once having confirmed objectives and deliverables, the next step in the planning for planning process is to decide on *how* to achieve the target. In practice this may have been decided well in advance, but it is still valuable at this point to confirm that the approach and techniques are appropriate.

'In our opinion, the quality of the procedure is not the most important factor but it is the factor which can be influenced most easily. Any procedure which is simple and acceptable to the members of the planning team will do for a start' (Nagel).

There is certainly no perfect comprehensive method. Many strategic information systems planning projects have foundered on the rock of 'method selection'. No method will, by itself, guarantee success. Responsibility for successful outcome, rests very heavily on the project leader. It is this person's responsibility to understand why each step in the process is being done, and why each document or diagram is being produced. Failure to do this results in the endless diagram production syndrome. This comes about commonly because the team is using a generalised method and diligently producing the diagrams mentioned, simply because 'the method says to do it!'

In a project the size of a strategic IS plan, however, some sort of method is obviously necessary. The selection committee should bear in mind the following major reasons for use of any method:

(1) *Overview* The method(s) chosen should include a way of obtaining an overview, or top-down view, of the whole area to be studied. One of the biggest dangers in an information systems strategy study is the attraction of using a detailed tool (e.g. normalisation for data analysis) which is a very good tool in itself, but completely inappropriate for the top-down view needed in a strategic study.

(2) *Consistency* The philosophy of the method(s) and the techniques used, need to be consistent between the various stages of the process. It would be inadvisable, for example, to be obliged to redraw diagrams containing essentially the same information simply because a particular method advocates using different schematic diagrams in two separate stages.

Furthermore the outputs from the various stages in the process should be consistent with other company methods, e.g. the outputs should be in a form which can be used as direct input to any subsequent systems development cycle methods.

(3) *Communication* One of the major reasons for using any standard method is to facilitate communication between team members and their user community, and between individual team members within the team. This means that the methods advocated should be relatively easy to learn and use. In particular, they should not be so complex as to dominate the whole study.

(4) *Documentation* The principal end-product of the process is a report. This implies that any method should give clear guidance as to the contents and form of the 'deliverables' and supporting appendices contained in this document.

(5) *Rationalise decisions* Any strategic planning methodology should provide management with a vehicle to make rational decisions. These decisions should be made at a series of clearly defined checkpoints which break the whole project up into easily comprehended units of work. The method chosen should give guidance on how to conduct these checkpoint reviews and what supporting intermediate deliverables are needed. It is especially important to record the reasons why various alternatives were not chosen. This avoids fruitless discussions at regular intervals about whether or not an apparently attractive alternative was ever considered.

Whichever method, or combination of methods, is chosen, it will have to be adapted to fit the environment, culture, organisational maturity and skills existing in the organisation.

In summary, the methods chosen should have the following characteristics:

- emphasis on deliverables,
- clear checkpoint stages,
- recognition of interactive nature of the study,
- recognition of importance of the human side of the process,
- modularity,
- simple diagramming tools.

The approach needs to accommodate the building blocks of the strategic IS/IT planning process as illustrated in Figure 3.10. The process also needs to include ways of understanding and interpreting the business and IS/IT inputs, to enable strategy formulation to take place. Figure 4.1 shows the main components of the process, briefly described below.

Understand and Interpret the Business Needs

This step can take various forms from studying existing documents to holding brainstorming sessions with groups of users.

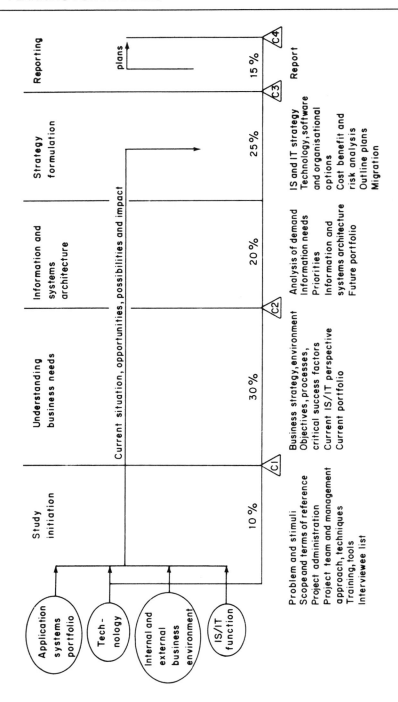

FIGURE 4.1 Phases of a strategic IT planning process

Its purpose is to develop a good understanding of the business in its environment, and of its current, planned and potential needs. This falls into three categories:

(1) Analysis of the business objectives, critical success factors, critical problems, and processes in order to determine the information needs and thus the focus for investment in systems to meet these. This is covered in Chapter 5.
(2) Evaluation of the current IS/IT provision to determine its coverage and contribution and where improvements would be beneficial. This is also covered in Chapter 5.
(3) Innovative analysis of the business to identify potential applications of IS/IT. This is covered in Chapter 6.

Very high level information analysis, critical success factor analysis, value chain analysis, and innovative techniques for identifying opportunities are techniques put to use here. They are described in the appropriate chapters.

Define Corporate Information and Systems Architecture

This step needs to take the results of the analysis of processes and information needs in order to build a global architecture for the business. It represents the future 'ideal' in systems terms, and is needed to plot a direction when developing migration plans. This step is also described in Chapter 5.

Formulate Business IS Strategies

The work here is to consolidate the findings which represent business needs and formulate the business IS strategy. This is described in Chapter 7.

Formulate IT Supply Strategies

Once a required application portfolio has been determined, then the remaining tasks are to define the elements of the IT supply strategies. These are addressed in Chapters 8 to 12.

Report and Present Findings

This is the final step to be achieved, which has already been mentioned in this chapter.

RESOURCES

The resources required can be broken down into three components:

- Team members
- Automated support facilities
- Physical facilities

Team Composition

The quality of the products depends on the quality of the team selected. The team leader and members should have:

- Knowledge of organisational objectives, management styles, culture, processes and people.
- Good communication skills.
- Ability and authority to make and implement plans and decisions which may affect the whole organisation.
- Respect of management and staff.
- An interest in areas other than their own and an ability to analyse objectively.

It is therefore likely that team members will come from different parts of the organisation.

As the main focus of the planning process is the development of information systems strategy, it is probably inevitable, and indeed advisable, that MIS be represented, but the team should be balanced. For example, if four people are required, then two should be from the user community and two from MIS. This is also important as some of the techniques employed require a certain level of MIS-type expertise (see Chapter 5).

In selecting the right group there are a number of factors to consider:

- The enterprise, as a whole, needs to be convinced that the planning exercise is important. If high level people work on the project then this message will come across.
- The participants in discussions will be from very senior levels. They must know and respect the team or they will not have confidence in the resulting strategy.
- During discussions or workshops the planning team must recognise if they are being deliberately or unconsciously misled or the resultant strategy will be rejected.
- A large part of the information requested and given will be sensitive and confidential. This will be more readily given to peer group members than to subordinate group members.
- During the analysis and strategy formulation stages, team members have to be capable of taking decisions which will ultimately affect the whole organisation.

So the organisational level of these team members has to be high, for both the user and MIS team members. These people, with the qualities mentioned above are precisely those executives who do not have time to spend on such a study!

Usually, if the management committee has agreed to finance the planning study, they will recognise the importance of the type of person on the team and provide the requisite managerial backing. The acid test of involvement is the decision to physically relocate the prospective team member for a major portion of his working time. This avoids the syndrome where a manager will say he is available anytime, but in practice, is impossible to contact in his native habitat.

Another catch here is the person who is only available for, say 30%, of the time. This occurred during one study where, right up to the start of the study, all the planning had been done assuming that the person in question would be a full-time team member. His explanation, and his manager's explanation, was that, as he thought he knew only about one third of the area in question, he would only be needed for one third of his time. It should be impressed on all concerned that a substantial commitment is needed from all team members, with the exception of the sponsoring management and steering committee members who are required to read reports, attend review meetings and be available for *ad-hoc* discussions when required.

It is perfectly feasible to conduct one of these projects using senior people for 40% of their time, and indeed, this is often what is actually practical. They need to be convinced of the value of the study. This can be achieved by selling the concept to them. For example in a major UK retailer, a consultant was commissioned to carry out the situation appraisal prior to the commencement of the study proper. His analysis of the situation, endorsed by the MIS Director, was that there was considerable scepticism about MIS at the senior management level and that any recommendations out of the strategy study would need to be 'sold' properly to senior management if there was to be any chance of success. To achieve this the selection of team members was obviously going to be important.

The consultant reviewed the list of executives and identified three people who had the right characteristics, one of whom was key as he was a dominant coalition member (see Organisational Modelling in Chapter 5). The Managing Director initially baulked at releasing any of them for such a project, even for two days per week, but agreed to it provided the individual executives concerned were, themselves, convinced of the benefits of their participation. The three people were then 'sold' the concepts and the benefits which would accrue to them from their participation, either in helping them in their immediate jobs, or in assisting them to realise their career ambitions.

It took two elapsed months before the team members became available, and, incidentally, it was easier to release the senior user executives than it was to release the corresponding senior MIS executives to complement them on the team!

In addition to the senior end-users and MIS staff it is often appropriate to use one or two MIS support staff who can document interviews using diagramming techniques and to assist in the subsequent information analysis. Also, if the strategic planning process is new to the organisation it may be appropriate to retain a consultant who specialises in this area.

Team composition is further discussed in the next section on process management.

Automated Support Facilities

Word Processing facilities are obviously extremely helpful, but much more sophisticated automated tools are now becoming available. There are two major requirements of such automated tools:

1. The graphical ability to construct any necessary diagrams, e.g. matrices, flow diagrams and data models.
2. The provision of a suitable data dictionary structure for the recording of such things as descriptions of data and activities, interview results and definition of business objectives.

Before deciding on the use of any automated tool, the team must decide on what information it wishes to record and how this information is to be structured, i.e. connected. For example, it is important to know such things as: how much detail is to be recorded from each interview; is a standard interview record format required? (normally the answer is yes); what is to be recorded about each major business activity and data group?

A typical combination could be:

- A good word processor for text and simple diagrams,
- a spread-sheet tool, such as Lotus, for matrices,
- a tool for drawing flow diagrams and data models; normally such tools also provide data dictionary facilities for the recording of definitions of major items in the diagrams, e.g. Excelerator, IEW, or Automate.

Physical Facilities

At the very least there needs to be one room dedicated to the team. It is usual to keep lists and tables and diagrams of general interest (e.g. company structure charts and process models) permanently on the walls of this room for easy reference.

The amount of paperwork generated tends to be immense. Even though team members may choose to do some diagrams themselves on micros, there is still a need for full-time secretarial assistance.

The information collected, both from desk research and from discussions is usually highly confidential and sensitive. Therefore the project room must be secure at night, or facilities provided for the locking away of such sensitive material.

It is preferable to have rooms set aside for discussions, equipped with white boards, flip charts, etc., and arranged so as to be conducive to a good interview. It is infinitely preferable if meetings, especially with these senior executives, can be held physically away from their own offices. This is preferred for three main reasons:

- reduced likelihood of interruption;
- the executive is away from 'today's' problems;
- recording facilities are at hand.

PROCESS MANAGEMENT

A suggested structure for managing and steering the process is as shown in Figure 4.2.

Management Sponsor

This person, who is preferably a director of the organisation, should fulfil the following functions:

- chairing the steering committee,
- assuring management participation and commitment,

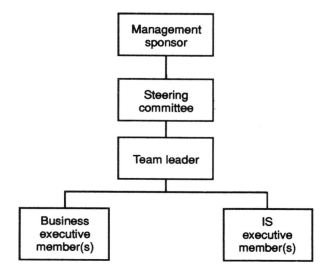

FIGURE 4.2 Planning process management structure

- heading the PR effort (which should not be underestimated),
- reviewing reports before publication.

Steering Committee

Depending on the size of the project, it may be necessary for this group to meet once every month, or simply to be present at the appropriate checkpoints. A minimum requirement is that the management sponsor should function as a one-man steering committee and report to the board of directors where necessary.

Typical steering committee functions are:

- checking out the team leader's plans,
- conducting interim reviews,
- reviewing final strategic plans,
- authorising continuation of work on the next project stage.

Team Leader

The team leader's role is to plan, manage and do much of the day-to-day work. As such, it involves a major time commitment on his or her part.

Team Members

Team members, as stated above, will be drawn from both the user and the IS communities. In general at least two full-time members are needed. They may require the assistance of other part-time members, such as technical specialists. The number of people required will vary with the size of the project and the desired completion date. The critical factor is normally the number of people to be interviewed as this is the most time consuming process in the study.

There is a further factor to consider in team selection. Acceptance and commitment from the members of the 'formal' management team is obviously needed. What is not so obvious is the need to involve people who, although they do not have the formal titles, are the effective powers behind the throne. Such a person could, for example, be the bright young economics graduate in the finance department who has set up an elementary, but much admired, budgetary system for the directors on his semi-legal PC. These people are sometimes known as 'gatekeepers' because they effectively control the gate of acceptance or rejection of any information systems proposals. Whether or not they are included in the team is a matter of judgement, but the team must be aware of their existence and importance.

One final point here is that, although it is possible, and perhaps necessary, to use external personnel in the team, it is essential that the organisation itself provides at least one full-time team member if not from the user community then from the IS organisation. This is because the project should result in the specification of a number of subsequent projects and someone from the organisation, who has participated in the study, is needed to guide these projects during implementation.

Business Participation

It is necessary to identify right at the start of the planning process, those members of the organisation who will participate in discussions, interviews or workshops. They can be briefed about what is involved, sold to, if necessary, and appointments set up in their diaries.

Other participants may be identified later, but the great majority should be prepared at the start. A few of these may be included purely for political reasons, rather than for any positive contribution they can make.

PLAN FOR THE STUDY—INCLUDING COSTS AND BENEFITS

The various topics covered in the planning process were indicated in Figure 4.1. This shows the process broken down into five stages which can be undertaken either as a single project, or as separate stages. Individual topics, such as organisational modelling can also be undertaken separately. However, from the point of view of planning it is a convenient model to use.

It is suggested that reports be produced at check-points C1 through C4 so that management can review the outcome from the various stages to ensure that the process is still on the right track.

The percentage figures at the bottom of each stage give a good rule of thumb for the proportion of time required for each of the stages as a percentage of total project time.

As mentioned previously, the number of people to be interviewed is perhaps the most critical factor in stages 2 and 3 of a planning study. On average it takes 1.5 to 2 elapsed days to conduct an interview, write-up the results, discuss them in the team and give feedback to the interviewee. Since at least two team members need to be present at each interview, the effort can be considerable. The situation is further complicated by the fact that the managers to be interviewed are almost certain to be unavailable in a timescale which is optimal for the planning schedule. It is often the case that the organisation has the choice of increasing at least temporarily, the team size, or increasing the elapsed project time.

It is important that there is a clear end to the study with clear deliverables. The project leader should strive to complete tasks on time. There will be no end of tempting possibilities to plunge further into the details in specific areas. These temptations should be resisted because management and user patience has an approximate 6 months' tolerance limit.

There are many aspects of the study which are iterative, so that the accomplishment of such tasks as 'strategy formulation' may already have been done by the time the team arrives formally at the relevant point in the study.

Costs and Benefits

One of the most important aspects of the scoping study is that it enables the appraiser to develop an understanding of the business needs which prompt the start of strategic IS planning. This is required in order to 'sell' the need for a strategic planning study.

The basic principle behind selling is to identify clearly with the problems (needs and wants) faced by the purchaser. In this instance it means ensuring that the person proposing the conduct of the strategy study can demonstrate clearly and precisely that he understands the problems faced by top management, their objectives and basic strategies.

The next stage of selling is to show that the service being offered will resolve some, or all, of the buyer's perceived problems. In the case of the strategy study it must be shown that the conduct of the study and the resulting strategy will assist management in achieving its corporate objectives and resolve the key problems, thereby satisfying both the 'wants' and 'needs' of management.

The third part of selling is reconciling the purchaser to the fact that the price and the time taken to deliver the service are worthwhile. So, in the case of the strategy, that the cost will be repaid by focusing future investment in IS and IT more precisely to the achievement of corporate objectives. It may also be useful to quote case studies.

The costs of the study are relatively easy to derive—they are people costs for the team, consultants, interviewees and management, and hardware and software.

The benefits can be more difficult to estimate. One client, though, described the benefit in the following way:

> We spend on average 3 man-months on every feasibility study. We perform about 20 feasibility studies every year, and reject about 20% as being too costly to implement. We therefore waste about 12 man-months of high level resource every year. Strategic planning will develop, amongst other items, a prioritised list of applications with a direct link between the systems and the business objectives, which will avoid the wasted effort at the feasibility study stage. The strategy study would take 4 people 6 months, therefore recovering the cost in two years without reference to any further benefit which cannot be quantified.

SUMMARY

Planning for planning results in the establishment of the planning process. Success can only be demonstrated by reference to the objectives of the planning study, but, in general, can be measured in three ways:

- completing the project on time and within budget,

- having the recommendations accepted by senior management and
- having the recommendations actually implemented.

Completing on time and within budget should be relatively easy provided the approach satisfies the terms of reference, the scope is adhered to, and the critical success factors followed.

Even if assessed as successful on that one count, this by no means guarantees that the recommendations will be accepted. For this to happen each team member, the business participants and the management committee must all feel confident in the results. Confidence is not generated simply by producing a good report. The building of confidence starts on day one and must be developed and sustained. Confidence would be generated by having a professional approach, by choosing good people to take part and by using an approach which involves people and which they feel is valuable.

The third criterion concerning success, that is having the recommendations implemented, requires commitment on the part of the organisation. Commitment to implementation of the results does not start on the date that the report is published but, again, starts on day one. On that day there is a commitment from senior management to conduct the study and then to seriously consider implementing the findings. That commitment must be nurtured and strengthened, so that once the report is produced then the enterprise is prepared to go to the next stage, which is to initiate feasibility studies in each of the designated systems. As in the paragraph above, confidence and commitment are developed and reinforced by a professional approach, the feeling of being involved and the sentiment that it has been worthwhile. It is very easy to sow doubt in people's minds which would lessen both confidence and commitment. The method of study must not allow for such seeds of doubt to be sown.

The chapter has discussed how the study is initiated and it is during this part of the study that the infrastructure is established which will lead to success— getting the team structure right and determining proper objectives and scope.

Chapters 5, 6 and 7 will describe the techniques which will be used to generate the strategy itself.

Chapter 5

IS/IT STRATEGIC ANALYSIS— ASSESSING THE CURRENT SITUATION AND FUTURE REQUIREMENTS

INTRODUCTION

Earlier chapters have considered the evolution of IS/IT in organisations from a strategic perspective, and then approaches to business and IS/IT strategic planning which can enable the required improvement in the integrated planning of both. More specifically in Chapter 3 'what is involved' in IS/IT strategic planning was examined in terms of the tasks to be undertaken and who needs to be involved.

Chapter 4 described how to approach the IS/IT strategic planning tasks the first time round via a planning project, which is often the only way to transform piecemeal, wish-list based planning to coherent business driven planning. The project focus enables the process to be managed more effectively in terms of establishing mechanisms, achieving timetables and using resources beneficially. Ideally, the planning process should not be seen as an 'event' or project, especially one separated from the process of business planning. Ideally it should be an integral part of whatever process develops and monitors business plans. Being pragmatic, however, the project/study approach can establish the disciplines, responsibilities and specific tasks to be carried out whether as part of a project or not.

In order to devise an IS strategy it is necessary to understand the business strategy, and that means examining three interlinked perspectives:

- the business as it is today,
- as it should be through meeting its stated objectives,
- as it might be if strategic direction changes from choice, competitive or other dominant pressures.

As introduced in Chapter 3, various tools and techniques are needed to achieve this multidimensional approach—analytical, evaluative, creative. All three demand a good understanding of the business's current position in relation to the industry structure it inhabits, and the opportunities and threats encountered in the external environment. An objective opinion of its strengths and weaknesses overall, and within its IS/IT environment are also needed.

This chapter will focus on a combination of analytical and evaluative methods primarily, although creative ideas can arise at any time in the strategic analysis. The next chapter will add the concepts for the more creative dimension, although they in turn are techniques which may provide new insight into results from this more logically structured and comprehensive analysis. Chapter 7 will then bring together the various approaches considered into a framework for overall formulation of prioritised information systems requirements for the business. It must be remembered that the focus at this stage is primarily on the 'IS strategy', i.e. **what** is required—the needs and priorities from a business perspective. Later the 'IT strategy', i.e. **how** to deliver it, will be discussed. But as the requirements are identified the current ability of the organisation to 'supply' or satisfy those requirements will inevitably be assessed. Hence, this part of the analysis will also focus on the IS/IT capability as reflected in the existing applications and information resources of the organisation.

Overview of Techniques

Several techniques can be used to evaluate the current situation and to analyse the demands of the business strategy:

- business strategy analysis to identify the components of the strategy and its associated information needs,
- critical success factor analysis to crystallise the essential characteristics of success in meeting objectives,
- information analysis to model the logical activities and inherent information elements of the business and to devise an idealised architecture showing how the enterprise's information and activities might be structured,
- current portfolio evaluation to determine the inventory of information systems in use and in development, and to assess their contribution and potential,
- value chain analysis to identify the most important information flows through the business, and to bring into focus potential opportunities for improving the value delivered by information, or potential hazards, where success may be jeopardised by poor interfaces, etc.

Whilst value chain analysis is very useful in analysing business needs, it is invaluable when considering external opportunities and threats, and so is described in Chapter 6 where external influences are especially relevant in considering the potential impact of IS/IT.

INVESTIGATING AND INTERPRETING THE BUSINESS NEEDS

The value of the IS/IT strategy is dependent upon the depth of understanding of the business and its needs, and the constructive interpretation of these needs into information and systems of value. To this end, there has to be a 'fact-finding' part during strategic planning which elicits and assembles all of the necessary information. Whatever techniques and approaches are used, the results have to be recorded in a manner that facilitates analysis. The approach described here relies on the building of models, showing the organisation, business and information requirements. A potential major problem of strategic planning is drowning in a sea of data. What is required is sufficient understanding of the business and information environments to be able to develop sensible and realistic strategies—not to actually design and code systems.

Much of the key information required for IS/IT strategic planning is in people's heads and needs to be elicited through discussion. However, interviews and workshops will be wasted effort if used to establish facts that can be obtained from available documentation. Not only does it waste time but also will mean important opinions expressed will not be seen in a factual context. Such problems can be avoided by reviewing as much available documentation as can be found. For example, the formal statements of objectives and mission can usually be derived during this preparation stage. If they are not already available from the annual plans, budgets and forecasts then they would almost certainly be included in statements issued by the company such as the annual report or in prospectuses supporting the raising of capital. These documents provide the official, financial view of the company's objectives and general direction.

An additional source of useful information about the organisation is the job descriptions. Many organisations today have job descriptions for management level staff and these often include statements about the main activities of the job holder and his accountabilities. These will be useful as preparation prior to interview but can also, at this very early stage, give a view as to the overall direction and purpose of individual parts of the business.

At this point it is also time to look at the IS/IT organisation within the business unit and to catalogue all of the hardware and software being used by the organisation and to describe the functions performed by each of the systems which are being run. This is basic data for analysing the current applications portfolio and internal IS/IT environment.

The 'inputs' model described in Chapter 3 (see Figure 3.10) included external and internal business environments and external IS/IT environment, for all of which information has to be gathered and analysed. This information, both fact and opinion needs to be organised as it is gathered, and an organisational model can aid the process.

ORGANISATIONAL MODELLING

Organisational modelling is a structured technique used to ensure comprehensive examination and documentation of a business and its IS/IT environment.

Information collected from available documents is used to begin the building of a model of the organisation to which information can be added to as discussions take place. There are a number of different models which can be used. The organisational model described here is based on original work by John Kotter.

This model of the organisation is made up of seven elements: a central 'process' element, labelled key organisational processes, and six 'structural' elements, labelled the external environment, employees and other tangible assets, formal organisational arrangements, the internal social system, the organisation's technology, and the dominant coalition. In his book, Kotter (1978) has developed a set of questions which enable the questioner to understand the organisation, but it is not intended that the questioner would thoroughly answer all of the questions. What is needed is a sensitivity to the potential relevance of each element or variable or question highlighted in the model. This sensitivity when combined with the understanding of the activities within the organisation and the data needed to support these activities is enormously helpful to both management and organisation specialists when considering alternative strategies, in implementation, and in providing an historical perspective.

The original work by Kotter has been substantially modified and enhanced for the particular purpose of information planning. Generally the questionnaire approach is conducted on a macro basis for the organisation as a whole and in micro form for the IS organisation itself. The questionnaire is not tackled as a separate exercise but as part of the overall fact-finding process, where the main focus is on determining objectives, activities and information flows, with additional questions being asked concerning the organisational model so that at the end of the process, an appropriate representation of the organisation has been developed, and understood by the senior management.

Figure 5.1 shows the organisational model. It has the following elements:

(1) The formal organisational arrangements—the plans, budgets, organisation charts, job descriptions are reviewed in order to develop an understanding of the way which the organisation records the way in which it operates.

(2) Employees and other tangible assets—questions are asked about the quality and quantity of people, their skills and training and the level of turnover and also about the fixed assets and financial assets of the organisation.

(3) Social structure—here the formal arrangements within the company are reviewed along with trade practices, relationships with trade unions. The informal arrangements, attitudes towards management, attitudes towards other workers, towards overtime, retraining, etc. are also reviewed.

(4) Technology employed—the level of use of technology within the enterprise itself is reviewed and the available technology, industry wide, is also determined. This section would include the catalogue of all the hardware and software within the enterprise.

(5) The external environment—questions are asked concerning the level of legislative change, the impact of fiscal policy, the challenges of competition in the particular industry, industry standards, competitor practices and products.

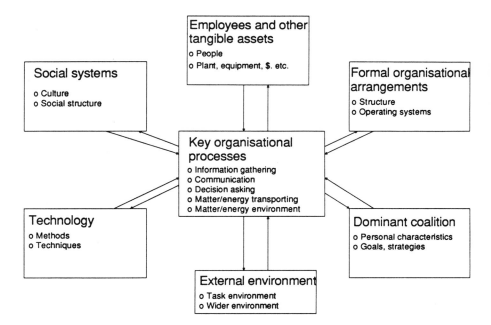

FIGURE 5.1 The organisational model—environment and culture (Source: J. C. Kotter, Organizational Dynamics, ©1978, Addison-Wesley Publishing Co., Inc., Reading, Massachusetts, Fig. 3.1 on page 25. Reprinted with permission of the publisher)

(6) The dominant coalition—these are the key internal influencers and in this section the people are described who constitute the driving force behind the organisation; what are their values; what are their aims; how do they work together as a team. It searches for the source of their power and influence and for how they see the future of the organisation. It is essential to identify this group as they will need to be convinced of the need for changes in information systems for competitive advantage and without their commitment there is little likelihood of success.

(7) The key processes describe the current products and activities within the organisation which convert the raw material into the finished products or services.

Extracts from the model questionnaire, developed by the authors from Kotter's original are enclosed as Box 5.1. Sample questions only have been included from a complete set of over a 100. They are intended to give an indication of the depth and breadth of detail which may be elicited. Without this kind of model it is very difficult to develop strategies for information systems which are consistent with the values and culture of the organisation. In his book, Kotter described how to use the model to bring about organisational change. This is often a feature of implementation of strategy and in its subsequent management. It provides further justification for adopting this technique.

There are three main reasons for developing the organisational model.

(a) When embarking on strategic information systems planning there are a multitude of options available to the organisation. It may want to develop new management information systems or there may be a focus on obtaining competitive advantage. However, the information planning process needs to be completed quickly so that the enthusiasm and commitment which develops during the process can be sustained, and so that work can start, to achieve the benefits of these improved systems. It is necessary therefore to have an effective filtering system so that the most relevant, realistic and implementable applications are considered for the future. The organisational model provides a very effective filtering mechanism. The basic premise here is that it contains substantial information about the resources which could be made available to implement systems, the culture of the organisation, its values and priorities, and supposes that it would not be sensible to propose systems which would be unable to be resourced or which would be totally foreign to the culture.

(b) However it may be essential to implement new systems and strategies which run against the culture of the organisation. If such systems are indeed in the best interest of the organisation then the culture itself needs to be modified. Here the organisational model is of considerable benefit because it describes the current situation in such a way that the cultural changes which are required can be understood within the framework of the model, to determine their impacts and considerably assists in implementation of the new systems and the organisational changes required. It is for this reason that it is suggested that two models are developed; the macro version for the organisation as a whole and the micro version for the DP organisation since almost inevitably there will be changes required to both.

(c) The third important use of the organisational model is that it provides a rigorous and essential understanding of the environment, both external to the organisation and internally at the point in time at which the strategic decisions were taken. This is important because when the strategy is revisited questions may be asked as to why certain options were discarded or why certain decisions were taken. Without this detailed historical perspective it would not be possible to answer those questions and could result in work being performed again or, worse, a decision being reversed to the detriment of the organisation. It also provides the perspective against which changes can be monitored. There will be a finite elapsed time between revisiting the strategy. During that time changes will take place in the external environment concerning competitors, the legal environment, the financial situation and also internally concerning the way in which employees work, new salary structures, and so on, and it is important to know the impact that these may have on future strategy.

The model provides a way of examining those changes to determine their impacts.

It will enable systems to be developed and implemented which are consistent with culture and values and sensitive to the influences of the various pressure groups and stakeholders. In this way the architecture which results will be in harmony with the organisation and will therefore be accepted by it. This is essential if IS is to be removed from the boardroom battleground where it is so often found.

As mentioned above, it is worth considering developing a second organisational model for the information systems organisation itself. This is often necessary because the IS organisation has its own particular culture and values and methods of working which may be quite different from the rest of the organisation. It may be possible to develop a good information strategy which fulfils all the criteria of supporting the business and being accepted by senior management but which is unimplementable due to its not being accepted by the IS organisation or by being foreign to its culture. One particular characteristic which has been noted on numerous occasions is a divergence between users and IS on the innovative uses of technology. Increasingly users want to push forward the use of technology but are being held back by an innate conservatism within the IS organisation.

ANALYSIS AND INTERPRETATION OF BUSINESS STRATEGY

The objective of analysing the results from fact finding is to ensure that as complete a picture as possible of the information needs of the organisation can be defined with a relative priority on each. Once this has been established the information needs can be grouped into logical subject data areas, which might eventually be implemented in databases and the business functions which access the information assessed, to identify potential application systems.

The list of information needs can be compared with current systems and databases to determine where the new information will come from or whether new sources must be found. Quite often, new information needs can be fulfilled by relatively minor modifications to existing systems or databases. Obviously these could be tackled in the short term. Other information needs may only be satisfied by developing new transaction processing and management information systems and will take longer to be implemented. The various techniques for analysing the information gathered are now considered in more detail.

BOX 5.1 *Organisational modelling — extracts from a sample questionnaire to elicit required facts and opinions*

A. *The external environment*

   1. What are the key groups in the outside world that the organisation has to take notice of?

   2. Who dominates/determines the development of the industry?

   3. What is the industry—growth, maturity, size etc?

   4. What makes for success in that particular industry?

   5. How dependent is the organisation on the external groups and what influence does it have over them?

   6. What is the basis of its own power?

   7. What is the value chain in the industry and how intense is the information value added?

   8. Could IT be used to increase customers' switching costs?

   9. How are competitors/suppliers/customers using IS/IT?

  10. Is there potential for pre-emptive use of IT with customers/suppliers?

B. *The dominant coalition*

   1. Describe individually for the key power holders, personal skills, attitudes and motives and how they see the organisation should be run.

   2. How do they work as a group?

   3. How do they seem to look at the future of the organisation?

   4. How powerful are they really, in the organisation, and where does such power come from?

C. *The formal organisation arrangements*

What formal procedures exist for:

   1. Corporate planning.

   2. The financial control of unit performance. The measurement of individual or unit performance.

   3. Controlling information, i.e. is information being managed as a resource?

   4. Deciding directives for information systems—users or DP.

   5. Determining policy with respect to distributed processing, use of personal work stations, etc.

   6. How is corporate, or SBU, strategy determined?

   7. Where does IS report; is DPM part of the senior management team?

   8. Is there an IS strategy and does this relate to corporate strategy?

D. *Employees and other tangible assets*

   1. What are the organisation's main physical assets, and financial assets?

continued on next page

continued

2. How many employees are there and of what general types?
3. Are the physical assets in good condition and up to date?
4. Are there strict financial limits imposed on the IS function or can projects proceed on the basis of justifications?
5. Comment on the existing application portfolio—how adaptable is it; how integrated, how cohesive?
6. Comment on the relative maturity of IS organisation.

E. The internal social system

1. What are the attitudes of the employee groups to company loyalty, hard work, co-operation with management and co-operation among themselves?
2. Are there any special cultural values which employees hold which affect the organisation?
3. Are IS personnel formally organised into groups or unions?
4. What is staff turnover and what are recruitment and career development policies?

F. The organisation's technology

1. What *main* techniques are used to produce the most important 'product' of the organisation?
2. What are the products, and potential substitutes?
3. What is the information content of the products/services?
4. Can IT change the products/product life cycles/production economics?

With particular reference to company-based information systems:

5. Is the installation relatively large or small?
6. Is CPU power centralised or distributed?
7. What is the degree of flexibility within the IS environment?
8. Does the IS technology have a high or low impact on the enterprise itself?
9. How much is there by way of telecoms; office automation; new technology etc?
10. How are the costs of IT passed on to the users?
11. How are IS investments evaluated, and prioritised?

G. The key organisational processes

1. What does the organisation take in to itself so that it can operate:
   e.g. raw materials
        energy
        information
        special skills etc.
   Are any of these especially costly or difficult to obtain?

continued on next page

continued

2. How are these resources converted into goods or services?
3. How are the goods or services disposed of?
4. How does change come to be considered?
5. In IT are there any steering committees or groups giving guidance and direction?
6. How are key decisions made in IT? Are there any user consultative groups; are consultants used for second opinion; how much authority does management have?
7. How is IS performance measured/objectives set?
8. How is any R&D funded?
9. What formal systems are used for development (methodologies)?
10. Is there an information centre and does it include PCs?
11. How does use of resources compare with strategic importance of applications?
12. Is maintenance separate from development and does it include enhancements?

Interpretation of Business Strategy

For the purposes of this particular part of the analysis the model shown as Figure 5.2 can be used. It describes the relationship of:

- Mission
- Objectives
- Tactics—or means
- Operational activities
- Internal and external information
- Performance measurement activities
- Critical success factors

all of these being part of 'strategy'

There are three main reasons for analysing and interpreting the business strategy:

(1) The activities which must be performed in order to contribute to the achievement of the business objectives, and the supporting information needs have to be identified. For example, an objective may be to launch a new product or service. The associated information that is required concerns the market size, competitor products and services and customer requirements.
(2) Secondary activities which have to be performed in order to measure performance towards achieving those objectives and which may then be used to modify goals must be identified. For example, once a new product has been launched it is necessary to monitor the takeup of the product or service to

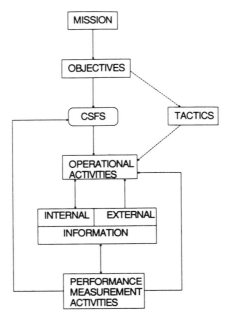

FIGURE 5.2 Business strategy framework

see if additional funding is required for advertising and to plan the resourcing
levels required to sustain the sale of the product in its particular market.
(3) The third reason is to provide a framework within which to critically assess
the information strategy itself so that systems can be properly prioritised to
focus the attention on those areas which deliver maximum value to the
organisation as a whole.

By analysing the business strategy in this way it is possible to consider a disparate
set of information system requirements across the whole organisation and put them
into proper context related to the benefit to the business. For example, the
production engineering department may wish to invest heavily in systems which
will enable the factory to respond quickly to customer orders and the marketing
department may want to spend money on developing systems to segment markets
and the sales department may want to spend money on developing a system to
help the sales force be more productive in generating orders. It would be very
difficult for anybody to say which of those three systems should be developed first
without reference to the overall activities and priorities of the organisation.
    Before going further it is necessary to define the terms used in Figure 5.2.

Mission

The mission is a broad philosophical statement that ties an organisation to certain activities and to economic, social, ethical or political ends. It provides a general framework within which the organisation operates. It contains statements of 'what we believe in' or 'what we are' and 'what we do' at a very general level, or statements of an inspirational nature such as:

- 'To be the World's Number One Airline', or, for example, the mission of the World Health Organisation 'to eradicate all communicable diseases worldwide'.

As an example of a mission statement, the following is taken from a large public company.

> The company engages in the retail marketing on a national basis of petroleum products and the equitable distribution of the fruits of continuously increasing productivity of management, capital and labour amongst stock holders, employees and the public.

Three further examples of 'mission' statements taken from public documents, for DuPont, General Motors and Honda are shown in Box 5.2.

Business Objectives

Objectives are general statements of future results or steady states that the organisation wants to achieve and are considerably more specific than 'mission'. Objectives are quite often quantified but may or may not be tied to dates or deadlines.

For the purposes of defining IS strategy, objectives need to be:

- unambiguous and results oriented,
- measurable, verifiable and not too numerous,
- established by those involved in their achievement,
- relevant, achievable and encouraging high performance,
- consistent with any higher level objectives.

To give an example, the following Mission Statement was for an engineering company:

> —Maintain close relationships with key customers
> —Provide an outstanding level of quality and service
> —Provide products tailored to the needs of the customer
> —Maintain technical lead by identifying market needs before competitors and developing new products
> —Develop a lean organisation promoting people from within and link rewards to results
> —Achieve a well above average growth in Sales and Profits.

BOX 5.2 *Sample mission statements*

General Motors guiding principles

'1. We will establish and maintain a Corporate-wide commitment to excellence in all elements of our product and business activities. This commitment will be central to all that we do.

2. We will place top priority on understanding and meeting our customers' needs and expectations.

3. General Motors is its people. We recognise that GM's success will depend on our involvement and individual commitment and performance. Each employee will have the opportunity, environment and incentives to promote maximum participation in meeting our collective goals.

4. We recognise that our dealers, suppliers, and all our employees are partners in our business and their success is vital to our own success.'

Honda Motor Co., Ltd

Company principle
'Maintaining an International viewpoint, we are dedicated to supplying products of the highest efficiency yet at a reasonable price for worldwide customer satisfaction.'

Management policy
—Proceed always with ambition and youthfulness
—Respect sound theory, develop fresh ideas and make the most effective use of time
—Enjoy work, and always brighten your working atmosphere
—Strive constantly for a harmonious flow of work
—Be ever mindful of the value of research and endeavor

Dupont

Principles
A significant factor contributing to our success is adherence to a distinctive set of guiding principles and commonly shared values.

Customer orientation
We must focus our energies on customers and markets, constantly striving for excellence in understanding, anticipating and serving their needs faster and better than our competitors.

Competitive position
We must serve those markets in which we can be the best . . . markets where our human, technological and financial strengths give us opportunities to establish and maintain leadership positions and achieve profitable growth. Further, we must be aggressive in both acquiring and divesting businesses to enhance those positions.

The objectives associated with the above included the following:

(a) *General business objectives*
 - obtain the highest prices,
 - achieve target operating profit (15%) etc.

(b) *Manufacturing*
 - reduce rejected batches to zero and raw material waste to 2%,
 - install extra finishing capacity by 1 March,
 - reduce manufacturing costs by 10%,
 - deliver 98% of orders on time etc.

(c) *Customer service*
 - achieve zero overdue orders,
 - enable sales team to concentrate on selling by reducing administrative load etc.

(d) *Commercial*
 - achieve 15% minimum growth in Sales,
 - win 15% of strategic market sectors (x and y),
 - develop technical competence of sales staff to reduce dependence on technical staff when dealing with customers,
 - (export) identify and contact at least 10 new prospects per month.

(e) *Procurement*
 - reduce staff turnover to less than 15% p.a.,
 - develop better understanding of the suppliers and their developments in raw materials,
 - extend potential supplier base within Europe etc.

Tactics—or Means

The tactics describe the manner or the way, or the policies, with which the objectives would be achieved. In other words the tactics describe how the appropriate resources would be used to achieve the desired objectives.

Operational Activities

The operational activities are the tasks that the enterprise actually performs. For the IS strategy it is only necessary to identify the main business functions (manufacturing, sales, etc.), and the principal business activities (analysing sales trends, handling customer enquiries etc.). Lower levels of detail, needed for systems design are not relevant here (create purchase order, reconcile invoice and order details etc.).

Activities need to be both analysed (decomposed) and appropriately structured for the understanding of the information and systems requirements and constraints. The existing organisation, as has been said, may not be the ideal way of structuring activities and may be limiting the information systems opportunities. Hence the activities should be analysed in terms of **business functions** not organisational groups. It may be necessary to 'list' activities under organisational headings to establish what is happening, but then they need to be reassessed. Box 5.3 shows such an analysis for a manufacturing and services company. As can be seen the activities elicited from the current business and organisation are regrouped for the purposes of identifying information needs and systems. For instance 'Processing of Sales Orders' includes activities currently located in Sales, Commercial, Manufacturing and even Finance. This activity decomposition/recomposition is essential to identify information relationships and consequent databases and systems.

This method of activity decomposition also enables costs of the business to be allocated to the various activities/relationships in order to identify the potential benefits available from systems investment.

Information

Information is required by every activity. At the strategic level of analysis, it is broadly defined, but, in an exact parallel with the activities, it can be decomposed during successive stages of analysis to a point when the information becomes elemental data which might form a field in a database. It can be derived from either internal or external sources.

Performance Measurement Activities

These are used to measure how well an activity is supporting the achievement of an objective and are quite distinct from operational activities. They are essentially information based activities.

The identification, documentation and analysis of these information activities is considered in more detail under the techniques of information analysis.

Whilst it is important to identify all of these elements in the business strategy context, the last one, critical success factors, enables a further degree of precision to be obtained in interpreting the business requirement in information systems terms. It is considered separately as a technique in its own right.

CRITICAL SUCCESS FACTOR (CSF) ANALYSIS

Critical success factors can be used in a number of different ways and for different purposes. In this particular context, they are used for the purpose of interpreting more clearly the objectives, tactics, and operational activities in terms of key

BOX 5.3 *Example of activity analysis for a manufacturing and services company*

1. *Current activity analysis*

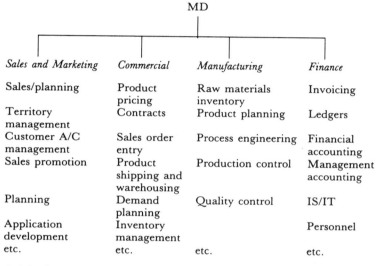

MD

Sales and Marketing	Commercial	Manufacturing	Finance
Sales/planning	Product pricing	Raw materials inventory	Invoicing
Territory management	Contracts	Product planning	Ledgers
Customer A/C management	Sales order entry	Process engineering	Financial accounting
Sales promotion	Product shipping and warehousing	Production control	Management accounting
Planning	Demand planning	Quality control	IS/IT
Application development	Inventory management		Personnel
etc.	etc.	etc.	etc.

2. *Activity decomposition* by subdividing into components
   e.g. *Sales planning*:   Obtain/review market intelligence
   Analyse recent performance
   Set immediate targets
   Provision resources etc.

   Territory management: Set regional targets
   Plan direct and distributor sales plans
   Procure sales
   Obtain market information
   Distributes sales literature
   etc.   etc.

3. *Major business functions and activities involved are analysed*

   For the organisation above major business functions were defined as:

   Processing of sales orders
   Distribution of finished product
   Selling the product
   Technology development
   Administration and finance

   Each major function is then constructed from the components above (plus new requirements).

information needs of the organisation and its managers and strengths and weaknesses of existing systems.

They can be used at the macro level to look at the overall industry, the company overall, or a particular business unit. They can also be used at individual executive level to determine which of those activities that he performs are the most important for overall achievement of success in a particular objective. In this way the CSF process can assist in prioritising activities and information requirements, both at individual manager and SBU level.

In both cases the CSF technique helps to focus attention on the key issues. So, what is a critical success factor?

Rockart (1979) defines critical success factors as being 'for any business, the limited number of areas in which results, if they are satisfactory, will ensure successful competitive performance for the organisation'. They are the few key areas where 'things must go right' for the business to flourish. . . . As a result, the critical success factors are areas of activity that should receive constant and careful attention from management. The current status of performance in each area should be continually measured, and that information should be made available.

As stated above they can exist at a number of levels as shown in Figure 5.3. Every firm in an industry may have some common CSFs, e.g. access to raw materials, timely delivery etc., due to pressures on or in the industry. The overall organisation which could have units in many industries will have CSFs relative to its objectives of diversification, return on investment and portfolio mix. The *key* area for determining CSFs as part of strategic IS planning is for the business unit, since as stated in Chapter 3 this is the practical level to determine strategy. A consensus of the business unit managers as to what these CSFs are is important in obtaining consensus on the major IS/IT investments.

There will also tend to be a structured relationship in a large organisation between objectives and CSFs.

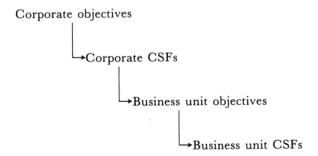

Corporate objectives
→Corporate CSFs
→Business unit objectives
→Business unit CSFs

The determination of CSFs should be started only when objectives have been already identified. The first stage is to identify CSFs against each objective and

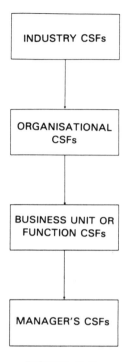

FIGURE 5.3

then secondly to consolidate them across objectives, since many CSFs will recur. Only then should the importance of information or systems in achieving those CSFs be considered. 'How can IS/IT help achieve the CSFs?' is really the first question to be explored. Equally 'How do existing systems inhibit achievement of CSF?' is important to consider and this implies a SWOT (Strengths, Weaknesses, Opportunities and Threats) analysis of existing systems against the CSFs. By implication if the CSF is achieved, the probability of achieving objectives is increased. That assumes a reasonable number of CSFs per objective—5 to 8 per objective is a useful rule of thumb. Too many suggest the objective is unachievable, too few and it is not ambitious enough!

With reference to an oil company example the CSFs can be seen to directly relate to the objectives and tactics. Take, for example one of the objectives of the company

● to achieve 1% growth in market share.

Supporting tactics are:

● to improve performance across all regions at rates in excess of the industry average,

● to improve performance in those regions which are currently under-performing to match the national average.

There are probably many factors which are required to achieve the objective using those particular tactics but the CSFs which were identified by the company were:

(1) competitive pricing,
(2) the remuneration of site managers,
(3) distribution of sites,
(4) the level of advertising.

Corresponding with each of those critical success factors there are specific measures which can be determined which will assist in achieving the objective.

For example, with the CSF of competitive pricing then a measure is the comparison between the company price against the average price.

The CSF of remuneration of site managers, for example, can be measured by looking at the salary paid to the site managers and comparing with the national average.

So, putting these side-by-side, shows:

Critical success factor	*Measures*
Competitive pricing	Company price versus average price
Remuneration of site managers	£ paid versus industry average
Distribution of sites	
● key sites	Proportion of top turnover sites
● geography	Site density/market size ratio
Level of advertising	
● national	£ spent versus industry average
● regional	£ spent versus industry average

This, in turn leads the organisation to identify more activities, i.e.

1. Survey prices.
2. Review and survey salaries.
3. Review demographics of site locations.
4. Compare advertising expenditure against industry average.

These, in turn, each have information requirements, and have associated performance measurement activities.

This example shows how the objectives, tactics and use of CSFs will lead to the derivation of operational activities and the identification of both the internal and external information required by those operational activities and for performance measurement. Ranking of objectives and the number of people sharing the same CSF will give a relative priority to the achievement of CSFs.

In summary, therefore, CSF analysis is an integral part of the IS/IT strategic planning process, as it should be in any business planning process. CSFs enable management to use their judgement in IS/IT matters in two ways, as shown in Figure 5.4,

(a) to assess the relative importance of systems opportunities in terms of how well they support the achievement of business objectives,
(b) to identify the information required by management to manage and plan the business—executive information needs. It is always better to have a crude measure of something important rather than a refined measure of something that does not matter! CSFs help differentiate the two.

From the above description it may appear that the CSF is the universal management tool. This is not the case for the following main reasons:

1. To be of value, the CSF should be easily and directly related back to the objectives of the business unit under review. It has been the experience of people

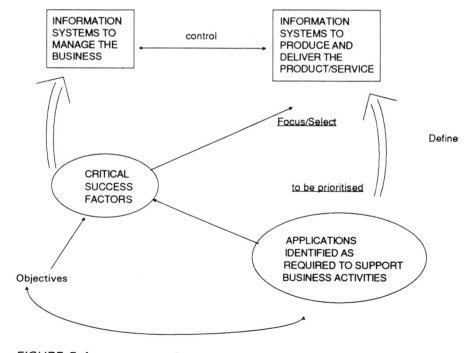

FIGURE 5.4

using the technique that generally it loses its value when used below the third level in an organisational hierarchy.

2. CSFs focus primarily on management control. As such this is fine because this is a difficult area, largely ignored by the applications portfolio due to the difficulty of defining the information needs. CSFs tend to be internally focused and analytical rather than creative.

3. CSFs, partly, reflect a particular executive's management style. The chief executive of one airline judged performance by load factors. His predecessor judged performance on the number of complaints letters. Both are valid but reflect different approaches. To use CSFs as an aid in identifying systems, with the associated long lead times for developing these systems, may lead to giving an executive information that he, personally, does not regard as important.

The process of using CSFs is summarised in Figure 5.5. It is important to remember that consensus of the senior managers must be achieved in order to get eventual agreement on IS/IT strategies. Therefore it can be said that the process is as important as the product. It forces analysis of the strengths, weaknesses, opportunities and threats and ensures a proper understanding of the mission and objectives, often for the first time!

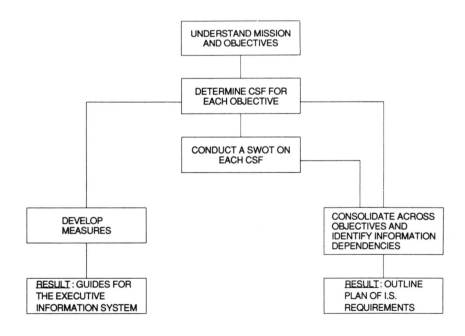

FIGURE 5.5

INFORMATION ANALYSIS

Information Models—as a Means of Documentation and Analysis

It is very advantageous when undertaking IS/IT planning to have a set of automated tools available—preferably integrated with one another and with the set of tools used within information resource management and systems development in the organisation. Even a simple diagramming tool and matrix manipulator makes the creation and manipulation of models, matrices and tables a great deal easier than when working entirely by hand.

The main models which are produced during planning are entity models, activity decomposition diagrams and data flow diagrams. Naturally they are all high level models, obtained from top-down analysis of the business unit. Nevertheless whenever possible these models are built and recorded in such a form that they can become initial input to the successive stages of feasibility and systems development.

Entity Models

Very high level entity models are developed when analysing the business's activities (real and conceptual). These entities comprise the key elements of fundamental importance to the business, about which the information is essential although it is by no means necessary to hold this in computerised systems. They may include people (customers, suppliers), objects (products, invoices), places (workshop, laboratory), or abstractions such as events (sale, order).

The model, apart from showing these key entities, also indicates the relationships between the entities (optional or mandatory, etc.). The entity models produced in a strategy study are purposely retained at a high level, and tend to be somewhat imprecise, since so much of the detail is absent, but clearly are capable of successive decomposition so that they become increasingly more precise, and thus effective at the systems development level. An entity–relationship (E–R) model is shown in Figure 5.6 (Rock-Evans, 1987). They are frequently called 'fuzzy' models at this stage as in this example.

The entities appearing in these models are likely to become the focus of the databases subsequently developed and maintained. They are also the starting point in the definition of an information architecture for the business unit.

In a large organisation with several business units it is likely that separate entity models will be created for each unit, and there will be no attempt to create a global model for the whole organisation. However, where there is a good deal of similarity between the units, or business synergy, then reconciliation between common entities becomes important, when the interfaces are explored. Similarly when consolidation of information from various units up to corporate level is considered, reconciliation may also be desirable.

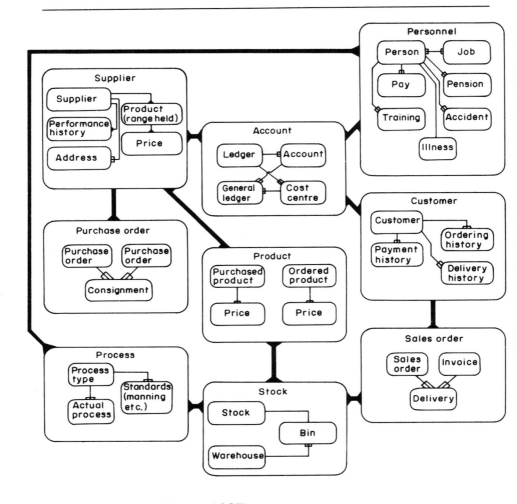

FIGURE 5.6 (Rock-Evans, 1987)

E–R models are essential components of the information and systems architecture for a business.

There are three main reasons why they are drawn:

(1) To define the underlying data architecture which is independent of functional considerations.
(2) To clarify company language and provide the initial entries into the business unit's data dictionary.

It is quite common for organisations to have different understandings of a particular term used within the same organisation. For example one particular Managing Director commented that, at a board meeting, he had four different parts of the organisation giving him four different answers to a question about sales. The production department said that they had produced for sale a certain quantity of goods and that was their 'sales figure'. Marketing department had another set of figures for 'sales' which were independently derived from their forward marketing projections. The sales department had a figure based on customer orders while the finance department had a figure based on actual invoiced sales. Now each of those directors was talking about what they thought was the same information but clearly there were four entirely different sets of figures involved. Entity–relationship modelling will help to resolve these issues.

(3) To identify some high level redundancies of data. At the same time it is almost certain that it will indicate areas where considerable further investigation will be necessary and thus illustrate that this first level of entity model is not precise, but rather a first, albeit useful, approximation.

It can also identify high level redundancies of activities. An analysis was conducted at a financial institution using the techniques of data flow diagramming and entity modelling. One particular part of the organisation was reviewed and it was found that while a lot of activity was taking place within the department, and information was coming into it, nothing, in fact, was leaving it. This had arisen because, some years before, exchange controls had been introduced by the government of the country concerned and this department was then established to monitor exchange control. However when the exchange controls were relaxed the department carried on, but there was then no purpose to it. It was with considerable embarrassment that the management accepted the results of the exercise because 30 people were involved in the department, busily working, but actually producing nothing of any value.

Activity Decomposition Diagrams

Sometimes called functional decomposition diagrams, they describe the business unit's activities, under the broad activity grouping that the unit is set up to do (banking, retail etc.).

When undertaking strategic IS/IT planning, activity decomposition diagrams are usually created at the global level, and at each major functional level, but only decomposing activities down to two or at most three levels below the broad grouping level. An example is given in Figure 5.7.

Once all the activity diagrams have been built, it is usual to rationalise them, and create what is the fundamental activity set for the future that meets the business objectives. After rationalisation this may bear little resemblance to the organisational layout of the business, and its current activities.

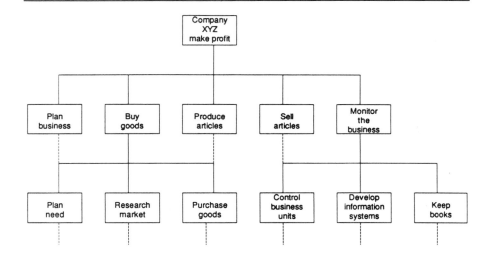

Each activity can be decomposed into more detailed activities

FIGURE 5.7 Activity decomposition diagram

Its purpose then, is having clarified the essential activities of an organisation, it can point to a likely set of information requirements and thus the basis for identifying future information systems.

Data Flow Diagrams

A Data Flow Diagram (DFD) is a network representation of business information systems and shows the logical dependency of one activity upon another for its data. It shows where 'parallel' activities (which are not dependent on one another for data) and where 'dependent' activities (which are dependent upon one another for data) can take place. All activities are represented, whether they are currently implemented as manual tasks or computer programs and whether they are what is done now or what the business would like to do.

Figure 5.8 (Rock-Evans, 1987) gives an example and illustrates how a client sends payment details (the payment is for an order delivered to him). The payment is 'processed' (validated), checked against the unpaid invoice (for which details are required) and a receipt is sent to the client. The checked payments are used to prepare a deposit to go to the bank. Details of the business's account with the bank are used to create a deposit which is then sent to the bank. In order to prepare the deposit, checked payments must be available. Thus, the activity 'prepare deposit' is logically dependent for its data on the 'process payment' activity which is also logically dependent on the data of payments and unpaid invoices. This

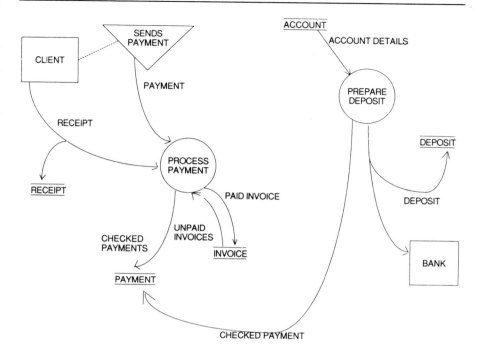

FIGURE 5.8

implies that another activity will have put unpaid invoices into the data store of invoice, ready for the process payment activity to use. The 'prepare deposit' activity is dependent on the checked payment details and on account details, implying that there is another activity which provides account details to which the 'prepare deposit' activity is logically dependent.

The most significant characteristics of DFDs are that the situation is represented from the viewpoint of data, not a person or organisation. The diagrams are graphic and can be partitioned and layered so that rather complex flows can be easily shown. They can be structured so that functions can be decomposed into more detailed self-contained models.

Data flow diagrams (DFDs) also form part of the conceptual information architecture in so far as they describe the activities of the organisation in a structured form. They are also particularly useful for the following reasons:

(1) To develop a clear understanding of what actually happens within a particular activity, and to clarify its information needs. This facilitates the identification of conceptual activities during the later stages of analysis in a comprehensive manner totally independent of the management structure. This is important

when it comes to developing systems where it is necessary to have a clear understanding of the activities that the system is to support and the data which the activities must use.

(2) Organisations and organisational structures develop over time and reflect not only activities which are grouped together but often the strengths and weaknesses of people who have a responsibility for those individual units. It is quite common for example to find that a particular executive has an aptitude for planning and when organisational change takes place that executive takes the planning responsibility with him into his new job. Thus, the planning department may well be part of marketing at one point in the life of the company and then may be part of production or retailing at some other point. This organic development of organisational structure manifests itself in all parts of the organisation and there needs to be a rational and logical view of activities otherwise it is somewhat difficult to develop systems.

(3) The data-flow diagram facilitates the review of the merits or faults of organisational structures. This is not primarily for the purposes of restructuring, although this may happen as a consequence of adoption of a particular strategy, but rather for the future logic within application systems.

Matrices and Tables

There are several matrices that can be produced during the planning process, once all the analysis of information systems needs has taken place. Collectively the matrices and models represent the total corporate or business unit architecture, conceived to satisfy business requirements.

The matrices provide a tabular representation of the business, and illustrate the relationship between information entities, business activities, and conceptual application areas. These are supported by other tables of objectives, critical success factors and derived information needs.

Since the architectural representation of the business is maintained at a high level, it necessarily lacks the analytic precision possible at lower levels of detail. Nevertheless it enables a first pass attempt at matching application areas to the important business needs of the business, and shows how information will be shared across applications. This step represents the beginning of the business-wide information architecture, which when completed, should enable optimal distribution of systems and information across the business's computing infrastructure.

The most useful matrix which can be built, is the activity–entity matrix (Figure 5.9). This plots the usage of information entities against the business activities. It also records whether the particular activities create (C), use (U), or modify (M) the entities.

The rows and columns on this example have been shuffled around so that the 'create' elements are clustered along the diagonal. This clustering into groups

Entity–activity (CRUD) matrix. Entities are listed as rows; business activities as columns.

Entities \ Business Activities	1 Financial registration	2 Incoming cash flow	3 Outgoing cash flow	18 Approval of incoming invoices	5 Sales support	7 Sales	8 Order registration	9 Order validation	19 Order receipt and planning	20 Service	26 Advice	15 Suppliers management	17 Ordering of goods	6 Product management	12 Storing of goods	13 Stock control	14 Stock taking	22 Personnel management	24 Time and cost registration	23 Wages and salary administration
1 Debit/credit	C																			
2 Incoming payment	C	C																		
3 Invoice	C	C		U																
4 Financial contract	C		C	U																
5 Outgoing payment	C												U							
6 Incoming invoice			M	C								U	U							
7 Client	M				C	M	M	U	U	U										
8 Sales contract	U				C	C	U													
9 Mailing					C	M														
10 Order	U				U	U	C	M	U	U	U	U			U					
11 Service contract	U				U	U	C	C	M	U										
12 Delivered order	U				U	U	C	C	C	C										
13 Client/goods registration					U	U	C					U		U						
14 Article-package-supplier	U		U									C	U	U		U				
15 Supplier			M									C	M	U		U				
16 Purchase order	U		U	U								U	C							
17 Goods	U					M						U	U	C	M	M	M			
18 Calculation algorithms		U										U	U	C						
19 Depot	U					U									C	C				
20 Receipts of goods			U	U								U		C	C	M	M			
21 Education											C									
22 Function																		C		
23 Employee				U		U	U	U		U	U	U				U		C		U
24 Department	U			U		U	U	U		U	U	U	U	U				C		U
25 Employee action																		C	U	U
26 Time capacity																		C	M	U
27 Time and cost registration	U			U														U	C	U
28 Employee payment	U																	U		C

C = created
M = modified
U = used

FIGURE 5.9

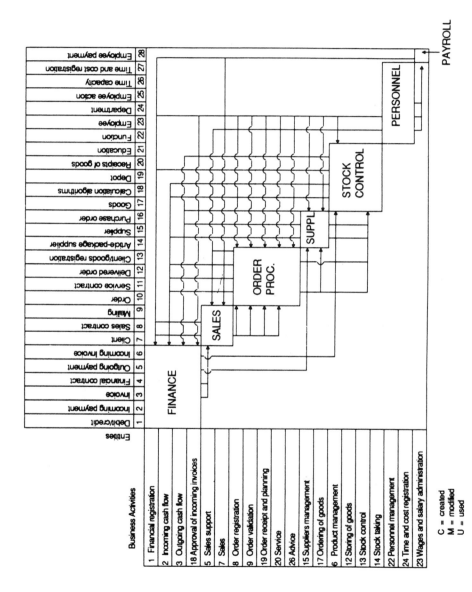

FIGURE 5.10

which demonstrate a high degree of autonomy and low level of dependence on other groups, enables a first pass attempt at identifying the architecture matrix showing proposed subject databases and application areas. Figure 5.10 is the same matrix, with the groups defined and interrelationships indicated.

As the analysis of findings, and formulation of information strategies begins, other matrices can be created, for example:

- Function–entity matrix, summarising the information usage of the separate business functions against the entity set.
- Function–application area matrix recording the correlation between application area and business function. This matrix is most useful if it confines the linkages to those illustrating where applications are used directly by the function, and does not include those representing occasional usage of information produced by the applications.
- Application area–entity matrix indicates which applications create, modify and use entities, and how the entities may be clustered into subject databases. It is useful in determining the contents of the applications portfolio to be developed, and the order of development, since dependencies are indicated. Clearly, the lack of detail may be a drawback, but any potential inconsistencies can be highlighted and resolved before firm decisions are taken.

The models shown in Figures 5.9 and 5.10 are simplified in order to show the concepts. However, the techniques can be used very effectively in the real world to generate the total information and systems architecture.

This is embodied in the set of high level models and matrices which represent a global, long-term view of the organisation's information elements, relationships and flows, and the consequent information systems and databases needed to support the business requirements.

CURRENT PORTFOLIO EVALUATION

Since the current portfolio of systems in use and under development represents the starting point of a migration path, and contains the current assets in systems terms resulting from substantial investment, it is extremely important to evaluate its contribution to current and future business needs. As a result of this evaluation, the following deliverables are produced:

- Assessment of coverage and contribution of systems to business needs.
- Unrealised potential in current systems and enhancements required to increase contribution.
- Common elements and differences between current portfolio and required information and systems architecture.

In order to do this evaluation, information needs to be systematically collected about the current portfolio, and then a strengths/weaknesses analysis conducted. This analysis and the risks of failure are part of the formulation of strategy, and are discussed in Chapter 7. At this stage, all that is necessary is to collect the information to go into the analysis. This involves collecting for each system:

1. What business activities are 'contained' within the system.
2. Which of these are critical processes, with reference to objectives, CSFs, value chain, etc.
3. How they map on to DFDs, entity charts and the architecture matrices. What gaps, poor links, duplications etc. are revealed.
4. How they contribute to meeting information needs determined in business strategy analysis.

The task is not trivial for a number of reasons, for example:

● Existing system titles and new information needs rarely compare easily. This is often because the latter refer to strategic and management information systems whereas the bulk of existing systems are core operational systems.
● Entity descriptions developed by the planning process will have different meanings from those at application system level. A comprehensive data dictionary, and mapping tools are very helpful here, although usually the process has to be manual.

At the end of this process the entities can be classified in several different ways:

1. Readily available occurrences of the entity, i.e. records, are available, in a database with sufficient attributes, i.e. fields, to satisfy application area requirements.
2. Available with minimal effort:

    ● records are stored in a database, but additional fields from underlying systems need to be stored.
    ● records are complete but not stored in a manner which supports the application area requirements.

3. Available with substantial effort—records are available but some required fields just do not feature in underlying systems.
4. Not available—the entire entity has never been used by any application system. This happens quite frequently despite organisations having spent many years in data processing. A common example is the entity 'competitor', which rarely features in computer systems.

It is also important at this point to describe each of the current systems in terms of the four quadrants of the application portfolio, to get an indication of its overall contribution to business strategy.

The likelihood is that factory and support quadrants will be well populated, and that a few systems will indicate an emerging interest in strategic use of IT. Very often there are a number of high potential systems created by end-users experimenting independently with innovative ideas.

SUMMARY

There are two main stages involved in establishing the current situation and logical requirements, i.e. fact finding and analysis. The processes occur iteratively and rely heavily on each other. The purpose is to identify the activities and business processes which support the objectives and strategy of the business, and the associated information requirements.

The 'fact-finding' results in a mass of information which needs to be recorded in a way which facilitates analysis. The data can be effectively recorded in a textual form, in an organisational model, developed for the entire enterprise, and also for the information systems function itself. Data can also be recorded in the graphical form of information models, entity–relationship models, activity decomposition diagrams and data flow diagrams. The drawing of these diagrams is a key element in the analysis stage.

During the analysis stage a set of application areas is produced which represents all of the systems required by management to achieve their objectives. This set of systems requirements is then mapped against the existing portfolio and the resulting list of new systems represents the required applications for future development.

Formulation of the IS strategy is considered in Chapter 7, after examining the future potential for IS/IT. As with the two earlier steps of understanding and analysing the business requirements, it is another part of the overall iterative process of determining business IS strategy.

The key points to draw from this chapter are:

1. There is a process for fact finding which must be followed if the data are going to be useful.
2. The techniques for fact finding must provide sufficient data for developing strategy, but no more.
3. The analysis task is not trivial—the time spent in analysis is at least as much as that spent in fact finding.
4. The processes of fact finding and analysis are essentially logical, not creative. Going through the processes will, however, generate a multitude of original and creative ideas. These need to be captured and developed. This will be further discussed in the next chapter.

REFERENCES

Kotter, J. P. (1978) *Organisational Dynamics Diagnosis and Intervention*, Addison-Wesley.

Rockart, J. F. (1979) 'Chief executives define their own information needs', *Harvard Business Review*, March/April.

Rock-Evans, R. (1987) *Analysis within the Systems Development Life Cycle*, Pergamon Infotech.

Chapter 6

IS/IT STRATEGIC ANALYSIS—
DETERMINING THE FUTURE POTENTIAL

INTRODUCTION

In considering the future IS/IT strategy for a business, the techniques of assessment so far discussed enable the current role IS/IT is, and should be, playing in the business to be analysed critically and constructively. It is always important to understand where you are—a situation appraisal of the systems that exist and how they support and enhance operational performance and management control and development of the business. A key aspect of this is how well the systems enable separate activities and functions of the business to perform harmoniously. This implies an understanding of the information and data relationships of the business as well as the processing requirements. Techniques for analysing the effectiveness of IS/IT applications and their actual business contribution (or lack of it) have been developed mainly from an IS/IT viewpoint—to enable IS/IT management to deploy its resources more effectively in developing appropriate systems and supporting services. They bring together the activities, organisation and information needs of the business *as they are known to be*. Often the analysis reveals areas of systems deficiency, obsolescence, ineffective linkages and poor utilisation of data. Dealing with the critical inadequacies—ensuring IS/IT is not hindering current business success is a key part of the strategy—ensuring IS/IT is not a potential or real source of competitive disadvantage!

Directing resources and actions towards areas which will affect the achievement of future, known business objectives is then the next step in developing the strategy. The use of 'critical success factors' is a valuable way of achieving this appropriate concentration of management attention and resources. The technique is designed to put IS/IT on to the 'management agenda', to ensure they pay it due regard where it will offer potential business opportunities and/or pose potential threats within the horizon of management's prevailing business attention. This probably implies within the objective setting horizon of 1–2 years.

Therefore, these are analytical techniques which enable firm foundations of systems to be established which deal with current business requirements and provide appropriate management information. This should enable IS/IT to be a 'net asset' of the business until requirements change.

Those requirements will change for two main reasons—external factors changing what the business is required to do and internal factors changing what the business wants or is able to do. This assessment of potential IS/IT application areas requires a degree of creative thinking as well as analysis of business options—to determine what *could be* the impact of IS/IT on the business. The tools and techniques that have been described so far are not sufficient to carry out such an 'impact analysis', neither do they easily express the options and issues in terms familiar to line managers. The tools and techniques of business strategic thinking and analysis offer another approach which will be more easily adopted by the business managers, the people whose commitment is critical to converting good ideas to actual strategic uses of IS/IT, i.e. those that will enable business strategies to be achieved.

Many of the tools and techniques of business strategic analysis were described in Chapter 2. A number of these are explored in more detail below. They are undoubtedly not all those that could be used, but they are techniques and tools which have often been successfully adopted in assessing the potential future impact of IS/IT on various businesses. Together the tools offer a more 'focused brainstorming' or 'creative analysis' approach.

The objective is to discover strategic information systems opportunities which could be exploited.

TOOLS AND TECHNIQUES IN OVERVIEW

The approaches described below can be considered in three main groupings of interrelated techniques:

  (i) Business portfolio analysis,
 (ii) Competitive strategy analysis,
(iii) Value chain analysis.

In addition, 'critical success factors' (CSFs) can be used in a creative mode, often in conjunction with an IS/IT SWOT (Strengths, Weaknesses, Opportunities, Threats) analysis to elicit new ideas. CSFs will be considered again in this role, in relation to the other approaches, later.

One problem with a 'tool-bag' approach is deciding which tool to use when. It is always convenient to have a methodology, which clearly indicates which tool to apply when, what result to expect and what to do next if you get (a) the right result or (b) the wrong result! Unfortunately, such a clear definition of an IS/IT strategic planning process is not, and probably never will be, possible. EDP Analyser (1986) in an edition entitled *Uncovering Strategic Systems* discussed many of the techniques described below and concluded similarly that a 'tool-bag' is necessary.

Although no methodology can be proposed, in the next chapter each of the tools will be considered as part of a framework of approaches which can be adopted for this aspect of IS/IT strategic planning, within the overall model of the processes required described in Chapter 3. Also the types of strategic applications that each technique is most likely to elicit will be considered at the end of this chapter, in terms of the four categories of strategic applications described in Chapter 1.

The focus of this part of the strategic analysis is primarily to identify 'strategic applications' in terms of the application portfolio matrix first described in Chapter 1 (see Figure 6.1). However, the approaches may also suggest 'high potential' possibilities which need further investigation before their value can be decided. They may also identify whether existing or planned key operational ('factory') systems either provide a good basis for exploitation or could be a constraint to future business IS/IT options.

BUSINESS PORTFOLIO ANALYSIS TECHNIQUES

Development of business strategies can be carried out in a variety of ways but as discussed in Chapter 2, this is probably most effective if the organisation is considered as a group of (strategic) business units. This enables the market/product relationship to determine strategic thinking and functional/organisational aspects become secondary—ensuring external strategy drives internal strategy rather than vice versa. Within a business unit the portfolio of products/customers can be analysed to identify how each grouping contributes to or makes demands on resources available. The business unit is also the level at which the generic strategic concepts of Michael Porter best apply—low cost, differentiation, niche—since it is both possible and essential to develop and operate a coherent set of business

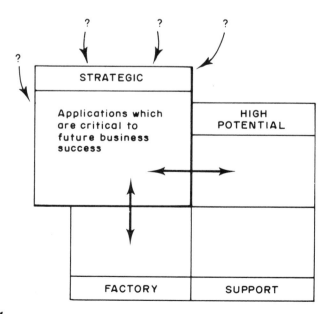

FIGURE 6.1

behaviours for a business unit. Low cost versus differentiation conflicts within a business unit will cause confusion and sub-optimal or even contrary decisions to be reached. But within a corporation, two business units operating in two different environments might adopt low cost and differentiation strategies within the corporate umbrella.

For these reasons alone it is important that IS/IT strategic analysis should align itself to the business unit approach. Two quite different business attitudes to investment, including investment in IS/IT, are likely to prevail in units following differentiation or low cost strategies and the resulting IS/IT strategies are unlikely to be the same. Applications for similar functions, such as order processing, could well be very different in practice due to the different relationships the two generic strategies imply will be sought with customers.

As discussed earlier, the most significant difference in the SIS era is the external focus of systems. Organisations have adopted the strategic business unit approach to business planning in part to achieve the more effective strategic decision making implied to phase 3 of approaches to strategic management discussed in Chapter 2 (see Figure 2.10); i.e. more effective (externally oriented) planning based on

- situation analysis and competitive assessments,
- evaluation of strategic options,
- dynamic allocation of resources.

IS/IT planning needs to change similarly.

Business unit based IS/IT strategic planning should therefore enable it to be related more effectively to business strategies and requirements, as explained in Chapter 3 and reflected in Figure 6.2.

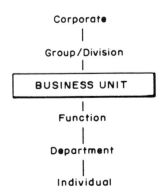

FIGURE 6.2 Relating IS/IT strategy to the business (PIMS (MPIT) data base 1984)

DEFINING SBUs FOR IS/IT STRATEGIC PLANNING

A strategic business unit is defined in Chapter 2 as

> sells a distinct set of products or services, services a specific set of customers and competes with a well-defined set of competitors.

It might be reasonable to add 'is an identifiable source of revenue and profit'.

Defining such units in many organisations is difficult but rarely impossible. For instance, in a building society, lending to customers for mortgages is a different logical business from taking in customers' savings, even though they may be dealt with in the same branches and deal with the same customers. The profitability of 'mortgages' is far higher than 'savings' and the competitive environment is different.

In large manufacturing companies in related markets, the manufacturing plants may make the same basic products which are 'packaged' for different types of market. The company may therefore have several marketing business units *and* a manufacturing business unit. The marketing and manufacturing units may have a customer/supplier relationship especially if the company does not directly make all it sells.

The organisational structure may not reflect the business unit structure for geographical, historical or power-base reasons. For instance, two business units may report to the same general manager even though the businesses are essentially different. This could lead to the false conclusion that the systems could be the same based on 'control' needs rather than operational needs. One manufacturer of heavy specialist vehicles (e.g. dust-carts, fire-engines, etc.) *and* coaches attempted to transfer the systems from one company to another. It failed; the requirements are essentially different in terms of customisation and the areas in which value is added. A distributor of cakes and pastries to corner shops did not understand the different information systems required when the business expanded to sell to a major supermarket chain. The original business is a high value added marketing and wholesaling operation whereas the distribution to supermarkets is a low value added delivery business. In the original business the only real competition is other wholesalers whereas the supermarket's own distribution network is potential competition. The company tried to service the major customer in similar ways to the large number of minor customers. It went out of business.

Whilst determining the business units is not always easy it is important that in order to identify strategic IS opportunities (and threats) logical business units are identified within the business. Both external and internal relationships of those units then need to be considered to maximise both the external benefits of specific IS/IT and internal benefits obtained from synergistic investments. When market/product business units have been identified there will inevitably be service functions 'left over', which cannot easily be allocated. These secondary or support functions are normally cost not profit centres (e.g. legal, personnel, accounting, information systems). These can be considered 'internal business units' providing services to clients within the business. They are less likely to provide IS/IT opportunities, but sophisticated manpower planning systems, for instance, may provide an organisation with competitive advantages. They should not be ignored in considering the opportunities.

Having identified the various business units, each needs to be considered in terms of how IS/IT investments can be focused to improve its competitive performance. Throughout the rest of this chapter the tools and techniques will be initially considered within this SBU approach to segmenting the business. However, the potential synergistic benefits from exploiting common information resources and even common or integrated systems across units will be considered. The degree of commonality will in due course affect the services and technologies requiring to be supplied to the business, but any commonality of supply should be aimed at achieving business synergy rather than minimising IS management problems and costs.

USING BUSINESS UNIT AND PRODUCT PORTFOLIO ANALYSES TO IDENTIFY IS/IT STRATEGIC OPTIONS

The various product and business portfolio analysis approaches described in Chapter 2 are based on the concept of product and industry life cycles. Figure 6.3 shows typical aspects of these profiles, especially those key business activities which could be enhanced by more effective IS/IT deployment in the various stages of the industry cycle. Strategies for a business unit will be different in emerging, growth, mature and declining industries and, therefore, IS/IT investment would be targeted differently as would other investments. For a particular product, investments in its promotion, distribution channels, production capacity would be for different purposes at different stages of the life cycle, and will vary in accordance with its market position. Using any of the matrix analyses considered in Chapter 2, by placing a business unit or product into its relevant segment, an indication of the types of opportunities IS/IT should be targeted at can be identified. Figure 6.4 shows such a matrix which combines the state of the industry and the relative strength of the business position.

This matrix is derived from one developed by Synnott (1987). The terminology is a composite of Boston Consulting Group and Michael Porter market based strategic analysis.

1. For a *'wild cat' product* (low market-share in a high growth market) the route to eventual success is likely to be through innovation in the general marketplace or selecting a clearly focused niche in the market—a size of market segment that can be effectively addressed. Thus the IS/IT strategy is likely to focus on product and/or process development or alternatively be used to identify potential customers, segment customer types and then ensure that effective information exchanges occur about the product/service with the chosen segment of customers, to enable exact specification of service and product requirements.

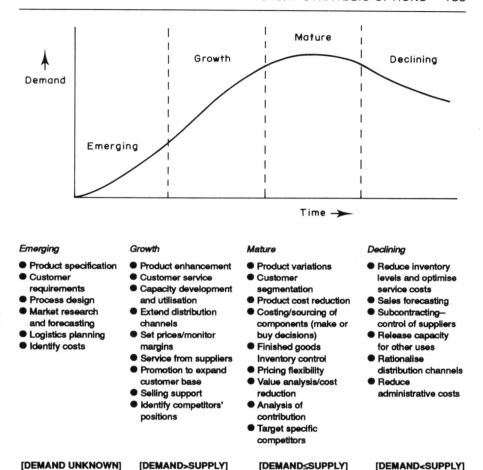

FIGURE 6.3 *Industry and product life cycles — information and systems focus. (Source: derived from an analysis in J. M. Higgins,* Strategy, *pp. 130–135 (Dryden Press, 1985))*

2. *Star* products and businesses (strong market position in an attractive or high growth market) imply a leading role for the company. Keeping ahead of or at least in pace with developing customer requirements and competing product offerings is vital to success as well as is matching sales growth with market growth. Systems and information focus will be towards the customer — identifying customers and their requirements to achieve a better understanding of demand than actual or potential competitors, based on leading position. The systems might also be aimed at allowing growth in business, handling greater order volumes or variety of product mixtures, or types of customer

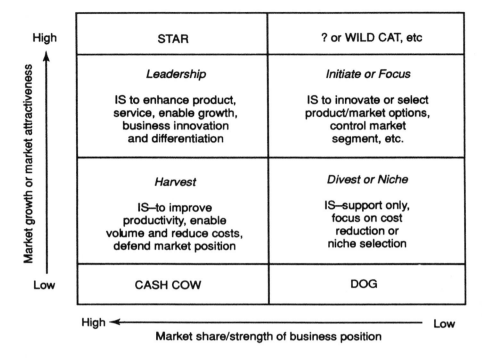

FIGURE 6.4 *Relationship of IS/IT investment focus to business and/or product portfolio*

service. The main emphasis will be on business innovation—to satisfy market requirements and differentiate the firm in that market place. Systems investment focus should therefore be to add value and cope with growth.

3. *Cash cow.* Products and businesses (strong market position in mature, lower growth markets) are to be 'harvested'—in Porter terminology, although 'milked' might be more apposite! Defending the current position, ensuring costs are lower, or at least as low as competitors and that demand is satisfied in the optimum way. Matching the details of supply and demand volumes is important to keep customers satisfied, but also 'batching' requirements to obtain the best economics or capacity utilisation must be achieved. Business productivity and control of customers and suppliers to defend a market position is the main aim—not to allow competitors to gain advantage—and systems will tend to focus on control of the business environment rather than innovation.

4. *Dog* products and businesses (weak position in a low growth or declining market) are unlikely to attract much of the corporate investment funding, unless it can clearly be seen to increase market share and/or improve deliverable profits. Divestment may be the eventual aim and so it is often undesirable to consider

integration of IS strategy with the rest of the business. Alternatively a niche market may be carved out by segmenting the products/markets. In general, IS/IT investment should follow the business direction—selective, strongly financially justified investments to improve profit performance by reducing costs or securing customers. Very little innovative IS/IT use can be expected.

The process of analysis will involve an assessment of both

1. the business unit in its industry, and then
2. the products in the portfolio.

Each stage in analysis can reveal opportunities or threats from IS/IT investments. For example, consider a leading door manufacturer in the UK. The market is low to steady growth overall and the business unit could be defined as a 'cash cow'. The emphasis of IS/IT had been to improve productivity in manufacturing and logistics. However by examining its product portfolio there are clearly two different products:

(a) standard doors—steady growth, high market share (cash cow),
(b) specialist doors—high growth, medium market share (star/?).

The standard doors are sold by catalogue directly to merchants and builders, where quality, delivery, and cost are all key parameters. Existing systems met these needs well. Specialist doors are designed to meet specific requirements—size, shape, durability, style, security, safety, etc.—defined often by architects and specialist contractors to be installed by builders, etc. The systems to support such products effectively must link to different customers, enable quotations and designs to be produced quickly, and track specific orders from enquiry via ordering specific raw materials, through manufacturing, testing and delivery and potentially after sales servicing. The existing systems were not primarily designed for such products. The profit margin per door is significantly higher on specialist doors. In order to keep pace with (or capture a greater share of) a high growth market, new systems tailored to meet the specialist doors requirements were needed to support the high value added nature of the product. In practice existing systems were being overlaid with additional informal, mainly manual systems to cope with the complexity for which existing systems were not designed. Whilst the company planned to increase its market position across the product range, specialist doors were clearly recognised as the main opportunity area for highly profitable growth.

These suggestions may seem rather too generalised, if only because the matrices themselves make no claim to be precise investment guidelines, but there should and will be different opportunities and threats, and therefore different targets and thrusts for IS/IT investments, within a product or business portfolio. During the industry evolution cycle, a firm will change its business focus from customers to

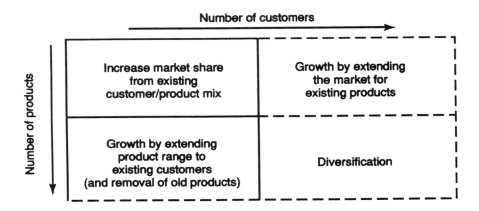

FIGURE 6.5 (after Ansoff, 1968)

products to customers etc. as the cycle evolves in order to achieve market growth and improved market share (see Figure 6.5). Growth is more manageable if at any particular time either the product or customer base is relatively stable. Either existing products are marketed to wider customer base or new products are developed for a known set of customer needs. Information systems focus can be expected to follow this pattern, being used to establish links with potential new customers and broaden the logistics of delivering to those customers or support the specification and processing of new, better or lower cost products to achieve growth through existing market links. At no stage will the other parameter be ignored but the emphasis is likely to be on product or customer 'development'.

Obviously once a product or customer base has been extended the scope of the firm's coverage has moved. Once better or more or cheaper products have been developed for a known market it probably means a broader market has become available. Equally, given a broader market for a restricted product range has been established, a wider variety of needs are known and can be economically satisfied, and justify further product investments.

In Box 6.1 a few example business and product portfolios from real organisations are briefly examined to show the conclusions for IS/IT strategy that could be drawn. These are inevitably first cut high level views for the potential forms of IS/IT investments. These are an input to the thinking in the next stage of the process, but an important input. That next stage is to consider the particulars of the competitive forces that are determining the future of the industry and the component firms, and how IS/IT can affect those forces and as with all good strategies, exploit those forces to the advantage of the company.

BOX 6.1 *Examples of business/product portfolio analyses*

1. *Gillette* (circa 1983) (*Source:* Harvard Business School case study 'Gillette Long Range MIS Planning' (No. 9-184-003))

Toiletries	
Electrical appliances	
Razors	Pens

Market attractiveness (vertical axis label)

Market strength (horizontal axis label)

Discussion: Within the strategy for IS/IT the need to invest in systems which ensured the products were available on the retailers' shelves to coincide with marketing initiatives was a critical area for toiletries and electrical appliances. Equally large IS investment in pens was not advisable until its business future was decided. Razors required systems which improved productivity and lowered costs as enhanced products were developed.

2. *Hammermill Paper Company* (circa 1982) (*Source:* Harvard Business School case study 'Hammermill Paper Company' (No. 9-183-199))

Industrial papers	
Distribution	
Fine and printing papers	Converted papers Forest products

Market attractiveness (vertical axis label)

Market share (horizontal axis label)

Discussion: The company had diversified within the paper industry from a base of fine papers. This core business was now threatened by price based competition and the systems investment was focused on internal productivity from manufacturing and improving service levels to merchants. Industrial papers were well positioned with an extensive range of innovative products

continued on next page

continued

in a high growth market but based on a small customer base. Its IS strategy focused on acquiring raw materials, logistics and production/plant management systems to meet growth of volume. Additionally, its critical dependence on a few key customers required a new order servicing system to give customers information on the status of all their orders and be able to expedite large urgent orders.

Distribution companies had been acquired to the extent that distribution provided 40% of the revenue but poor profit margins. The company aim was to 'win on service' but poor systems and different systems across the group meant business was won locally on price. Integration of systems was required across the outlets to enable a common value added strategy, to avoid internal competition and enable the cost base to be controlled. However, in 1982 the company had not realised the value of synergy across the various business units—vertical as well as horizontal integration—and was not exploiting the base of market data held in the distribution part of the business.

3. *Union Carbide* (circa 1982). (*Source:* Harvard Business School case study 'Union Carbide Corporation—Information Technology & Strategy' (No 9-183-197))
(a) **Business portfolio** (partial)

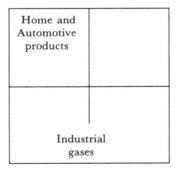

Discussion: The strategy for industrial gases was essentially to reduce operating costs and be able to gain a greater share of the growing markets for industrial gases. Its IS/IT thrust was for productivity in plants, optimisation of distribution logistics and improved forecasting of demand. Its traditional plants were no longer located close to the newer customers and its low cost base could easily be eroded if these key operational systems were not effectively integrated. Energy costs in particular had to be controlled. Home and Automotive division was a market leader in a fast growing, but unpredictable market place. Sales growth had not delivered a similar profit growth. Its primary strategy was to maintain market share leadership with high quality differentiated products. IS strategy needed to be geared more to the particular products and markets due to their disparate nature, but across the products was a need to improve materials management, systems and interfaces with suppliers (see below).

continued on next page

continued

(b) **Product portfolio** (home and automotive)

	Speciality automotive products
Plastic wrap products Antifreeze products	

Discussion: The antifreeze market was very competitive and traditional brand loyalties were being eroded. It split into three areas: manufacturers, garages and consumers—the last two being very seasonal and each required different marketing and distribution systems. Raw materials were a critical factor in cost and availability and systems focused clearly on procuring supplies (from potential competitors). Plastic wraps (bags, etc.) required continuous development to meet the demands of a small number of powerful customers as well as effective control of raw materials and process costs. Systems linking to customers to provide differential service were important. Speciality products were consumer products and required extensive marketing systems support to track consumer demand and ensure product promotion was linked to product availability in 'retail' outlets.

4. *Banc One* (circa 1982). (*Source:* Harvard Business School case study 'Banc One Corporation and the Home Information Revolution' (No. 9-682-091))

Card processing services, inc. M. Lynch Visa, etc.	Home information services, inc. Home Banking
Traditional banking services, inc. ATMS	

Discussion: By the early 1980s Banc One was the number one bank in Ohio and had used IT to automate traditional banking services. To grow further it had to develop businesses outside the restrictions of banking legislation. Its card processing services, based on leadership in providing computer services

continued on next page

continued

to Bank America and others was very successful and their expertise and low unit costs gained them the processing franchise for Merrill Lynch's Cash Management Accounts. The strategy was to remain ahead by investing in computing resources and retain leadership through innovation in the services provided. Home Banking and Home Information Services provided another vehicle to nationwide markets. The development of the service was led by marketing who carried out a successful local pilot proving technical capability but not the criteria for market acceptance. Whilst trying to find 'like minded partners' to extend the venture, they lost control to larger organisations—who subsequently lost many millions of dollars due to public apathy!

COMPETITIVE STRATEGY ANALYSIS TECHNIQUES

The concepts of competitive strategy analysis derived principally from the works of Michael Porter (1980, 1984) were outlined in Chapter 2. The process of assessing competitive strategic options is considered at three levels:

- Industry analysis
- Competitive forces
- Generic business strategy

These basic concepts of analysing competitive opportunities, threats and strategies have been used by a number of people as a basis for considering IS/IT and its potential to impact a business and its strategy. Parsons (1983) and McFarlan (1984) in particular used Porter's models to examine how IS/IT had and could impact certain industries and affect any particular firm in that industry, depending on its business position in the industry and its adopted business strategy. The importance of the various issues will depend on the state of the industry in terms of growth. This implies that the opportunities and threats that IS/IT can offer and pose will vary over time in an industry. But as with product innovation, IS/IT innovation can stimulate new industry growth or in some cases hasten the decline of certain industries. IS/IT has for instance rejuvenated the mail order industry in the UK. The customer information base offers new possibilities, extending potentially as other technologies develop, to true 'Home Shopping'. How will this affect the various sectors of conventional retailing? IS/IT impact is often obvious but in many cases the effects are secondary and will require other changes in business economics, social behaviour or parallel developments in other fields before they become fully effective.

Industry Analysis

At the highest level the ideas of analysis to identify IS/IT opportunities will be similar to those developed earlier in this chapter. However, more specific assessments can be made. Parsons and McFarlan both address this area by a 'questioning' approach: 'Can IS/IT . . .?', suggesting management should ask questions regarding how IS/IT could affect:

(a) the products and services,
(b) markets,
(c) economics of production,

i.e. fundamental bases of the industry, its size, economics, etc. Obviously if IS/IT can have a major effect on any of these, the implications for *all* the competing firms are significant, and management must consider in more depth how those effects will or could manifest themselves. Parsons suggests some of the ways IS/IT can affect these areas, a number of which can be seen in the examples quoted earlier in the book.

(a) *Products and services*—how can/could IS/IT affect the nature and value of the product or service and its life cycle?

- Financial and business information services, such as Dun & Bradstreet have developed new services for commercial organisations to interrogate directly. Banks, such as Hong Kong Bank, have entered the same markets, offering services to financial managers in companies.
- Merrill Lynch developed the Cash Management Account for both business and consumer customers—new services enabled by IS/IT. Allied Dunbar offer customers a free financial planning service as a front-end to selling pensions, insurance and other financial services.
- Life insurance companies can develop new insurance policy types from concept to mass marketing via database marketing systems to defined market sectors in two to three months. This can render older products uncompetitive very quickly. Using CAD in manufacturing, or, like Benetton, even in clothing design, can deliver the same effect.
- Otis lifts put microprocessors in their lifts to record details of problems and diagnose faults to improve the servicing. The computers also recorded the lifts' patterns of movement so that they could be programmed to match movement patterns more closely and reduce waiting times, etc. The same data could be used to help plan department/building layouts to minimise 'commuting' time throughout the building. A basic, traditional, utility product had been upgraded and differentiated by Otis, enabling them to increase their market share from 18–25% over three years after many years of steady decline.

In general terms the questions to be asked are: can IS/IT generate a new product or a new line of business; or enable products to be designed/delivered more quickly; or be used to add additional features or services to increase the products' value—as perceived by the consumer/customer to change the basis for purchasing?

(b) *Markets.* How can/could IS/IT affect the demand for products and services, segment markets more effectively or extend them geographically, or provide new distribution channels to reach the market?

● An example which could have been quoted under (a) above is Home Banking, pioneered in the UK by Nottingham Building Society and the Bank of Scotland. Undoubtedly it is a new service, extending national banking services into the home. But the main objective of the organisations concerned was to extend their markets electronically beyond the extent of their branch networks. It has not been the success that was hoped because the infrastructure of 'communicating home computers' did not materialise as they anticipated. However both organisations have exploited their innovative market posture to achieve a higher market profile and attract new business. Derivatives of the services offered—Office Banking etc.—have been more successful in certain market niches (a likely successful strategy—see Figure 6.4). Other building societies, notably Nationwide Anglia, have implemented subsets of the concept, enabling customers to make direct enquiries on their 'computer' account via a telephone.

● Timber importing businesses have been affected by agents who 'trade' containers of timber while they are being shipped. Previously an importer bought a cargo of timber from the supplier and sold it to customers while it was being shipped, then offloaded the timber and broke it into customer orders for shipment onwards. Now much of the timber is loaded on to the ships in containerised loads and then sold via agents on an international network to specific customers to collect on arrival, to some extent by-passing traditional importers. Trading in oil has been similarly affected, to the extent that British Petroleum developed a system to help the trading process rather than swim against the tide.

● Most auction-based markets have been revolutionised over the last twenty years by IS/IT. The effects on the share dealing, securities and currency markets are well known—parochial markets are now global and the firms dealing in those markets are no longer dependent upon the services of specialist or 'licensed' traders. Much of the trading is actually done by the computer systems, implying the systems are *causing* market behaviour!

These changes are to be expected where the product is itself 'information', using technology to actually buy and sell the product. However, changes have been equally significant in other auction-based trading—cotton, grain, and even flowers can be bought and sold remotely via electronic auctions. Flower wholesalers in New York can buy flowers at Dutch flower auctions and arrange shipment and payment automatically. This has certainly extended the potential market for the products.

● A final example of the rise of IS/IT to affect a market place is the development of Financial Services by major retailers, notably Sears in the

USA and Marks & Spencer in the UK. Marks & Spencer did not historically accept payments other than cash or cheques. The Marks & Spencer charge card—an exclusive credit card—has enabled them to exploit a number of avenues: first, to sell higher priced goods such as furniture and furnishing, which require extended credit financing; secondly to exploit new point-of-sale systems to identify not only what is bought in what patterns in which shops, but also who is buying what; thirdly a catalogue-based mail order service has been developed which targets customers with particular short catalogues based on the information held about the customer and what they have bought; lastly, in conjunction with a banking licence to accept deposits, Marks & Spencer can offer a range of financial service products, even emergency cash, to its customers. Many mail order companies are using IS/IT to analyse their customers and develop segment-focused catalogues.

Again the typical questions to be asked are—can IS/IT enable us to reach more or more appropriate customers: or enable us to match our different products/services to customers more appropriately: or enable the product or service to be distributed in new ways to the customers: or can we use IS/IT to get closer to the market place rather than deal through intermediaries?

(c) *Economics of production*—How can IS/IT affect the cost base of the key processes in the industry or change the balance in the trade-off between flexibility and standardisation?

- An obvious example is the publishing industry where the use of IS/IT from the basic preparation of material by authors to the final printing process has dramatically changed the basic economics of producing newspapers, journals, magazines and books. The revolution in newspaper production is well documented. Journalists can produce stories remotely and transmit them electronically, the edition of the paper can be set on even 'desk-top' publishing systems and transmitted for printing to as many locations as necessary. Not only has the production cost base been dramatically altered, so have the economies of distributing the newspapers. The revolution in book production may not be so obvious but given the reduced set-up time per book the economic batch runs become much smaller, enabling

  (a) lower-selling books to become profitable,
  (b) more books to be available on the market due to lower launch costs, and
  (c) ability to respond to demand changes more accurately.

- Automated warehouses, linking physical goods access to logistics and inventory systems, enable some wholesaling companies to stock much wider ranges of goods and respond to customers' orders more quickly and anticipate changing demand earlier. Delivery routes and order profitability can be optimised.

● Robotics for flexible manufacture combined with effective manufacturing logistics systems such as 'Just-in-Time' management enables unit costs of special and standard products to become more similar, enabling a lower cost for higher value added products. Where companies produce 'designed' products to order, CAD systems enable derivative designs from previous similar designs to be produced very quickly and at much lower cost than traditional design/drafting methods.

Once more these are only examples but they should prompt the following types of questions to be asked—can and could IS/IT enable the product/service to be produced more economically; or can IS/IT enable production and associated logistics to be integrated to produce greater flexibility of resource use; or can improved logistics and control change the basic working capital structure of the industry: or can IS/IT enable a higher quality of product or service to be offered at a much lower cost than traditionally?

This first level of 'interrogation' of IS/IT potential in the industry focuses on products, markets and economics and considers options available to all the firms in the industry and, importantly, to potential new entrants who can exploit their existing information or systems to develop and sell new products or identify and deal with an extended customer base, or both. Gaining an advantage at this level will be difficult for others to counter except by 'following' or by risking more dramatic and effective innovation. Consequently many of the anecdotes of sustained success derive from companies who have fundamentally changed one of these aspects. These changes are irreversible in that if the factors for success in the industry and the relevant capabilities required by companies wishing to succeed in the industry are fundamentally altered, the competitive game will have a new set of rules!

Analysis of Competitive Forces to Identify IS/IT Opportunity and Threats

The five competitive forces affecting an industry, as described by Michael Porter and described in Chapter 2, are depicted in Figure 6.6. McFarlan suggests that each of these forces should be examined by questioning whether IS/IT can affect the key parameters which govern the degree of impact that force has on determining the future of the industry. These factors were outlined in Table 2.1.

These questions flavoured by IS considerations are summarised in Figure 6.6. MacFarlan (1984), Porter and Millar (1985), and Cash and Konsynski (1985), all quote examples to support how companies have actually achieved changes in the relative impact of these forces by the use of IS/IT. The examples are often

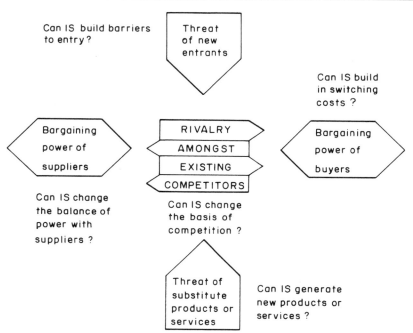

FIGURE 6.6 Competitive forces in an industry (adapted with permission of The Free Press, a Division of Macmillan, Inc. from COMPETITIVE ADVANTAGE: Creating and Sustaining Superior Performance by Michael E. Porter. Copyright © 1985 by Michael E. Porter)

similar to or even the same as those quoted under 'Industry' impact but used to demonstrate a particular aspect of the 'forces' argument. This is not unreasonable given that the reality came first, the rationalisation to 'theory' came later! It may be more useful to use one industry to demonstrate how this approach can be useful (albeit with hindsight). In the airline industry *all* the competitive forces have and are still being affected by the use of IS/IT, as described in Table 6.1.

A similar analysis could be carried out for the travel industry and the more recent impact of holiday booking systems such as Thomson's 'TOP'. One interesting aspect to consider is that 'TOP' has increased Thomson's leverage over its suppliers, including the airlines whose reservation systems can actually be exploited by large buyers of seats such as holiday companies. Like a holiday, an airline seat is a perishable commodity and in terms of complexity is much simpler than a holiday. Why IS/IT has had a considerable impact on all forces in the industry is determined essentially by the nature of the product, how it is purchased and the information needed to be exchanged in order to complete a transaction.

TABLE 6.1 The airline industry—how IS/IT has affected the competitive forces

1. How can IS/IT build barriers to entry?	• by increasing IT entry cost for reservation systems (£50m +) • by tying in distribution channels (travel agencies)
2. How can IS/IT build in switching costs for customers?	• by linking purchasing and remittance systems to reduce overheads of customer • discount/volume packages to discourage piecemeal purchase
3. How can IS/IT change the basis of competition?	• lower costs: optimise yield per aircraft • differentiate service: reconfiguring aircraft due to demand • niche/focus service into high yield sectors, e.g. business travel
4. How can IS/IT change the balance of power in supplier/customer relationship?	• agent is constantly aware of seat availability of competing airlines • airline can readily promote unsold capacity via chosen agents
5. How can IS/IT generate new products/services?	• integrated travel package to high mileage business customers—bypassing agencies • new routes/schedules to cater for demand • reservation/wholesaling—'bucket shops'

The product is a 'difficult to differentiate' commodity in spite of attempts to promote different airline images of comfort, service, glamour, etc. Therefore service to the customer in obtaining the commodity becomes a basis for competition, making it easy to buy (reducing buying cost) and risk free (certainty of availability). It is purchased by individuals and companies based on a clearly defined need to travel from a to b and although the route, price and other parameters might vary, the customer is certain of his basic need, simplifying the information a 'system' has to contain! The information exchange is also predictable—date, time, route, class, price—and it has been demonstrated that the customer will, 80% of the time, select the first flight that meets the basic criteria. The whole airline industry can be defined as 'information intensive' and therefore IS/IT use has always been a potentially powerful weapon. Other industries, such as Financial Services and Publishing, are even more information intensive in that the product itself is information. In most industries the bases of competition are not as dependent on information as Airlines, Travel, Financial Services and Publishing. But in many other industries one or more of the forces has been significantly impacted by an organisation using IS/IT quite deliberately to achieve a competitive advantage. For any firm in any industry the questioning process should proceed in two stages.

First—what forces are determining the future of the industry and our potential success? Who dominates the industry and by what strategy? For example,

- Who might enter the industry, why and what would the effect be?
- What substitute products might affect the market for existing products?
- On what basis are we currently competing and how might that change?
- What leverage do suppliers exert and how could the control of key resources affect success?
- How much power and discretion do buyers (customers) have and how will this change market/product possibilities?

These are all business questions, the result of which may be that only one or two of the forces are critical. Once that has been established then the IS/IT questions should first focus on these areas of concern—opportunities or threats and prompt consideration of available options. A final stage should then be to reverse the thinking process by looking at the other, less critical forces, to identify whether IS/IT could change their importance in the future.

Cash (1988) takes this view with particular reference to inter-organisational systems (IOS)—how can IOS affect particular forces if they are the main determinants of success in an industry. A modified version of his analysis is presented in Table 6.2.

Generic Business Strategies

How can IS/IT be used to enable/enhance or support specific business strategies?

As considered in Chapter 2, companies that succeed in an industry in the long term need to out-perform the competitors by either achieving *lower costs* or by *differentiating* themselves in the view of the customer, enabling them to obtain a price premium. Some companies, for a period of time at least, can achieve both. For instance Kodak in the 1960s and early 1970s achieved this in the colour film market and IBM in the 1970s with mainframe computers. Sainsbury's, as the leader in UK grocery retailing, in the mid to late 1980s has probably also achieved both. Most companies, however, have to strive for one advantage or the other at least in the short to medium term. The other critical decision is to define the extent of the market within which the company wishes to gain that advantage. The scope can be defined as 'industry wide', implying that the company must have a range of products to meet the requirements of the majority of potential customers.

Ford and General Motors in the car industry are good examples, as are the big four UK banks in the Financial Services industry. Other companies choose a segment of the market place, focus on a particular niche to obtain an advantage

TABLE 6.2 Impact of competitive forces and potential IS/IT opportunities

Key force impacting the industry	Business implications	Potential IS/IT effects
Threat of new entrants	Additional capacity Reduced prices New basis for competition	Provide entry barriers/reduce access by: ● exploiting existing economies of scale ● differentiate products/services ● control distribution channels ● segment markets
Buyer power high	Forces prices down Demand higher quality Require service flexibility Encourage competition	Differentiate products/services and improve price/performance Increase switching costs of buyers Facilitate buyer product selection
Supplier power high	Raises prices/costs Reduced quality of supply Reduced availability	Supplier sourcing systems Extended quality control into suppliers Forward planning with supplier
Substitute products threatened	Limits potential market and profit Price ceilings	Improve price/performance Redefine products and services to increase value Redefine market segments
Intense competition from rivals	Price competition Product development Distribution and service critical Customer loyalty required	Improve price/performance Differentiate products and services in distribution channel and to consumer Get closer to the end-consumer—understand the requirements

Adapted from J. I. Cash, 'Interorganisational systems: an information society opportunity or threat?' *The Information Society*, **3**(3) (1988).

by matching their products and services to the needs of a subset of the potential customers. BMW, Volvo, Jaguar and Mercedes are all examples of companies focusing in the motor industry. The Giro bank, whilst offering similar services to the major banks, has tended to focus its services on the lower income end of the consumer market.

Many examples of companies who have enhanced these strategies directly by the use of IS/IT have been quoted. Some well known examples are overlaid on the basic matrix in Figure 6.7.

Type of advantage sought

	Low cost	Differentiation
	General Tire Use telemarketing for soliciting routine orders from existing customers and handle customer queries (i)	**American Express** Providing an information service to corporate customers which analyses the travel costs incurred by employees in categories required by the customer (iii)
	Caesar's Palace Analysing data on gambling customers, rating the players to reduce the cost of complementary services by offering them only to 'high rollers' (iii)	**BMW** Dealer/customer car option selection systems linking to operations system to allocate a car and identify delivery date (ii)

FIGURE 6.7 Examples of IS/IT enhanced strategies. (Sources: (i) J. Wyman, 'Technological myopia — the need to think strategically about technology', Sloan Management Review (1985); (ii) J. Large, 'Information's market-force', Management Today (August 1986); (iii) M. E. Porter, and V. E. Millar, 'How information gives you competitive advantage', Harvard Business Review (July–August 1985))

The opportunities available to support each of the fundamental generic strategies—low cost and differentiation—will be considered first.

Low Cost Strategy

Cost leadership strategies require the organisation to identify the lowest cost approaches to the direct activities of the business, minimise the indirect/overhead expenses *and* provide management with detailed reporting on all aspects of fixed and variable cost incursion and recovery. The essential emphasis is on process efficiency and tight control systems, taking advantage of technology to increase profitability through a demonstrated return on investment through cost reduction. Parsons (1983) and others have identified ways in which IS/IT can deliver these benefits to the various direct and indirect business activities. Since IS/IT has traditionally been employed by most companies as a means of reducing cost (even if the business strategy was essentially 'differentiation'!), many of the areas of potential are familiar. For example,

Order handling and sales accounting,
Labour recording, incentive payment and control,
Centralised supplies and services purchasing,
Cost recording, analysis and allocation.

Low cost is achieved through structure and conformity and 'value engineering' the processes of the business plus accuracy in control and measurement of performance, and early identification and action when variances occur from expected results—a 'systems' environment. Traditionally IS/IT has been employed process by process, often causing inefficiency between processes. If that inefficiency is moved into the customer and passed back to the supplier then the low cost may be offset by other problems. But again IS/IT offers potential solutions. Black and Decker, for instance, achieves low costs by moving stock into dealers early in the product season (e.g. lawn-mowers) and does not want returns! Dealers, however, may well mis-estimate demand and either end up with too many or not enough to satisfy their customers. Black and Decker did not want unhappy customers, and provided a network for dealers to exchange shortage/surplus stock information, which B&D would then help in redistributing—anything to avoid returns!

In such an environment systems will be required to deal with basic business information processes efficiently and link them together effectively, not necessarily to produce a highly integrated information resource. Flexibility in systems increases their cost of development and operation—simple, standard systems, often packages, are more cost effective and force user adherence and conformity. Integration can reduce the opportunities to improve efficiency of any particular process as technology offers further particular savings. Information is not seen as a key resource for exploitation, but as an overhead cost to be processed efficiently with minimum additional IS/IT overhead! Integration produces added value potential but incurs overheads. Electronic Data Interchange (EDI), for example, will probably provide cost advantages if it is used to avoid processing paper (orders, invoices, statements)—i.e. more efficient transaction handling. It also enables invoices to be rendered unnecessary by triggering funds transfer at a certain period after goods receipt (to be reconciled later). The relative costs to both customer and supplier of paper work processing and debtor funding can be optimised. This is linking two systems together to produce greater efficiency in both. Similar relationships can also be continually improved by better systems within the organisation. The ability of IS/IT to support a low cost strategy is best exemplified by Thomson's Holidays, who, via 'TOP', as well as providing a better booking service to agents, have avoided operating and overhead cost increases claimed at £28m per annum while an additional one million holidays were handled—all bottom-line profit.

Differentiation Strategy

The majority of organisations have to follow a differentiation strategy, since, theoretically at least, only one company can be the 'low cost' producer of a product or service at any one time. Not surprisingly, therefore, the majority of documented strategic uses of IS/IT have been in support of a differentiation strategy. The essential emphases are innovation and creativity, market orientation, and people-driven rather than systems-driven management controls. For instance, incentive schemes will be market or sales based, not production based. Often key components of differentiation will be the creation of strong brand and corporate images and close, mutually beneficial links with distribution channel firms. The strategic use of IS/IT will focus on enabling new things to be achieved or existing things to be done better. That is not to say that opportunities to use IS/IT to reduce cost will be ignored.

Anglia Building Society (now Nationwide Anglia Building Society) provided its branch managers with personal computers to enable them to sell insurance to customers requiring mortgages, etc. Managers who previously had been reluctant to 'sell' products they were not certain of, trusted the process of evaluation and selection provided by the system and became confident enough to advise customers. The commission on life insurance premiums alone paid for the system in a few months. The system differentiated, at least for a time, Anglia Building Society by the service its managers could now offer.

McKesson differentiated itself in serving the drug stores by taking over many of the 'systems' aspects of running a small business—stock control, ordering, sales analysis, prescription insurance processing, etc. These systems became most effective when the druggist dealt with only one supplier! Other distributors took the matter to court, crying 'foul' over 'one supplier agreements'. The druggists supported McKesson, denying that they were under any obligation to buy only from McKesson—they just preferred to!

Whilst basic business process systems will need to operate efficiently in dealing with the bulk of transactions and basic calculation and reporting requirements, the value of having flexibility to extract information from an integrated 'database' will drive the systems towards sophistication and user tailoring rather than standardised or packaged solutions. Each user will need to be satisfied as fully as possible, implying high overheads in development and operations, i.e. value added, differentiated systems.

The opportunities for strategic advantages will derive from asking such questions as:

How can IS/IT help

- Find out more about customer requirements?
- Monitor customer perceptions of service?
- Provide faster delivery on urgent orders?
- Reduce product change lead times?

- Enable market intelligence to be available to R&D staff?
- Get customers through to the *best* source of an answer to a query?
- Improve quality control on key components?
- Integrate the management decision making and planning processes?
- Provide individuals with pertinent information from which ideas can be developed, etc.

In overall terms IS/IT will provide many potential areas of benefit if such words as '*improve, enable, more, better*' are used in the questions.

Companies that achieve greatest success realise that costs must be controlled *and* value must be added. For IS/IT this means that in any organisation cost reduction and value adding opportunities will exist—but the driving forces will be different where the different generic strategies prevail.

Niche/Focus Strategy

Within a market niche a company will need to adopt a differentiation or low cost strategy to achieve long-term success in that niche. All that has been said above will then apply. However, in addition IS/IT may be a competitive weapon in identifying and then establishing a strong hold on a particular niche. A small company described by Meyer and Boone (1986)—Cardiopet—providing electrocardiogram (ECG) analysis for animals to veterinary hospitals, used public databases to analyse the veterinary industry, identifying the potential expenditure on clinical services. The data also enabled them to identify competitors and then select a range of services to offer which would not bring them into contention with major organisations but would differentiate them to medium-sized veterinary practices *vis-à-vis* other small companies offering only a subset of the services.

Another example quoted by Meyer and Boone is of a relocation service firm who developed systems to enable them to provide comprehensive services to people who were moving house due to company relocation in New England, i.e., a market sector of 'enforced moves'. The service not only located suitable housing but could satisfy other specific requirements such as schooling, leisure facilities, mortgage arrangements. Not only was it a service to buyers, but also to sellers where houses on offer could be channelled towards 'enforced movers' who would be likely to be more reliable purchasers. The total service advantage to an individual both buying and selling was significant. Companies were keen that employees used such a service to minimise the delays and stress involved in moving employees around locations. The service would not have been possible, at an economic service cost, but for a comprehensive system linked throughout the office network.

In general terms the use of IS/IT to achieve success in a limited subset of a general market will be in:

(a) identifying the target market, and/or
(b) developing a unique base of information about the selected market and its needs, and/or

(c) establishing a specialist process via systems to produce a clear cost advantage *vis-à-vis* general market servers, and/or

(d) linking the organisation via systems into the business of the customers to increase switching costs and establish potential barriers to re-entry from general market servers.

In addition, as mentioned earlier, IS/IT can enhance the chosen generic strategy of lowest cost or differentiation within the selected market segment.

VALUE CHAIN ANALYSIS

The concept of the value chain is considered at length by Michael Porter (1984). He says 'every firm is a collection of activities that are performed to design, produce, market, deliver, and support its product. All these activities can be represented using a value chain. Value chains can only be understood in the context of the business unit.' His classic value chain for any firm is shown in Figure 6.8. The primary activities form a linear flow from suppliers through the business to customers. These are things the business must do to exist and not only must each activity be carried out effectively but they must link together effectively if optimum overall performance is to be achieved. The secondary activities are required to control and develop the business in aspects which are required because of a corporate identity, which are common across the primary activities or which require additional capabilities. They add value indirectly but that value is only realisable through primary activity results.

An example of a manufacturing company's value chain is shown in Figure 6.9.

Each activity adds value in terms of customer willingness to pay or enables value adding activities to be co-ordinated, or ensures value has been added. Some activities, as shown in Figure 6.9, only add value if effectively co-ordinated across the primary and secondary areas. These are often information intensive activities such as forecasting—estimating the potential sales, calculating activity levels and capacity requirements and identifying inputs required, etc—and pricing—which requires input from all parts of the chain.

This basic value chain model is a form of business activity analysis, another way of decomposing a complex enterprise into its component parts for analysis and eventual derivation of information systems. It has a number of special features, however:

(a) it separates primary and secondary activities of the business;

(b) concentrates on how the business adds value to satisfy customer requirements;

(c) follows a business unit approach linking to other approaches to strategic analysis and formulation;

(d) is independent of organisational structures. (How the value chain and organisational modelling interrelate will be considered in Chapter 7.)

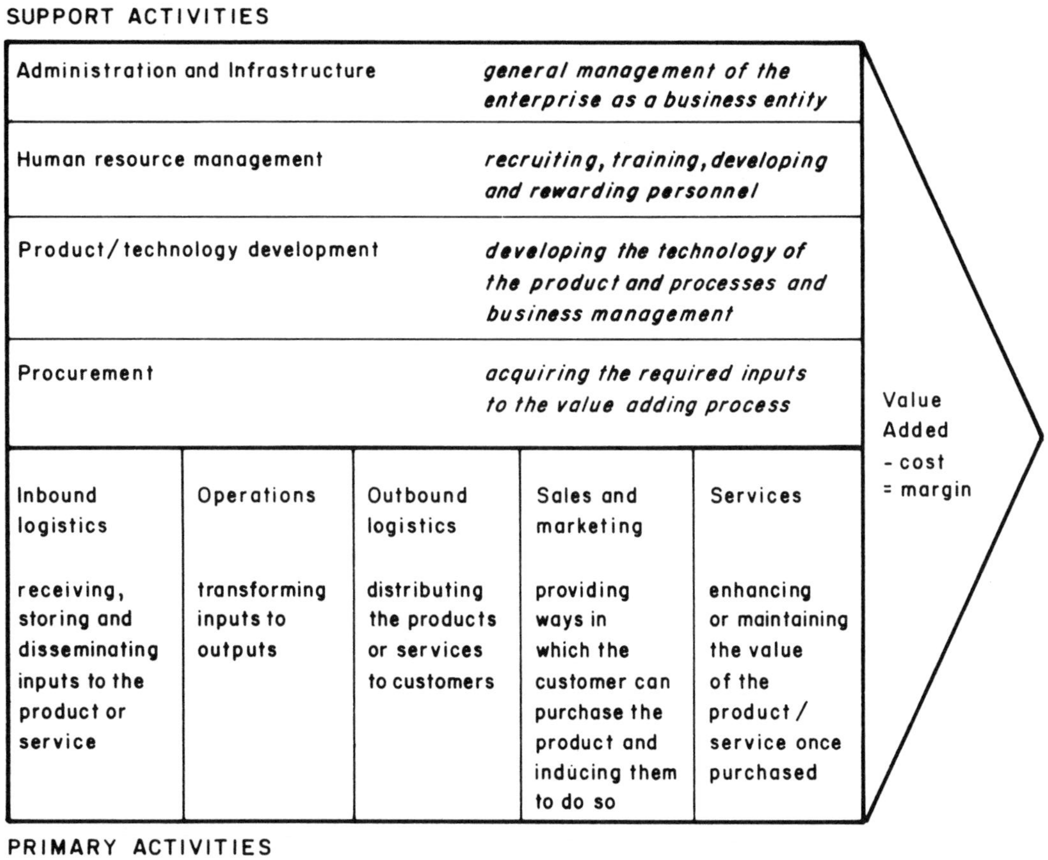

SUPPORT ACTIVITIES

Administration and Infrastructure	*general management of the enterprise as a business entity*			
Human resource management	*recruiting, training, developing and rewarding personnel*			
Product/technology development	*developing the technology of the product and processes and business management*			
Procurement	*acquiring the required inputs to the value adding process*			
Inbound logistics	Operations	Outbound logistics	Sales and marketing	Services
receiving, storing and disseminating inputs to the product or service	transforming inputs to outputs	distributing the products or services to customers	providing ways in which the customer can purchase the product and inducing them to do so	enhancing or maintaining the value of the product/service once purchased

Value Added
– cost
= margin

PRIMARY ACTIVITIES

FIGURE 6.8 *A firm's value chain (Adapted with permission of The Free Press, a Division of Macmillan, Inc. from COMPETITIVE ADVANTAGE: Creating and Sustaining Superior Performance by Michael E. Porter. Copyright © 1985 by Michael E. Porter)*

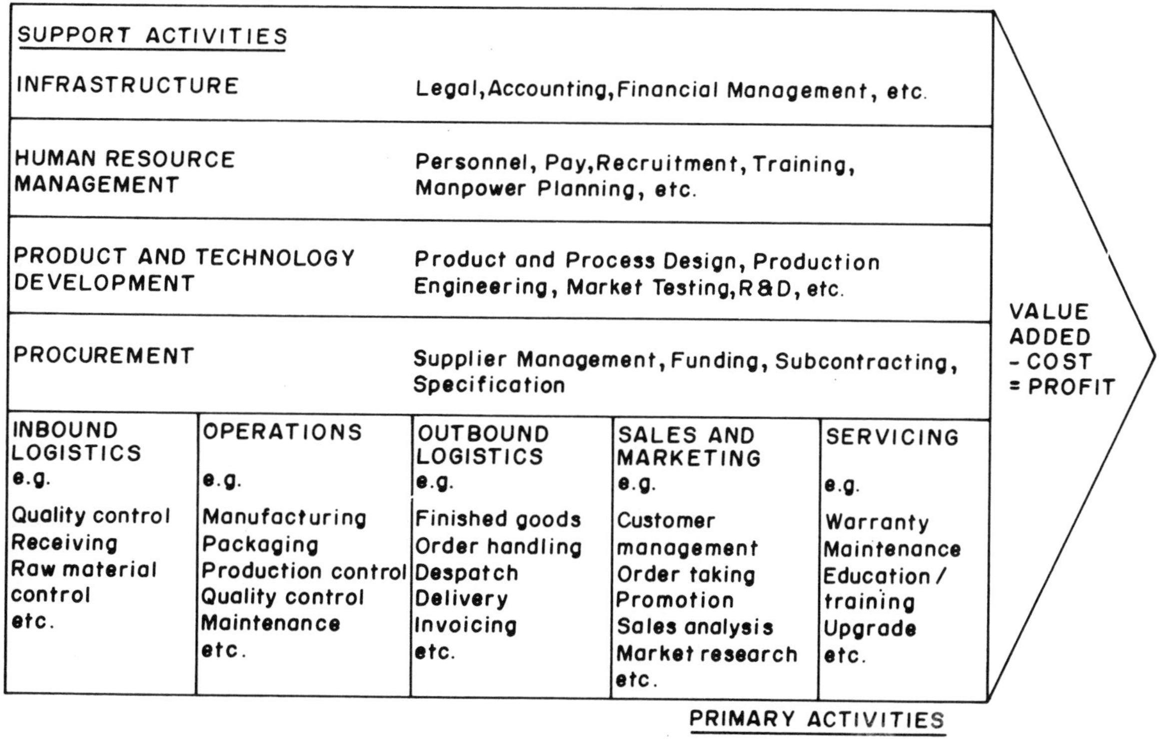

FIGURE 6.9 A value chain for a manufacturing company

Many activities cross the boundaries – especially information – based activities such as: sales forecasting, capacity planning, resource scheduling, pricing, etc.

The diagram contains the following labels:

SUPPORT ACTIVITIES

INFRASTRUCTURE	Legal, Accounting, Financial Management, etc.
HUMAN RESOURCE MANAGEMENT	Personnel, Pay, Recruitment, Training, Manpower Planning, etc.
PRODUCT AND TECHNOLOGY DEVELOPMENT	Product and Process Design, Production Engineering, Market Testing, R&D, etc.
PROCUREMENT	Supplier Management, Funding, Subcontracting, Specification

INBOUND LOGISTICS e.g.	OPERATIONS e.g.	OUTBOUND LOGISTICS e.g.	SALES AND MARKETING e.g.	SERVICING e.g.
Quality control	Manufacturing	Finished goods	Customer	Warranty
Receiving	Packaging	Order handling	management	Maintenance
Raw material	Production control	Despatch	Order taking	Education /
control	Quality control	Delivery	Promotion	training
etc.	Maintenance	Invoicing	Sales analysis	Upgrade
	etc.	etc.	Market research	etc.
			etc.	

PRIMARY ACTIVITIES

VALUE ADDED – COST = PROFIT

All of these features make it a useful tool of analysis in identifying how IS/IT can be used to enhance or enable business strategies and also improve the management control of the business. A value chain can be identified for each business unit with the prime 'driving force' being the customer/product relationship. The value chain of the firm does not exist in isolation, it exists as part of an *industry value system*, or set of value chains that eventually link from the source of raw materials of a product to the eventual consumption of the product. That value system will consist of the value chains of suppliers, customers, and competitors. The profitability of the industry system will ultimately depend on the demand for the end product—how much the final consumer will pay, for what quantity of the product or service—less the cost incurred by the component firms in getting the product to the consumer. It is important to realise, as Porter points out, that a firm's ability to achieve a satisfactory profit is not only dependent on the performance of competitors, but also the effectiveness of its customers and suppliers in bargaining for a greater share of the profit available in the chain. The firm *competes* with suppliers and customers for the profit available. Many of the successful strategic uses of IS/IT have involved increasing the overall profit available by the firm becoming the key to the most effective route through the system. This additional profit can be shared with suppliers or customers or both to ensure they realise greater benefit by dealing with the firm rather than competitors.

An overall value system is represented in Figure 6.10—throughout the chain the component firms are adding value and incurring cost, and, if stability is to exist, making appropriate profits. If any firm or group of firms is failing to make profits then equilibrium is destroyed, and either rationalisation of directly competing firms must occur or vertical integration will follow to reduce the cost structure. From an information management perspective one aspect of the value chain approach to analysis stands out. Demand information flows back along the chain from the end consumer, and supply information flows in the opposite direction. Ideally to maximize performance a business needs to match demand and supply precisely. This explains why many firms have been pushing IS/IT tentacles outwards to capture this information earlier and more accurately.

Various aspects and limitations of value chain analysis as a source of IS/IT strategic options are considered below, and some areas are dealt with in more detail based on refinements of certain parts of the analysis. However, first this basic value chain approach needs to be considered in regard to some other business realities.

First, large multi-business companies may possess business units in various parts of the industry value system, as in Figure 6.11 which outlines the value system of the paper industry and shows the disposition of business units of the Hammermill Paper Company described earlier (Box 6.1). The chain is much simplified. Hammermill's basic philosophy was 'profit centered, free market', more like a very diversified financial holding company than a specialist industry company,

For the entire chain...

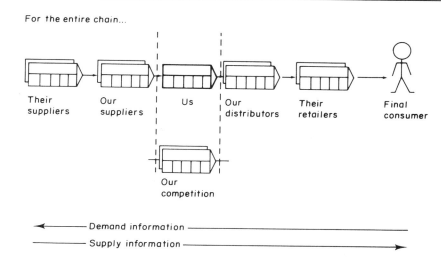

FIGURE 6.10 *The industry value system (adapted with permission of The Free Press, a Division of Macmillan, Inc. from* COMPETITIVE ADVANTAGE: Creating and Sustaining Superior Performance *by Michael E. Porter. Copyright © 1985 by Michael E. Porter)*

although all its companies were in the wood/paper industry. This strategy of 'internal competition' for markets and resources provides incentives and opportunities in high growth stages of an industry cycle, when creating and meeting demand is more critical to profitability than fighting for market share. By 1982 the industry was mature, even entering decline which, with high energy costs and environment factors increasing the cost base of the industry, meant intensified competition amongst the few major firms in the industry. Additionally traditional wood companies were moving downstream into pulp and paper, and traditional glass and metal packaging companies were moving into paper packaging. The industry was under severe stress. Hammermill's strengths lay in brand image and extensive distribution coverage, plus its knowledge of the industry. However, by 1982, only 1% of its sales of its forest products were to its own manufacturing companies (the rest was sold to potential competitors). Only 20% of its fine and printing papers were distributed by its merchants (the rest by its merchants' competitors). Only 15% of its own merchants' sales were of its products (the rest were mainly competitors' products). Its industrial and packaging companies distributed their own products direct to customers. The information systems were developed to the requirements of the units at the various stages of the chain— many of its fine and printing manufacturing companies had different systems and even worse many of the distribution branches had local systems! There was obvious potential to achieve vertical synergy through information exchange

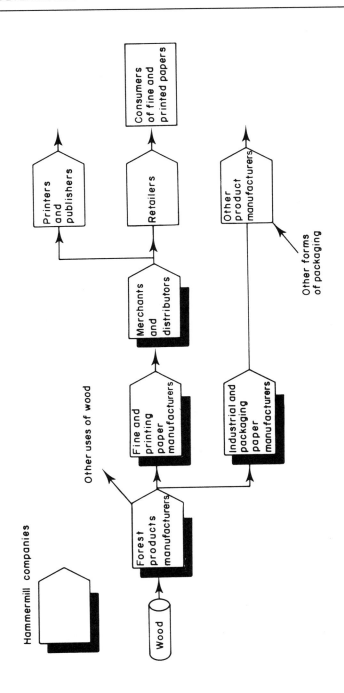

FIGURE 6.11 Paper industry value system

of both demand and supply plus considerable opportunities for more effective procurement of vital raw materials and delivery of products to customers. The marketing data held by its merchants, *because* they distributed competitors' products, was an asset which could have produced competitive advantages. None of these opportunities were taken advantage of, and eventually, in 1986, Hammermill had to engineer a friendly takeover by its biggest competitor to ward off the threat of takeover by a corporate raider.

Interestingly, had Hammermill developed highly integrated and interdependent systems it would not have been an attractive prey to an asset stripper since each component company would not have been an attractive resale—unable to operate effectively outside the umbrella of information systems. Hence effective information systems investments would have at least protected it from competitive disadvantage.

This extended example shows that in using industry and value chain analysis the potential for mutual business advantage of component businesses in the same or related industries should be identified to obtain benefits available from information exchange. The analysis can also show the potential for synergistic and rationalisation benefits from intra-company systems and shared systems. In addition, the analysis should reveal additional benefits particular to any business unit.

Viewed in reverse, if a competitor is spread through the chain and hence has opportunities to develop such information systems linkages then this will pose a threat to companies whose business involves less stages of the chain.

A particular problem of applying the value chain approach has often been encountered. The basic, rather structured concept of the value chain—'the big arrow'—is sometimes difficult to apply to non-manufacturing industries where the product is not tangible and there are no obvious 'raw materials'. A bus company, the police, car hire, building societies, estate agencies, the inland revenue and education are all examples where the five linear components of the value chain are difficult to identify. However, the concept is still valid since each provides a service to a customer and has to link together several activities effectively to provide the customer with value. And all the activities cost money. The process of analysis can be made more flexible if used to describe 'freehand' the relationships between the customer, the service/product and the resources consumed. Then the various activities involved can be separated into *primary* (essential) and *support*. Then the primary activities can be broken down into linear activities concerned with resource acquisition, carrying out the key operation or process, delivering the service, and where appropriate, selling it and providing follow-up services. However in most cases primary value chains can be established, even when they share a set of support activities.

The main objective in all cases is to represent the main activities in the business and their relationships in terms of how they add value as to satisfy the customer and to obtain resources from suppliers—not in terms of how the organisation currently is structured—i.e. to focus on core business requirements. By considering that value chain as a component of an industry value system a broader view of systems implications and opportunities can be determined. For instance the value chain for providing primary education needs to be considered as part of the education value chain from pre-school to postgraduate. At present each school *and* the education authority keep and re-input the same information many times throughout a child's education at great and probably unnecessary overhead cost!

However crudely the value systems and value chains are drawn they will enable further analysis of any or all of the following:

(a) The information that flows throughout industry and how critical that information is to the functioning of the industry and the success of the firms in it; and by determining where and when that information is available, who has it and how it could be obtained and be turned to advantage or be used against the firm.

For instance in some industries, such as fashion goods, 'demand' information is the critical factor, but in others such as confectioners (the price and availability of cocoa) and timber (the price and availability of wood) 'supply' data can be critical to success. Manufacturers who have good information can out-compete those without. Again in the UK timber industry the price of softwoods will be affected over a six-month cycle by the US building industry—'housing starts' in the USA determining availability and price elsewhere. As the world's largest purchaser of wool, Benetton would find huge stocks on its hands if it failed to anticipate and satisfy demand—hence the importance of its point of sale system in its franchised shops to obtain daily sales data in a volatile market.

(b) The information that is or could be exchanged with customers and suppliers to improve the performance of the business or lead to mutually improved performance by sharing the benefits; and also the information that is required for the customer or supplier to either sell on the product/service or acquire his input resources.

Suppliers of particular components or resources may have longer lead times than appropriate, given the volatility of the company's business. Providing plans for forward requirements, even buying on his behalf to spread both companies' risks might help. The information links between companies are far more complex than often appreciated and the value chain approach allows them to be analysed.

(c) How effectively the information flows through the primary processes and is used by them

   (i) within each activity to optimise performance, and

(ii) to link the activities together and avoid unnecessary costs and missing opportunities,

(iii) to enable support activities to contribute to the value adding processes, not hinder them.

Historically most systems have been developed to meet functional needs—and often the links between them, from marketing to outbound logistics for instance, are added later. This often results in 'armies' of people working at the interfaces, with the generic job title of 'professional reconciler', working to overcome the weaknesses at the system interfaces. Porter suggests that the companies who succeed with IS are those who link their systems together along the value chain most effectively. For instance it may be most effective to supply daily sales data in its raw form direct to the procurement and inbound logistics activities to determine ordering requirements much earlier. Otherwise these could effectively hinder the marketing effort in the long term.

One area where effective integration of information can be exploited to advantage is in pricing. Pricing is purely an 'information-based' activity. Increasing prices to the highest obtainable in the market also offers the easiest way of increasing profits. Beath and Ives (1986) consider in detail how companies have gained an edge by developing pricing systems which are responsive to changing demand and supply and are sensitive to the relationship of fixed and variable costs. Figure 6.12 shows the fundamental pricing strategies available ranging from supply/accounting based 'cost' to sales based 'value-pricing' ('What will the customer pay?'). Each strategy requires knowledge of both supply and demand and cost information, and IS/IT can help in all cases to determine prices or price ranges and then inform people of the price to be charged. Computerised price books, i.e. prices on the screen, are often more effectively used than traditional catalogues of prices and pages of price updates. Supermarket chains via networks and point of sale systems can change shelf prices of items instantly in all stores or selectively in certain stores depending on sales, stocks available, competitive pressures or local price wars, etc.

Pricing is just one example of how, in detail, information on the value chain can be brought together and exploited to gain advantage. The value chain approach enables an information flow model of the industry and the firm to be defined in order to identify areas where information gathering, exchange and processing will affect the performance not only of the firm but also its suppliers, its customers and competitors. The next questions could be: 'what can we do about it' and/or 'how far do we want to tie ourselves into other parts of the chain'. The first stage is to identify which force—customer chain, supplier chain, competitor—can be influenced by IS/IT and the importance of doing something about it. Then we need some further stages of analysis—more specific techniques which can be used within the value chain framework to determine what to do.

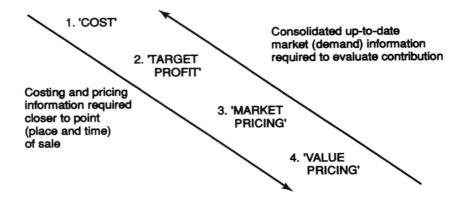

FIGURE 6.12 Choosing the price strategy. (After C. M. Beath and B. Ives, 'Competitive information systems in support of pricing', MIS Quarterly (March 1986))

STRATEGIC OPTION GENERATOR

The 'option generator' technique for identifying strategic IS opportunities in relation to customers, suppliers and competitors is based on an approach developed at GTE, a diversified international electronics company. The approach was described by Rackoff *et al.* (1985) and is explored in great detail in Wiseman's book (Wiseman, 1985).

As mentioned above, the first stage in the analysis is to define the targets:

Suppliers: Anyone supplying essential resources—it may be necessary to subset them either by the nature of what they supply or their strength, ability to exert pressure on you and other customers.

Customers: This could include the consumers as well as direct customers if the latter are essentially distributors. Again the customers need perhaps to be classified in terms of what (and what else) they buy or how much leverage they exert.

Competitors: Obvious competitors selling very similar products or services should be supplemented by potential new entrants into the market and 'threatening' substitute products and services should be included as competition. Competitors' strategies (differentiation, cost, niche) should also be understood.

Having determined the strategic targets, for each of them a number of alternative 'strategic thrusts'—major offensive or defensive moves—can be made by the firm. Wiseman *et al.* recognise five alternative thrusts, producing a matrix as shown in Figure 6.13.

Differentiation: Being better and ensuring that quality is perceived and leads to premium pricing—the thrust could be to be not only a better supplier or competitor by differentiating the product or service but also being a better customer of suppliers to obtain preferential service.

Cost: Being cheaper or enabling suppliers or customers to reduce their costs (sharing the benefit) and thereby prefer to do business with the firm; alternatively ways may be found to increase competitors' cost.

	SUPPLIER	CUSTOMER	COMPETITOR
DIFFERENTIATION	Ford putting quality control systems into component suppliers	ICI Counsellor system	BMW system for car allocation and delivery
COST	American Hospital Supplies *vis-à-vis* primary materials suppliers	Banc One Card Processing services	Thomson's Holidays— administration cost reduction
INNOVATION	Merrill Lynch cash management account	Thomson's Holidays (via agents)	ICI Counsellor system
GROWTH	Thomson's Holidays to enable more holidays and flights to be sold	Aalsmeer Flower Auction by speed of process	Aalsmeer Flower Auction by ability to process volume of product supplied
ALLIANCE	?	McKesson with drug stores	Joint ATM networks among building societies

STRATEGIC THRUST ↑

STRATEGIC TARGET ⟶

FIGURE 6.13 *Framework for assessing strategic IS opportunities.* (Source: N. Rackoff, C. Wiseman and W. A. Ullrich, 'Information systems for competitive advantage: implementation of a planning process', MIS Quarterly *(December 1985)*)

Innovation: Introduce a new product, service, process or way of doing business which transforms the relationships and competitive forces in the industry. This may require the active involvement and cooperation of suppliers and/or customers.

Growth: Enable volume or expansion in geography or increased flexibility of production of product varieties without indirect or overhead increases.

Alliance: Forging agreements, joint ventures, joint investments in systems to prevent new entrants or competitors achieving advantage or to increase the effectiveness or durability of the other thrusts above.

As said above, it may be that a number of different thrusts are appropriate with different groups of suppliers or customers or even competitors, implying that an action may be possible in all 15 segments of the matrix!

On Figure 6.13 some examples quoted earlier in the book are placed in the various boxes of the matrix. Notice that some examples appear in more than one box.

To identify what you wish to do and what benefits are available, a questionnaire approach is suggested. Table 6.3 shows some sample suggested questions which

TABLE 6.3 IS/IT opportunity analysis — questions

1. *Suppliers*—Can we use IS/IT to:
   - gain leverage over our suppliers (improving our bargaining power or reducing his)?
   - reduce buying costs?
   - reduce the suppliers' costs?
   - be a better customer and obtain a better service?
   - identify alternative sources of supply?
   - improve the quality of products/services purchased?
   etc.

2. *Customers*—Can we use IS/IT to:
   - reduce customers' costs and/or increase their revenue?
   - increase our customers' switching costs (to alternative suppliers)?
   - increase our customers' knowledge of our products/services?
   - improve support/service to customers and/or reduce the cost of existing services?
   - discover more about our customers and their needs?
   - identify new potential customers?

3. *Competitors*—Can we use IS/IT to:
   - raise the entry cost of potential competitors?
   - differentiate (or create new) products/services?
   - reduce our costs/increase competitors' costs?
   - alter the channels of distribution?
   - identify/establish a new market niche?
   - form joint ventures to enter new markets?
   etc.

might lead to the identification of options. Some of the questions imply a degree of lateral thought. For instance, 'reduce suppliers costs' tends to go against the grain! The full question should be perhaps 'reduce the suppliers cost, when he does business with us' (in order to create more profit in the chain and share the benefit).

Earlier in the chapter a confectionary wholesaler was mentioned who did business with corner shops and multiples. Using the 'strategic thrusts' ideas it would seem that a differentiation (value added) approach to the corner shops might be appropriate, but from a systems point of view the thrusts towards the multiple might be low cost—essentially an efficient delivery business. However in its relationship with the suppliers a differentiated approach might be appropriate to discourage potential by-pass by the suppliers direct to the multiple. In general, it is likely for any firm that customers/suppliers/competitors will have to be segmented and potentially different 'thrusts' made towards different groups.

Having decided the strategic targets and thrusts, it is important to consider the basic objective—is it to be *offensive* to gain or increase an edge, or *defensive* to reduce a competitor's edge or prevent a potential disadvantage. This will affect the way the eventual project is managed.

The strategic option generator approach relies on a thorough understanding of the state of the industry, the firm's competitive position, the determining factors for success and the industry value system plus a clearly understood business strategy. It is a very effective way of refining the options available within the overall SIS treasure-hunting process. One final 'technique' will now be considered which refines the options still further.

Resource Life-cycle Analysis

This approach under the heading 'customer resource life-cycles analysis' is described in detail by Ives and Learmonth (1984). They state that by examining its customer relationships via the model, companies can determine not only when opportunities (and threats) exist for strategic applications but also when specific applications should be developed. They imply that the Resource Life-Cycle (RLC) model should be viewed from one end only, i.e. towards the customer, but the same possible options will apply in reverse in relationships with suppliers. Hence the RLC model could be a customer or supplier resource life-cycle model, depending on point of view!

The RLC model relies on the fact that an organisation's products/services go through a typical life-cycle when viewed as a *resource* by the customer. The four main stages of this life-cycle (as defined in IBM's Business Systems Planning Process, 1981) are:

- Requirements determination.
- Acquisition.

- Stewardship.
- Retirement or disposal.

Each of these stages involves a number of processes of information exchange—between buyer and seller—to enable the stage to be managed effectively, thereby ensuring maximum benefit to the buyer and seller. If at any stage the exchange breaks down, either the current transaction or future business will be adversely affected. The further through the life-cycle the information exchange has gone, the higher the switching cost to the customer, who will have to retrace the steps at additional cost and risk with another supplier. The full resource life-cycle model proposed by Ives and Learmouth is outlined in Table 6.4. They list a considerable number of good examples of how IS/IT has been used to improve the relationship at one or (in most cases) several stages of the detailed interaction required to maximise the customer's benefits from the supplier's products and services.

TABLE 6.4 Resource life cycle analysis (after B. Ives and G. P. Learmonth, 'The information system as a competitive weapon', Communications of the ACM, **27** *(12) (December 1984))*

Requirements	
Establish requirements	To determine how much of a resource is required.
Specify	To determine a resource's attributes.
Acquisition	
Select source	To determine where customers will buy a resource.
Order	To order a quantity of a resource from the supplier.
Authorise and pay for	To transfer funds or extend credit.
Acquire	To take possession of a resource.
Test and accept	To ensure that a resource meets specifications.
Stewardship	
Integrate	To add to an existing inventory.
Monitor	To control access and use of a resource.
Upgrade	To upgrade a resource if conditions change.
Maintain	To repair a resource, if necessary.
Retirement	
Transfer or dispose	To move, return, or dispose of inventory as necessary.
Account for	To monitor where and how much is spent on a resource.

In essence the RLC model forces consideration of what happens to the product or service once it has become part of a customer's value chain or while it was part of the supplier's value chain and thence leads to extended information relationships between buyer and seller over an extended timescale while the product/service is being consumed or in reverse while it is being developed and made available. Most historical uses of IS/IT have dealt only with stages 1 and 2 in the model, and then from the view of the company only, i.e.,

how can we find out what is available to meet our needs and get our requirements understood?

and

how can we best take delivery, test, handle, and pay for the product or service when we decide to buy?

The RLC model suggests that the information relationship is an extended one, eventually resulting in a replacement sale or purchase. The life-cycle may be very short (days) for consumable items but many years for capital items. Two examples may serve to conclude consideration of this approach.

First, the Gas Boards (Regions as they became) in the UK during 1965–70 collected data on every domestic gas appliance in the UK as part of North Sea Gas conversion. Without any vision as to what to do with the data, it was disposed of in the early 1970s. Until the late 1970s, domestic gas appliances could only be purchased from Gas Board showrooms, hence every appliance sold was known. This data too was kept for a limited period only! Since the mid-1980s, Gas Regions have been trying to persuade (via warranty schemes) consumers to provide them with details of the appliances (especially central heating systems, cookers and fires) they have so that long-term replacement marketing plans can be developed for the 1990s when gas may be less attractive in many ways than electricity for the replacement appliances.

UK electricity boards are considering how they might exploit their existing customer database asset more effectively. A possibility is a 'one stop appliance repair service'. Irrespective of where the white goods (fridges, freezers, cookers, washing machines, dryers, dishwashers, etc) appliance is purchased, the board could offer a warranty/repair service by phoning one number, provided they are informed early of the purchase. The warranty would cover all such appliances, the premium based on the age balance of the particular products. This would be an excellent stewardship service to the consumer, paid as part of the electricity bill, and would provide the board with extensive data for the increasingly competitive appliance replacement market place and provide leverage with respect to the major manufacturers. None of their competitors could easily or economically replace such a system based on business strategy because of the electricity board's existing database of *all* the people who possess such appliances.

VALUE CHAIN-BASED TECHNIQUES—A SUMMARY

Information systems have always been part of the value adding processes that comprise any enterprise, whether it be a commercial company, a public service or charitable body. Historically though, IS/IT has been mainly deployed to improve individual component processes or activities of the enterprise. In some cases this improvement has been focused on the supporting rather than the primary activities of the business. When systems have been focused on primary activities it has tended to be on the main operational activity of the business, ensuring its optimisation and then 'spin off' systems which help in dealing with suppliers and customers, as long as they do not jeopardise the effectiveness of internal operations. The focus has been on

- internal operations and control,
- key processes in the organisation,
- internal CSFs,
- the firm not the industry,
- short-term use of information.

The value chain analysis techniques suggest that the firm's information systems should be considered in an extended context—that of the industry value chain—in order that it achieves maximum leverage from IS/IT investments and benefits from industry and internal developments. The value chain represents the flow of goods and services and use of resources through the industry and there is a simultaneous, parallel flow of information about what is happening running through the industry. The value chain analysis tools make the organisation consider how much of that industry information flow affects the firm and how much they can and want to influence it, where to intercept it and where it is worth investing to achieve superiority with respect to others by exploiting the information and its flow. The techniques lead to opening up new opportunities or exposing potential threats, and then enable the means of exploitation and counteraction to be considered. This form of analysis also enables the assessment of existing systems and known requirements to be considered in a broader and longer-term context.

This broader view is represented in Figure 6.14 which shows how the main concepts discussed above relate to one another. The diagram mentions another technique described in Chapter 5—Critical Success Factors (CSFs)—whose usefulness can be extended into this part of the process. Critical success factors occur at many levels

- for the whole industry, affecting all the component firms,
- for a corporation based on corporate objectives,
- for a business unit based on the corporate objectives and CSFs, plus the unit's own objectives,
- for functions, activities, even individual managers in the business unit.

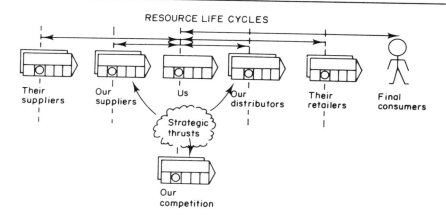

FUTURE IS/IT FOCUS
- external links and control of relationships
- focus on the links between processes in the industry
- the CSFs of customers/suppliers/competitors
- the entire industry and its information flows
- long-term acquisition of information

FIGURE 6.14 The industry value added chains

In the first three mentioned above the technique can be used to consider what customers, suppliers and competitors might also attempt to do or what might be their response to any strategy adopted. Would a selected group of customers be responsive to closer ties via systems? It will depend on *their* critical success factors— if securing supplies is critical, they may be keen to develop mutual links, etc. The idea of sharing the benefits was mentioned early on—helping to satisfy critical success factors is a sharing of benefits. The questions should be raised—what are the CSFs likely to be for key suppliers, competitors and customers and what are the implications? Obviously this cannot be accurate but by looking at the firm from the critical success factors of others may reveal new options or consolidate or amend ideas developed through other processes of assessment.

SUMMARY AND CONCLUSIONS

In planning the future information systems and technology for an organisation it is important to identify the business opportunities and threats presented by increasing and developing use of IS/IT in the firm's industry. The objective is to identify strategically important applications, those applications which directly support chosen business strategies or enable new business strategies to be developed and implemented. These will help the organisation gain competitive advantages or avoid future disadvantages. If the organisation is not in a strictly competitive environment, strategic applications will be those focusing on meeting organisational objectives. These strategic applications are only a part of the organisation's IS application portfolio, but a very important part.

This chapter has described a number of approaches which can be taken to analyse an organisation's information and systems possibilities and the potential business benefits. The use of each technique has been exemplified by what others have done. The various techniques have been described from the 'top down', from the industry down to particular aspects of information exchange with customers or suppliers. Beneficial options can arise at any stage of the analysis or equally by inspiration. The various models used also offer a basis for testing the value of *ad hoc* inspiration.

The various tools of analysis mentioned will tend to uncover a variety of potentially strategic applications. In Chapter 1 a classification of such strategic applications was proposed. Four types of different strategic uses of IS/IT were described from a broad analysis of actual examples. The immediate use of such a classification is to enable the firm to search for potential benefit in four areas. These four areas are summarised on the horizontal axis of Table 6.5. In Chapter 1 the implications of the different strategic applications were discussed and who in the organisation will need to become actively involved in the determination and management of each type was reviewed. This chapter has described techniques for analysing the business and its environment to discover potential opportunities. The tools are listed down the side of Table 6.5. Each tool

TABLE 6.5 *Strategic uses of IS/IT and the techniques for uncovering them*

	Application type			
Technique	1 External linkage systems	2 Internal integration	3 Product/ service enhancement and innovation	4 Executive information

(a) SBU/product
   portfolio
   analysis
	* *	*	* * *	*

(b) Competitive analysis	* * *	*	* *	*

(c) Value (ext)
   chain
   analysis (int)
	* * *	* * *	* *
			*
				*
				* *

(d) Critical
   success
   factors
	*	* *	*	* * *

The number of asterisks show the varying degrees of emphasis.

and technique will tend to lead to a different mix and emphasis in terms of types of applications that result. Table 6.5 attempts to demonstrate the likely differences of emphasis.

For instance: competitive analysis and external value chains will primarily provoke issues of external linkages, but each will also suggest means of product or service enhancement.

The table also clearly shows that no one technique will assess business implications of IS/IT sufficiently to identify all possible options. But use of all the techniques in combination can produce a comprehensive set of options.

There are undoubtedly other techniques which could have been considered here—the most widely accepted ones have been included. Over time more techniques will be developed to supplement these. All these techniques have a common theme—they must be used by people with knowledge of the business and its environment and therefore cannot be tools for IS specialists alone to use. Senior management and line managers as well must become familiar with the basic approaches to this type of analysis. All of the tools and techniques described are really IS/IT subsets of business strategic analysis tools which should enable such managers to become actively involved in determining the future potential, both potential opportunities and potential threats, IS/IT has to offer the organisation.

In the next chapter the ideas of this and the preceding two chapters will be considered together—how can they be used so that the results can then be integrated into the process of strategic planning and through into successful implementation of the strategy.

REFERENCES

Ansoff, H. I. (1968) *Corporate Strategy*, McGraw-Hill.
Beath, C. M. and Ives, B. (1986) 'Competitive information systems in support of pricing', *MIS Quarterly* (March).
Business Systems Planning Process (1981) 'Business systems planning: information systems planning guide', GE20-0527-3, IBM Corporation.
Cash, J. I. (1988) 'Interorganisational systems: an information society opportunity or threat?' *The Information Society*, 3(3).
Cash, J. I. and Konsynski, B. R. (1985) 'IS redraws competitive boundaries', *Harvard Business Review*, March–April.
EDP Analyser (1986) 'Uncovering strategic systems' *EDP Analyser*, **24**(10) (October).
Higgins, J. M. (1985) *Strategy*, The Dryden Press.
Ives, B. and Learmonth, G. P. (1984) 'The information system as a competitive weapon', *Communications of the ACM*, **27**(12) (December).
Large, J. (1986) 'Information's market-force', *Management Today* (August).
McFarlan, F. W. (1984) 'Information technology change the way you compete', *Harvard Business Review* (May/June).
Meyer, N. D. and Boone, M. E. (1986) *The Information Edge*, McGraw-Hill.

Parsons, G. L. (1983) 'Information technology—a new competitive weapon', *Sloan Management Review* (Fall).

Porter, M. E. (1980) *Competitive Strategy*, Free Press.

Porter, M. E. (1984) *Competitive Advantage*, Free Press.

Porter, M. E. and Millar, V. E. (1985) 'How information gives you competitive advantage', *Harvard Business Review*, July–August.

Rackoff, N., Wiseman, C. and Ullrich, W. A. (1985) 'Information systems for competitive advantage: implementation of a planning process', *MIS Quarterly* (December).

Strategic Planning Institute (1984) *Management Productivity and Information Technology (MPIT)*, Overview Report.

Synnott, W. R. (1987) *The Information Weapon* (Ch. 3, Integrating business and information planning, pp. 43–62), John Wiley.

Wiseman, C. (1985) *Strategy and Computers*, Dow Jones–Irwin.

Wyman, J. (1985) 'Technological myopia—the need to think strategically about technology', *Sloan Management Review* (Winter).

Chapter 7

DETERMINING THE BUSINESS INFORMATION SYSTEMS STRATEGY

INTRODUCTION

By a series of analyses of the business environment, the strategy of the business and the role that information and systems can and could fulfil in the business, a set of known requirements and potential opportunities can be elicited. These needs and options will result from business pressures, the strategy of the business and the organisation of the various activities, resources and people in the business. Information needs and relationships can then be converted into systems and an appropriate organisation of data. To enable these 'ideal' applications to be developed and managed successfully, resources and technologies will have to be acquired and deployed effectively. In all cases systems and information will already exist and normally IS resources and technology will already be deployed. Any strategy, therefore, must identify what is eventually required and must also understand accurately how much has already been achieved. The strategic plan must determine a migration path which overcomes existing weaknesses, exploits strengths and enables the new requirements to be achieved in such a way that it can be resourced and managed appropriately. A strategy has been defined earlier as 'an *integrated* set of actions aimed at increasing the *long-term* wellbeing and strength of the enterprise'. The plan must therefore be integrated not only in terms of information, systems and technology via a coherent set of actions, but also in terms of the evolving needs of the business. Long term suggests uncertainty, both in terms of the business requirements and the potential benefits the various applications and technologies will offer. Change is the only thing that is certain! Those changing circumstances will mean that the organisation will have to be capable of effective responses to unexpected opportunities and problems.

The strategic approach must therefore not define a rigid plan but define a business information systems environment which can be adapted as circumstances change.

This chapter will consider how the models for the scope and processes of IS/IT strategic planning from Chapters 3 and 4 and the various tools and techniques of analysis from Chapters 5 and 6 can be consolidated to produce a strategy for the business which defines the appropriate application systems and information resources it requires. Later the management of a diverse portfolio of application requirements will be considered as the first stage in defining the options for the technology and resourcing strategies that are available to achieve the application strategy successfully.

The requirement to determine the business information systems strategy over an extended period demands that a consolidated approach must retain the flexibility to respond to changing business and organisational needs and IS/IT options. In order to do that the processes used to analyse situations and assess opportunities must be capable of being revisited in part at any time to assess the implications without a major rethink of the whole strategy.

STRATEGIC PLANNING MODELS AND THEIR RELATIONSHIPS

In Chapter 1 a simple model for describing the IS application portfolio of a business was developed. This model suggested that IS/IT applications could be described in terms of 'STRATEGIC', 'TURNAROUND', 'FACTORY' or 'SUPPORT' applications (see Figure 1.8). The main factors which will determine the balance of that portfolio for any business—i.e. which applications reside in which sectors and the relative strategic importance and criticality of each could be described as:

(a) External long term
  —the state of the industry in terms of profitability, growth and structure.
  —the degree to which IS/IT is, or is capable of, changing the products, markets and interrelationships of the industry.
(b) External short term
  —the actual use of IS/IT by competitors and others in the industry to gain a relative advantage,
  —the opportunities created by IS/IT to change the balance of competitive factors and influences on the industry both in the existing value chain and by new entrants or product/service substitution.
(c) Internal long term
  —how new IS/IT applications could more effectively support or enhance the business strategy of the enterprise,
  —or enable the business to adopt a more appropriate strategy to suit the future business environment.
(d) Internal short term
  —the degree to which existing systems support the chosen strategy and criticality of those systems to sustaining existing business advantages,
  —the existing approach to IS/IT management and its appropriateness to the business strategy and the current stage of development of IS/IT in the industry.

These are closely related to the inputs to the strategy described in Chapter 3.

External long term—External business environment
External short term—External IS/IT environment
Internal long term—Internal business environment
Internal short term—Internal IS/IT environment + current applications portfolio

These are conclusions drawn from the previously developed arguments, and they mainly focus on determining *what* could and should be done rather than *how* to do it. This therefore relates to the *demand* management part of the basic demand/supply or IS/IT rationale of strategic management described by Earl and depicted in Figure 3.5. *How* to achieve the appropriate supply will be considered in depth in later chapters, as will the detailed issues of the management of the portfolio. In Chapter 5 the focus was on the internal factors both short and long term, which determine the overall structure of the portfolio, whilst Chapter 6 focused mainly on external factors. The models in Chapter 3 considered in more depth the issues of both demand and supply management. There is obviously an iterative relationship, supply can constrain the demand and modified demand will require different strategies for supply.

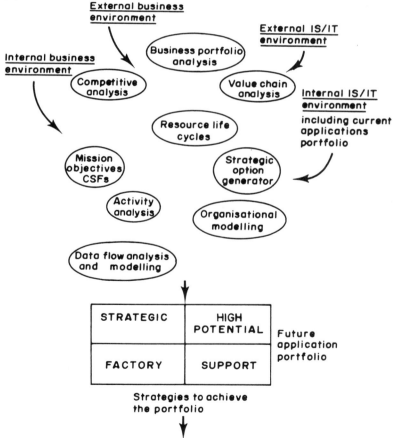

FIGURE 7.1

The processes for determining the strategy described in Chapter 4 emphasise the need to determine requirements before deciding how to satisfy them—but the ability to conceive the requirements will be coloured by a historical pre-disposition based on a knowledge of the organisation's ability to deliver. Despite these convolutions which can potentially result in an inability to do anything!, the determination of *demand* is the primary driving force in the early stages of strategic IS/IT planning. Consequently, the use of the various ideas to determine that demand needs to be brought together to ensure that a coherent set of demands are formulated.

Demand for IS/IT in a particular business unit can be most easily described as a 'business information systems strategy' using the portfolio concept above. The previous two chapters have described techniques for trying to 'fill' the portfolio with applications. Figure 7.1 summarises the inputs to the strategic planning approach and techniques used to 'create' the portfolio. Whilst it might appear from previous discussion that the 'STRATEGIC' box is all important, all the components of the portfolio offer the business major contributions to improved performance. An inability to manage support or factory systems successfully will both reduce the ability to extrapolate potential and will absorb resources on applications of lower importance. The objective at this stage of strategic planning is to determine what future applications would be appropriate for the business. So far a model has been developed which has inputs, tools and techniques and a conceptual product! The next stage is to consider how the various techniques and approaches can be brought together to ensure the products of analysis are consistent and can be reconciled during more detailed planning.

A FRAMEWORK WITHIN WHICH THE MODELS AND TECHNIQUES CAN BE USED EFFECTIVELY

It would be convenient if a 'methodology' or structured, repeatable process could be proposed but this is not realistic given the need to simultaneously relate existing situations to requirements to ideas. However, a framework within which the various concepts can be used more effectively than as isolated techniques, is essential if the determination of the business systems strategy is to be a manageable task. Also, as circumstances alter and progress is made the strategy will need to be updated, without having to reappraise all the analysis and resulting conclusions.

The main objective is to identify the required applications, their priorities and be able to deploy resources to achieve them successfully. The outline framework depicted in Figure 7.2 shows as the end-product the portfolio divided into three components.

1. The existing applications—those currently in place and currently being developed to be installed in the near future—say one year. These need to be assessed in terms of their contribution to existing business processes and

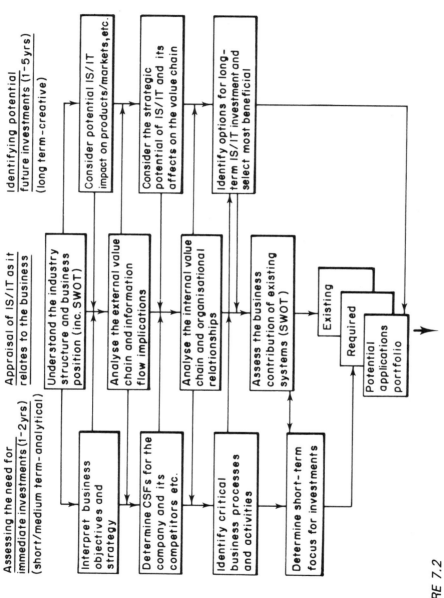

FIGURE 7.2

performance *and* in terms of future requirements and potential. The strengths and weaknesses of each need to be understood but in a future as well as current context.

2. The required applications—those that will be necessary to achieve the business objectives and strategy within the business planning horizon *and* can be shown to have specific contributions to make.

3. The potential applications—those that might prove valuable in the future provided they prove feasible and can be shown to have a particular contribution to make, either to the strategy directly or by significant indirect effects through improved efficiency of performance.

The different types of applications and their implications are likely to result from (respectively) a thorough situation appraisal of the business and its information requirements, an analysis of the business strategy and objectives and a creative assessment of possibilities for IS/IT in the business environment. The products of each type of process need to be interrelated and consolidated and this implies that the process will be somewhat iterative. Ideas as they crystallise will have to be reconsidered in relation to each other and the overall business options.

The overall framework described in Figure 7.2 will now be considered in more detail both in terms of the processes and products of each process and their interrelationships. All the various tools and techniques have been described in previous chapters, and this framework is a more detailed description of the overall processes and deliverables described in Chapter 3, see Figure 3.12. The first part of the discussion will consider the steps which essentially address the opportunities and threats that IS/IT poses for the business (see Figure 7.3). This involves the first six 'boxes' on the diagram mainly.

UNDERSTANDING THE INDUSTRY AND BUSINESS POSITION

As mentioned earlier, this is prerequisite to any development of an IS/IT strategy. This has to be done by the business management. The key issues to be considered are:

● the business units and their relationships to each other and to the corporate body;
● the stage of maturity of the industry or industries within which the businesses compete;
● the product portfolios of the business units and the contributions to revenues and profits and demands on resources each group of products/markets make;
● the competitive forces affecting the business units and the corporation and their impact on the business. This in turn leads to a SWOT analysis (**S**trengths, **W**eaknesses, **O**pportunities and **T**hreats) of the companies' positions with regard to each of the forces to identify areas of greatest concern and need for action.

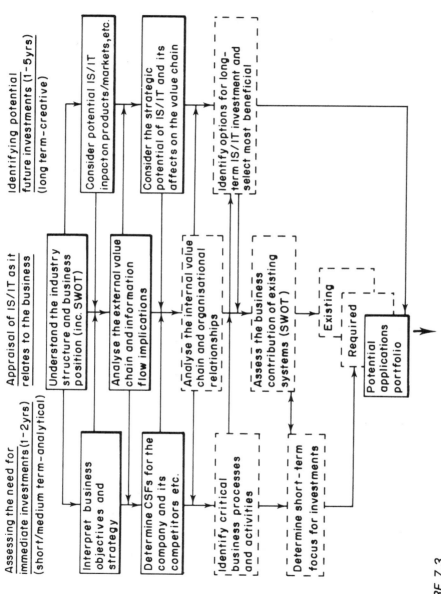

FIGURE 7.3

This stage is essentially the business strategic analysis process described in Chapter 2 and leads immediately in two directions:

(a) to consideration of the business strategy and objectives in the established business environment (see Chapter 5), and
(b) to the identification of ways in which IS/IT could impact the industry in terms of products/services/economics and be used to affect the relative strengths of the competitive forces (see Chapter 6).

Perhaps the key product of this stage of analysis is the understanding of the organisation in terms of business units, their relationships and the similarities and differences between them and the environments in which they operate. This enables a basic investment stance on IS/IT to be adopted—innovative, aggressive, defensive or survival—and this will act as guidance to the types of opportunities to be sought.

In the discussion below it will be assumed that *a* business unit will be considered and the additional implications across business units and for corporate information will be considered at the end.

Interpreting Business Objectives and Strategy (see Chapter 5)

Business objectives and strategies are the products of a number of considerations;

- what the organisation *might do* based on the environment within which it operates or by moving into new environments;
- what the organisation *wants to do* based on the values and wishes of chiefly the senior executives and stakeholders;
- what the organisation *must do* if it is to survive in its environment depending on the pressure groups and their influence;
- what the organisation *can do* based on its resources and capabilities.

Overall business objectives can be classified in a number of ways for further analysis and formulation of strategies. An adopted overall strategy will result in specific objectives for parts of the organisation which will then develop functional strategies to achieve them. The subsidiary strategies and objectives will reflect how that part of the organisation will contribute to the overall objectives of the organisation. The process can be formalised into a strict 'management by objectives' (MBO) scheme which allocates responsibility to individuals for achieving each of the objectives.

A structure of objectives and strategies is often the result and the relationships need to be established. The objectives need to be prioritised if only into high, medium and low and as far as possible measurement criteria established. One useful structure adopted by a major retailer for structuring objectives for use in determining IS/IT requirements considers 'objectives' at three levels:

(a) 'Permanent objectives' which reflect the mission and overall goals of the company—what the company might do in the long term.
(b) Strategic objectives which the company wants to achieve in the medium term.
(c) Tactical objectives which the company and divisions within the company can and must achieve in the short term to make strategic and permanent objectives attainable.

In terms of 'usable objectives' in IS/IT strategic planning (b) and (c) are most relevant and can be assessed in terms of critical success factors, etc. The 'permanent objectives' give essentially the 'why'—why the company needs or intends to do things.

Whilst objectives should be driven by the business and be set primarily in relation to external demands, often they reflect the way the current organisation and managers of it interpret that external world in terms of what they see as required to be done. They may not therefore consider enough options or may address only some of the issues. IS/IT may change objectives due to its potential impact on the business environment.

It is, therefore, at this point that we need to bring together the potential impact of IS/IT on the industry and the objectives of the organisation to either develop new objectives or qualify the priority given to existing objectives based on IS/IT threats and opportunities.

Before, therefore, looking at critical success factors it is worth considering both the objectives and potential impact of IS/IT on the business in more detail in the light of the initial situation appraisal.

Analysing the Industry (External) Value Chain and the Information Flow

The industry value chain is effectively a high level information flow model which can demonstrate the role information plays not only in terms of achieving business objectives but also in terms of how it can be used by suppliers, customers and competitors to affect the potential achievement of those objectives. The product of such analysis is an understanding of the information 'entities' which *all* the players in the industry need to manage to achieve success and this can lead to an extension of the IS requirements and potentially new or modified objectives. Considering *the potential impact of IS/IT on products/markets*, etc. identifies what could happen.

Appraising these possibilities in the light of business objectives and strategies and by overlaying them on the overall industry value chain enables consideration of what the organisation wishes to do to take advantage or otherwise of the options.

The result will lead possibly to refinement of objectives and should lead to a more focused consideration of the potential opportunities or threats, requiring some creative thinking. It will lead naturally to the extended CSF model described in Chapter 6—to consider the CSFs of customers, suppliers and competitors.

The external value chain and high level entity models then form a framework within which more detailed considerations and more specific techniques such as data flow analysis and modelling can be used.

Determining Critical Success Factors

Critical success factor analysis under many guises ('Key Issues Analysis', 'Do Wells', etc.) is the most commonly used tool in the IS strategies tool-kit. Why? When used effectively it achieves a number of requirements all vitally important to the strategic planning process. These are:

- involving top management in strategic IS planning and gaining their commitment;
- developing a consensus view of IS applications in the business;
- linking IS activity to business strategy;
- providing guides to executive information needs.

When used ineptly the approach can cause frustration, even despondency and even turn management against the planning process.

The strengths and weaknesses of the CSF approach are well documented. Shank *et al.* (1985) list practical guidelines as to their use. They highlight the needs to:

- use them in a formal structured way,
- educate people in advance regarding the process,
- not to link them explicitly to information needs.

In addition, from experience, the eliciting of CSFs probably works best (and is certainly done more quickly) in a group working process rather than by conducting interviews with numerous individuals and then trying to collate the results.

CSFs are not a technique peculiar to IS planning. They can be used to develop many aspects of business strategy. The value of a group approach is demonstrated by Hardaker and Ward (1987) when CSF analysis was used as part of a concept called Process Quality Management in IBM. The CSF process must produce agreement to move in a coherent direction which is very difficult to achieve by later consolidation rather than achieving consensus as the analysis proceeds. This also enables the CSFs to remain focused on the management 'business agenda' rather than the personal agenda of an individual. It avoids ambiguity being left unchallenged.

It can be summarised by saying that the process is as important as the product, since it achieves commitment to the outcome. If well prepared for the process senior managers find little difficulty in articulating CSFs, since they are often merely overt statements of issues that they are aware of, or are already addressing anyway.

Guidance in establishing an effective process is given in the articles mentioned above (Shank *et al.*, 1985; Hardaker and Ward, 1987) and by Rockart and Crescenzi (1984). All three are based on case history use of the technique in large organisations.

The establishment of a set of critical success factors against a set of business objectives needs a consolidation into a matrix of objectives and relevant CSFs, as described in Chapter 5. This is reasonably straightforward provided there are not too many of either one. The priority for dealing with the CSFs is not determined by the CSF ('Critical' implies no priority can be set), but by the priority of the objective which caused the success factor to be identified and the number of objectives which will be affected by its satisfactory achievement. The next stage in the process is not, however, as straightforward—interpreting CSFs in terms of information and information systems. This cannot easily be done without reference to the activities of the business and its organisation structure, which is considered below.

In order to ensure that the activities and organisations are considered in their overall context in terms of the potential impact of IS/IT the next stage is to consider in more detail how they relate (in information and systems terms) to the industry value chain. The *strategic potential of IS/IT and its effects on the overall value chain* should now be identified.

The refinements of the value chain analysis described earlier namely the Resource Life Cycle Analysis and Strategic Option Generator enable consideration of how far/over what timescale, who in particular and in what way we can and should extend the information systems beyond the internal value chain to exert appropriate influence. The critical success factors define how important it is for the organisation to do so (if at all) in order to meet the business objectives. This analysis by itself should lead to the definition of information needs and potential systems options. How feasible it is to actually develop such systems to take advantage of such opportunities will depend on the effectiveness of internal systems in linking the chain together as well as obtaining additional information and the co-operation of suppliers and customers.

To summarise the process so far. Figure 7.3 shows how far the analysis has progressed through the framework of tools and techniques. The overall products are effectively a view of the **opportunities and threats** that IS/IT offers the business, based on its relationship to the business environment and its objectives. No consideration has been made of its ability to deal with these—to take advantage or avoid being disadvantaged. The remaining steps in the process are essentially to assess the **strengths and weaknesses** of the existing IS/IT applications and information within the context of the broader business issues and identify priorities for action and needs for enhancing the capability. So far the analysis and thinking has taken an external ('outside-in') and top-down view of the business. This needs to be counterbalanced by an internal, bottom-up analysis before selecting what and how application areas are to be addressed.

Before proceeding, however, it is worth considering how long this first 'half' of the analysis should or can take and the resulting implications for the rest of the strategic planning process. It should not take too long because at this stage it is important to obtain a senior management buy-in to the potential of IS/IT in terms of business opportunities and threats. If management interest cannot be obtained at this stage sufficient to commit the organisation to the second, more internally focused stage of planning then there is little chance of later success. Given the types of analyses required most of which require predominantly business inputs, preferably in a group analytical and creative thinking process, the time available to do the work will not be great and continuity needs to be maintained to avoid repeated reworking of ideas. It is realistic from experience of companies doing this to expect 2–3 months elapsed time at the most, with the main working done in a series of workshops, led by a business manager. The IS role is to facilitate the process and perhaps document and consolidate the conclusions, without attempting to initiate action unilaterally on ideas arising unless it is apparent that resources are currently being seriously misused, or that decisions being taken are obviously inappropriate.

During the next stage of the process the IS role is significantly increased in providing management with input to help strategic decision making and identify specific implications of options available. That does not mean, however, that the second stage task should take too long. From identifying the opportunities and threats to eventually describing an outline business systems strategy for the business unit should again be no more than a 2–3 month process. If it takes much longer, earlier work may have to be repeated or management will have lost interest, since nothing appeared to result from the time they spent.

The second half of the process will now be considered in more detail (see Figure 7.4).

ANALYSING THE INTERNAL VALUE CHAIN AND ORGANISATIONAL RELATIONSHIPS

One thing is almost certain at this stage: the analysis of the internal value chain to identify what the business does and the analysis of the organisation to show how it is structured to do it, will produce a mismatch. When the dynamics of how the organisation structure works are considered this will confuse the picture even more! Equally inevitably existing systems and information resources will have been established more from an organisational than value chain perspective.

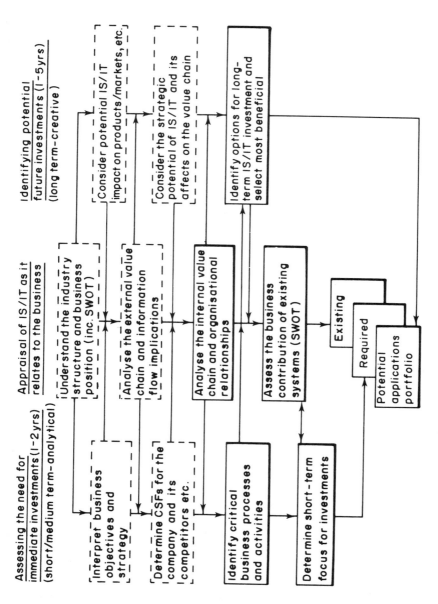

FIGURE 7.4

Also, the situation is not static. The business may be changing, developing or retrenching, and reorganisation of functions and people, structure and dynamics, will be a continuing process.

Of the three dimensions to the problem, the value chain offers a firmer foundation for analysis than organisational structure or dynamics in terms of analysing the key businesses' activities and identifying information and systems requirements. It is, therefore, important to identify the primary activities of the business, those essential to the value adding process, and describe the key information requirements of each and the links between them. These can then be considered as part of the information flow through the industry in relation to suppliers and customers and if necessary the existing value chain can be 'extended' or redefined in terms of those external relationships. The internal primary chain essentially describes how the business operates, not how it is controlled or developed. Control and development involve both primary and support activities and information to enhance these processes will be derived from and overlaid on to the information and systems in the primary activities. Control and development activities are more dependent on the organisation and its dynamics than the basic business value adding structure. The value chain model is less useful in analysing the 'support' activities.

Opportunities for gaining advantage from IS/IT exist in both primary and support functions as do 'opportunities' to incur a disadvantage, although in the latter case the disadvantage incurred will be more immediately obvious due to failure in the primary functions. This reinforces the need to establish a clearly understood *internal primary value chain* within which to evaluate the strengths and weaknesses of existing applications. This primary value chain is essentially a high level information flow model for the operation of the business.

Having established the model, the organisation structure can be examined to allocate functions which do fulfil a primary role into the model. Many organisational units will contain primary and support functions, and these need to be separated. Some 'support' activities will exist merely because of poor linkages with other functions, their existence the result of 'failure' in another part of the organisation. Many of these will be due to systems or information management weaknesses elsewhere and these problems need to be cured at source. The value chain is likely to expose such problems—organisational analysis may obscure them.

As has been said, support activities are more organisationally dependent and either assist in controlling the primary activities where integrated and/or consistent controls need to be applied, or are instrumental in the planning and development of the business by co-ordination of planning etc., of the business across primary and secondary functions. They need to be analysed in terms of the contribution of information they need from primary functions, plus any additional information they require and also in terms of how primary functions can obtain information from them in order to manage their activities successfully.

Information and systems can be used to improve efficiency, enhance management's effectiveness or add value to the business in terms of external perception. To focus attention appropriately, therefore, it is important to identify where costs are incurred, where success depends on management effectiveness and how and where value is added.

Accounting systems offer a basis for cost allocation although they will inevitably reflect organisational rather than value chain groupings of cost. It is not impossible and obviously desirable to reallocate the costs of the business to the value chain functions to identify areas of most potential benefit. This again will separate 'primary' and 'secondary' costs. Business objectives and critical success factors offer a basis for assessing management effectiveness, through their achievement or otherwise. A very fruitful step in the analysis is to overlay all the CSFs on the value chain to identify which parts are more critical to overall business success than others—to identify the business critical activities and their interdependence. CSFs which cannot be so allocated need to be questioned, since organisational ownership of a CSF is important if it is to be dealt with. The external view of the business developed earlier in the process offers guidance as to how and where the company adds value in relation to suppliers/customers and in comparison with competitors. This can be transposed into the value chain to highlight areas for enhancing the value adding aspects of the business. Figure 7.5 attempts to consolidate these ideas, using a retailing type company value chain.

From this stage it is now possible to *identify the critical business processes and activities* based on CSFs and the way the company adds value/incurs cost and is managed. The overlay of CSFs will also show up the interdependence of functions. By following the more detailed data flow analysis processes described in Chapter 5 the information and systems implications can be analysed into those which are critical to current business success, those which are likely to affect future success and those which merely support the business processes—i.e. Strategic/Factory/Support information and systems. Again, the DFDs and Data Entity models will show the dependence of processes on sources of data across the organisation, and the need for integration or otherwise of information resources.

Having overlaid the value chain and organisation it is now possible to assess the value of the various IS/IT opportunities developed through the 'creative' thinking route in terms of whether they could have an immediate impact or are of longer-term potential. They need to be reconsidered in terms not only of whether they could provide the company with potential advantage or reduce threats, but also whether and how they contribute to the chosen business strategy and how they would improve the operations and development of the business. This will depend on how they affect the objectives/critical success factors and whether they address critical business activities. Because of the rationale of the overall process the ideas should not be totally independent of the prevailing business needs. Some, however, may be beyond the current objective horizon but should be kept within the portfolio as high potential ideas which may

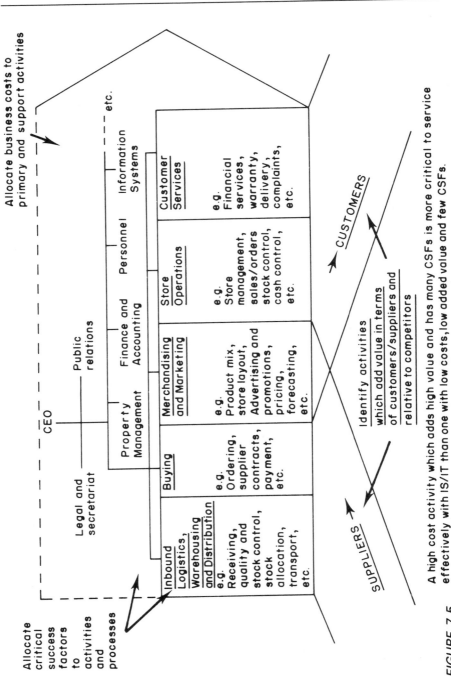

FIGURE 7.5

become more valuable as the business moves forward and the environment changes. That is especially true of ideas which would equally well apply to competitors. The selection process is essentially a decision on each idea in terms of *why* it should be pursued or not in the next few months or year, i.e. is it strategic to the business?

The overall route through the 'creative' chain can be summarised as:

- what could IS/IT do for all the firms in the industry, in terms of changing business parameters?
- what could IS/IT do for the company based on its particular position within the industry?
- which things offer most immediate benefit in terms of the business objectives/strategy and the way the company operates and is managed?

Two steps of the overall process remain to be considered. It is only at this stage that the existing applications need to be brought into the assessment. The process of 'fact finding' in Chapter 5 determines what needs to be known about them, the remaining task is to assess them in terms of current contribution and potential future contribution to the business. This is effectively a strengths and weaknesses analysis. In order to do this an application or system may need to be broken down into its component functions.

For example, the 'Accounts Receivable' system may consist of several functions:

- customer account maintenance,
- sending out statements,
- bad debt control,
- cash flow forecasting,
- information to marketing on customer purchases.

Some of these are more critical to business success than others. It is functions that are important, not system names and both are more important than the acronym given the system for IS and user convenience. These systems functions can be mapped on to the DFD and entity models to identify gaps, weak links, duplication, etc. as previously described. Equally, this may show how complete and well integrated some functions are and as such are an asset that does not need attention or could even be a strength on which to build.

At the two extremes: some applications are entirely worthless and should be discontinued: some applications may have considerable potential which is under-exploited. In between, the strengths and weaknesses can be assessed in terms of potential actions required. Figure 7.6 attempts to show such a classification. The analysis should include all applications, whether centrally managed, departmental or on personal computers.

Exploit strengths

e.g.

- high future potential, currently under-exploited

  - can be extended, enhanced to be of more value

    - could be more valuable if integrated more effectively or used more extensively

      - critical to the business but data quality is poor

        - needs to be developed to meet current and future business needs

          - needs to be redeveloped to meet changed business requirements for future

            - system required but needs to be reimplemented to absorb less resources or overcome technology obsolescence

              - system will be less important in future—needs to be simplified/reduced to real needs

                - system is no longer of value—should be discontinued

                    Overcome weaknesses

FIGURE 7.6

This approach can then be followed through in terms of where in the organisation action needs to be taken. Looking at the problem in reverse, it is worth considering why systems fail, and who is responsible for the failure, according to its reason for occurring. The diagram in Figure 7.7 is adapted from extensive research into the reasons for information systems failure by Lyytinen and Hirschheim (1987). The 'face' of the box is the prime concern here, although the dimensions of failure obviously encompass the development process and system operation as well as the achievability of objectives.

Failure can occur in five domains which, from the inside outwards are:

(a) *Technical failure*: This is clearly the domain of IS/IT who are responsible for the technical quality of the system and the technology it uses. Technical failure is now usually the easiest and often the cheapest to overcome.

(b) *Data failure*: This is a shared responsibility between IS/IT and the users who input the data. Obviously good data design, processing integrity and sound data management practice are the IS/IT responsibility but not everything can be legislated for and effectiveness of user procedures and data quality control fall clearly in the user domain.

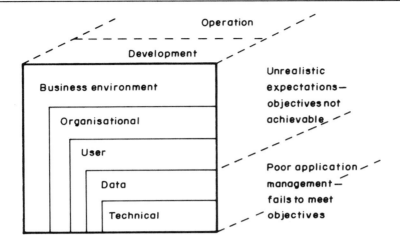

FIGURE 7.7 Failure of information systems—areas for potential failure

(c) *User failure*: Whilst blame for the user misunderstanding the system or being ineptly advised or trained may accrue to the IS/IT professionals, the primary responsibility for using the system appropriately and to its maximum capability must rest with the user management. Many systems become less effectively used over time as staff change and training investment is insufficient.

(d) *Organisational failure*: Systems may be satisfactory in meeting particular functional needs but may fail because they do not satisfy the organisation overall, its operations and their interrelationships. For example, a budgetary control system specified for and by accountants at the centre may fail to meet the needs of line managers to plan and control different types of business expenditure. Responsibility here clearly lies outside the IS/IT domain and must be shared by users and senior management for not aligning systems to organisational needs.

The Lyytinen and Hirschheim analysis considers only these four domains, but a fifth and potentially more serious area of failure exists and coping effectively with this will become more critical as the IS/IT investment becomes more strategic to the business.

(e) *Failure in the business environment*: the systems are or become inappropriate to the market requirements due to changing business practice instigated by others, or by not supporting a changing business strategy adequately or by simply not coping with volume and speed of business process needs economically. The responsibility for this is essentially senior management's, although without active user and IS input they cannot be expected to identify the problems, but they must underwrite action to correct them. The front page of *Computing* on 6 October 1988 carried the headline: 'Catalogue King Looks Up Cost of TP Shortfall' and went on to describe how Great Universal Stores estimated it had lost £133 million of sales because 'its computer systems are out-of-date'. With modern on-line integrated systems 'there is no doubt that we could have done an extra 5% on our current sales' to quote a director. The systems had clearly failed to meet the needs of a rapidly changing mail-order business environment, although they have a 45% market share.

Some applications will be weaknesses due to more than one of the above reasons and corrective action may have to become a collective responsibility. However, it is important to ascertain the cause to avoid merely, if expensively, changing or redeveloping a system to overcome its weaknesses only to find the problems recur once more. This has happened!

The process outlined throughout this chapter has been designed to avoid the more serious domains of failure, namely organisational and business environment from causing the enterprise to fail to achieve its objectives because of IS/IT!

Each of these last steps in the process is focused on defining the future portfolio of applications. The creative route will produce ideas which will be generally categorised as:

(a) High potential—worth evaluating further, and
(b) Strategic—the idea relates to the business strategy.

The current portfolio analysis will probably highlight some applications in each quadrant, though they are likely to fill the factory and support boxes more than the other two. From this will come a need to consolidate strategic and high potential applications derived from various routes plus a need to address the weaknesses in terms of the current contribution of factory and support systems to the business. Determining which weaknesses to address first will depend not only on current impact but on whether it will be increasingly or decreasingly important in the future. That in turn depends on how critical the activity it supports will be or whether it can impact any critical success factors. Will, for instance, not integrating a system make a further strategic application impossible? CSFs determine what is of strategic importance, what offers the highest potential, and what are the key weaknesses to be overcome. They have little, if nothing, to do with Support applications where decisions must be based on economic, resource consumption and technological arguments. These arguments will be expanded on in the next chapter. At this stage it is perhaps worth emphasising that it is perhaps of more importance that weaknesses are addressed first, provided they are serious in terms of turning into a real threat to the business or are precluding opportunities being taken. In addition, some opportunities which are not dependent on anything else are invested in, in particular where they build on existing strengths, giving more chance of success.

The overall process has been described completely. It is not a methodology but a way of bringing together the various techniques of analysis to ensure that the overall product is more complete and of greater value than the sum of the parts. No one technique exclusively addresses only one segment of the portfolio, and no one technique can produce certainty of conclusions. Figure 7.2 has one additional arrow showing the need for the next stage—managing the portfolio. Before moving on to that stage, one further aspect needs to be discussed—how would this process be used in a multi-SBU company and what are the implications?

DEALING WITH LARGE ORGANISATIONS, MULTIPLE SBUs AND THEIR CONSOLIDATION

Most multi-business unit enterprises will have some opportunities to benefit from looking not just at one business unit, but also across them, before deciding on how best to meet the needs. Figure 3.7 described in Chapter 3 demonstrates the basic relationships.

The potential synergistic and economic opportunities will be affected by a number of factors, not least of which is corporate management's desire to gain such benefits across the business units. Each business unit may be seen merely as part of a 'portfolio' which is continually being changed by buying and selling businesses for primarily financial reasons. In such a case synergistic and economic benefits will at best be short-lived, if achievable at all. In most other circumstances, however, the overall corporate benefits from IS/IT opportunities will often exceed the sum of the parts.

The factors which can effect the corporate as opposed to purely business unit 'value added' of IS/IT, are in outline as follows:

(a) Whether the units compete in the same or different industries. This is obviously true—a financial services unit will have little in common with a plastic bag manufacturing unit. However, there may be similarities elsewhere.
(b) Whether the units are in similar relative positions in their industries (strong, average, weak), whether the industries have similar rates of growth (or decline) and whether the types and mix of competitors is different.
(c) Whether they have the same customers and/or suppliers, where information can be shared and value chain links could be mutually developed.
(d) Whether they trade with one another, i.e. are related in a value chain where IS/IT links could give the company overall an advantage.
(e) Whether they carry out similar activities, e.g. two retail units could have different customers and sell different products but essentially consist of the same functions (e.g. DIY retailing and haberdashery), i.e. are the internal value chain components similar?
(f) Whether they have similar objectives and are adopting similar strategies and as a consequence have similar critical success factors or not. Units with different CSFs will have significantly different IS/IT priorities.

(g) Whether the parent company requires a consistent, even standard structure of information from all the units.

(h) Whether support activities are broadly similar and organised in the same basic structure.

(i) Whether the existing applications are based on the same hardware/software/data infrastructure or at least are not incompatible.

These imply opportunities exist in all the 'inputs' to the strategic planning process (i.e. external and internal, business and IS/IT environments) for the corporation overall to gain from synergy and economies. Opportunities or threats in one business unit may expose a weakness, which can be overcome by a strength in another business unit. It is, therefore, important to compare results of the analyses and share ideas. Any of the techniques, at any stage of the 'process' outlined above could reveal such cross-unit opportunities, so all results need to be 'pooled' for others to adapt, adopt, or join in the development if appropriate. An idea from one part of the business, adapted by another may even offer more benefits.

If the effort of strategic IS planning is worthwhile, then additional extra work to build on or share ideas could yield significantly greater benefits and avoid considerable duplication of effort across the overall business. This will be considered further in Chapter 8 from the point of supply management. Obviously, if similar opportunity led demands can be identified the scope will be greater to gain benefits from co-ordinated supply management.

SUMMARY

Chapters 3 to 6 described models for IS/IT strategic planning, an overall process for planning and tools and techniques of strategic analysis. This chapter has attempted to bring these together in order to describe a framework by which the business information systems strategy can be developed and then represented in terms of *what* information and systems the business must, should and might have to achieve maximum benefit in its business environment.

The IS/IT strategy consists of much more than this but without business needs and opportunities so identified and defined the rest of the strategy is worth very little—*how* to improve the achievement of things that are not very important! Whilst not every threat can be anticipated, every opportunity spotted, each strength exploited or weakness overcome, the framework for using the tools and techniques should enable fewer threats and opportunities to be missed and IS/IT strengths and weaknesses to be understood better in terms of their business implications.

The framework may seem rather conceptual, even theoretical, and it may be that various steps can be short-circuited and appropriate conclusions drawn much earlier in the process. There is no point in exhaustive correlation when ideas obviously make sense, but many ideas cannot be evaluated without consideration from a number of viewpoints. The approach taken in this chapter assumes that little correlates until it is viewed from a number of angles, or arises from various analyses or creative thinking processes.

The framework attempts to bring together analytical processes and focused creative thinking approaches to enable the products of both to be considered *as they arise*. This is more realistic than waiting for all the analysis and all the ideas to be generated and then to examine them all together, to distil all the resulting conclusions.

That is not the way the best ideas and strategies evolve and develop. Good ideas and insights will occur throughout the process, and they need to be capitalised on there and then, as far as possible, not put on the shelf for later consideration when their 'value' may have been forgotten.

Whilst the framework is therefore somewhat 'ideal', it does include all the tools and techniques, which are generally considered useful, in a logically linked process. It also ensures all the types of strategic input, both external and internal are assessed in relation to one another. It does enable an outline business IS strategy to be identified and achieve a consensus of agreement and attract management endorsement in a matter of a few weeks or, at worst, months—in time for it to be planned and implemented to achieve its benefits.

It must also be remembered that planning is a continuous and continuing process and the formulative framework described above will have to be repeatedly revisited to ensure the portfolio as foreseen is still relevant. As factors inside or outside the business change, in the business or IS/IT environment the conclusions to be drawn from each step in the framework may change and therefore some paths through the process will have to be readdressed to identify implications and reflect these quickly in the expressed portfolio. However, it is equally important not to need to repeat the whole process if any particular factor changes.

The management of such application portfolios is considered in depth in the next chapter, in terms of ensuring demand for applications based on needs and ideas generated, as above, can be successfully supplied. Later chapters then consider in more detail strategies for managing key aspects of the delivery of that supply to satisfy the variety of requirements inherent in the applications.

REFERENCES

Hardaker, M. and Ward, B. K. (1987) 'Getting things done—how to make a team work', *Harvard Business Review* (Nov.–Dec.).

Lyytinen, K. and Hirschheim, R. (1987) 'Information systems failures—a survey and classification of the empirical literature', *Oxford Surveys in IT*, **4**, 257–309.

Rockart, J. F. and Crescenzi, A. D. (1984) 'Engaging top management in information technology', *Sloan Management Review* (Summer).

Shank, M. E., Boynton, A. C. and Zmud, R. W. (1985) 'Critical success factor analysis as a methodology for MIS planning', *MIS Quarterly*, **9**(2) (June).

Chapter 8
MANAGING THE APPLICATIONS PORTFOLIO

INTRODUCTION

In Chapter 1 various application portfolio models were considered and a model developed from McFarlan's 'Strategic Grid' has been used as a key idea in subsequent chapters (see Figure 1.8). The model proposes an analysis of all existing, planned and potential applications into four categories based on an assessment of the current and future business importance of each application. An application can be defined as 'STRATEGIC', 'TURNAROUND' (or HIGH POTENTIAL), 'FACTORY' (or KEY OPERATIONAL), or 'SUPPORT' depending on its current or expected contribution to business success.

The original McFarlan Strategic Grid was devised as a way of plotting the *overall* expected contribution of IS/IT to the business success. This is of limited value since every enterprise is likely to have some strategic, some factory, some support and some turnaround applications. Over time the contents of the portfolio will change and for any organisation the contents of segments of the portfolio will be influenced by a variety of internal and external factors as described in Chapter 7. The usefulness of this derivative matrix is borne out by the ease with which management are willing to and can categorise applications according to their perceived business contribution and potential. The limitations of the original strategic grid are also borne out by the research of Hirschheim *et al.* (1988) who found when surveying the views of IS management, that 'it was an unhelpful way of categorising (the whole) IS function since virtually every company had systems in all four categories'. This derivative model has, however, proved effective in providing a framework by which agreement on the portfolio of business applications available and required can be reached from the often divergent views of senior management, functional line managers and the IS professionals. Once that agreement has been reached the organisation can move forward along mutually agreed paths toward the delivery of the required portfolio. It is a simple concept which enables consensus to be achieved both as a strategy is initially conceived and later as the business and its requirements evolve.

The 'McFarlan Grid' is not the only matrix approach to have been developed to aid the definition of strategic options and the implications of the evolving application portfolio. Other such models, whilst considering marginally different aspects of IS/IT strategic management, offer additional insight and enable the basic model to be extended to provide more value as a tool in IS/IT strategic planning. Some of these ideas are summarised in the early part of the chapter.

The similarities of this matrix to the well known and previously described Boston Matrix, developed for managing product portfolios, are immediately obvious and offer a source of ideas well understood by business management from which further insight can be gained.

Other work, which describes successful IS/IT management approaches can be overlaid on to the grid to offer guidance towards the most appropriate mix of strategies to achieve the required portfolio. These propose a cause and effect relationship—a particular strategy causing by its intrinsic nature certain types of application to be developed.

This approach to application portfolio management offers considerable help in determining the strategy. However, like any simplification of a complex problem, it has its limitations. Precision should not be expected, merely guidance to support the process of management decision making. However, as will be seen subsequently, it does offer significant overall guidance when considering the details of IS/IT strategic planning and implementation as described in later chapters. It is a valuable 'framework', which helps link together and reconcile the difficult issues involved in managing the demand and supply components of IS/IT strategy.

CONCLUSIONS FROM VARIOUS MATRICES AND MODELS

A number of matrices have been produced to help management decision making with respect to IS/IT planning, utilisation and resourcing. These have been analysed in detail in an article by one of the authors (Ward, 1988). Some of the conclusions from that analysis are useful to show how the ideas are generally complementary, even convergent. A composite matrix, including some key ideas, is shown in Figure 8.1.

The main models on which the composite matrix is based include the following:

(a) *The Sullivan matrix* (see Sullivan, 1985)—has already been described in Chapter 3 and considers the types of IS/IT planning approaches required, depending on the combination of *infusion* and *diffusion* of IS/IT in the organisation.

Infusion is 'the degree to which IS/IT has penetrated a company in terms of importance, impact or significance', and diffusion is 'the degree to which IS/IT has been disseminated or scattered throughout the company'.

He identifies the need for new demand driven and decentralised planning approaches to improve the management of the strategic and high potential quadrants in addition to the better understood planning approaches required for 'backbone' (factory) and 'traditional' (support) systems. These new approaches are based on the identification and use of critical success factors plus an 'eclectic' planning method to deal with the strategic aspects when IS/IT is considered in establishing the objectives or is being used to transform business processes—i.e. when there is a complex relationship between IS/IT and the business.

(b) *The ITAA* (Information Technology Assessment and Adoption) *matrix* developed by Munro and Huff (1985) based on work by Rockart *et al.* (1984) considers how organisations have adopted IS/IT as a competitive weapon. They consider the relative roles and importance of business issues and technology in the process of developing so-called strategic systems. Most companies it seems are either 'technology driven'—looking for ways of deploying new technology to advantage—or 'issues driven'—looking for new business opportunities within the known possibilities of existing technology. These relate to high potential and factory type environments mainly and few companies achieve 'normative' planning where issues and technology are effectively matched—an 'ideal' planning relationship as they describe it.

(c) Two matrices developed by *Ives and Learmonth* (1984) and *Galliers* (1987a) rely to some extent on earlier work by McLaughlin *et al.* (1983). Both consider how the 'value adding potential' of IS/IT in the business and the 'quality of IS resources', i.e. the ability of the organisation to affect what is done with IS/IT and how it is managed. They consider how vision of what is possible plus strength of resources are essential if IS/IT is to be used as an offensive weapon—i.e. strategic—and how the two are often interrelated. In most organisations the lack of vision reduces the ability of even good resources to do more than 'explore' opportunities as issues arise. Low quality of resource implies a 'safe'/support systems only approach and the company will become very vulnerable due to its inability to respond to new high potential or strategic applications developed by competitors. In such a case 'vision' is not enough—the resource must be improved at the same time and it must 'beware' of IS/IT investments by competitors.

(d) *Galliers* (1987b) developed a matrix based on analyses of IS/IT planning approaches described by Hirschheim (1982). Like the Sullivan matrix it considers factors affecting planning methods but this time in relation to

  (i) long- and short-term thinking—strategy or issue driven, and
  (ii) business issues versus technology driven planning (rather like the ITAA matrix).

He separates the need of IS/IT to react to current business issues (factory) from the need to react to changing future objectives (strategic) and compares these to the proactive IS/IT stance required for high potential opportunities. Like most others he identifies an efficiency, problem-solving basis for managing support type systems.

In most of the matrices, all of which address similar issues from different directions, clear differences can be seen in the way applications in each of the four quadrants of the matrix need to be planned and managed. Not all ideas map precisely on to the original grid and there is not always full agreement on the specific needs

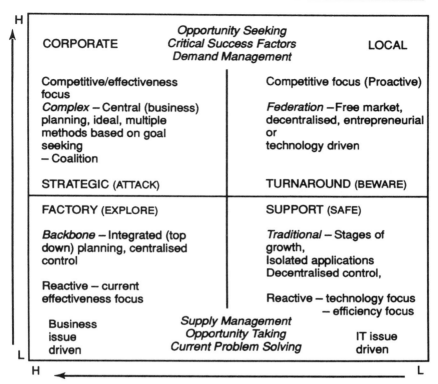

FIGURE 8.1

of the strategic and high potential segments, perhaps due to their more uncertain and newer nature. However, the agreement in the factory and support areas is very close. The composite matrix in Figure 8.1 attempts to reflect the key ideas and the terminology used in the analyses briefly summarised above.

The axes chosen are derived primarily from the McFarlan matrix. The horizontal axis attempts to reflect the ability of an organisation to control its destiny whereas the vertical axis reflects the uncertainty due to external forces of future IS/IT impact.

Matrix analysis approaches are attractive because they reduce an apparently infinite continuum of alternatives to a manageable, pertinent number of discrete options from which high level directions can be determined. They demonstrate relationships which evolve over time, but which will normally have to be managed to success simultaneously in the organisation.

Like many such models developed to assist management they are often over-simple and more complex models would be needed to reflect the diversity of reality. As complexity is added, however, clarity of perception often dims! Without intending to introduce confusion by complexity it is worth considering a fourth aspect of the models.

All the models seem to address the relationship between two or more of four variables or forces determining the role of IS/IT in the organisation:

- Business requirements,
- Competitive pressures,
- IS/IT potential,
- IS/IT delivery capability.

In various ways most of the matrices address the need to manage IS/IT *supply* (which traditionally predominates) in harmony with IS/IT *demand* (which is not entirely under the control of the organisation in a competitive environment).

Also, they address the need to accommodate *centralised* and *decentralised* management approaches which will depend on the degree of integration, both desirable and feasible, required in the applications of IS/IT, or at least how those application requirements are likely to manifest themselves. These various issues are brought together in Figure 8.2.

Particular competitive opportunities and uses of new IS/IT will address singular or few applications and, initially at least, can be exploited most advantageously close to the business opportunity. Applications which produce benefits by business integration or sharing of assets require centralised co-ordination which will only be achieved by effective planning within the business planning

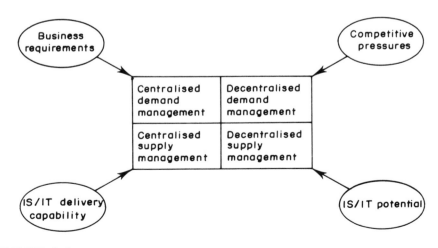

FIGURE 8.2

framework and will need competent IS/IT management to achieve long-term goals.

All of the matrices generally suggest this overall pattern.

GENERIC IS/IT MANAGEMENT STRATEGIES

Based on extensive observation of the realities of IS/IT management processes in many organisations Parsons (1983) describes six strategies which are prevalent as the means by which organisations link the management of IS/IT to the corporate or business management processes. His linking strategies (called 'generic strategies' hereafter) are 'general frameworks which guide the opportunities for IT which are identified, the IT resources which are developed, the rate at which new technologies are adopted, the level of impact of IT within the firm, etc.' The six strategies described are 'the central tendencies which firms use to guide IT within the business', hence the adoption of the word 'generic' since this definition is similar to the Porter concept of generic business strategies of low cost and differentiation, etc.

Generic strategies are ways of succeeding in the management of IS/IT in the long term provided the appropriate strategy or mix of strategies are adopted in a given set of circumstances. Parsons describes the characteristics and implications of each strategy in detail. Those characteristics and implications will be summarised here sufficient for an understanding of each strategy and the differences amongst them. How they can be employed as part of the IS strategic planning processes will then be considered.

Parsons' strategies are:

Centrally planned
Leading edge
Free market
Monopoly
Scarce resource
Necessary evil

They are well titled since the very names evoke a basic understanding of the attitudes and behaviour that each is likely to produce. The key points of each, and their pros and cons, will be outlined before considering the implications.

Centrally Planned

- IS/IT strategy is totally integrated and interdependent with corporate strategy through a centralised, senior, dedicated agency.
- This enables understanding of competitive opportunities and requirements, resources to be optimally deployed and large investments to be undertaken, especially those which span a number of proposed applications.

The strategy is very demanding of senior management time, and can be difficult to make effective in many organisations. It can also become removed from 'sharp end' business realities and may inhibit innovation.

Leading Edge

- Implies an intrinsic acceptance that IS/IT will create competitive advantage and hence 'state-of-the-art' technology must be sustained.
- Involves R&D expenditure and often many wasted investments, and requires senior management commitment to the concept, if not heavy involvement.

It can be expensive and requires adept management to convert entrepreneurial ideas to effective applications. It is not a strategy which can be adopted for all IS/IT applications, but is required if technology developments are to be exploited. 'Leading edge' implies relative to IS/IT use in the particular industry.

Free Market

- Implies that user management knows what is best for the business, including IS/IT.
- Internal services must compete with outside vendors and expect little attention from senior management.

It can cause duplication of investment and differential rates of development across the organisation, but will lead to business/user driven innovation in IS/IT usage. It is not a strategy which produces integration of systems.

A true free market implies that if users can choose how to resource their applications, any IS group must be allowed to sell its services outside the corporation.

Monopoly

- IS/IT is a sole source utility or service within the organisation.
- User satisfaction with services is the main measure of its effectiveness.
- The overall expenditure on IS/IT is easy to identify.

It can mean innovation is slow and hence unable to respond to competitive needs, since the users do not perceive IS in that role. However, a well-run monopoly will provide a very professional service in terms of systems quality. The ability to satisfy all user demands implies having excess capacity to respond to urgent needs. The existence of an IS application backlog implies a failure to satisfy user requirements.

Scarce Resource

- A budget is set in advance and applications compete for a share of the resource available.
- A very popular strategy which ensures careful management of IS/IT resources using financial controls.
- Investments must be well justified in hard financial terms, and a tendency to focus on the returns on investment in setting priorities prevails.

Given management's view that IS is a cost centre and the objective is controlled well justified use of IT, it is not conducive to IT being exploited or speculated with as a business weapon. The strategy does not recognise changes in demand, and priority setting will be a major issue in the planning process.

Necessary Evil

- A strategy of only deploying IS/IT to meet legal requirements and for very high return investments, i.e. using IS/IT only where no other alternative is available!

The strategy has many disadvantages, unless IS/IT is almost entirely irrelevant to the business, or the business itself is being treated as a low priority for investments of any type.

A necessary evil strategy normally occurs by mistake or neglect, perhaps due to over-zealous scarce resourcing. Symptoms of such a situation are high staff turnover and very defensive IS managers unable and unwilling to take any risks. Demoralisation then leads to a lack of capability. Such situations can, however, be observed in many companies in many industries at certain times—they are very difficult to get out of. As a strategy in the context of this book it is of little relevance, except where it exists!

Figure 8.3, derived from Parsons' work, summarises a number of other attributes and issues provoked by the strategies.

In practical terms these strategies as described above have certain key differences, some of which are more obvious than others.

Central planning and monopoly have certain similarities but central planning is essentially a demand management strategy by which the business and IS together plan the best route to achieving all the main demands for applications. Monopoly is a supply management strategy—controlling the supply of technology and resources, not funds, to satisfy the evolving user needs. It does not mean that the IS group does all the work—but gives permission for users to solve problems within the preferred supply strategy.

	Centrally Planned	Leading Edge	Free Market	Monopoly	Scarce Resource	Necessary Evil
REQUIRES	• knowledgeable and involved senior management • a mechanism for planning IS/IT within the business planning process	• commitment of funds and resources • innovative IS/IT management • strong technical skills	• knowledgeable users • accountability for IS/IT at business or functional level • willingness to duplicate effort • loose IT budget control	• user acceptance of the philosophy • policies to force through single sourcing • good forecasting of resource usage	• tight budgetary control of all IS/IT expenses • policies for controlling IS/IT and users	• very tight IT control • meet basic needs only
MANAGEMENT LOGIC	• central co-ordination of all requirements will produce better decision making	• technology can create business advantages and risks are worth taking	• market makes the best decisions and users are responsible for business results • integration is not critical	• information is a corporate good and an integrated resource for users to employ	• information is limited resource and its development must be clearly justified	• information is not important to business
INTERNAL IS ROLE	• provide services to match the business demands by linking closely with business managers	• push forward boundaries of technology use on all fronts	• competitive and probably profit centre intended to achieve a return on its resources	• to satisfy users' requirements as they arise but non-directive in terms of the uses of IS/IT	• make best use of a limited resource by tight cost control of expenses and projects. Justify investment projects	• maintain minimum resources and skill levels and respond to well justified needs only by ROI
USERS ROLE	• identify the potential of IS/IT to meet business needs at all levels of the organisation	• use the technology and identify the advantages it offers	• identify, source and control IS/IT developments	• understand needs and present them to central utility to obtain resources etc.	• identify and cost justify projects passive unless benefits are identified	• very passive and no role in the IS/IT resource development

FIGURE 8.3 (From Gregory L. Parsons, Fitting Information Systems Technology to the Corporate Needs: The Linking Strategy, Note 9-183-176. Boston, Mass.: Harvard Business School, 1983. Reprinted by permission)

Scarce resourcing is a financial management strategy which asks users and IS to explain the value of investments in financial terms. It is not the negative attitude to IS/IT that necessary evil implies.

Free market and leading edge are strategies for innovation, the former led by business demands, the latter driven by technological developments.

These strategies can be overlaid on to the evolutionary models discussed in Chapter 1. As overall or predominating strategies each (with the exception of necessary evil) can be seen to have a span of time when it will have most appeal to management. Figure 8.4 attempts to show this and also overlays the main stages in the evolution of the IS/IT planning processes.

The match is not perfect but that is to be expected from an attempt to overlay three simplified models. However, it does correspond to a common path of evolution found in many companies, as different strategies dominate the management approach at different stages of evolution.

In the early days of IS/IT either individual departments began to develop systems independently and/or the investments were justified by return on investment—offsetting the capital and development costs against calculated efficiency benefits. As investments increased resources were often centralised to achieve economies of scale, integration and higher quality of results in the long term. Large monopolies, however, became constrictive, backlogs built up and users became frustrated with the limited supply options available. By the early 1980s personal computers enabled users to overcome some of these constraints and seek their own solutions. Often this caused a major rift between the monopolistic centre and the newly liberated users. At about the same time senior management attitudes to funding the ever-increasing IS/IT cost centre initiated

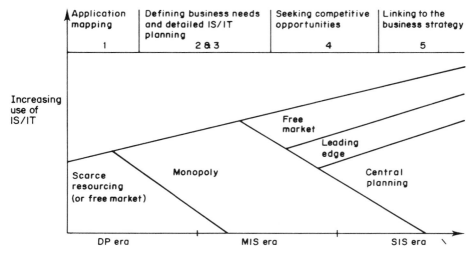

FIGURE 8.4 Stages of IS/IT planning evolution

attempts to improve its contribution by forcing a 'profit centre' motivation— deliberately forcing a free market. The response of many previously inert IS/IT monopolies to market pressure was to extend their technology base into newer technologies which had been previously resisted. As the full understanding of strategic IS potential arrives in organisations, processes of central planning are developed to enable links with business strategy to be made.

That may be oversimplified but the behaviour of many companies is typical of the trends. After initially haphazard beginnings to computing, it was often centralised under the financial function, often the main user and the scarce resourcing strategy is a natural consequence of financial control of IS. Many organisations still have IS as part of Finance. Most major corporations set up monopolistic style utilities in the 1960s and 1970s to provision the business with IS/IT. Many of these were restrictive monopolies and still are. Companies like British Leyland (ISTEL), Imperial Metals (IMI), the Burton Group and BTR evolved to free markets in the late 1970s and early 1980s setting up independent IS/IT companies. This trend has been followed by many others, including local government bodies in the 1980s (Warwickshire County Council, even West Wiltshire District Council). Some have found problems with this approach as the IS/IT company succeeds, develops strategic applications and then seeks a market (potentially competitors) in which to profit from those developments. Others such as ISTEL were able to price themselves out of the market for source company business as BL struggled to afford IS/IT. Major UK retailers in the 1980s have developed central planning mechanisms to enable major point of sale and network investments to be managed effectively. Financial service companies have attempted, less successfully overall, to achieve central planning as products and services begin to integrate. Banks with a long history of devolved IS/IT strategies are finding more problems than building societies who have been less IS/IT dependent historically and also have a more centralised culture. However, as they expand their business following deregulation into estate agency, insurance, banking, etc. the central planning approach is becoming strained. One significant observation is that once a free market strategy dominates it is very difficult to convert to any other, it is very expensive to 'buy out'.

It is at this level of dominating strategies that Parsons describes the implications, pointing out for instance how a scarce resource strategy will seriously inhibit the development of strategic applications because

(a) business strategy is not known or understood by users making requests
(b) business strategy is unknown to the (IS) group doing systems work
(c) strategic benefits are hard to quantify
etc.

He argues similarly with regard to each strategy, but as he points out, historically at least, management has generally adopted one approach to managing IS/IT, implying one generic strategy is prevalent. Given a limited portfolio of applications this may at some point in the past have been sufficient if not ideal. He then examines how each strategy fits on to an applications portfolio to identify the best approach available to the systems in each segment of the portfolio. He concludes that in each segment one or two strategies will work best but also that other strategies can work, although they are not ideally suited. It is from this simple and logical correlation that the generic strategies become a valuable consideration in the process of IS/IT strategic planning.

His overlay of generic strategies on the portfolio model is depicted in Figure 8.5. The strategies in capitals are the ideal strategies and those in lower case are those which can work, less effectively.

His rationale is straightforward and easy to relate not only to the portfolio management requirements but also to the issues of demand and supply, and centralisation and decentralisation raised earlier. The obvious conclusion is that an organisation will need to adopt a full range of generic strategies if it is to manage an extensive application portfolio.

Central planning is a demand management strategy whereas monopoly is essentially a supply management approach and both obviously mean strong

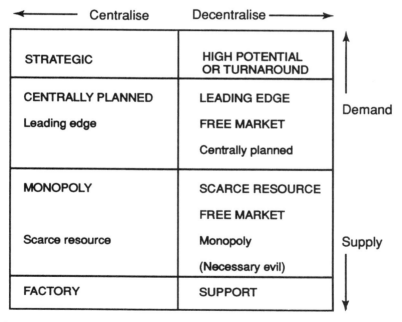

FIGURE 8.5 *Viable generic strategies related to strategic importance of systems (from Gregory L. Parsons, Fitting Information Systems Technology to the Corporate Needs: The Linking Strategy, Note 9-183-176. Boston, Mass.: Harvard Business School, 1983. Reprinted by permission)*

centralisation of control. Free market and leading edge are demand management approaches, letting users decide and/or new technology initiate demand. Free market is obviously decentralised and leading edge is dependent mainly on external supplies of technology. Scarce resource is obviously a supply management strategy and is decentralised in that once the justification rules are set the ability of any user function to satisfy them will determine what is done.

Examining some of the main reasons behind the different application types and resulting issues helps demonstrate why certain strategies are more appropriate in the different parts of the matrix. In each case the strategies correlate closely with the issues and requirements as expressed in the composite matrix (Figure 8.1).

Strategic Applications

Based on earlier discussion some key aspects of strategic applications could be restated as:

Driving Forces

- market requirements and competitive pressures,
- business objectives and management vision,
- obtaining and sustaining an advantage.

Requirements

- speed of development to meet business need,
- flexibility of solutions,
- links to associated business initiatives.

Central planning, integrated IS/IT and business planning satisfies these parameters best.

High Potential (Turnaround) Applications

Again, the driving forces and requirements can be summarised as:

Driving Forces

- business idea or technology opportunity,
- individual initiative,
- create an advantage and demonstrate its worth.

Requirements

- rapid generation of prototypes and ability to reject failures,
- understanding the potential in relation to business strategy,
- identify the best way to proceed.

Over-planning of such applications can restrict progress when uncertainty prevails. The two strategies which fit best are leading edge and free market, both of which are risky but cause innovation.

Factory Applications

Using the same format again:

Driving Forces

- improving performance of existing activities,
- integration to avoid misinformation or duplication of tasks,
- avoiding a business disadvantage.

Requirements

- high quality and long life of solutions and effective data management,
- balancing risks/costs and benefits,
- evaluation to identify most effective option.

A monopoly strategy, whilst potentially restrictive is ideal to reduce risk, providing quality solutions over the long term as IS requirements arise from business issues.

Support Applications

Driving Forces

- improved productivity and efficiency of existing tasks,
- legal requirements,
- most cost-effective use of IS/IT funds and resources.

Requirements

- lowest cost solutions in long term,
- avoiding obsolescence by evolution at pace of IS/IT industry,
- objective cost/benefit analysis to reduce financial risk.

Scarce resourcing is ideal in controlling such investments, requiring certainty of expected outcome before allocating resources. Alternatively, due to their low criticality and the low emphasis on integration each user could be allowed responsibility in a free market mode.

Parsons suggests that the secondary strategies may also work even if they are not ideal.

- Leading edge could be used (at least in part) for *strategic* applications but will be risky and potentially expensive.
- Central planning could be used to manage *high potential* applications but may reduce the pace of innovation.
- Scarce resourcing will perhaps work for *factory* systems but may increase the risks of systems failure in both business and technical terms and integration will not easily be justified.
- Monopoly is an indulgent way of meeting *support* needs and will waste resources.

The relationship with the model for IS/IT planning evolution also shows how the mix of generic strategies will have to develop and evolve over time to enable the whole mix of applications to be managed appropriately. Combining the contents of Figure 8.5 and the version of the matrix in Figure 1.11, the result is as shown in Figure 8.6. The numbers 1–5 refer to the stages of planning maturity in the Earl model in Figure 1.10.

Whilst none of the correlations amongst the various models is perfect, consistent patterns are easily identified and this consistency should enable the strategy to be developed with more confidence of eventual success. Whilst so far the use of the ideas has been expressed in general terms and exemplified in trends, etc. the next stage is to show how they can be used as high level IS/IT strategic planning tools in practice. Then more detailed aspects of portfolio management can be introduced to the framework.

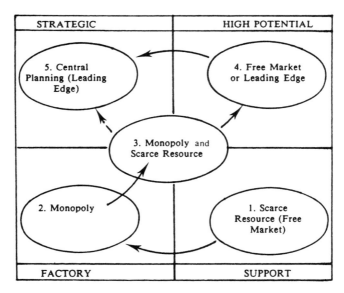

FIGURE 8.6 Portfolios, generic strategies and planning evolution

USING GENERIC STRATEGIES IN DEVELOPING THE IS/IT STRATEGY

The 'generic strategies' have primarily two uses in the process of developing the IS/IT strategy.

(a) *Diagnostic*. They are a way of assessing the current strategies being used—a clear way of expressing the ways in which IS/IT is being managed. There is a strong correlation between the applications developed and the strategies adopted. The 'generic strategies' can encapsulate the apparent complexity of the existing situation, explain it and describe it succinctly. In Box 8.1, such an analysis is exemplified for a multi-business unit company.

(b) *Formulative*. Once a future portfolio of applications can be identified using the various techniques described in earlier chapters, and the strengths and weaknesses, opportunities and threats resulting from the existing applications assessed, the generic strategies can be used to identify a migration path towards the required mix. It is superficially attractive to say 'central planning' is needed, but it might be an overkill and it is impossible to centrally plan everything. Allowing more freedom, using new technology or tighter, monopolistic control may be more appropriate in the short term. More rigorous scarce resourcing of support systems might yield resources to be deployed on strategic systems. No definitive mixture can be prescribed for every situation but the generic strategies provide a limited number of basic options from which to select an appropriate mixture which matches the application portfolio requirements. This approach avoids the need to 'invent' the strategy entirely from the 'ground up'—it is easier to define the strategic approach by modification from proven approaches to suit the particular need and then identify the action necessary to achieve the migration path.

In the second part of Box 8.1 the potential application portfolio is described and then the mix of strategies required to make it happen are outlined.

In a single business unit company these concepts are reasonably easy to apply. In a more complex, multi-business unit organisation the use is inevitably more difficult.

However, as has been emphasised throughout, the IS/IT strategic planning process must concentrate initially on the requirements of a business unit, within which the portfolio and generic strategy analyses can be utilised. In a multi-business unit organisation there then occurs another level of strategic analysis and formulation.

In a diversified conglomerate evolving through acquisition and divestment of business units the *Corporate* IS/IT generic strategy is likely to consist of a minimal centralised component—perhaps financial control systems—with an otherwise free market philosophy. This is appropriate to the business.

However, if the company is predominantly in one industry where synergy is a potential source of advantage the business unit strategies are likely to be supplemented at a corporate level by some central planning of IS/IT applications

BOX 8.1 *Using application portfolio and generic strategy techniques to develop a business information systems and management strategy for the Hammermill Paper Company (as described in Harvard Business School Case 9-183-199)*

The basic business of Hammermill, their competitive positions and the business environment in 1982 have already been outlined in Box 6.1 (case 2) and the relationships of the businesses in the value chain are shown in Figure 6.11.

Based on details of the applications in place and planned for each business and the corporate body and descriptions of the management approaches, summarised application portfolios can be drawn for a number of typical group companies and the prevalent generic strategies assigned.

1. Fine and Printing Papers

	(Electronic invoicing) (Modelling/Planning) (Links to Merchants from HILITE) (Large order system)
HILITE* Purchasing Cost control Merchant sales analysis	Various accounting and other support systems

Prevailing strategy = Monopoly.
*Integrated, on-line, order handling and production control and scheduling system.
Systems in ( ) are proposed and others exist.

Discussion: Being the original core business of the company and until recently the largest part, Fine and Printing Papers had attracted a considerable part of the IS/IT investment as with other investments. The company's central IS group (CIS) was geographically close to the main plant and provided a central resource which had been employed to develop a good base of factory systems. However, whilst new IS/IT ideas had been identified, little was being done to try them out—more 'free market' prototyping of the ideas would have probably identified the strategic value. The monopoly was generally limiting the innovative possibilities.

continued on next page

continued

2. Industrial and Packaging Papers

(Order management and customer service) (plant utilisation —optimisation)	(Wood procurement)
(New integrated order services and production/inventory control) Payables/receivables Costing/budgeting	(Personnel) Accounts, etc. Inventory management and production control

Prevailing strategy = Scarce Resource *but* a major planning exercise had produced the new application requirements (? some central planning).

Discussion: In the seventies a non-integrated set of factory and support systems had been satisfactory and resources had been reduced. However, as the business strategy changed to 'growth' the systems became a limiting factor. A strategic IS/IT planning approach had identified required replacement for factory systems with an integrated suite and also a few high potential and strategic systems. The scarce resourcing strategy of old meant the timeframe would be too long, unless significant resources were made available. However, the factory systems functions were very similar to those performed by HILITE for Fine and Printing Papers.

3. Distribution

	(Vendor analysis) (Management information systems (VIPS))
(Integrated vendor, inventory, price and sales analysis system) Financial returns	Accounting* Price Book* Stock Control* Order Processing* Receivables*

Prevailing strategy = *Free market*.
*A mixture of computerised and manual systems

Discussion: Distribution companies had been acquired over time. The systems acquired with them varied widely. The profit centre orientation of the branches discouraged

continued on next page

continued

a centralised approach due to the free market attitude of entrepreneurial managers. These two factors combined meant that although significant resources were available they were deployed maintaining a variety of largely ineffective and non-integrated systems. A BSP study identified the factory systems' requirements but they were not implemented—probably because of the monopoly approach implied—counter to the business culture. Instead further 'dreams' of MIS systems were devised—but the database would not support them.

4. Corporate

	Office automation
Financial reporting and control	

Discussion: There were very few corporate or corporately initiated systems. The attitude to IS/IT was a confused combination of Monopoly—central CIS group, scarce resourcing—budget limited and IS reported to Finance, Free Market—especially in the rapidly acquired Distribution area. Consequently, no real strategic systems were planned for corporate management or within the group. Neither were resources and skills allocated to the most worthwhile areas.

Potential Strategic IS/IT Applications

Using the types of analysis tools described in Chapters 5 and 6 a number of strategic and high potential IS applications can be clearly identified, as can the potential for rationalisation of factory and support systems. The potential future portfolio could be seen as:

Potential applications	
Market analysis product mix/profitability Communication links Overall stock management Internal trading systems Pricing Business unit strategic systems, etc.	Links to large customers/end users Corporate procurement and links to suppliers Business planning and decision support + local ideas, etc.
Distribution operational systems (VIPS1) Manufacturing operational systems (derived from HILITE?) Customer + product databases Local process control Financial reporting	Common support applications (packages) or local discretion where justified + information centre(s) Local decision support

continued on next page

---

continued ─────────────────────────────

This implies that a whole mix of strategies are required including:

(a) some central planning at corporate level and within each business unit;
(b) better resource allocation and application transfer from a monopoly centre to provide high quality factory systems;
(c) that distribution systems are a priority, both to improve operations and provide key data on the market place to other units and the corporate centre. Central planning/monopoly—not free market!
(d) Central and local scarce resourcing of support systems;
(e) some leading edge/free market business unit driven initiatives to try out high potential applications within the corporate central planning 'umbrella'.

This mixture is quite different from that prevailing.

---

and a monopolistic control over the ways of meeting key operational needs to avoid proliferation and incompatibility of solutions.

Where the organisation cannot benefit from vertical synergy, but consists of like types of companies (e.g. manufacturing, or retail, or financial services) similarity of functional requirements might be more effectively or economically satisfied from a central utility (monopoly) for those systems which are needed by many companies. For each corporate situation a suitably structured mixture can be arrived at. Box 8.1 considers such a more complex situation.

The management of the portfolio is considered in more detail below and from different viewpoints, but those views and the detailed ideas are entirely consistent with the generic strategies outlined above.

PORTFOLIO MANAGEMENT PRINCIPLES— APPLIED TO THE APPLICATION PORTFOLIO

The obvious resemblance of the strategic grid to the better known Boston Consulting Group matrix has already been mentioned. The main rationale for that resemblance is that component products or applications must be managed according to their contribution to the business over an extended life-cycle. The contribution is determined by both internal and external factors—in the case of IS/IT the external factors, market driven are becoming more and more important.

More specific parallels can be drawn:

1. Application and products both have *life-cycles*, and will move around the matrix over time.

   Turnaround applications and wild cat products are both risk investments which need to be carefully assessed as to whether or not they are of strategic importance or can become star products. As the competitive balance is restored and the application is commonly in place across the industry it moves into factory, as should a star product become a cash cow as market growth slows up. Finally as the industry moves on to a new competitive basis applications may be of support value only and similarly products move from cash cows to dogs eventually.

   It is important in both cases to avoid turnaround or wild cat investments from drifting straight down into the support or dog quadrant due to indecisive management.

   For example, on-line order handling systems, pioneered by airlines, were strategically important and provided a competitive edge to those companies who succeeded in developing them before proprietary on-line software became generally available. But once everyone in the industry had the systems they lost their strategic value, but in most cases are still of critical importance (factory) since no other viable method exists for handling the transactions efficiently and feeding product delivery and replenishment systems reliably.

2. Both applications and products require *investment funding*. This is easily seen with products where the cash generated by today's profitable products is reinvested in cash hungry future products. For applications this reinvestment is in terms of reinvesting the benefits derived from today's systems into new applications. What are those benefits?

   - Skills and experienced resources which can develop and manage effective business systems.
   - Management commitment to the use of IS/IT in the business, based on successes achieved and a perception of the value of IS/IT investments.
   - Data (or information) held in the existing applications, if well organised, is a potential source of advantage if re-invested into strategic applications.

   Lack of reinvestment will in all cases cause the accrued benefits to depreciate.

3. Both applications and products *need to be managed and have resources allocated in accordance with their business importance*, not their technical or operational peculiarities. Management capability and resources are normally in short supply and need to be continuously reallocated to obtain the best business results from the overall portfolio. Balancing the available expertise with the portfolio needs is critical to long-term success.

Overall, the main reason that the product portfolio model offers useful input to the application portfolio is that it reflects the competitive business environment. The model was developed to assist in managing and planning in an uncertain, market driven environment where management decisions are made within a total environment they can only influence not determine. IS/IT in the new competitive or strategic era is now subject to the forces of the market place—external parameters will now define the effectiveness of an organisation's IS/IT management.

Of the various analyses and conclusions that have been drawn from product portfolio models, some have particular relevance to the IS application portfolio and strategies for managing IS/IT in the new competitive era.

Figure 8.7 superimposes the two matrices. Maximising the long-term contribution to profitability of products depends on successful management in the relevant quadrant *and* successful transition management across quadrants as determined by prevailing market forces. Strategic IS application management depends on the same two factors. The particular parallels will be drawn by following the evolution of an application around the matrix.

Turnaround (Wild Cats)

IS/IT turnaround applications resemble wildcat products due to the degree of uncertainty of success—the amount of risk. Many will fail. Identifying and then transforming the successes into the next phase of the life-cycle is the objective. This implies dealing effectively with the failures and not pouring good money

STRATEGIC (STARS)	TURNAROUND (?)
● Continuous innovation ● Vertical integration ● High value added	● Process R & D ● Minimal integration ● Cost control
● Defensive innovation ● Effective resource utilisation ● High quality	● Disinvest rationalise ● Efficiency ● Sustained quality
FACTORY (CASH COWS)	SUPPORT (DOGS)

FIGURE 8.7 The business/systems portfolio matrix

and resources after bad. Three particular approaches to management are appropriate to achieving this:

- *Process R&D*—not 'product'. From the business lessons—*how* to make, market, distribute, resource the new product not just achieve the ultimate in product design. A weakness of British industry is 'over-engineering' products— satisfying the designer, not the customer! A similar problem exists in IS— satisfying the technical professional not the user. Any prototype or R&D should be undertaken to find out *how* the organisation can make best use of new IT, not to discover all it can do. Many prototypes of office automation, decision support and computer aided design have failed—not because the organisation could not benefit from the technology, but because it failed to discover how to implement it appropriately.
- *Minimal integration*—Risky ventures should be separated from mainline activities while being evaluated. Should they fail, aspects of the business should not have become dependent on them and at low cost the prototype can be aborted. Neither will the evaluation be clouded by issues not directly relevant to it. A key part of the evaluation is to decide how the integration can be best achieved—therefore, any initial integration could preclude the most effective options. Again many current new IT applications are producing disappointing results due to evaluations which are prejudiced by existing activities to which they are attached.

  Non-separation of new products has caused similar problems—contribution to the business being impossible to assess, and commitments having been undertaken which make decisions to pull out expensive.
- *Cost control*—the only common factor which applies across prototypes is money. A budget is the only consistent link with normal management processes, where the unknown is being explored. This need for strict budget control reinforces the need for non-integration to ensure the financial implications are correctly assessed. Controlling activity on time is not really feasible—how long will it take when it is a unique R&D project?—and by pre-specifying required results, opportunities may be missed. Strong cost-based management is the only effective control available and it must be understood the 'investment' may have to be written off.

Strategic (Stars)

A star product or strategic application is one that the company is dependent upon for future success in a competitive, changing market place, where any advantage gained can be expected to be eroded quickly. The value of the application can only be judged by its effectiveness *vis-à-vis* competitors. A system to link customers directly to a firm's order-taking systems will only work if it is of value to the customer—a judgement the firm can influence but not make!

Again particular approaches should be adopted:

- *Continuous innovation*—This applies to what the system does and how it does it, to increase the value added by the system as an integral part of the business. These improvements will be business driven, based on the need to sustain the perceived advantages. Whether to spend money will be a user decision, based not simply on return on investment calculation, but on the risk to the business if the system fails to stay ahead of the competition. 'Customer contact and channel' systems are often pre-emptive—the customer will not want two terminals! If, however, a competitor has a more attractive systems offering, the 'one-terminal' may be replaced by someone else's!

- *High value added and vertical integration*—In order to achieve appropriate innovation the business system user has to decide *how* the system adds value to the business process and then have the capability to implement the needs as and *when* required. This implies business control of IS/IT resources and the right to satisfy the unique needs of the particular situation without prevarication or accepting lower value added compromises. The processes of systems management should be vertically integrated with the business unit management process to obtain maximum strategic advantage from information as a value adding resource. Most applications in this strategic box should be associated with a highly information intensive part of the business and the business manager will be inadequately served if he has insufficient discretion over IS/IT deployment.

    This process of value adding is expensive and resource intensive and is only justified where IS/IT can change the business environment sufficient to gain a worthwhile, sustained advantage. As the rest of the industry catches up, diminishing returns come from adding value and greater returns become available from reducing the cost of adding value to industry norms.

Factory (Cash Cows)

Like its cash cows, an organisation depends on its factory systems to deliver a high marginal contribution to the business. This depends on keeping the product or system in line with current market and business demands in the most cost effective way.

The particular business lessons in this case are:

- *Defensive innovation*—the system should only be enhanced and redeveloped in response to changes in the business which threaten to put business at risk through a reduction of competitive capability. This risk should be quantified as far as possible to ensure that the expenditure involved gives a net benefit over time. Deciding on innovation now requires a joint evaluation—users deciding the benefit or risk of action or inaction and IS professionals identifying the costs and risks of any action.

● *High quality*—Factory systems are expected to have an extended life over which they make a significant business contribution. Compromises on system quality will reduce that effective economic life—due to increased user costs overcoming system deficiencies and increased IS/IT costs dealing with increasing numbers of system problems. In the long term, the low cost of support depends on thorough quality control—data and processing integrity and consistency of the system within the network of the organisation's systems.

● *Effective resource utilisation*—Factory systems cannot be afforded the dedication of resources given to strategic systems—it is not justified. This implies the integration of the support for the system with other systems—sharing resources and expertise to reduce the costs. This is a familiar lesson from systems development—transferring the management of a system from a dedicated development team to a general support group after implementation. This both reduces the cost, but also improves development quality control and discourages continuing poorly justified system 'tuning'. There is another important reason. Integrating the system's support activities will allow opportunities to further reduce costs from general improvements in IT capability/cost developments whose justification is from general use.

The general approach to managing factory systems is to reduce costs whilst not reducing the business value of the system. Integration of the system and resources with other applications will provide this net gain.

Support (Dogs)

Support systems like dog products are not critical to an organisation's future unless they waste valuable resources or the market place changes. The business lessons are therefore:

● *Disinvest/rationalise*—Reducing the organisation's commitments to systems can be achieved in a number of ways—facilities management, bureau processing or using packages. Each involves the substitution of resources—money for scarce skills—and the decision is essentially a financial one, which often gives very good returns. Alternative solutions are available for these applications, because they offer no competitive advantage and service/package providers can make a profit from the volume of similar applications in many companies.

● *Sustained quality and efficiency*—The quality of the system should be maintained in proportion to the costs of failure and if necessary calculated risks should be taken—based on the efficiency of resource use involved. In general, the system should not be enhanced unless there is a very demonstrable economic case—to ensure that resources are only consumed where a return is certain. The disinvestment process discussed above will automatically reduce the pace of enhancement to that of the generally available service or package.

A number of immediate observations can be made from the above analysis.

1. The rate of enhancement to any application should reduce as it progresses around the life cycle.
2. The balance of control of the application moves from business driven to information systems management driven as the system is consolidated.
3. The justification for application investments becomes more quantifiable over the evolution and financial evaluation becomes both more meaningful and more decisive in the factory and support quadrants.
4. To achieve the appropriate balance of resource dedication to business contribution, different management processes are involved in the different boxes—which implies that often the system may have to be rebuilt when it crosses the quadrant boundaries to enable those new practices to be effective. For instance, the degree of enhancement and probable expediency of the methods of change in the strategic box will mitigate against effective resource use in the factory box unless some consolidation is undertaken during the transfer.

Another important concept developed from the product portfolio is how the management style should change during a product's life cycle. Since managers cannot be totally adaptive in style this implies changing the manager! Equally, different styles of management are required to successfully develop and deliver the different types of applications in the portfolio. The lessons of product portfolio management offer significant guidance. When an application evolves over time through different segments of the portfolio the style will need to change.

1. *High potential* (Turnaround) applications require a similar style to wild cat products, namely *entrepreneurial*, to champion the application through phases of doubt or decide to stop if the potential is not realisable. Entrepreneurs are strongly personally motivated, expecting recognition of their personal success. At the same time they recognise that they must not be judged to have failed by others, and will either be adept at avoiding failure or be the first to decide it is not worth proceeding.

   They also do not obey the rules and hence will cause change and innovation which implies changing preconceived ideas or ignoring or by-passing accepted custom and practice. This mode of operation is very appropriate for the turnaround situation, but would be wholly inappropriate elsewhere in the matrix.
2. *Strategic* systems require more nurturing, to gain organisational acceptance through demonstrated contribution to the achievement of organisational goals

and objectives. A style of '*developer*' best describes the type of manager required. A developer is someone who will acquire and develop the resources necessary to achieve the task or business objectives. Other terms to describe this are 'organisational climber'—someone whose career ambitions will be met by being related to the achievement of organisational success—or 'empire builder'—a much maligned term! A developer is a planner who achieves results through others, a team manager who moulds the resource to match the needs of achieving the strategic objective, and will be flexible to changing circumstances —adapting the means to achieve the end result.

3. *Factory* systems require a different style of management entirely. '*Controller*' is an appropriate term. A controller is risk averse, wanting everything to be done correctly and failure never to occur. Assurance of success implies reducing risk to a minimum via quality control, strict adherence to procedure and standards and building an organisation structure and mentality which is self checking and control conscious. The best way of achieving quality control is to build it into the organisation by cross-checking procedures.

   The controller approach is essentially inflexible, resistant to change, since change causes confusion and error. Within clearly defined parameters the status quo will be defended and ideas carefully scrutinised and evaluated before changes will be allowed. This is a key requirement if factory systems are to be managed to avoid disadvantages due to failure.

4. *Support* applications are ideally best managed with a *caretaker* approach. Caretaker managers get their satisfaction from achieving 'the impossible, with no resources, repeatedly' and have to be congratulated for it! It is a reactive, problem-solving approach where planning and resource management are less important than getting the job done expediently and efficiently to the satisfaction of the client. This implies a multi-tasking, flexible approach to achieving results which are not of any strategic impact but which will cause a major distraction from strategic objectives if not dealt with in a timely and adept manner. Support systems have no great future potential impact but will be a constant source of irritation if mismanaged.

An entrepreneur is impatient to achieve results to demonstrate his personal capability whereas a developer has longer-term career aims of achieving success through the organisation. A controller wants to prevent the failure of the organisation and a caretaker wants to be recognised as effective user of limited resources in solving problems. The nature of these management styles reflects the generic strategies required to manage the various components of the portfolio:

- an entrepreneur is a free marketeer, who pays little attention to established procedure,
- a developer is a central planner, close to the organisational goals who builds resources to achieve results,

STRATEGIC	HIGH POTENTIAL (TURNAROUND)
Developer ● organisation goal seeker ● risk accommodating ● 'Central Planner'	*Entrepreneur* ● personal achiever ● risk taking ● 'Free Marketeer'
Controller ● long term/quality solutions ● risk reducing ● 'Monopolist'	*Caretaker* ● immediate/efficient solutions ● risk avoiding ● 'Scarce Resourcer'
FACTORY	SUPPORT

FIGURE 8.8

● a controller is a monopolist, uncomfortable with anything outside his control,
● a caretaker is a scarce resourcer—proving he can achieve as much with less!

If the strategy is to be achieved overall then the appropriate management styles must be adopted and the strategy will not be achieved by managers who are 'square pegs in round holes'—a developer managing support systems will develop ever larger, more significant versions of relatively inconsequential systems; a controller expected to develop a turnaround opportunity will never take the first risk! And so on . . . .

These particular management styles will also be reflected in the types of organisational structures and job roles which will be appropriate to the various segments of the portfolio. This will be considered in more detail in a later chapter.

It must be remembered that all these roles are equally important and each has a major part to play to managing a complex portfolio over time. The basic attributes are summarised in Figure 8.8.

APPROACHES TO STRATEGIC IS/IT PLANNING IN RELATION TO THE APPLICATION PORTFOLIO

Based on a study of eight major organisations, Pyburn (1983) identified three basically different approaches to IS/IT planning which enabled organisations in different situations to link the IS/IT planning approach to the business strategy.

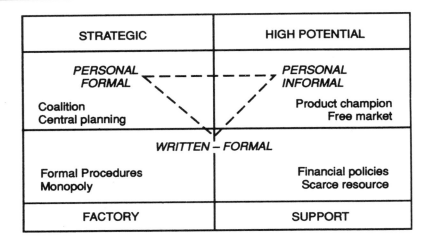

FIGURE 8.9

His ideas can easily be overlaid on the application portfolio—implying different strategic management approaches in different segments.

His three different approaches can be summarised as follows:

(a) *Written—formal*   The approach is very structured and procedural resulting normally in a document describing application plans and policies for the acquisition and deployment of IS/IT in the organisation. It is normally linked 'downstream' from business strategic planning as an IS response to business requirements. This is ideal in relatively stable circumstances where supply management strategies can be adopted and should be clearly enforced to avoid, over the longer term, ineffective solutions and misuse of limited resources. As can be seen in Figure 8.9 this is both possible and required in the factory and support segments. Formalistic strategic studies based on 'business systems planning' top-down approaches are ideal means of achieving this discipline and conformity. The emphasis will vary from factory to support quadrants— resource utilisation and financial control policies predominating in support, software and information quality issues being important in factory. It tends to demand a centralist philosophy of overall controls, although rules for free market activity of a clearly support nature can be established.

(b) *Personal—formal*   This is a 'partially structured' approach which relies on individuals reaching agreement within a formally constituted group process. 'Steering groups' are the most obvious manifestation of this approach. The process of reaching agreement is the most important aspect. The formally communicated agreed actions effectively become the strategy. An effective process will ensure organisational 'buy in' to the strategic decisions. Obviously most of detailed planning occurs outside the formal meetings, but the key job of the steering group is to ensure IS/IT progress reflects business priorities as they evolve. This is essential where the business opportunities and issues will change relatively quickly and also where IS/IT developments will have a considerable impact on the achievement of business objectives and success factors. It is therefore appropriate in the strategic box and is a means of achieving a coalition of actions and enabling integrated IS/IT planning with the business.

That is not to say that all 'steering groups' achieve these aims. The practical implications of such overlays on the organisational structure will be considered later in the book.

(c) *Personal—informal*   No formal planning relationship exists between IS, senior and line managers. At its worst this can mean IS activity is only accidentally linked to business objectives! This is not an approach suitable for complex or critical aspects of IS/IT in business terms. However, like a free market, the user is entrusted with making business based judgements about the value of potential IS/IT applications, after consultation with IS specialists, or the IS department may 'sell' ideas based on technological developments to users. This relates to the idea of a 'product champion' (or entrepreneur) who has licence to develop his ideas and solutions within a broad understanding of his business responsibilities. It will create innovation but will need some mechanism of planning and control to subsequently evaluate and probably fund the further, strategic investment. It does equally allow failure, provided the business is not fundamentally put at risk! Overall it is an ideal approach to the high potential box and like the 'free market' may not be too risky in the support quadrant.

Pyburn's findings are most easily considered as a 'triangle' with the three approaches at the corners and a continuum of variations between them. He does point out that the dominating approach will depend on the overall criticality of IS/IT to be business, the organisation structure/culture, its geography and the personal and business capabilities of the IS management team. Even with these considerations taken into account the basic ideas map very well on to the portfolio management concepts and provide further insight into options available.

THE APPLICATION PORTFOLIO—THREE-DIMENSIONAL ASPECTS

The Business Dimensions

As stated earlier, the analysis of applications into the four components of the matrix is most appropriately carried out for a business unit. Indeed, each business unit should assess the IS/IT contribution in such terms and hence determine how IS/IT can best be managed to achieve success.

However, few real organisations consist of a single business unit and an overall approach to IS/IT management has to be developed for the 'corporation' *and* its various component businesses. The components will be of different sizes, making a greater/lesser contribution, absorb more/less resources and probably operate in different market environments. The extent of the differences will determine how similar the application portfolios are and hence how cohesive the strategies should be. In some organisations, even with considerable product and/or market overlap and even where there is significant information based synergy, developing deliberately diverse portfolios has become almost a policy to prevent mutual interdependence and sharing of resources. Unless the organisation envisages early break-up this is inevitably a sub-optimal strategy. Others have, historically at least, pursued a policy of 'common systems' forcing units to compromise their real requirements and accept a less than ideal set of applications, ensuring additional business costs will be incurred or opportunities forgone.

The application portfolio concept enables the matrix of approaches to be adopted to satisfy the individual business unit and to take advantage of similarities of need and economic routes to common solutions.

Figure 8.10 depicts the minimum gains to be made by a co-ordinated approach across the organisation.

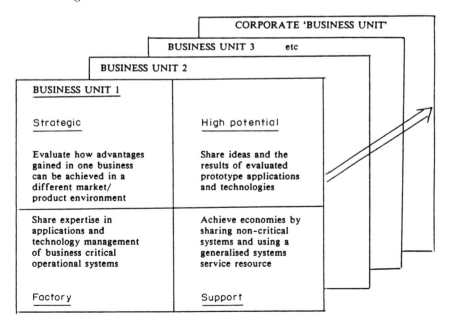

FIGURE 8.10

In the support box, even if the businesses are diverse, the applications are likely to address similar administrative requirements and 'packages' are a common choice. At worst a limited number of packages should be used, at best a common suite of applications could be used. This will obviously depend on the diversity of the business. Manufacturing and financial services will require different systems—but several types of retail companies in different market sectors could easily use common accounting systems, etc.

The same logic applies throughout the matrix but the areas of potential commonality of actual applications are likely to decrease as we progress from support to factory to strategic, although the potential in the last box may be realisable through different uses of the same idea.

Providing similar technological environments in the different units even if the businesses are as different as health care and financial services may enable 'supply based' expertise to provide better quality factory solutions to both.

Sharing the advantages gained from one organisation to another may accelerate the development of strategic applications—this implies business-based sharing of *how* to achieve the benefits available, even if the details of the applications vary. Links to suppliers, for instance, are likely to achieve similar benefits to manufacturing and retail companies.

All this will require a corporate view of the portfolios of the various units and the concepts of the 'generic strategies' can be extrapolated to a higher level—not to drive the strategies but to ensure opportunities are not missed or resources and funds needlessly wasted.

The IS/IT Management Dimensions

If the portfolios of business units can be consolidated into a corporate portfolio, so can each portfolio be considered in more depth.

Figure 8.11 identifies some aspects of the component strategies required in order to achieve overall IS/IT success. From all that has been said before it follows that different approaches will be needed to the detailed processes of resource and technology development and deployment in the segments of the matrix.

- different development methodologies, process and application development tools will be more or less appropriate;
- different technologies in terms of maturity and complexity will deliver differing results implied by the importance and criticality of applications;
- different IS organisational structures, services provided and interface relationships with users are implied, as also is the allocation of responsibility across IS and user departments;
- how IS/IT investments are justified/evaluated, prioritised and costs allocated will vary. A singular approach will tend to produce one type of application to the exclusion of others.

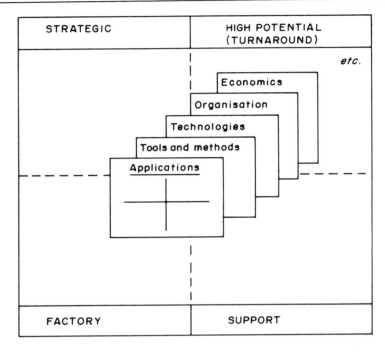

FIGURE 8.11

These and other aspects of the issues of IS/IT strategic management that lie across and behind the portfolio will be considered in depth in later chapters. The real objective is not to have a strategy but to develop the appropriate set of business applications in the most effective way. As has been said before, this requires appropriate demand and supply management strategies in each segment *and* coherent means of moving systems around the matrix in relation to their evolving business contribution.

SUMMARY AND CONCLUSIONS

This chapter has tried to demonstrate the rationale behind adopting an application portfolio management concept as a core part of the IS/IT strategic planning approach. The rationale consists of two parts:

(a) the need to use business strategic planning concepts wherever relevant to ensure the closest possible linkage between business and IS/IT strategy;

(b) the end-result of the process is inevitably a set of applications and hence the ways of producing and managing them must always be a focus of attention, before, during and after the development of a strategy.

The basic 2 × 2 matrix model has been explored from a variety of directions to identify the potential advice and guidance it can offer in determining and selecting strategic options. Whilst not all the advice is identical, it after all has been derived from many diverse sources, it is never contradictory and the patterns that emerge are generally consistent. However, it must be reasserted that the simple model does not reflect the full complexity of the IS/IT strategic management environment. In reverse it does allow much of the complexity to be analysed and categorised to enable the issues to be understood better in devising their resolution.

Figure 8.12 attempts to summarise the critical issues involved in managing the portfolio quadrants.

The next four chapters consider the more detailed aspects of strategic planning and management under four main headings:

- Organisation
- Information
- Applications
- Technology

Throughout the detailed considerations the basic portfolio concept will be referred to as appropriate to keep a coherence and comprehensiveness of perspective across related issues.

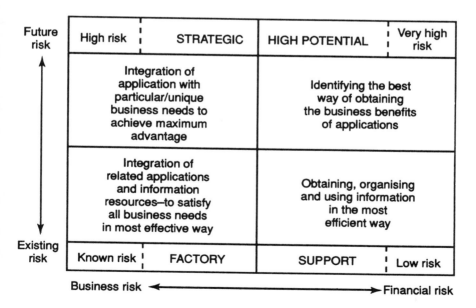

FIGURE 8.12 Critical issues in managing segments of the portfolio

REFERENCES

Benjamin, R. I., Rockart, J. F., Scott Morton, M. S. and Wyman, J. (1984) 'Information technology: a strategic opportunity', *Sloan Management Review* (Spring).

Galliers, R. D. (1987a) 'Information systems and technology planning within a competitive strategy framework'. Published in Pergamon Infotech State of the Art Report (Griffiths (Ed.), *The Role of Information Management in Competitive Success*).

Galliers, R. D. (1987b) 'Information technology planning within the corporate planning process'. Published in Pergamon Infotech State of the Art Report (Duling & Berry (Eds) *Controlling Projects within an Integrated Management Framework*).

Hirschheim, R. A. (1982) 'Information management planning in organisations', *LSE Working Paper*.

Hirschheim, R., Earl, M., Feeny, D. and Lockett, M. (1988) 'An exploration into the management of the IS function: key issues and an evolutionary model', *Proceedings of the Joint International Symposium on IS* (March).

Ives, B. and Learmonth, G. P. (1984) 'The information system as a competitive weapon', *Communications of the ACM* (Dec.).

McLauglin, M., Howe, R. and Cash, J. (1983) 'Changing competitive ground rules—the impact of computers and communications in the 1980s', unpublished working paper.

Munro, M. C. and Huff, S. L. (1985) 'Information technology and corporate strategy', *Business Quarterly* (Summer).

Parsons, G. L. (1983) 'Fitting information systems technology to the corporate needs: the linking strategy', Harvard Business School, Teaching Notes (9-183-176) (June).

Pyburn, P. J. (1983) 'Linking the MIS plan with corporate strategy: an exploratory study', *MIS Quarterly* (June).

Sullivan, C. H. (1985) 'Systems planning in the information age', *Sloan Management Review* (Winter).

Ward, J. M. (1988) 'Information systems and technology: application portfolio management—an assessment of matrix-based analysis', *Journal of Information Technology*, 3(3) (Dec.).

Chapter 9

STRATEGIC MANAGEMENT OF IS/IT— ORGANISATION, RESOURCES AND ADMINISTRATION

INTRODUCTION

So far the book has demonstrated how the potential IS/IT offers a business or organisation can be assessed in relation to the environment, objectives and strategy of the enterprise. In terms of the overall IS/IT strategic planning models described in Chapter 3, the focus so far has been on the inputs to the strategy and the tools and techniques of analysis and formulation. The previous chapter used the application portfolio matrix to show how the ways in which IS/IT is managed in an organisation is inextricably linked in a cause and effect relationship with the portfolio.

High level (generic) management strategies were reviewed, from which organisations can derive a mix appropriate to their needs. These generic strategies when related to business portfolio management lessons, lead to a rational set of management approaches to achieving success in all areas of the portfolio. But as shown at the end of the last chapter, the matrix has a third dimension, behind the applications, which reflects how each system, project or infrastructure development is itself defined, developed and managed. All these aspects can really be considered under four main headings which represent the four most tangible aspects of IS/IT management, and hence require clearly defined strategies. These key strategy areas are:

- for managing the *information* and data resource of the organisation to ensure its business value is fully exploited and protected;
- for managing *applications* as projects and operational systems from the establishment of requirements to successful long-term use in the business;
- for managing the introduction, development, utilisation and eventual replacement of information *technologies* to greatest benefit to the organisation;
- for organisational management of the range of IS/IT related *resources*, the activities they perform and the administration of IS/IT in both its unique features and its relationships with other parts of the business.

This chapter deals with the last of these in order to establish an organisational context for the more specific strategies for the 'physical' components of any business information system—the application as represented by the 'code', the information and data it uses and the technology it operates on.

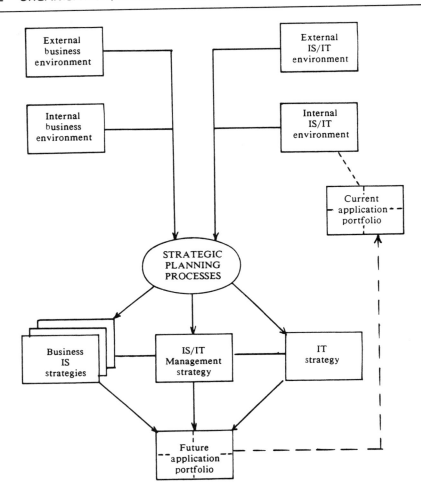

FIGURE 9.1 The IS/IT strategic model

The 'organisational' strategy for IS/IT management cannot be prescriptive. The strategy must evolve over time as the organisation becomes more dependent upon, and demands more from, IS/IT. More freedom of action or tighter control of resource use will be appropriate at different stages of development.

The formulation of strategy is only the first step on the road to successful IS/IT management. Delivering the results and updating the strategy to reflect changing business and IS/IT environments are obviously critical to eventual success. Failure to achieve success is often the result of organisational, political and cultural issues being inadequately addressed.

THE STRATEGIC MANAGEMENT REQUIREMENT

In overall terms the enterprise must ensure that an appropriate IS/IT strategy is developed and implemented.

Referring back to Chapter 3 this implied that the inputs, processes and outputs involved in strategic planning are all managed successfully over an extended period. The basic building block model Figure 3.10 is reproduced in a simplified form in Figure 9.1. This model, however, ignores the inevitable 'refinement' of strategy during planning and implementation and its continuing update as achievements (or otherwise) occur or any environmental input changes. As stated in Chapter 2 and illustrated in Figure 2.3, strategic management is a combination of formal planning, informal thinking and opportunism all of which must be effectively exploited. From establishing the strategic direction, through defining specific strategies to eventual achievement, the balance moves from formality to relative informality and opportunism.

In order that the formal process does not inhibit the realisation of each step in the implementation of strategy and changes to the strategy, policies and practices must be established to avoid IS/IT planning slowing up business progress. At the same time many organisations have suffered the consequences of lack of co-ordination in IS/IT management which can cause the existing (and potential) portfolios effectively to disintegrate. Figure 9.2 considers how this might happen as the strategic direction is disregarded by totally opportunistic achievements.

This failure results in the long term in three major effects:

(a) the systems do not meet overall business needs:
(b) resources are misused;
(c) planning is essentially a retrofitting process producing enormous rework.

Any or all three can occur. The cause can usually be put down to two main reasons

(i) unco-ordinated management of supply and demand (see the basic IS/IT strategy model of Earl in Figure 3.5);
(ii) over-centralisation or decentralisation of control of IS/IT investment.

McFarlan and McKenney (1983) consider the implications of the latter point and some of the key effects they identified in many organisations are summarised in Table 9.1. The use of the strategic matrix and appropriate generic strategies to prevent these causes of disintegration of the portfolio were summarised in Figure 8.5. It will be the effectiveness of the overall IS/IT management strategy and resulting policies and practices which will determine whether all other aspects of strategy development and implementation succeed.

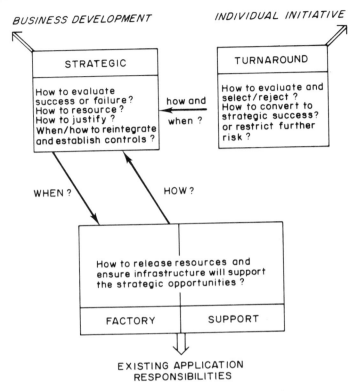

FIGURE 9.2 The disintegrating portfolio?

TABLE 9.1 Effects of excessive dominance of . . .

IS departments	User departments
• Forcing new systems to fit existing data structures—integration and tailored systems focus	• Short-term problem focus, growth of incompatible systems
• Little innovation with new suppliers, technologies or services	• Hidden maintenance overhead due to proliferation of services/suppliers
• Insistence on feasibility and cost/benefit studies in response to all requests	• Lack of quality control of data
• IS organisation based on technical specialisations not user need	• Lack of experience/skill transfer duplication and differential rates of development
• 'Maintenance' absorbs bulk of resources—up to 80% +	• Little cost/benefit analysis or objective justification of systems
• Users frustrated, senior management often not involved. 'Secret' growth of user machines and staff	• Rapid growth in (duplicated) technical staff
	• Central IS group degenerates

The management strategy must not only deal with the 'rational' aspects of strategy such as investment appraisal, but also with the behavioural and cultural considerations. Whilst defining strategies is predominantly an intellectual process, implementing them requires appropriate behaviour throughout the organisation.

Some of the objectives of this management strategy are listed in Table 9.2. The rest of this chapter will consider how these can be addressed, in practical terms and in conjunction with the need to manage the development of the application portfolio and supporting technologies and resources.

In Chapter 3 the aspects of strategy to be addressed at this corporate management level were suggested as:

- Organisation,
- Human impact policies—see Chapter 13,
- Vendor policies—see Chapter 12,
- Investment and priority setting policies—see Chapter 11,
- IS accounting policies.

It might be tempting to also include 'corporate information systems'—the set of applications required by the corporate body—in this strategy but these are really an IS strategy to satisfy corporate requirements, not issues of management policy. Equally potential synergy between systems or benefits from rationalisation of systems across the business are obviously of interest to corporate management, but again these are application or technology strategy issues. A 'management edict' to produce common systems will only work if the businesses concerned can see the benefits in their applications. The investment and organisational policies should encourage these approaches and, if necessary, a 'task force' of involved users can be delegated the task of devising application and technology strategies to enable these corporate benefits to be achieved.

Hayward (1987) in an article on 'Developing IS Strategies' argues for a similar structure for the IS/IT strategy in terms of a planning model. He identifies a 'management strategy', an 'applications strategy' and a 'technology strategy' as the components, as in the model used in this book.

TABLE 9.2 Requirements of strategic management

- To ensure IS/IT strategies, polices and plans reflect business objectives and strategies.
- To ensure potential business advantages from IS/IT are identified and exploited.
- To ensure strategies, etc. are viable in terms of business risks.
- To establish appropriate resource levels and reconcile contention/set priorities.
- To create a 'culture' for the management of IS/IT which reflects the corporate culture.
- To monitor the progress of business critical IS/IT activities.
- To achieve the best balance between decentralisation and centralisation.

Within the management strategy he lists five main components—reporting structure, 'centralisation/decentralisation', standards, security and education. The first two are equivalent to the more general 'organisation' heading used here, and education is a subset of the 'human impact strategies'. The impact of IS/IT on people within organisations and the need for appropriate strategies and policies is considered in the final chapter of the book. IS/IT will not only change what people do but over time the structure and nature of organisations. In terms of standards, the management strategy is to ensure they are developed, or adopted from outside and then adhered to, rather than define the standards. In this book standards are considered as part of information, application and technology strategies.

The heading of 'security' covers both information and physical security of equipment, networks and applications. General management may be unaware of the security issues in using the latest technologies. Again, the management strategy should address the issue of how security will be audited and provide re-enforcement by action when security standards have been ignored. It could be argued that some aspects of information management, especially concerning its confidentiality and security, will require corporate policies to be established. This area of strategy is considered in the next chapter, not because it does not deserve management attention, but information management strategies need to be seen as an integrated set of approaches in user, senior management and IS/IT terms.

ORGANISATION STRATEGIES

This section will not only consider aspects of overall organisational alternatives, and the position of IS functions in the organisation, but also IS organisational options and resourcing strategies. Whilst these depend on the approaches adopted to information, application and technology management it is most critical that the IS organisation is structured to satisfy its 'customers'' requirements as well as manage itself effectively.

In addition to defining organisational responsibilities concerning IS/IT management, corporate management need to decide if and how that structure needs to be overlain by committee or steering group structures. Most large private sector and public bodies have realised that no one organisational alternative can achieve appropriate management of all aspects of IS/IT. To overcome this, upwards of 80% of major US and UK organisations have constituted some form of IS/IT management steering group.

However, in many of those organisations the 'steering group' is seen as a failure or at best an irrelevance by both user line management and IS managers, and even by the senior executives. Others, however, are very effective as an approach to develop more concerted, strategic management of IS/IT. The reasons for those differing realities will also be explored and an overall 'ideal' model for effective steering groups will be outlined.

The positioning of the main IS resource of the organisation in the organisation structure has been problematic since computing began, but the problems have become compounded as IS/IT has pervaded and affected many parts of business life. A 'tug of war' has often developed, as stated earlier, between centralised and decentralised control in many organisations. The overall 'IS Manager' job has moved, normally migrating up the hierarchy to perhaps 'IT Director' or 'Chief Information Officer'. Much has been written about both the positioning and structure of IS/IT functions in organisations. Some of that will be drawn on in this section. Getting it wrong can be very costly, but how can an organisation know what is right?

In a decentralised engineering group, a very centralised monopolistic IS/IT group was failing to provide a satisfactory service. Rather than evaluate why, the management bowed to political pressure from the operating company managers and rapidly devolved IS/IT resources to the units. Systems development virtually ceased! and support for existing systems became very poor. Many of the best people left and at no site was there sufficient resource to achieve major developments and local management had no experience of running an IS/IT group. Gradually it was realised that some aspects should be recentralised to avoid duplicated expertise, etc. and some aspects, reinforced by user resource investments, should remain in the units.

The rest of this section will address the organisation of IS/IT resources and then the positioning in the organisation, although they are interdependent.

Organisation of IS Resources

Undoubtedly much application expertise is devolving into the user organisation, though in the process the quality of many systems and integrity of data is declining. At the same time the need to develop technical infrastructures and information architectures are forcing more centralisation of certain functions. First, the 'things' required to be managed will be considered, then the pros and cons of the various 'positioning' alternatives.

A good assessment of what needs to be managed and how it is changing was put forward by Zmud (1984). He describes the traditional, often very centralised, structures developed for IS/IT organisations in the 1960s and 1970s as those demanded by the *manufacturing* role IS/IT was seen to perform in producing systems. This normally led to a structure which included:

systems development (and maintenance),
operations,
technical services,
administration,

and activities were allocated to each. Many of these activities are still very critical, but he argues that new roles have evolved whereby *distribution* (or technology transfer) of solutions becomes equally important, forcing a service rather than manufacturing structure to be developed. This not only introduces new functions but also changes or extends the role of the above or reallocates tasks. His extended model is summarised in Table 9.3.

TABLE 9.3 Evolving information system roles

Delivery systems	Computer operations including job scheduling, etc.
	End-user facility operations support
	Database support
	Telecommunications support
	Maintenance (hardware, systems software and applications software)
	End-user liaison and quality assurance for production systems
	Capacity planning
Systems development	System design and software development for production systems, for critical systems, for sensitive systems, for corporate-wide systems, and for software tools
Support centre	Internal consulting service for organisational analyses, modelling, feasibility studies, and systems analysis
	Broker for packaged software, external data services, word processors and microcomputers
	End-user and systems personnel training
Information centre	Internal consulting service and support facilities for end-user applications development via microcomputers, decision support systems, modelling languages, data inquiry systems, and automatic applications generators
Research and development	Monitor technological developments
	Develop technical infrastructure
	Technological forecasting
Technology diffusion	Develop organisational infrastructure
	Investigate potential for applying new technologies within organisational areas
	Plan and manage system implementations
	Plan and manage pilot studies
Planning	Overall information planning
	Liaison with corporate strategic planning
	Overall evaluation of organisational use of information systems
	Establishing information policies
Internal auditing	Standards development
	Evaluation of adherence to controls
Administration	Budgeting
	Personnel management
	Document management

Reprinted by special permission from the *MIS Quarterly*, Volume 8, Number 2, June 1984. Copyright 1984 by the Society for Information Management and the Management Information Systems Research Center at the University of Minnesota

In his model many traditional 'systems development' functions have been split up to separate the 'construction' process from 'enabling' processes. Administration is greatly reduced from traditional roles. *Planning* becomes a main activity and technical services are split into several subfunctions. He also believes these various activities have to be structured or focused and therefore organised to reflect the dynamics of the task performed. He classifies these as:

'Hierarchical'   to achieve economies of scale by work separation and specialisation (internal efficiency focused).
'Product'   to provide responsive services to enable subgroup to complete the job (external effectiveness focused).
'Matrix'   to achieve the best from resources available by team work and adaptability to change (task focused).

Analysis by the authors drew similar conclusions but in relation to the different demands of the types of applications in the portfolio. Different types of structure and services are required to develop and sustain applications in the different segments in line with the generic management approaches developed in Chapter 8.
  Relating these (summarised in Figure 9.3) to Zmud's ideas:

- 'Hierarchical' relates to 'functional' in the Factory box.
- 'Product' relates to 'individual' and 'cross-functional' in the High Potential and Support boxes respectively.
- 'Matrix' and 'matrix' in the Strategic box imply very similar things.

This rationale is saying that wherever in the organisation functions are located, the same issues have to be managed. In addition, depending on the location, the amount of co-ordination or communication effort will vary and Zmud suggests that some organisational overlay will normally be required to overcome the weaknesses of any chosen structure. This is considered later in the chapter.
  Combining these subfunctions into an organisation structure suggests a number of service functions which may be subdivided further to meet application portfolio variations. In addition some specialist functions peculiar to the nature of IS/IT remain, plus some 'staff' tasks (see Figure 9.4).
  Remember that so far these are considered to be all the functions required—where they should be placed will be considered below. Based on the various demands of the segments of the portfolio the key domains of the various 'services' are likely to be different, as suggested in Table 9.4.
  All this implies that the IS/IT organisation structure should evolve as the organisation matures in its use of IS/IT, a maturity reflected in the development of the portfolio of applications, and by the need to implement a simultaneous mix of generic strategies. This not only involves developing new organisational alternatives to meet new demands but also to reduce the resource commitment

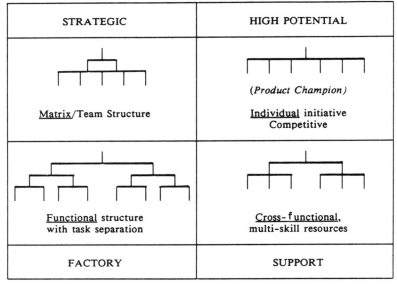

FIGURE 9.3 Structures for resourcing IS/IT applications. Note: a flat structure (as in high potential) causes innovation and change, whereas a very hierarchical structure (as in factory) is designed for control, retaining the status quo and reducing risk. Matrices are most effective when there is a clear task objective which overrides 'department' views and a strategic application will require a flexible/evolving team structure. Support applications need less rigid quality control and multi-tasking people ('Jack of all Trades') is a more expeditious way of getting things done than the task separated method implied in Factory

to old demands. The emotive picture of the disintegrating portfolio (Figure 9.2) is as much the result of the organisation failing to manage its legacy from the past, as the development of new demands.

Henderson and Treacy (1986) consider this need to adopt an evolving organisational approach with particular reference to the effective development of 'end-user computing'. They identify the criticality of achieving balance between '*control*'—to focus resources in areas most critical to the business —and '*laissez-faire*'—to enable innovation and broaden the organisational capability. The criticality is compounded by the phenomenal rate of growth and consequent spending on end-user computing.

They suggest that the overall organisational learning curve implies changing management issues over time and hence the management perspective has to change through the learning period. They describe this in terms of implementation, marketing, operations and economic perspectives and the key objectives, etc. of each are summarised in Figure 9.5.

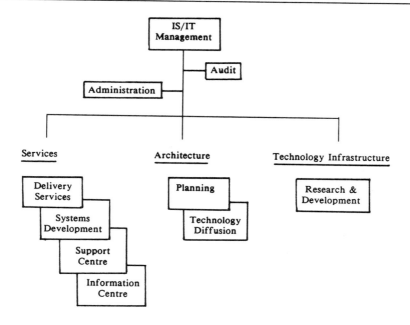

FIGURE 9.4

TABLE 9.4

Service utilised	High potential	Strategic	Factory	Support
Delivery service	LOW	HIGH	HIGH	LOW
Systems development	LOW	HIGH	HIGH	LOW
Support centre	MEDIUM	LOW	LOW	HIGH
Information centre	HIGH	MEDIUM	LOW	HIGH
Architecture and infrastructure	MEDIUM	HIGH	HIGH	LOW
Organisational approach	Innovative	Matrix	Functional	Cross-functional

These concepts, whilst developed for managing end-user computing, are not inconsistent with the overall migration path suggested for the organisational management of IS/IT. They emphasise in conclusion that the framework is pragmatic but needs to be initiated early to ensure organisational learning follows a smooth curve, not a conflict driven zigzag path.

Management perspective ⟶ Time

Implementation	Marketing	Operations	Economic	
Increase use and user satisfaction	Market growth – diffusion	Integration and efficiency	Business advantage	*Objective*
Opportunistic educational	Improved services	Standards and policies	Targeted investments	*Strategy*
Central help and *ad hoc* consultancy	Local support groups	Central control and local support	Distributed operations control	*Structure*
Resources available	Departmental accountability	Centralised policies	Formal business justification	*Control by:*

FIGURE 9.5 *(derived from J. C. Henderson and M. E. Treacy (1986) 'Managing end-user computing for competitive advantage'*, Sloan Management Review *(Winter) with permission)*

POSITIONING IS/IT RESOURCES IN THE ORGANISATION

It is not easy to produce a general statement of the ideal organisational arrangement for IS/IT resources. A number of factors will always have to be weighed for any organisation:

- its stage of maturity in terms of its application portfolio;
- the geography of the enterprise, especially for international companies;
- its business diversity and rate of change of the types of business and competitive pressures in each business;
- the potential benefits of synergy between businesses in both trading goods and services and information exchange;
- the economics of resourcing, obtaining and deploying skills.

EDP Analyser (1986) in an edition entitled 'Organising for 1990s' focused on how the role of IS/IT is changing and will have to change further, and with it the positioning in the organisation. They identify the following main existing organisational approaches which have evolved over the last 10–15 years:

(a) totally centralised (i.e. monopolistic),

(b) totally decentralised to business functions (plus some co-ordination of company wide activities),
(c) geographically placed data centres and resources,
(d) business unit control, even where resources are centrally located,
(e) by class of user—large users have own resources, small ones share from the centre,
(f) by activity—operations centralised, development decentralised, etc.,
(g) by type of resource—networks, computers, software data, etc.

They observe the trend away from 'production' to 'service' and to providing the architectural support for the applications and conclude that the data or information architecture will become a critical component of strategy which 'someone' in the organisation must tackle.

A 1988 study for the Society for Information Management (SIM) reported in *Datamation* by Lodahl and Redditt (1989) concluded that the pressure to get competitive information systems in business units is the main driving force for positioning IS resources.

They considered the pros and cons of the various organisational strategies being adopted by major companies and identified four major approaches:

1. Decentralise IS resources—i.e. IS resources under the control of the business units. Traditional IS/Business barriers often remain because traditional systems development methods are maintained by 'professionals'.
2. Disperse (IS) resources—unlike decentralisation IS resources are not kept together even at business unit level but dispersed into the functions within the unit. This reduces professionalism, architectures disintegrate and IS people have no career paths.
3. Convert IS to a profit centre—is really a service bureau mentality, competing for 'project'-driven business. It produces new contractual problems between IS and the business.
4. Set up a separate IS business entity—takes the profit centre into a business in its own right and means new functions including marketing have to be developed. Business users can often lose out to 'sales' outside the company.

None of these is an ideal solution but the analysis favours the first option—very much along the lines of the Manufacturers Trust Co (see below)—followed by a further stage of realignment between the business unit and its IS resources to produce a 'partnership' within the unit.

'Whither the IT Organisation?' was the question posed by La Belle and Nyce (1987) who discussed how the IS/IT resource was reorganised in Manufacturers Trust Co to respond to a major company reorganisation. The resulting structure is similar to that being arrived at by many multi-unit organisations.

Manufacturers Trust Co as reported by La Belle and Nyce considered many alternatives before arriving at the need to 'recentralise' (as they put it) some aspects of IS/IT in order to support a decentralisation of the business into five units to match the customers each served. Previously IS/IT had been steadily decentralising but in support of a different business structure. They concluded that whilst the business units should be responsible for applications—architecture, development and operation—certain areas should be centralised. These included:

● Telecommunications.
● Hardware and software architecture.
● Information architecture.
● Risk management and security.
● Shared services and utilities.
● Human resources.

In each of these areas the central IT group would be able to assist, advise and, if necessary, control the activities of the business units where they could provide improved economics or supply-related options and/or demonstrate added value from the corporate synergy. To do this the activities of the units had to be co-ordinated with the central architectural development via a 'steering group' infrastructure, which is similar to that described later in the chapter.

This brief description does scant justice to the detail of the restructuring involved and the careful planning and implementation required to change not only organisation but also the culture to accept the implied changes in responsibility. Table 9.5 summarises the divisions of responsibility for one aspect—'IT architecture management'.

If the overall application strategy is to fit the business strategy the business unit management must be accountable and responsible for the deployment of resources in developing and maintaining the applications. This applies whether they are employed as part of the business unit or contracted from a central or even outside agencies for the duration of a project, or the life of the application. This responsibility includes the application architecture for the unit, even if some applications are also part of the corporate portfolio and/or shared with other units. Where there are significant potential gains from synergy, sharing experience or resources, or from economic optimisation, an additional corporately sponsored 'central planning and control' of the application architecture and delivery will be beneficial. The more geographically dispersed the organisation the less attractive the concept of co-ordinated planning becomes in the short term, but perhaps the more attractive are the long-term benefits of not resourcing very similar applications separately in multiple places.

The degree to which information is a shared business resource will determine how centralised the information architecture and data control processes will become. Similarly, how closely technologies need to be co-ordinated will depend on the relationships amongst applications and data utilisation as much as the economies of supply or technical simplicity or flexibility achieved.

TABLE 9.5 Division of responsibility: IT architecture management

Function	Central IT group	Business Sector operations
• Develop and maintain information architectures	• Monitor process; provide assistance if requested	• Complete business architectures defining business (within sectors) by location • Complete translation of strategy into technology requirements • Define information architecture
• Develop and maintain applications architectures	• Set standards; monitor process • Review architectures and report on adequacy to Technology Committee • Ensure appropriate commonality	• Define requirements and develop architecture • Coordinate between sectors for common business
• Develop and maintain data architectures	• Co-ordinate development/establishment of common database management processes • Create/maintain corporate databases	• Define requirements; develop in accordance with standards
• Develop and maintain hardware/operating systems architectures	• Monitor development/implementation within sectors • Develop and maintain architecture for corporate users support operations	• Develop in accordance with corporate standards business requirements • Request variances as appropriate; make change recommendations
• Develop and maintain telecommunications architectures	• Develop in accordance with standards and business requirements	• Define requirements • Report performance/responsiveness problems

From A. La Belle and H. E. Nyce, 'Whither the IT organisation?' *Sloan Management Review* (Summer 1987), with permission.

Undoubtedly in every major organisation other than the most diversified conglomerate, there are potential gains from the centralisation of some resources. But as described in all the models these centralised functions are primarily required to service the various needs of the business units—their *raison d'être* is that if the resource was distributed it would be less effective. In addition, where there are potential benefits to the organisation as a whole which are greater than the sum of the parts (of the business units) then some planning and co-ordination at the centre can add value to ensure these additional benefits are achieved.

In the case of the Hammermill Paper Company examined earlier in the book, there would have been considerable benefit in managing applications at the business unit level, except where through either improved or more efficient trading or exploitation of information, additional benefits were available. In that case, additional application strategies were required at a corporate level and the information and technology strategies needed strong direction from the centre in order that application benefits were not forgone *and* to stop the very wasteful use of resources that had developed due to operating companies (*within* business units) choosing their own solutions.

It should be remembered that *balancing demand and supply in the long term* is the objective, not achieving the next batch of projects in the most expeditious way.

The People Resource—Strategic Issues

One aspect of the Manufacturers Trust Co. strategy which deserves more comment, is the need to manage the *Human Resources* as a corporate resource. Undoubtedly one of the critical factors for any organisation in achieving the best results from IS/IT is the quality of people it deploys. The ability to obtain, develop and retain highly skilled IS/IT resources in adequate numbers, will determine in the long term how well the business and IS/IT strategies are brought together. Whether these staff are located centrally or decentralised does not matter—the issues are the same. Good IS/IT staff are in short supply and in great demand.

There are essentially three solutions to the basic shortage of skills, other than ensuring that the turnover of staff is kept to a minimum by good 'hygiene factors' plus career and personal development options.

The three ways are:

(a) training new recruits from school or university, which is expensive. Also people early in their careers are more likely to move on within 3–5 years;
(b) training existing non-IS people—especially in application skills in user areas;
(c) using external resources.

Whilst training is initially expensive, using external resources is potentially a higher long-term financial commitment unless it is to deal with a known and controllable peak load.

Consider the following scenario which has become increasingly common.

The existing IS/IT resource is 'bogged down' in factory and support systems, mainly maintenance and rewrites. A new major strategic development is conceived, but cannot be resourced internally in the time required. Decision—bring in external contract-based resources to develop the strategic application. What are the potential long-term consequences?

1. An open-ended contract to meet an ever-changing requirement for the strategic development?
2. No one in the IS/IT department is capable of understanding and supporting it in due course?
3. What will the 'contractor' do with the knowledge?
4. Demoralised staff who have to do the 'boring stuff' while others get the 'good jobs'? They leave—often to join the contractor!—and the situation worsens.

It can become a vicious circle. By referring to the rationale of the strategic grid, it should be clear that the one area that must not be handed over to outside parties is that which provides the future business advantage! Equally, the one area that can be handed over with purely economic consequences is the 'support' quadrant, or much of what it contains. Facilities management can even be considered to release resources to use elsewhere. If the organisation is to develop its capability *and* provide an attractive environment to its skilled people, its own resources, IS and user must be deployed on the challenging strategic or turnaround systems as well as keeping the factory systems up to the business needs. If anything, it is even more appropriate to pay outside resources to deliver factory systems to a clear contractual specification rather than use scarce internal resources. Quality control could be maintained by a strong quality assurance process applied to the contractor.

It may of course be necessary to buy in some special skills that the organisation does not have to help develop even a strategic application. This resource should be bought with the objective of extracting that special knowledge for the benefit of the organisation, by using it not just to deliver results but also train internal staff.

Overall the organisation's IS/IT resource must be developed as part of the strategy—it must be consciously planned. The long-term aim is to move resources out of the support quadrant by finding less resource intensive means, and whilst ensuring factory systems are adequately resourced, develop a capability to carry out strategic and turnaround projects. Any alternative strategy will reduce the long-term capability of the organisation, and increase the unit cost of every application development and amendment in all parts of the portfolio.

These ideas in terms of the Strategic Grid are summarised in Figure 9.6.

Peter Keen (1988) discusses similar issues in more detail and considers not only the types of people required and their likely sources, but also the job roles and skills, experience and career paths for each. He considers the spectrum of skills from business to specialist IT and defines four major role categories:

(a) Business services—requiring strong business, organisational and planning skills.
(b) Business support—business and organisational plus some technical skills.
(c) Development support—strong technical and good business skills.
(d) Technical services—strong technical skills.

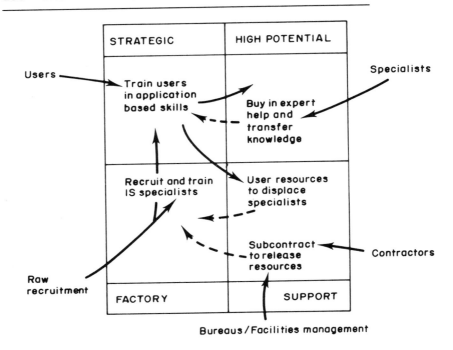

Bureaus/Facilities management

FIGURE 9.6

Many organisations are developing such new roles to link the traditional programmer and analyst via business based but dedicated people (e.g. business systems analysts) to the real business management. These roles are required irrespective of where IS/IT reports in the organisation.

WHO SHOULD MANAGE IS/IT AND WHERE SHOULD IT REPORT?

Positioning of IS/IT in an organisation is obviously related to, and should perhaps determine who manages it and the level at which he or she reports. Ultimately someone at Board level (represented at the highest executive level of the company, not necessarily with Director status as defined by Companies Legislation), even the Chief Executive by default, is accountable at that level for IS and/or IT—although many Board members are in practice responsible for IS/IT, given the diffusion of systems throughout the whole organisation. Even then someone will probably be primarily responsible for IS/IT, although often that will not be his or her main responsibility at Board level. But should that be the case? Should not someone be charged at Board level with responsibility for all (or most, or some?) aspects of IS/IT management within the organisation and have that status based on primarily an IS/IT management task?

This question has no doubt been discussed in the boardrooms of most major organisations. A variety of answers have resulted.

At some level in the organisation an individual (or in a dispersed business, several individuals) will be responsible solely for IS activities and for a significant resource and budget. For simplicity he or she we will call the '*IS/IT manager*'. In a multi-business unit company there are likely to be '*IS (biased) managers*' in each unit plus an '*IT (biased) manager*' at the centre, and this seems sensible given the earlier organisational arguments. The split of responsibilities discussed earlier would give application responsibility to the units, leaving some functions at the centre for economic and strategic reasons. The IT manager at the centre is the more problematic because his or her reporting position will affect his or her ability to do the job. Given any autonomy in the units they will be easily able to overrule or ignore the central role if it is too junior. The IS managers in the units will be considered below.

'IT Director' or 'Chief Information Officer' (CIO) faces a changing job role in the future. That is the conclusion of research by Benjamin, Dickinson and Rockart (1985) concerning the more extensively analysed CIO role in the USA.

They predict that as application development and operations are passed to the business areas to manage

(a) corporate IS departments will shift to a staff orientation, including coordinating strategic planning for IS/IT across the whole business. Any line responsibilities will be either to serve the corporate body's IS needs or to manage 'interconnection issues', amongst systems, data and networks,

and hence

(b) the Chief Information Officer (in charge of such departments) will increasingly concentrate on setting policy and strategy in a similar way that the 'Chief Financial Officer' executes his financial management responsibilities.

The survey also showed that the CIO job was steadily rising in most organisations and although most did not report directly to the Chief Executive few still reported to Finance.

In a more recent survey in the US in 1988 reported by Carlyle (1988) in *Datamation* only 27% of IS executives reported to the Chief Executive, although 59% of them considered they fulfilled the role of 'CIO' as generally accepted. Very few indeed had a title of 'Chief (or Corporate) Information Officer', a title many thought to be not only misleading but harmful! However, whatever the title the function had a 'toothless quality' in most major commercial organisations! Most not only had a formal line reporting role and accountability but had to operate through some form of executive committee established solely for IT.

Part of the problem is not perhaps the need for the job, but the origins of the person filling it. Merely promoting via a change in job title a career IS/IT specialist seems to be a failure. According to Carlyle they remain 'outsiders' in the executive team. Some individuals may overcome the problem of background but more success is likely if a high-flying non-IS/IT executive takes the role. This also upgrades the perceived importance of the task and should provide a business focus for its activities.

The previously mentioned Lodahl and Redditt article (1989) also identified two key aspects of the CIO approach:

(a) about 50% of the CIOs appointed are business people with little or no technical experience
(b) that appointing a CIO alone is not a solution to all the management issues.

All of these findings seem to relate to the UK experience of appointing 'IT Directors'. In a bank or similar information based company, having an IT Director is the equivalent of an Engineering Director in a manufacturing company. It is the technology of banking. However, he or she will not have jurisdiction over all applications. Equally in less IT dependent organisations IT may well report via another executive, preferably one with a primarily commercial or business development role rather than a service role such as Finance. IT will inevitably, for better or worse, be tarred with the brush of its 'superior' departments.

Within business units the 'IS manager' positioning faces similar problems and should depend on the criticality of the systems to the business—the more critical, the more senior and central should the role be to the running of the business. Again, indirect reporting should be through commercial activities rather than service to ensure 'primary' activities in value chain terms obtain the appropriate emphasis relative to secondary activities.

One conclusion in all this vagueness is quite certain—that as IS/IT becomes more critical to organisations the more senior will become the executive with IS/IT as a sole responsibility, both in corporate and business unit terms. Equally certain is that the success of such a senior role in ensuring strategies are developed and achieved will depend as much on the individual as the position on the organisation chart. Both issues should be on the management agenda for regular review.

No doubt some companies will succeed without a coherent strategy for organising, positioning and developing IS/IT resources—but most will need to address this aspect of strategy with considerable thought and insight. Whatever conclusion is reached it will not be entirely satisfactory from every viewpoint! and will need to be changed over time and probably overlaid with some other IS/IT strategic management processes in the meantime!

STEERING GROUPS FOR IS/IT STRATEGIC MANAGEMENT

As mentioned earlier in the chapter, the majority of organisations in both public and private sectors have established some form of 'steering group' for IS/IT. They are called many things but usually have the words 'policy' or 'strategy' or 'planning' in the title.

From discussions earlier in the book some of the main reasons for the establishment of such a grouping of senior managers, focused on the management of IS/IT, can be summarised.

1. In Chapter 5 the Kotter organisational model was used to differentiate between formal and informal organisational arrangements. The formal organisation structure reflects the way the business operates, whereas the 'dominant coalition' or informal structure essentially determines the future strategy of the organisation. This implies that members of that coalition are scattered through the upper layers of the organisation structure, but are not necessarily the most senior, and/or all of the senior management team. Using the jargon of Chapter 8, some senior executives may be 'caretakers' or 'controllers' by nature rather than the 'developers' and 'entrepreneurs' who drive things forward. It is important that the members of the 'dominant coalition' overtly include IS/IT on their agenda since

   (a) they are in practice establishing business strategy and therefore will miss opportunities, etc. if they ignore IS/IT. They are in the best position to identify and evaluate the impact of IS/IT on the strategy.
   (b) they, by their attitude and behaviour towards IS/IT, are determining the role it plays in the business.

   It means that the dominant coalition by intent or default is setting IS/IT strategy and needs to be aware of that and the consequences of its interest or neglect! Any steering group, therefore, must include the main members of that coalition or power group.

2. In Chapter 1 the Earl/Galliers model of the evolving nature of IS/IT planning showed how in the most mature stage, when the aim was to link IS/IT to business strategy, a coalition approach of users, senior management and IS staff needed to be established. This sounds very similar to the argument above but extends the potential franchise to users and IS people as well as the strategy formulators. In essence this may imply a steering or policy group is not enough to involve all necessary parties to the planning process. This will be considered below.

3. In Chapter 8 a number of issues in portfolio management point to the need for strong co-ordination of at least the strategic applications and the need for clearly defined management approaches in the other segments. In particular:

- central planning implies establishment of some mechanism for linking IS/IT and business planning;
- the 'personal–formal' mode of planning described by Pyburn suggests the role that an appropriately constituted steering group can and should play in IS/IT planning.

These arguments perhaps explain the appearance and contagious spread of the steering group during the last decade. Equally, some of the points made above may also explain why many of those groups fail to steer IS/IT in a beneficial or even consistent direction. Criticism of steering groups is often the only thing that users and IS can agree on! especially if they introduce delays, increase bureaucracy, fail to make decisions, etc. The list of comments is almost endless:

'wrong people/too many people attend',
'wrong terms of reference',
'discuss the wrong things',
'meet too infrequently/too often',
'make too many/not enough decisions',
'do not understand the real issues',
'are too remote from reality'.

The causes of these problems can probably be summarised into two major areas:

(a) The wrong people are involved—the group does not include enough (if any) of the 'dominant coalition' to be willing or able to establish strategy. If the right people are involved many of the other problems disappear—the 'agenda' will contain items of strategic value only and the less important will be dropped. Decisions can and will be made.
(b) The group has no infrastructure to support it and carry out its actions, which, as agreed, become the strategy. The steering group needs to address two basic areas:

- ensuring the applications that are strategic in business terms are identified, developed and implemented successfully;
- that policies for managing IS/IT as a key business resource are defined and adhered to.

Using the strategic management model first shown in Figure 2.3 and mentioned earlier in this chapter, the role of the steering group becomes a key part of the *formal* planning process—to *establish the strategic direction*, aligned to the business strategy. Two further stages exist which no grouping of senior managers can expect to carry out personally

- converting the strategy into viable plans for applications/resources,
- implementing the plans by delivering the applications.

These will be done by others but obviously there have to be strong links to and from the steering group, which cannot achieve much in a vacuum. It must both obtain relevant inputs from somewhere and have the means to ensure its decisions are actioned. Most good ideas will originate lower down the organisation. The steering group role is to evaluate opportunities resulting from those ideas in the context of the business, judge their worth, initiate appropriate action and then monitor whether success is achieved. Interpreting this in terms of the IS/IT strategic model defined earlier and shown in Figure 9.1, and considering the need to balance supply and demand effectively, a structure for a steering organisation for IS/IT strategy is proposed in Figure 9.7

This structure reflects the broad concept of coalition defined by Earl and Galliers as well as the high level strategic concept of the dominant coalition.

It also reflects the need for continuity, overlap even, and feedback between developing and implementing the strategy which should as far as possible be done by the same organisational groupings. It is very difficult in terms of knowledge and motivation to implement someone else's strategy.

The main roles and responsibilities are outlined below and summarised in Figure 9.8.

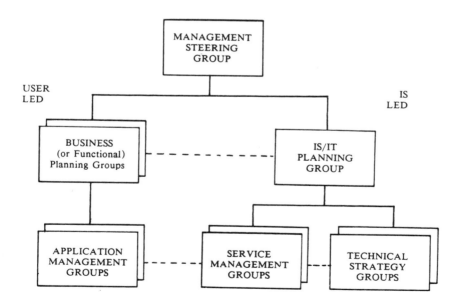

FIGURE 9.7 Steering organisation for IS/IT strategy. The same groupings are required to develop and implement the strategy—a coalition of the users, management and IS/IT professionals

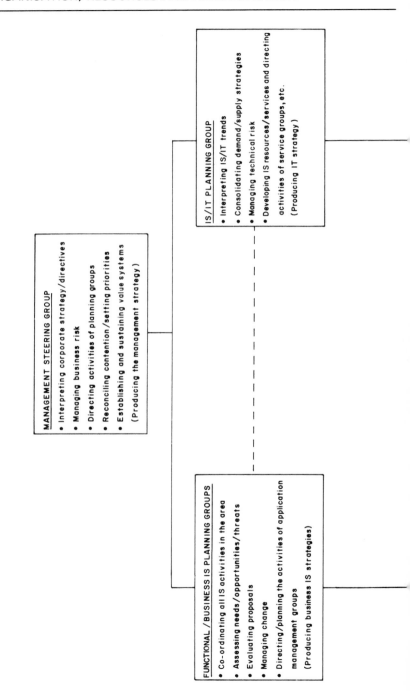

MANAGEMENT STEERING GROUP
- Interpreting corporate strategy/directives
- Managing business risk
- Directing activities of planning groups
- Reconciling contention/setting priorities
- Establishing and sustaining value systems

(Producing the management strategy)

IS/IT PLANNING GROUP
- Interpreting IS/IT trends
- Consolidating demand/supply strategies
- Managing technical risk
- Developing IS resources/services and directing activities of service groups, etc.

(Producing IT strategy)

FUNCTIONAL /BUSINESS IS PLANNING GROUPS
- Co-ordinating all IS activities in the area
- Assessing needs/opportunities/threats
- Evaluating proposals
- Managing change
- Directing/planning the activities of application management groups

(Producing business IS strategies)

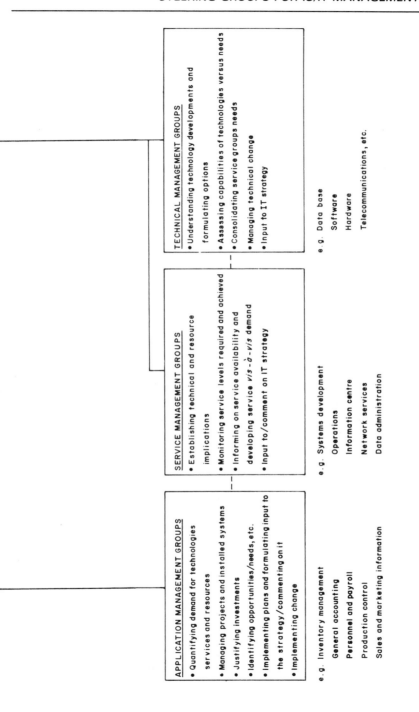

FIGURE 9.8

The Management Steering Group

This group is as critical to the whole structure as the keystone is to an arch. Its membership should reflect the dominant coalition which implies they are:

- able to recognise the potential of IS/IT in terms of the business strategy;
- keen to exploit IS/IT as a business weapon;
- able to influence the management of systems in the area of the business they represent;
- have the confidence of the executive to whom they report.

The steering group is a collection of people, not a collection of job roles. The individuals are what matter, not the role they currently fulfil, but it is important that all areas of the business are represented. That includes the IS group, though it is critical that an IS person does not 'chair' the group. Leadership must come from the business, preferably from the Chief Executive or his highly respected nominee.

The group should meet regularly if not frequently—probably 4–6 times per annum. The lower levels in the structure should get together more frequently— even weekly when a critical application is being developed.

The main purposes of the steering group are:

(a) To agree and produce the management strategy, the key components of which are outlined in this chapter, and ensure the overall objectives of strategic management of IS/IT listed in Table 9.2 are addressed effectively.

   Most of those objectives are impossible to measure and require careful judgement and also consensus agreement amongst senior management as to whether any particular decision made is appropriate to the situation and capable of implementation.

(b) To direct the activities of the planning groups and require responses in due time, and to consider ideas and issues submitted by the other groups.

(c) To address any issues which affect strategic applications and ensure their success is not jeopardised by organisational or resourcing problems. Equally they need to ensure the applications in the strategic segment (and related activity in the high potential and factory segments) are all still relevant to the business as the business environment and strategy evolves. They must be willing to stop activity as well as initiate it.

(d) To act as the final judges to reconcile or settle the short-term contention for resources. Such urgent decisions must be made with an understanding of the long-term implications for the business and its IS/IT capability.

(e) To justify to the executive of the company that expenditures associated with strategic applications and on related R&D or infrastructure improvements are worthwhile and will be controlled effectively.

(f) To ensure that experience is transferred across the organisation and that potential benefits of integration are not sacrificed merely for expediency in meeting local requirements.

It is not just what the steering group does that is important, but the way that it does it. Its process should be open not secretive; its decisions should be communicated quickly and widely; it should demonstrate its willingness to consider ideas from the planning groups which require such attention, and should be quick to redelegate trivial matters. These are all aspects of the IS/IT 'business culture' which must be established. Finally, it should ensure that successes are recognised as well as failures!

Functional/Business Planning Groups

Depending on the organisation's structure, these may be established for each business unit or major function (or both if the organisation consists of both units and service functions). In a one-unit business this role and the management steering group will clearly overlap.

Ideally, the representative of the business area on the management steering group should 'chair' the planning process, although equally, ideally, business IS planning should be part of the agenda for whatever business planning process exists. Either way the senior line managers involved in the business should be directly involved with the planning group.

Whilst the obvious responsibilities include ensuring business priorities and requirements are reflected in the planned application portfolio for the area, it is also this group's responsibility to ensure the plans interrelate with plans in other areas and are understood by the IS group. Where mismatches occur, problems should be resolved amongst the planning groups if at all possible rather than be escalated to the management steering group before alternatives can also be provided from which the best course of action can be chosen.

Having ensured the application portfolio, priorities and plans reflect the business requirements, a number of other aspects must be addressed at this level:

- that appropriate approaches to application development are adopted given the position in the strategic grid and the availability of central, local or external resources. Where the free market philosophy is appropriate the business IS planning group may make the decision without consulting the IS specialists;
- the group must ensure project justifications include all relevant costs and benefits, and can be adequately resourced by the user areas concerned. Lack of availability of key user resources is often as much the cause of project delays as IS resources;

- the group must determine whether the portfolio is being developed to take maximum advantage of experience gained and investments already made in the area and that the information resource is being managed effectively locally and as part of the corporate resource;
- implementation of systems will undoubtedly cause organisational change in the area. This is becoming an increasingly common aspect of systems developments. In time, most major systems investments will probably need related organisational adjustments if benefits are to be realised. Such adjustments will be needed within the area and at the boundaries with other functions. Understanding and suitable co-ordinated and consistent action needs to be established at this level as part of business planning;
- the group should establish appropriate application management groups for their own critical systems and developments and also ensure they are appropriately represented on other such groups on applications which effect the area. Those activities should be initiated, directed, responded to, and in time even disbanded by decisions at this level, unless the application is 'strategic' and cross-functional when the decision belongs higher up!

It is clearly this group's responsibility to produce an IS strategy that converts business requirements into demand for applications which are then managed to achieve the objectives identified. Establishing a coherent plan and associated resource and financial budgets are a key part of that process.

In most organisations business plans have often been developed in a way that satisfies external requirements and suits the business culture or style of management. That process may have excluded or ignored IS planning. That cannot continue if the link is to be forged between the corporate steering and policy setting of IS/IT and the management of each application. In general, business planning is rarely a weak link in this overall structure, but the inclusion of IS in that planning is often done with reluctance and without great effect if earlier mentioned surveys are to be believed (Galliers *et al.*).

Application Management Groups

Application management strategies are dealt with in detail in Chapter 11, and they are clearly focused on the responsibilities of these groups as well as the roles of service management and business IS planning groups.

Here, only the role of such groups in the steering structure will be considered. Every major project, group of related systems or major operational systems will demand significant user management and staff time to ensure it 'works'. During development it is critical that it is 'user project managed' and not seen as an 'IS project'. The users will have to live with the application's consequences. One of the commonest reasons systems fail in a business sense is that the project manager was not a heavily committed, knowledgeable and able user. Every organisation has learned this lesson, the hard way, over the last 30 years!

Establishing system and service requirements and monitoring achievement is a critical aspect of application management. Most such problems should be able to be resolved at this 'implementation' level unless they affect overall plans or resourcing. Then the planning group must become involved.

Major existing systems on which the area depends and interrelated groups of systems, whether developed centrally or locally, require the same ongoing application management attention to ensure they continue to fulfil requirements. Obviously less time and effort should be devoted to support than factory or strategic applications unless the value of investment is significant.

Obviously some applications cross organisational and/or planning group boundaries. 'Applications management' is required irrespective of planning structures and applications which cross organisational boundaries and/or have multiple users are notoriously difficult to manage coherently. There is therefore not a strict hierarchical relationship—an application management group may report to many masters and should conflict be unresolved, the 'application' may have to become an issue on the management steering group agenda.

IS/IT Planning Group (and Service Management and Technical Management Groups)

The IS limb of the structure consists of three parts, all of which have been discussed earlier in the chapter. Overall resource and technology planning and development is the responsibility of the IS/IT management team, but must also include or allow for IS/IT resources not directly under its control. The head of the IS/IT organisation should be a member of the management steering group, but in that role he or she is first a senior manager and second an IS/IT professional. Indeed, as suggested earlier, it might be best if he or she is not by career an IT specialist.

An infrastructure is required to support the management team's planning and production of the 'IT strategy'. The IS/IT planning group should consist of the IS/IT senior management team plus, if appropriate, senior user managers who control significant IS/IT resources or technologies. This split of responsibility is common in 'high-tech' companies where technological use of IT is separated from commercial application.

This group will bring together the resource implications of application plans as well as determine the main aspects of technology development and capacity. It should direct the activities of the service and technical groups which are probably departments rather than 'committees'.

One responsibility it must undertake is to interpret the implications of IS/IT developments and trends for the management steering committee in relation to the business. Some advantage will accrue by being technically advanced provided it can be exploited in business terms.

The role of the subsidiary groups is summarised in Figure 9.8 and described in more detail under considerations in IS/IT organisations earlier in the chapter.

Other issues to be managed under these headings are considered in later chapters. What is important is to appreciate that close co-ordination along the implementation level from the extremes of business and raw technology is just as vital to success as the effectiveness of the management steering group.

The effectiveness of the relationship between user biased application management and IS biased service management groups will determine not only how well applications are managed during development, but also whether the best application development approach is adopted in the first place.

The ability of service and technical management groups to work together will determine whether technology is employed on the basis of what it does for the business rather than just what it does! At the same time the choice of the best technology within strategic and financial constraints will depend on the mutual understanding of these two groups. Technical specialists have a very important role in the organisation, but they and business oriented users often fail to communicate. The service groups are the interpreters in both directions capable of understanding the language of business and technology. People working in such service groups will often have a split loyalty to the business and technology.

Summary

This structure or model brings together a number of facets of IS/IT strategic management:

- top management involvement where it is most useful;
- user and IS balance in determining strategy;
- strategy, planning, implementation requirements;
- exploitation of ideas generated from anywhere;
- command and control in effecting policy decisions;
- supply and demand management;
- co-ordination of the generic strategies and portfolio management;
- consistency over time in developing and implementing strategies;
- an ability to learn from and transfer experience.

From using the model in evaluating the management of IS/IT in many organisations it is clear that if one or more of the functions is missing, or is ineffective, or not linked properly to related functions, then either strategies are not being developed or they are not being implemented. Many organisations need variations on this model depending on size, diversity or otherwise of the business, degree of corporate control exercised, the stage of IS/IT development and the variety and sophistication of technologies deployed.

ALLOCATING AND/OR CHARGING OUT IS/IT COSTS

Few aspects of IS/IT management have attracted as much academic attention or user dissatisfaction as so-called 'chargeback systems'—ways of either allocating IS/IT costs to users or charging them for services used. Why is this rather irritating aspect of IS/IT management, which should perhaps be a minor accounting issue, be of any importance in strategic management? Because what may appear as charge-out to the accountant and IS department is seen as a *pricing mechanism* by the user. If the charge is a crude overall cost reallocation of a relatively arbitrary nature which the user can neither influence nor control he will probably ignore it. Otherwise the charging system can significantly affect the implementation of strategy as decisions are made on the price of systems and services prevailing at the time of decision. Box 9.1 describes briefly two examples of how charging systems deflected a strategy in two sophisticated organisations. They are probably not unusual nor extreme cases.

What must be remembered is that such charge-out systems are really *transfer-pricing* systems for the buying and selling of IS/IT products and services, and must be constructed as such. Should the IS group be set up as a profit centre or even a separate company then the charge to users is obviously a real price. The merits of such an acceptance of the pricing mechanism are strongly argued by Allen (1987) in terms of the benefits accruing when information service groups are made to 'pay their way'. He argues that when IS is managed as a profit centre it will provide a 'better service because it is rewarded for successfully responding to the users' and 'users determine their own budgets'. It must of course follow that:

(a) users can select the supplier (internal or external),
(b) the IS department can refuse 'unprofitable' work.

This arrangement is close to the definition of *free market* as described in Chapter 8. Allen concedes that the profit centre approach is not appropriate where the IS department is technologically backward or poorly managed because the users will choose outside suppliers in preference for most needs. If a free market strategy is appropriate then so perhaps is a profit-centre approach, but it could be seen as the need for effective charging and user accountability driving the strategy not the reverse. It should be feasible to devise a charging/pricing system which does not potentially risk the mix of strategies required.

Charging out/pricing of development costs is relatively straightforward since the majority of costs are identifiable deployed labour plus capital expenditure. Either a market or internal labour recovery rate can be used. The total project development cost can be identified relatively easily and performance against targets reviewed either against a fixed 'contract' cost or original estimate. Whether any over/under run is attributed to the IS 'supplier' or the user 'customer' is largely academic but may be a sensitive political issue!

BOX 9.1 *Examples of impact of charging systems on IS/IT investment decisions*

Example 1

The central computer facility was run as a number of separate cost centres but the two of concern are:

(a) batch computing—mainly overnight processing requiring a large number of operations staff to handle output, etc.
(b) online computing—mainly during normal working hours requiring a smaller number of staff.

The indices of charging for mainframe computer usage in a major corporation between 1980 and 1984 were as follows:

	1980	1981	1982	1983	1984
Batch	510*	515	500	370	200
Online	500	380	240*	260	290

*Major upgrade purchases.

The financial objective of each cost centre was to recover its full costs each year by means of a per unit charge-out rate to user departments.

In 1980 the charges for a unit of online use and batch use were very similar. In 1981, a major upgrade of the mainframe was installed to cope with an increasing overnight batch load. The cost of the upgrade was loaded on to the batch cost centre from the first year, although it was expected to provide sufficient batch capacity for three to four years.

Initially, the unit cost stayed approximately constant, in the first year—the cost of capacity matching increased demand. Unit costs of online use were falling due to the increased utilisation of the existing fixed resources and the greater spread of principally fixed costs. Most of this usage was for new systems made feasible by online use of the mainframe; i.e. the applications would not have worked in batch mode.

A manager in the personnel department calculated that he could reduce his department's costs if he could transfer the existing batch personnel records systems to run online. The 30% p.a. operating cost savings as seen in 1981 would 'pay for' the development. His divisional manager, under pressure to reduce his costs, endorsed the proposal. The online system was finally installed in 1983, by which time batch costs had reduced to the level of online in 1981—the savings would have materialised anyway!

But worse, in 1984 the trend reversed and his new system was costing more than the old one would have and considerable systems resources had been used to achieve this result.

What had happened? In 1982, the online resources became fully utilised—further capacity was purchased for the online cost centre which temporarily increased the unit charge. In the meantime, increased volume had more fully utilised the 1981 purchased 'batch capacity'—thus reducing the unit charge. Interestingly, the charge curves closely follow the actual cost of the resources offset by a capacity utilisation lag.

continued on next page

continued

The differential cost-recovery driven charging—differential 'pricing' to the users—of these arbitrarily derived cost centres caused a misuse of resources, due to the policy to recover all costs against actual utilisation in the annual budget period (rather than over the full utilisation for which capacity was purchased and the full asset life). In this example the personnel manager could presumably have made a financial case for reconverting his system to batch mode!

Example 2

A major public corporation purchased a new mainframe computer to meet the estimated demand from a number of interdependent new systems, proposed for installation over three to four years. Accounting policy stated that the cost had to be recovered evenly over four years, i.e. 25% of the cost each year. Utilisation of the machine was expected to grow by 15 to 20% p.a. up to a maximum of 60 to 70% over the four years.

Consequently, 25% of the cost had to be recovered with only 15% utilisation in year 1. The charge out rate in year 1 was therefore at least 200% of the expected average and 400% of the expected rate when the systems were all installed. Naturally, the first user objected to subsidising future users and finally purchased a minicomputer for the system—which cost his division less money on its budget. Obviously, the second user had an even worse financial balance to overcome and he too purchased his own machine. The new mainframe lay idle and the benefits of integration were never achieved! Two more computers than necessary had been purchased by the corporation as a whole.

Source of examples: J. M. & K. R. Ward, 'The transfer pricing of IT', *Management Accounting*, Feb. 1987.

Charging/pricing for other services is more problematic due to changing economic factors and usage of resources over an extended period.

The overall objective is to improve the accountability of both user and IS/IT management for the resources they consume and deploy.

The CIMA Management Accounting Guideline, No. 4, *Charging for Computer Services* recognises that:

> The problems of calculating a transfer price for computer services are complicated by the specialised nature of the services, their independence from the saleable end products of most businesses and the difficulty of matching the demand for computer services with their supply in the short and medium term.

Many charging systems for computer services are complex in design to address these problems, producing elegant accounting solutions but often ignoring the fact that transfer pricing is a matter of business policy, to enable overall business, not just IS/IT and accounting, objectives to be met.

Most writers on this subject describe some or all of the objectives that Olsen and Ives (1982) list for charge-out systems:

- to provide the basic accounting functions of cost recovery;
- to maximise IS/DP benefits;
- to ensure equitable resource allocation amongst users;
- to regulate demand for scarce resources;
- to assist in planning;
- to motivate and evaluate IS management performance;
- to make users accountable for resources consumed.

A study carried out by Bergeron (1986) showed that if users are to be held accountable for meeting their DP budget they must be involved in its preparation and they must be charged in proportion to the services they use.

In order for this to happen the charges to users have to be understandable to the users. If they are difficult to understand they will not be used. These findings are similar to those of Olsen and Ives, and apply to both project development and systems operational charges.

McKinnon and Kallman (1987) argue that the type of chargeback mechanism should relate to the stage of maturity of IS and its management in the organisation. They use the support–factory–turnaround–strategic rationale of an increasingly important application portfolio to demonstrate the need for increasing sophistication of charging/pricing mechanism. They argue that prices and the pricing mechanism should be clearly aligned with IS policy either encouraging use or trying to control it and either encourage freedom of user choice or directly influence priorities. Irrespective of the detailed methods used, pricing is, and must be employed as, an instrument of strategy.

Whatever pricing/charging system is selected it is clearly important that it reflects in user charges the real costs of IS/IT to the business, otherwise comparisons of alternative solutions and measurements of IS/IT utilisation and performance are based on artificial figures.

The cost allocation/transfer pricing problem has been resolved in some organisations by a 'utility' based system. Airlines are totally dependent on their systems and technology and can be considered as some of the most advanced IS/IT using organisations. One airline had suffered from the misuse of resources and antagonism caused by sophisticated charging systems as in the earlier examples. To overcome the problems and resolve conflicts a simple charging/pricing mechanism was established by treating IS/IT as a corporate resource to be paid for as and when used.

In outline the approach is as follows:

1. All computer and network operating and depreciation costs were pooled together as a corporate cost.
2. All transactions (the number of interactions with computers) were cumulatively monitored.

3. Users paid a charge per transaction (= total cost/total transactions), the same charge irrespective of the complexity, i.e. irrespective of the specific quantities of resources consumed. They paid on utility value not resource consumption.

This is both practicable and realistic as both a financial and a management performance measure. The rationale is as follows:

1. Across the organisation, total transaction demand can be forecast within $\pm 5\%$, even if particular applications cannot be predicted accurately.
2. Equally, in total, costs of IT follow a forecastable pattern of growth, at least over a one or two-year period.
3. A user manager has control over how much his department uses a system but not over how much resource the system uses.
4. IS management has control of the resource in total and responds to total demand, but cannot control the mix of usage, which varies with business activity.
5. The price paid by all users will reflect the decreasing cost of IT equipment, offset by a lag due to depreciation periods and capacity utilisation. This price should compare closely with outside services—which have the price-lag problems—provided the IT resources are well managed.

At the end of the accounting period a 'profit/loss' against budget recovery is calculated—this is a measure of IS management planning performance. The charge per transaction reduces year on year reflecting the decreasing cost of IT—again this can be compared with external price changes to measure IS management performance.

Budgeting and control of user charges is in the user's control. Variances from budget will only be volume-based and explainable within user management business performance measurement.

The system is cost effective in its administration, due to its simplicity, and is simple to understand—unlike many charging systems which are a total mystery to many users.

As a system of charge-out for cost recovery and transfer pricing it comes close to achieving all the objectives referenced above including reflecting real world costs of IS/IT in the prices users pay.

Summary of the Issues

Inevitably, no system of transfer pricing can be absolutely fair. However, not recognising that any system of IS/IT cost recovery via charge-out is a transfer pricing system will not only make it unfair but also cause misuse of expensive resources, reducing the profitability of the business. Charge-out is therefore an instrument of policy to promote effective use of resources. Those who have to pay for the services will make decisions on the price they have to pay in the short term. The charging mechanism must anticipate this buyer behaviour and influence it appropriately.

Rather than expend ever-increasing amounts of expertise in refining the cost recovery/charging/pricing system to accommodate the peculiarities of IS/IT, more time should be spent ensuring that the policy is effective. To achieve this, consolidation of IS/IT costs and usage, rather than detailed service analysis, is likely to provide the best solution. It is also likely to provide a simple enough mechanism for all to understand and use responsibly.

SUMMARY AND CONCLUSIONS

The previous chapter provided a framework of the strategic grid and high level (generic) management strategies for IS/IT. Subsequent chapters deal with aspects of strategy which in many ways are particular to IS/IT in terms of information, systems and technology. This chapter has attempted to consider the rationale for certain strategies at the interface between the particular of IS/IT and the general management of the organisation. These strategies essentially address the matching and integration of the IS/IT function to and within the business organisation, and as such have to be defined by general management.

If these issues are not addressed both at the corporate level and for each of the main business units and functions it is unlikely that throughout the organisation, behaviour will be consistent with the strategy. The result will be failure to implement the strategy. It is obviously important to devise appropriate business-driven IS strategies and then to think out appropriate IT supply strategies. But having a strategy is not going to lead to business success! Implementing and then updating that strategy as the business progresses is how success will occur. Mechanisms must be put in place to ensure that happens. A number of these mechanisms are considered in this chapter—primarily those concerning the organisation of resources and their positioning in the business in relation to its other primary and support activities, and ways of ensuring those resources are most appropriately deployed and accounted for as a business investment.

One conclusion and hence an extension of the discussion into organisational overlays, is that, except perhaps in the simplest businesses, there is as yet no ideal organisation structure for IS/IT within the business structure. This should perhaps not be surprising given the recent arrival on the business scene of IS/IT and its rapidly changing nature and importance. Many general managers perhaps wish the IS/IT management problem might 'go away' or become simple again—the DP manager reports to Finance—but it will not, and will need to be addressed in every organisation several times over the coming decade.

Equally, other issues concerning IS/IT that management would perhaps prefer not to have to deal with are those resulting from the specialist people IS/IT involves. These people often have a career versus company conflict of loyalty and do not easily conform to the culture of the company. But they are becoming in even shorter supply and without them business objectives may become unachievable. Strategies for ensuring these critical resources are retained and developed are an essential part of the management strategy.

These organisational, resourcing and administrative issues of IS/IT strategy are those that become very critical during implementation and can lead to the failure to achieve what should have been a perfectly feasible strategy, because they are ignored or dealt with ineffectively, by the senior management of the enterprise.

REFERENCES

Allen, B. (1987) 'Make information services pay its way', *Harvard Business Review* (Jan.–Feb.).
Benjamin, R. I., Dickinson, C. and Rockart, J. F. (1985) 'Changing role of the corporate information systems officer', *MIS Quarterly* (Sept.).
Bergeron, F. (1986) 'Factors influencing the use of DP chargeback information', *MIS Quarterly* (Sept.).
Carlyle, R. E. (1988) 'CIO: misfit or misnomer?', *Datamation* (1 Aug.).
EDP Analyser (1986) 'Organising for the 1990s', **24**(12) (December).
Hayward, R. G. (1987) 'Developing an information systems strategy', *Long Range Planning*, **20**(2) (April).
Henderson, J. C. and Treacy, M. E. (1986) 'Managing end-user computing for competitive advantage', *Sloan Management Review* (Winter).
Keen, P. G. W. (1988) 'Rebuilding the human resources of information systems', in M. Earl (ed.), *Information Management*, Clarendon Press.
La Belle, A. and Nyce, H. E. (1987) 'Whither the IT organisation?', *Sloan Management Review* (Summer).
Lodahl, T. M. and Redditt, K. L. (1989) 'Aiming IS at business targets', *Datamation* (15 February).
McFarlan, F. W. and McKenney, J. L. (1983) 'The information archipelago—Governing the New World', *Harvard Business Review* (July–Aug.).
McKinnon, W. P. and Kallman, E. A. (1987) 'Mapping chargeback systems to organisational environments', *MIS Quarterly* (March).
Olsen, M. H. and Ives, B. (1982) 'Chargeback systems and user involvement in information systems—an empirical investigation', *MIS Quarterly* (June).
Zmud, R. W. (1984) 'Design alternatives for organising systems activities', *MIS Quarterly* (June).

Chapter 10
STRATEGIES FOR INFORMATION MANAGEMENT

INTRODUCTION

An IS demand strategy, expressed as a required applications portfolio is determined by analytical and creative study of the business and its environment. Obtaining the maximum contribution to the business is then the primary objective in managing the portfolio. Chapter 8, in considering this objective included a comprehensive 2 × 2 matrix model which encapsulated several critical aspects of application management, in particular, the set of generic IS/IT management strategies and the various requirements associated with different types of applications throughout their life cycles. This chapter now focuses on one of the key strategies which contribute to attaining the required benefits from the portfolio—the information management strategy.

The expression, Information Resource Management (IRM), is a term frequently used to embody the comprehensive set of activities associated with managing the information resource. These include its acquisition, protection, utilisation and dissemination and the promotion and management of thrusts to derive maximum benefit from the resource. The effectiveness of IRM in a business relies on implementing coherent policies which aim to provide relevant information of sufficient quality, accuracy, and timeliness at an appropriate cost, together with access facilities suited to the needs of authorised users. A well managed IRM function is arguably an essential element in an effective IS/IT infrastructure. Whilst the components of IRM are described in this chapter, it does not set out to cover the subject in great detail. There are several books that are devoted to this, for example, Synnott's *Information Resource Management* (1981), and Holloway's *Data Administration* (1988).

Information is emerging as a recognised 'resource' following a period where production, complexity and demand have rocketed, but where access to the real information needs has been limited; partly because of a proliferation of stand-alone unintegratable systems, and also through lack of clarity in identifying business-driven requirements.

The importance of information will inevitably grow as more organisations accept its new role. Drucker (1988) predicts that the typical organisation of the 21st century will be information-based. He claims it will be flatter, having drastically slimmed down its management size and levels, and will be peopled mainly by knowledge specialists, working in fluid interdisciplinary teams. Everyone will be responsible for meeting their own information needs, and the organisation as a whole will need to have a unified vision (an information architecture), and to have abandoned former parochial views on information and its role.

It is true that some fragmentation of information has occurred as a result of the increase in the use of PCs, and that this will mean a harder job in convincing users that some of the information they customarily use in their PCs should be treated as a shared resource and managed accordingly. On the positive side, many users are now more aware of the value of information.

Promoting the management of information as a corporate resource does not infer building an all-embracing corporate database—'*The* MIS', but does support data independence. True data independence is achieved when there is no relationship between how information is stored and how it is accessed and applied by different users. They need to be able to vary their requirements without impacting the storage structure or accessing efficiency. Conversely it should be possible to restructure databases from time to time, without interfering with access demands. This can occur when organisation-wide needs change or when corporate data management policies or even basic information architectures change in line with business evolution.

This chapter focuses on the needs of an organisation undertaking strategic IS/IT planning, perhaps for the first time and identifying its information needs. Some of the questions that need to be answered in that process are:

- What information is strategic and what high potential information is likely to become strategic?
- Where is it to be found and how can it be obtained?
- When and how can it be delivered to where it will be most useful?
- How can it be verified and what other information is required to turn it into useful knowledge?
- What impact can it have and how can this be ensured?

These questions are addressed here by considering a framework for the sound management and exploitation of information defining:

1. Objectives for effective application of information.
2. How to introduce IRM to meet the objectives.
3. Conceptual information architectures.
4. Activities directed towards meeting the objectives.
5. Policies and implementation procedures.

OBJECTIVES OF INFORMATION MANAGEMENT

Levering Power from Information

The overriding objective is to lever maximum power using applying information as an integral resource in business strategy. In meeting that objective, the value potential of information, associated with business processes, especially the primary competitive processes, will be harnessed to its fullest extent. In Chapter 6, opportunities for gaining strategic advantage and techniques for identifying the opportunities, were considered. In setting out to manage information, it is presumed that such opportunities have been examined, and supporting information requirements confirmed.

Since information needs to be managed in line with its value to the business, it is helpful to 'weight' areas within the total information set, according to their contribution. A similar portfolio model to that used to categorise applications, can be used to rank the information portfolio (Figure 10.1).

Information, both internal and external, that is crucial to *strategic* business processes, and prominently associated with objectives or measures of success, represents the greatest potential value.

New information may be required about external bodies; customers, competitors etc. to improve competitiveness, and possibly enable electronic links to be established. In some cases restructuring of existing information may be needed in order to meet these external bodies' critical success factors. Alternatively, the requirement may be to provide very fast access to integrated information so that information based services can be delivered effectively, or unstructured information may be required to satisfy executive information needs relating to critical business issues.

These are all business-driven needs, demanding flexible and often high performance response. As long as it can meet the performance criteria, relational

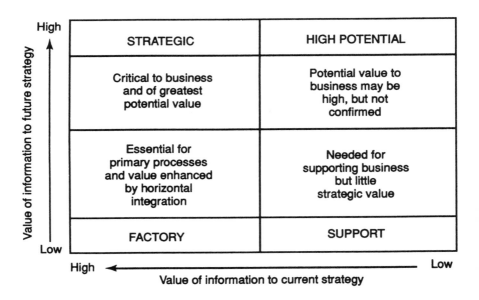

FIGURE 10.1 *Value of information to the business*

technology is probably the best means of supplying information in this area. Short-term interim solutions, depending on setting up intermediate bases of easily accessible information, may be needed to extract value from information in existing but inappropriate data structures.

There may be information, in the *high potential* category, with unproven value to the business, and so not yet classified as corporately managed information. Its sources, structures and relationships may not be fully understood, but as potentially valuable systems are being clarified, their data requirements must be confirmed, so that they can be taken under the IRM umbrella at the appropriate time. Single user systems need not necessarily be subject to corporate data administration as long as the reliance placed on their data is not greater than its integrity warrants.

In some cases it may be the possibility of exploiting latent information power that is the driving force in exploring a high potential opportunity. In others it is the desire to improve business performance that prompts the uplifting of information content and usage.

Information contained only in *support* systems, though necessary, is not likely to contain much latent power. In some cases it may even be a burden on the organisation when it is bound by legislation or corporate instructions to supply information, without any business benefit being recognised. Effort expended on data management or integration should be kept to a minimum, consistent only with efficiency and necessity.

The largest volume of information is probably associated with the *factory* systems, supporting primary operational processes, and essential for their effective day-to-day running. Its value can be greatly enhanced by creating navigable horizontal threads running right across the business, enabling rapid and consistent communication, especially to its external interfaces, where strategic requirements take over. There could also be opportunities to improve business productivity, remove duplication and risk of mis-information. These opportunities must nevertheless be assessed in terms of the benefit they may deliver against the almost certain high cost of imple-mentation, and the likely displacement of resources from strategic developments in the short term.

There is no assumption that to deliver value, information must be stored and transmitted via computer and communications technology. It may be transmitted verbally, or in hard copy paper form in books, journals, directories, instructions leaflets and so on. Within the automated environment requirements for information may result in several types of products

- databases for internal access or external distribution,
- application systems of many different forms,
- electronic information products—electronic mail, telex messages, voice mail, fax etc.

In all cases, to establish and exploit the potential power in information effectively it is imperative to acquire a profound understanding of the business needs. That is the aim of the first stage of the strategic IS/IT planning process. That is the time to determine what information is available and what needs to be captured in addition. A comprehensive, although high level knowledge of the information and activities that use it can then be built into structured models which serve as a blueprint for building an information architecture.

Making the Most of Current Systems

Within that primary objective for managing information, a second one exists: to ensure maximum contribution from current systems, and those still under development. This is achieved by managing the existing mass of information tied up, usually literally so, within them. It is frequently imprisoned in multiple corporate files and databases, exhibiting considerable duplication, and inconsistencies. More often than not it embraces the majority of relevant information. If any headway is to be made towards implementing IRM in an organisation, it is absolutely vital to provide efficient access to information in these databases. However, if multiple versions of key databases, such as customer, product, or order exist, then it is no easy task to rationalise the various versions, and harder still to integrate with the newly defined corporate information architecture. Until unique versions of subject databases, or identically maintained versions are available, managing information globally, implies managing the differences; between actual database versions and consistent data dictionary definitions.

As pointed out in Chapter 7, analysis of existing systems often reveals serious problems. Obsolete data, inconsistent definitions, ineffective linkages, poor exploitation of information, can all lead to competitive disadvantage and must be rectified.

Very frequently there is a huge investment in systems, and in most sizeable companies the cost of maintaining these can be as much as 70–80% of the annual expenditure on systems and technology. Very rarely can the investment be written off—and if it could, replacements could not be found overnight. Nor can support and maintenance be abandoned. So, part of migration planning is to obtain maximum support from current systems. Meanwhile the provision of critical business information in an appropriate set of databases should be the migration target, defined in line with the applications portfolio and conceptual model of information. This is likely to be a long multi-step process of progression towards an elusive goal.

Starting out in planning, the task of evaluating the contribution of data in existing systems, is then continued within IRM. Chapter 5 described how data referenced in current systems can be recorded. Some systems already have associated data and process models and some are recorded in dictionary systems. Frequently, however, this is not the case, and the contents need to be unscrambled from the total system, if their structure is to be understood, and their value assessed. The process serves several purposes

- Documentation of the information structure and processes, which helps in plotting the migration path to the desired systems and information architecture.
- Recognition of whether current systems are able to provide information to satisfy business needs, either directly or after enhancement.
- Evaluation of the contribution they deliver to business objectives.
- Identification of data which can be transferred to an intermediate base of consolidated information for subsequent accessing, perhaps to satisfy composite needs or unstructured enquiries.

Few tools are available for unscrambling the conceptual framework in existing systems, but CASE tools should provide reverse engineering facilities which will serve a very useful purpose in backward tracking and documenting components of systems.

The main aim is long-term benefit through delivering information power, and whilst perfection is seldom attainable, substantial advances can be derived from an IRM approach.

Further aims of managing information include:

1. Creation of a stable integrated information framework.
2. Provision of rapid response to dynamic business needs.
3. Improving efficiency and effectiveness in processing information, and in the business itself.
4. Improving the overall quality of information and systems.

Stable Integrated Information Framework

The business information environment is mainly stable, but business processes need to be responsive to changing demands. As a consequence, in a closely aligned business and IS/IT strategy, the applications that support processes and objectives, need to be flexible and easy to amend. The inference is that information should be maintained and managed independently from applications, whilst accommodating the need to share information from a variety of sources. Keeping the data and applications apart gives a better chance of providing a rapid, high quality response.

Having claimed that the information architecture is more stable than its companion application systems, it is necessary to qualify this by pointing out a few vulnerabilities. If the business undergoes radical change, such as merger, repositioning in a new market, or re-orientates its business strategy, then the conceptual architecture changes quite noticeably. If changes are more subtle, then the effect on information relationships is at a detailed rather than fundamental level. Volatility such as this must be expected.

The other facet of the architecture which is sensitive to change, and difficult to model, is where external factors are involved. There, the information required by the business is not necessarily under its own control, but determined by external influences—suppliers, customers, competitors, the marketplace, the government, etc. Satisfying changing information needs may require creating new unexpected views of information across the business, or linking more of the primary value-adding processes together, internally or across external boundaries. Increasingly, there is a need to meet unstructured requirements, to answer the ubiquitous 'what if?' queries.

If business strategy is subject to frequent change, especially in increasingly volatile times then it is important to:

1. Conduct information planning at a strategic level; involving executive management, and closely matching it to strategic business planning, so as to build future perspectives as far as possible into the envisaged architecture.
2. Regularly re-visit strategic information planning as part of the strategic IS/IT management processes. One of the strongest arguments for making information independent of applications is to cope more effectively with change. Change at application level, where the information architecture remains stable, is the easiest to accommodate. Change of a more profound nature is much trickier. However with sound information management procedures in place, the information infrastructure in good shape and automated support available, the impact of change and its consequences can be tackled with a stout heart.

In providing a stable information base, there are strong arguments for it being integrated, at least throughout the primary business processes. Prompted by many factors in the business environment, it is expected that there will continue to be a steady increase in the number of knowledge workers and growth in the volume and complexity of internal and external information needed to meet a variety of demands. As people become more involved in competitive activity, they want their finger on the pulse of the business, via their own particular pressure points. This means more people wanting more access to more information, distributed more widely. These increased demands call for improved gathering and dissemination across a wide area. Its use can vary from exchange of information within competitive systems, support within decision-making processes, *ad hoc* end-user enquiries, and board-room planning systems, to searches through external databases.

Widespread sharing of information from a variety of sources requires considerable integration, but this does not mean a single corporate database. More likely, the target is for several databases each representing a logical portion of the business, but all descendants of a representative high level global model. That way, fragmentation, the scourge of the non-IRM approach, is avoidable, since everyone can look at the same or consistently related models, the same meanings and definitions and by and large, the same occurrences of information.

Benefits of a well structured, stable, integrated information resource, that can be easily and quickly adapted include:

- Businesses better equipped with information to respond as necessary; to change direction, monitor market and customer needs, promote themselves, tie in their customers, etc.,
- Direct savings achieved in the long run. Even though introducing IRM is costly, fragmentation is even more costly when one takes into account multiple duplication of data capture, confusion caused by data inconsistencies, and the frustration and chaos in reconciling differing coding structures. It can be the cause of lost opportunities through lack of comprehensive information.
- Cross-functional and cross-organisational cooperation improved by making information available across boundaries to a broad community of authorised users. Some of these may be external users, having their own requirements for accessing information. For example customers placing orders, suppliers enquiring into the status of manufacturing schedules to meet Just-in-time delivery requirements, financial analysts collecting global economic figures. In these cases both user and (information) supplier are beneficiaries.
- Support for managing businesses in a more integrated way. Traditionally many businesses have been functionally oriented and IT has supported individual business functions quite effectively. Now there is a growing trend towards integration in order to be more customer and market oriented, and thus more competitive. This demands taking a horizontal view across the business, for example linking all activities relating to a customer, and reorganising information in such a way that the whole of the customer's relationship with a business is logically brought together and presented at the point of contact with the customer—face to face, on the telephone, when a written order, query or complaint arrives, or when an automated link is used.

A company may want to link information about its services to a customer in order to contain risk (e.g. a bad debt in one area would constitute a bad risk in another), or to maximise opportunities by being able to offer its complete range at one time. Finance offers several examples here, in relationship banking or in financial institutions offering a range of combined services.

Opportunities exist in many other fields, for example in government departments. The Department of Health and Social Security may wish to provide a potentially valid claimant with information and advice on a range of benefit entitlements, or alternatively to provide the authorities with a better chance of detecting false claimants. In these and most cases, the total view is needed at the business/customer interface, more so than at the centre, since the contact takes place in distributed branches.

The architecture represented in corporate or SBU data models, data flow diagrams and the entity/activity matrices should facilitate access to this information.

It may be needed for use in highly structured systems or for unstructured usage. In either case independence needs to extend beyond its separation from applications, to include independence of location, and technical medium, and transparent linkages. That is, the user should not need to be aware of any of these characteristics.

Rapid Response to Dynamic Business Needs

This is closely related to the previous aim. Not only should the information framework be stable and integrated, but also facilitate a swift response to an unexpected business need. The 'window' may only be open for a brief period. A completely healthy systems and data architecture that can enable a virtually instant response is a rare occurrence, but there is much that can be done.

The business models derived from top-down analysis and based on aligning business and information, reflect the information sharing requirements of the business throughout its internal value chain, and into the adjacent organisations. During the analysis of the value chain, and in particular in examining the information logistics of primary activities, opportunities for deriving competitive advantage by improving information flows will have been examined, and built into the required architecture. The ability to satisfy unexpected needs can best be provided if consideration is given to them during the processes of information planning. Applying informed second-guessing, potential information needs, and their sources, relationships and flows can be built into the initial information architecture.

The most appropriate structure for an organisation's information and systems is usually that which mirrors the organisation itself. Thus, if the organisation is divisionalised and highly decentralised, then the information resources, both applications and data, are probably also best disposed in that form. Determining how best to implement the conceptual architecture is part of the SISP process. Clearly it is also part of the process to look towards future business needs before embarking on what could be very extensive development or redevelopment of systems and information resource planning.

The benefits which can then be delivered, are swift responses to:

- exploit an opportunity,
- counter an unexpected attack,
- build a rapid defence against possible competitive threats,
- supply information to assess a business risk.

Improved Efficiency and Effectiveness of Information Processes

Improving IS productivity is an aim of many organisations, and good information planning and management should play a substantial part in meeting this aim, resulting in stable databases and flexible applications. There are a number of factors that contribute to improving efficiency.

- Initially, increased investment is required to create an appropriate infrastructure. Thereafter, whilst initial project development costs may be higher, benefits are reaped over a long period in reduced maintenance costs and greatly extended effective life and reliability of systems.
- Information is consistent across the business, and not plagued by incompatibility problems.
- If a good data dictionary is employed, fewer data related program errors are incurred.
- High level languages, associated with advanced and reliable database management systems reduce programming effort considerably, for example, in generating enquiries and reports.

In defining the information architecture along with new applications, many problems can be avoided. But in considering the current portfolio, it could be worthwhile seeking out long-standing culprits in the form of obsolete information or unmatched needs and supply.

- Archived information held longer than needed.
- Information disseminated when it is no longer needed. Where this used to apply to hard copy reports, it may now apply to files of information distributed electronically, but never accessed by users.
- Useful information available but not used.
- Inefficient methods of capture, manipulation, storage or distribution.
- Duplication in several activities; capture, storage, transmission.

Duplication in one or another of these forms is very common. It is usually a consequence of independent developments, and is often perpetuated out of lack of trust between system 'owners', than absolute necessity. It is clearly a source of potential errors when data is input more than once. It is not uncommon to find ten or even more different customer databases in an organisation where an extensive portfolio of systems has been built over a number of years. Few, if any of these will be identical, in definition or content. Overlapping will be extensive, even where the products of the enterprise differ widely from division to division, and thus database to database. The degree of overlap varies from case to case. For example publishers of journals and magazines will have one set of customers who are subscribers and another who are advertisers. In this circumstance there may be little overlap, nor much potential for generating business from combining the two.

Where multiple copies of data exist, whether the physical data need to be centralised or distributed more widely is an implementation and operational issue.

Multiple databases, which have grown out of independent developments can demonstrate a number of differences. They can contain entirely different coding structures and they may also incorporate different definitions of entities, ambiguous or conflicting meanings, and different logical relationships. In the worst cases they infer polarisation, mistrust and a widespread lack of confidence in combining and sharing information. In these cases, the task is more than one of data management, it requires major cultural change. One of the objectives for introducing IRM then involves gaining the confidence of disaffected business users, and sometimes their IS colleagues.

The risks associated with duplication of data input and storage can be greatly reduced by seeking to enter, update and store information once only. Duplication risks thereafter will be linked to the number of databases into which data is transferred, and their distribution around the organisation.

Other factors affect the effectiveness of information processes and of the users who depend on them, but most of these are tackled within the identification of business IS demand, and the resultant information architecture. Characteristics which then determine effectiveness include availability of required information, ease of access to end-users, timeliness, quality, integrity and consistency. These all fall within IRM policies and 'service' criteria.

Improved Overall Quality of Information Systems

The quality of systems will be covered in the next chapter, nevertheless, IRM has a very significant contribution to make towards quality. Much of this depends on the separation of data and processes and on the provision of a data architecture, matched to the business.

INFORMATION RESOURCE MANAGEMENT (IRM)

Background

After a slow start and patchy growth, IRM approaches are slowly gaining ground, having been introduced around 1970. There is no universal agreement about what precisely constitutes IRM, its component functions, scope, organisational focus, policies and tools. It is often called by other names, corporate data management being a favourite alternative. It is significantly different from data administration or data management applied at system or business function level, having a much wider significance and value.

IRM policies for managing information are defined and refined as part of the IS/IT strategic management process. Mechanisms are needed to carry out these policies; mechanisms for acquisition, protection, dissemination, and disposal, supported by appropriate tools and methods. Key functions of IRM are data administration, data dictionary administration, database administration and information access services. Watson (1987) describes IRM and its components briefly as follows:

- *IRM* is an holistic approach to the management of the information resources of an organisation. The emphasis is on integral, efficient, and economical management of all the organisations' information. It means getting the right information to the right people at the right time.
- *Data administration* is the identification and classification of business information and associated requirements, development of a corporate architecture, development of procedures and guidelines for identifying and defining business data.
- *Data dictionary administration* entails describing and cataloguing the information available.
- *Database administration* involves design and development of a data(-base) environment for recording and maintaining data (especially machine-readable data), development of procedures and controls to ensure correct usage and privacy of data, operational timing, monitoring and housekeeping.
- *Information access services* ensure provision of support services, and hardware and software to enable end-users to locate, access, correctly interpret and, where appropriate, to manipulate the information available.

There have been numerous attempts to classify the essential characteristics of IRM. Guimaraes (1985) observes that an organisation can claim to be practising IRM only if certain essential characteristics are evident. These are:

- the head of the information management function is on the board of directors,
- data administration as well as database administration is practised,
- information flows are modelled at a global level, and in more detail for the principal processes,
- strategic IS/IT planning has taken place, for the whole organisation,
- an IS management strategy incorporating corporate policies is in place.

Apart from his insistence on the appointment of a head of IS/IT at board level, which although increasing, is still not widespread, his other points are all included in effective IRM as described here.

On the other hand, Synnott's view of IRM (Synnott, 1983) goes far beyond the management of information. He claims that IRM consists of seven information resource building blocks, linked into a single architecture. Each block is designed, implemented and managed separately, but all bond together with increased strength and synergy.

The first of the building blocks is information policy, which is consistent with the IRM concept above. The policy determines the scope of the information which will be incorporated under the IRM function. Sources of information are computer-based (including the technologies of data processing, office automation and communications), paper-based and people-based. The IRM architecture may have to take into account distributed and variable technology resources, so that the ultimate user has no knowledge of physical location, technological differences, or application source. Technically this may not be possible, but conceptually, access difficulties are ignored. Information policy also addresses:

- IRM steering mechanisms,
- quality assurance of the information management functions,
- standards and guidelines for ensuring effective utilisation of the resource.

He also includes database management as a separate building block. The other components of IRM as conceived by Synnott include:

- Organisational structure.
- Computer hardware architecture.
- Communications networks.
- Office automation.
- A systems architecture built around alignment with business needs.

These are all covered within an overall IT supply strategy, but not here within the compass of IRM.

Martin (1982) uses the term information engineering to encompass a set of interrelated policies and activities needed to build an information model, which he terms a 'computerised enterprise', based on current information as used in the existing portfolio. Its focus is the set of information captured and maintained in computer systems, and other information derived from this source. Its central hypothesis is that data (information), is the heart of IS/IT, and that various systems are employed to create, maintain, manipulate and disseminate it. Whilst central to IS/IT, the information probably resides in multiple databases and locations. The second main hypothesis of information engineering centres around the stability of information definitions and relationships, and the frequency with which procedures using the information change. This has already been addressed at some length earlier in the chapter. Not surprisingly, Martin promotes data-driven (stable) rather than procedure-driven (fast-changing) systems, and indeed sees the role of data administration in creating and maintaining the information architecture as pivotal to the entire process of application development, all built on the foundation of the information architecture.

Appleton (1987) adds his weight to the arguments for data-driven IS/IT development, and for maintaining information independent of applications. He introduces an interesting dimension within his argument for promoting information asset management as the principal driving force within IRM. He believes that as asset management develops, then there will be far-reaching effects in the IS environment and especially on development of application systems. A workshop held in 1985 at the National Bureau of Statistics (Appleton, 1987), described information assets as horizontal structures transcending the vertical (application) structures. Five horizontal structures, sharing data as a common element are data acquisition, storage, manipulation, retrieval, and distribution—in other words they map across the information life-cycle. This shift from vertical to horizontal affects information planning, organisation, administration and control. It will in time affect traditional systems development, and IS as it is recognised today, shifting towards data-driven development, and much more widespread user led development. Signs of this shift are becoming more and more apparent at the end of the 1980s.

Principles of IRM

Having introduced IRM, a few further points need to be addressed concerning:

- Stimuli influencing its introduction.
- Extent of the managed environment.
- Relationship between IRM and strategic business units.
- Information as a shared resource.

Stimuli and Start-up

Along with the many factors that may trigger strategic IS/IT planning it is apparent that several further factors stimulate interest in global information management, such as:

- A growing awareness of, and dissatisfaction with information-related problems and the realisation that existing operational systems, or *ad hoc* derivatives of these cannot solve the problems, and even exacerbate them. They are usually associated with the risks and cost of handling obsolete, poor quality and locked-up information. All too often lines of communication within primary businesses break down, or are non-existent. The proverbial 'wheels' get reinvented, application systems do not interface, and the power of imprisoned information is severely diluted.
- Technology push, epitomised in this instance by the growing availability and improvement in tools such as advanced data dictionaries, computer-assisted systems engineering (CASE) tools and relational databases.
- Expansion in use of communications—wide and local area networks, and the increase in available and useful external data sources.
- The growing number of consultants who are committed to an IRM approach, and who inhabit major installations in large numbers, preaching its benefits!

● Growth of end-user computing and increasing IT literacy, prompting the demand for accessible, integrated information. This has also brought into sharp focus the problems and opportunities associated with widespread movement of information.

Once information planning is acknowledged as a necessary part of the IS/IT and business strategies, then the first step has been taken and the painstaking task of building the infrastructure can begin. The size and cost of the task must not be underestimated, nor the difficulty in framing a business case for implementing effective IRM. A considerable act of faith is often needed, based on the expected value of an eventually cohesive, accessible, consistent resource. It will then be independent of systems, and maintained in a flexible condition, paralleling the business, and capable of delivering value for money over an extensive period.

The introduction of IRM takes time, commitment and substantial investment, but the alternative; continuing an unintegrated approach, may be more costly and have a wider impact in terms of lost opportunity over a long period.

The Information Environment

There is a basic assumption within the tenets of IRM that information can be managed, and indeed should be managed, for the optimal benefit of the users and the business itself. But which information, and how much of it?

The information environment of a business is not confined to data in computers, and with expanding technology, automated information is no longer confined to data and text. It increasingly includes voice and image, and any or all of those can be combined with one another. Clearly, future technological developments will encompass much more convergence. The manual environment ranges from heaps of miscellaneous notes on desks to rigorously indexed filed records. Manual and automated information may be archived on microfilm or microfiche. The environment also includes the embedded experience, memory and creative output of its people. Much of this cannot be adequately captured by computer systems today, at least, not in such a form that it can be usefully accessed. However, with the growing use of expert systems and knowledge-based engineering, it is likely that a much greater proportion of this fund of knowledge and experience will be captured and made good use of in the future.

Most activities associated with information are dynamic in nature—information on the move. This is when it is acquiring and delivering its value. The static element—storage, is necessary, but its value is then latent. It is at its lowest when information is available but difficult to access, such as in archived media, or in 'tied up' forms. It has the highest value when it is easily accessible and in such a form that it can be accessed, combined and manipulated easily, as for example in a suitable relational database coupled with a powerful fourth generation development tool.

The information environment does not stop at an organisation's boundaries. It extends into the external environment, inhabited by customers, buyers, competitors and other organisations and influences. This external environment is never static and as stated earlier, can thus never be completely modelled, nor its contents easily captured and made accessible. A key issue in IRM is deciding what is the right scope for the information environment, and how it should be structured.

The starting point in a typical organisation may be where information is fragmented and growing evermore so, as users of personal computing build up their own caches of information. Systems designed to meet specific business needs are unable to communicate directly with one another, and often unable to share, exchange or combine information effectively, because of inbuilt differences in definition or usage. Figure 10.2 illustrates the various information environments associated with a typical business. Much of the information is automated, but the scope of managed information is not yet determined. The next figure (Figure 10.3), shows an idealised picture of an environment, where information is managed as an integrated whole, regardless of location, technology, or application and where a common user interface provides access to the whole environment.

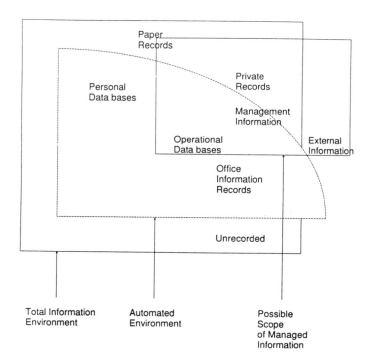

FIGURE 10.2 Information environments

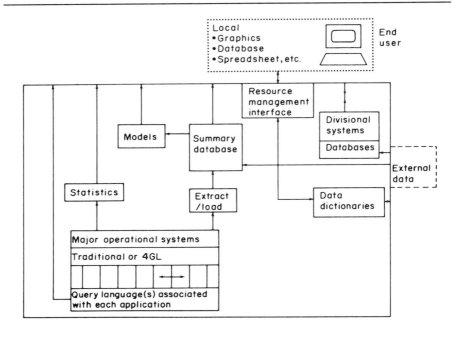

FIGURE 10.3 Integrated information environment

Introducing IRM into a Business

For any business, IRM has its foundation in its business IS strategy, where information needs are defined, and the information architecture for each business unit is constructed. When several business units have developed their own IS strategies, either independently or collaboratively, they may decide to compare and rationalise, and possibly combine all or part of their information architectures, or applications portfolios. As long as due consideration is given to likely long-term needs as well as to immediate requirements, it may make very good business, resource and economic sense to collaborate in this way.

Where two businesses have entirely different technology strategies then the collaboration can extend no further than the conceptual architecture level. More frequently a single business unit opts to introduce IRM within its own boundaries, and sometimes even in smaller sub-divisions of the business.

Whatever the business scope in terms of business units, the information architecture becomes the initial target for IRM in that business. At first, only certain parts of the architecture may be analysed beyond a global level, but piece by piece the information relevant to the business's key processes will be added until an information blueprint is complete to an appropriate level. This is likely to be a multi-year process and it will never be static, as new information is taken into the shared resource and perhaps other information is excluded as not having current significance and not warranting being managed under the IRM umbrella.

Remember there is no suggestion that the information in the business environment should be stored in a single comprehensive database. Far from it, it is almost certain that there will be a number of separate databases in use. However, every attempt should be made to retain consistency of definitions across all databases, and also to confine the entry of information so that it is only input once.

Information Sharing

In the original planning process attention becomes centred on the requirement for sharing information. Sharing can encompass interfaces within one business unit, several units, divisions or companies within the same group, and external organisations. This scope for sharing entails describing the information to be shared, and the community of users having access to it. The rationale will have also addressed the benefits derived from sharing and the practicalities of the provision (access mechanisms, security, risk, communications capability, centralisation or decentralisation, single or multiple copies of data sets). To make it really valuable, technical and cultural issues must be taken into account, such as:

- interworking across various technologies and software offerings,
- overcoming barriers brought about by differences in management style and local values and culture within an organisation,
- interdepartment or company rivalry.

It is less likely that cultural factors will pose problems if the information sharing requirement is largely restricted to a single strategic business unit, and its commercial partners in its value chain, than if the issues of shared information straddle business units in a larger corporate organisation, or international boundaries as in multinational companies. Logical arguments for sharing have to be weighed carefully against potential conflicts.

Sharing is not an issue that is normally raised by end-users. Henderson and Treacy (1986) refer to the findings of Quillard *et al.*, who found that over 80% of data used by end-users was hand entered, and only as growth of end-user computing sets in, in a given area does the need to coordinate the data and the necessity to maintain reliability become pertinent. All such issues must be addressed in the business IS strategy and in the management strategy when information management policies are created since they are fundamental to defining the terms of reference for IRM.

CONCEPTUAL INFORMATION ARCHITECTURE

When IRM is introduced, a conceptual model of the organisation is needed which reflects the business information structure. It may have already been constructed, but if not, it is one of the products when strategic IS/IT planning is first undertaken. Chapter 5 described the top-down process of information analysis, in which activities and data requirements associated with meeting stated objectives, and performance measures are derived and current activity and data usage recorded. The deliverables of information analysis are data flow diagrams, entity-relationship models and activity or functional decomposition diagrams, plus several architecture matrices. These may be recorded in paper-based hard copy form or on tools of varying sophistication, some of which may be interfaced into CASE tools, which span the analysis and design processes of the systems development life-cycle. When analysing future as well as current activities, the result is not one, but possibly a series of conceptual information architectures that reflect the business information status through time. They represent:

(1) The business information currently in use. There may be a corporate architecture in place that mirrors all or part of this more or less accurately or it may need to be built up. Some information currently collected, recorded and communicated may not be required any more, and may only be recognised as obsolete after analysis of information needs related to objectives and current essential processes has taken place. Such an example of obsolescence uncovered in a European financial organisation is described in Chapter 5. In one department some 30 people were effectively operating in a closed loop, collecting, analysing, reporting and transmitting information that was no longer needed by the institution!

(2) Data associated with the current applications portfolio and end-user systems. There may be several variations and subsets of current business data represented here. For example, in many companies there are several versions of one or more databases, two favourites being customer and product. Each will represent versions of data structures associated with their own systems, and the definition of data elements within them are not necessarily consistent.

(3) The data represented by the set of activities and data that would most effectively achieve the business objectives and satisfy performance measurement needs. This would be expected to be an extension of (1) with some redefinition, some obsolescence and some extension.

Figure 10.4 illustrates the changing environment for a dynamic organisation. When an ideal conceptual architecture is produced, this may have been after a process of rationalisation to remove common data elements and redundancies, and after rationalisation of business activities to end up with a logical enterprise wide function model, with embryonic data sets and application systems described.

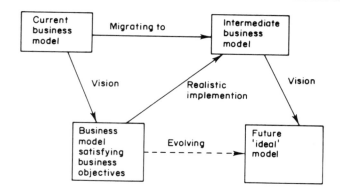

FIGURE 10.4 Evolving business models

Since it may be totally impractical to implement the 'ideal' model in the foreseeable future, it may well be that yet another variant is conceived that comprises a realistic and achievable set of data elements and business activities. Migration planning will focus on this conceptual framework, deriving it largely by enhancement and extension of the architecture representing the existing portfolio. This is very likely to be the case when business needs demand drastic overhauling of the business, whilst the embedded culture remains resistant to change.

As a whole the information architecture has several important roles:

● It is the information framework on which new systems are based.
● It is the valid base against which existing systems are matched, and if appropriate, their information elements are brought into the central information resource.
● It is a benchmark tool for evaluating packages, in terms of their adherence to information policies and their conformance with the architecture.
● It gives a global perspective across the organisation.

Products of Information Planning

As a result of strategic information planning, it may be decided to create a number of databases.

● *Subject area databases* These are databases that contain information relating to business entities that are important throughout the business, such as product, location or customer. These are then accessed by a number of applications each with their own purposes, including the maintenance of the information.

- *Corporate information databases* These are databases which have several sources for their information. These may include operational databases, external data sources, or end-user applications. Their contents are principally determined through investigating the needs of middle and senior managers, and very often contain information relating to measures of critical success factors. Automated bridges may be provided where appropriate, otherwise applications to capture information may be specially written.
- *Operational system databases* These usually exist already, although very often are out of step with the definitions and architecture defined within information planning. However, they must be maintained, often for some time, and it is necessary to take account of the differences between these and the evolving managed environment throughout the remainder of their active lifetime.

ACTIVITIES OF IRM

As mentioned earlier in the chapter, the principal activities undertaken within IRM are:

1. Data administration.
2. Data dictionary administration.
3. Database administration.
4. Provision of access services.

Together with information planning, their purpose is to manage the information resource on behalf of a business, as well as its use. In asset management terms, IRM seeks to build up the information assets of an organisation at an acceptable cost, so that they can be employed to deliver value to the business. The activities provide mechanisms for acquiring, storing and communicating information, conforming to predetermined criteria relating to accuracy, quality, timeliness, and cost.

It is assumed here that IRM is implemented, or upgraded as an outcome of strategic information planning. Otherwise the work performed during the planning process relating to defining the information architecture and in setting information management objectives and policies becomes part of the initial work in introducing IRM. However, without a top-down business focus, the rationale for the architecture is absent and genuine business commitment unlikely to be adequate for the purpose. Commitment is needed for two reasons, firstly because implementing IRM needs substantial investment. Secondly, since the role of IRM crosses all internal boundaries, it needs to have a broadly based interface with the organisation. Even after undertaking strategic IS/IT planning this is difficult to institute if the incumbent culture is strongly 'function' oriented, and business-wide cooperation is not common practice.

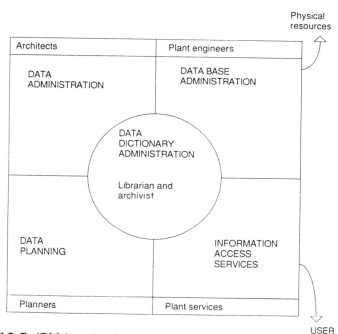

FIGURE 10.5 IRM in a business

Focusing on its component activities, Watson and Omrani (1988) liken the creation and implementation of effective IRM in a business to setting up an efficient industrial plant. Figure 10.5 illustrates the activities of IRM, matched with the roles required to set up and maintain the plant. Here, the designers and builders perform roles in systems development, interfacing with each of the principal IRM tasks.

Data Administration

Business-wide data administration entails implementing policies and procedures for identification, management, protection and provision of information and enabling sharing by authorised users. Holloway (1988) points out that data administration either controls or coordinates the definitions and usage of reliable and relevant data. He makes the distinction on the basis that internal information can be controlled, whereas external data which is used by an organisation can only be coordinated. Indeed he makes a more precise distinction by asserting that data administration does not even directly control internal data, which is 'owned' by the business, but only data about that data and data about itself (meta-data).

The precise responsibilities under data administration will vary from organisation to organisation, and depend on policies set up for managing information. For example, whether IS/IT is distributed or centralised, whether there are established methods for systems development and analysis, and on its use of advanced tools for database management, CASE, etc.

The tasks within data administration are performed by the 'architects and planners', and include the following:

- Data planning, which is a top-down task started in the strategic planning process, and continued at a tactical level in IRM.
- Identifying business information requirements, also undertaken in strategic information planning and continued thereafter.
- Setting data definition standards and procedures, including naming and abbreviation conventions. This may also entail selecting the medium and methods for recording the definitions, usually on a data dictionary, defining procedures and communicating them to business and IS/IT users. A further related task is to introduce monitoring procedures for compliance with standards, and to measure their effectiveness. Another is to assess the impact of changes in data definition or relationships, resulting from changes in the business. Data administration and data dictionary administration work closely together in this area.
- Data administration manages the corporate data models; determining their most appropriate form and their total scope, levels of decomposition, where separate models are relevant, and how they interface or overlap.
- It also has a responsibility for coordinating the solving of data-related problems. These may range from promotion and implementation of a policy to achieve single source of data entry, to internal disputes over data sharing and access rights.
- Communicating with the business, which includes promoting awareness of the role of information, and informing the business what information it possesses, where it is located, what its precise definition is in business terms, how it relates to other information and so on. Some of this is in conjunction with data dictionary administration.
- Establishing and implementing activity and data analysis. They may already be used at system level but there could be a requirement to introduce high level modelling. The task involves selecting methods, techniques, and tools, and developing standards and procedures for their use throughout the information life-cycle. They must integrate comfortably with systems development methods and end-user computing. Part of the responsibility is to promote their use and to provide advice, training and assistance where necessary. There is also a quality role, to ensure conformance and consistency of analysis deliverables.

The deliverables are data models, data flow diagrams, activity decomposition diagrams and architecture matrices as described in Chapter 5. The level of detail in the deliverables is determined by the type of analysis being performed. Rock-Evans (1987), distinguishes between strategic, overview, and detailed analysis levels. The top level is strategic analysis, and its aim is to produce a global structured plan of the business information and activities. Models at this level are necessarily lacking in detail. Rock-Evans describes them as 'fuzzy'.

In practice data administration takes responsibility for the global business models, or if they are not there, produces them. Business analysts produce the overview and detailed models. Where contention occurs, when for example the scope of two overview areas overlap, then this must be resolved by data administration.

- Establishing controls and procedures for data security and recovery, privacy (ensuring compliance under the Data Protection Act), and integrity.

Data Dictionary Administration

This is the function that coordinates and controls all the data about data, the meta-data. It is performed by the 'librarian and archivist'. Whilst it is usually performed by an IT professional, and sits organisationally within IT, this is a business responsibility. It provides data administration with its primary tool for storing and manipulating definitions.

The effectiveness of data dictionary administration is to a large extent determined by the quality of the dictionary tool which is sometimes called an encyclopaedia and more recently a repository. Some can only be used for storage and enquiry, whereas the most sophisticated are integrated with CASE tools, and into application databases. There are very few that currently offer full integration with the cycle from strategic IS/IT planning to application development and on to post-implementation tuning and systems maintenance.

They are potentially very powerful tools, which can impact an organisation at several levels, and in areas outside the IS/IT area. They can simplify the tasks of documentation and system audit, and provide an effective communications route between user and IS departments.

The tasks undertaken by data dictionary administration include:

- Provide an authoritative source of information to users and IS/IT groups on information. It has the unique opportunity of putting information in context for the business at large, but the data dictionary must be clearly seen as a general management communication tool, and not as the preserve of IT. In effect it is the glossary and dictionary of the business.
- Evaluate, select and implement data dictionary management software.
- Set up and coordinate the data dictionary contents, the meta-models of data and functions.
- Establish standards and procedures for use of the data dictionary, and monitor conformance.

- Work with data administration on data definition and impact analysis, and with development and database administration on application and database development and maintenance.

Database Administration

This is the function that supports data administration with responsibility for technical aspects of the database environment, implementing the databases, and supporting their day-to-day operation. The role is performed by the 'plant engineer'.

Tasks within its remit are:

- Undertaking design, development, implementation and operational tasks associated with the business's logical and physical databases.
- Setting technical standards procedures and guidelines for database activities, data input, update and access.
- Evaluating and selecting database management software to suit the technical infrastructure specified to support the business. Implementing and maintaining the software, and implementing change control procedures.
- Monitoring and controlling the environment and database services to the business. Protecting the integrity of the environment, and investigating security problems. Undertaking periodic reorganisation and restructuring, performance monitoring and tuning.
- Performing any necessary housekeeping tasks such as, back-up, archiving, recovery and restart.
- Working closely with data administration and data dictionary administration to ensure policies are followed, and the impact of implementation issues are assessed. Also keeping abreast of database technology, either new, or as yet unused by the business.
- Working with systems development in ensuring that database usage is planned effectively for new applications, and existing systems to give optimal user benefit, whilst complying with database standards and policies.

Information Access Services

As far as the growing population of end-users is concerned, there is little point in taking the bulk of the organisation's information resource into the IRM sphere unless access to that information is made very easy for those with access rights.

The tasks undertaken in providing access services, by 'plant services', are:

- Formulate, implement and monitor policies and procedures relating to ownership, responsibility, security and access rights.

- Provide tools and techniques that enable users to access information. They should also be equipped to improve their effectiveness by applying information innovatively, or by improving their decision-making effectiveness.
- Promote benefits of information management, shared information and appreciation of the value of information.
- Ensure that high quality information is available and accessible, whether in operational databases, extracted information databases, or external information.

POLICIES AND IMPLEMENTATION ISSUES

The general principle underlying IRM and its component activities and working products have been described, as have its objectives for meeting short- and long-term business IS needs. Policies and some implementation issues need further consideration.

Information planning, at a strategic level demands top management involvement, without which there could be an unhealthy IS/IT orientation to the plans. It is necessary for issues to be resolved at this level, and the outcome specified in policies. The type of policies which are set at this level affect the organisation as a whole. The following paragraphs indicate some of these policies. A few relate to physical issues, others to matters of central coordination, authority and responsibility, enabling access and the scope of managed information. There may also be a continuing need for marketing into the business community, to raise the level of commitment for treating information as a core business resource, and to educate the business about information's inherent cost and value characteristics. There will be other issues that reflect the particular requirements of individual organisations.

Scope of Information to be Managed

As indicated earlier in the chapter, the extent of the information resource to be 'managed' must be broadly determined. It will inevitably be smaller than the total set, even taking into account non-computerised and external information. Whilst it is unlikely that a policy will lay down the precise boundaries of managed data, guidelines are needed for data administration. However, hard-and-fast rules would be inappropriate since the status of information changes from time to time.

At any one time some user information will be corporate and some personal, and excluded from data management. Over time the personal may move into a managed status as, for example, it becomes more widely applicable, or its value grows. Butler Cox (1986) defines the two categories of data as authenticated 'corporate' data and unauthenticated 'local' data. Sometimes authenticated data becomes unauthenticated after it is extracted from the managed environment into a local environment where it is manipulated in non-standard ways. There has to be a method for identifying what information is held by users that may have a wider usefulness. The challenge is clarifying the definition of each information element, ensuring that it fits consistently in the relevant models, and recording the details in the data dictionary. Once the criteria for setting boundaries has been determined, the task of bringing information into a managed environment is relatively slow, and needs careful coordination and control.

Data planning needs to incorporate the definition, implementation and maintenance of the information architecture. This means that following the high level work undertaken during strategic planning, there must be guidelines in place for identifying and defining business information elements, and indeed monitoring the overall data needs and maintaining the global conceptual model.

Physical Factors

Several physical factors have to be taken into account.

- Deciding the most effective distribution of data, whether it should be centralised, or split into separate distributed portions, or if multiple copies of distributed data, linked by a common network should be set up.
- Adopting a method for maintenance of data. This is naturally more complex when multiple copies of information are maintained.
- Selecting the type and mix of database technologies to be used. These could include a mixture of hierarchical, network and relational databases, alongside other file management methods, the choice being determined by usage requirements tempered by inevitable justification criteria. Clearly within a long-term migration plan the mix may change, as information becomes available through new applications. Many organisations are opting to use relational technology combined with fourth generation tools for their 'management information' databases, where *ad hoc* access, and easy manipulation and presentation is needed.

Tools

Selecting an appropriate tool-set for managing data and accessing it, including data dictionaries, fourth generation environment tools, and in conjunction with application development, CASE and IPSE products. With all of these, it is necessary to balance the preferred business solution against economic constraints, technical viability, and organisational skills. For instance the cost of storage, transmission and tools, the quality of software offerings in providing good maintenance of distributed databases, and the ability of staff to embrace new methods, must all be considered.

Deliverables out of the strategic planning process usually include a high level conceptual model of the business, including a process model, data model, data flow diagrams and an information architecture. These deliverables are rarely linked directly into the systems development methods and tools, other than via a data dictionary. Where they are connected, then it is likely that CASE tools are in use. These tools will be discussed in the next chapter.

Organisational Responsibility for IRM

Responsibility for coordinating data management activities needs to be centralised, but certain elements may be delegated to one or more information centres, responsible for end user computing and access matters, or to local IRM units in each SBU in a decentralised business.

In certain instances, for example where several SBUs have almost complete autonomy, a central IRM function may not be desirable, and each SBU may set up its own. However, if the corporate body has a significant say in SBU IS/IT policy, and if any attempt is made to standardise systems and data architectures across the company, then central coordination is probably desirable. See Table 9.5 and the discussion on positioning the IS resources in Chapter 9.

A number of other organisational factors should be considered:

- Skilled specialists may be needed to set up and implement IRM, and to train the in-house people in the skills required.
- As it may be a large multi-year project, sufficient resources must be allocated.
- There is no one organisational structure which is universally appropriate. Two possible versions are shown in Figures 10.6 and 10.7. The first illustrates a structure with all IRM activities encompassed within the IS/IT organisation, and managed at the same level as IS/IT development etc., and the information centre. This could represent either a corporate or SBU structure.

The second example shows data management sitting outside the IS/IT organisation, which retains only database administration. In this case the structure contains corporate data management as well as data management at SBU level. This would be repeated for each SBU.

Authority and Responsibility for Information and for Marketing its Role

Criteria for determining ownership, and the responsibilities associated with this for acquiring, storing, maintaining and disposing must be decided. Standards for maintaining quality, privacy, consistency and integrity and for providing the required levels of security must also be determined, and responsibilities assigned appropriately. In addition access rules should be laid down.

These criteria, standards and responsibilities have to be communicated to all users of information, along with details of what information is available, and who has the responsibilities throughout the various stages of the information life-cycle.

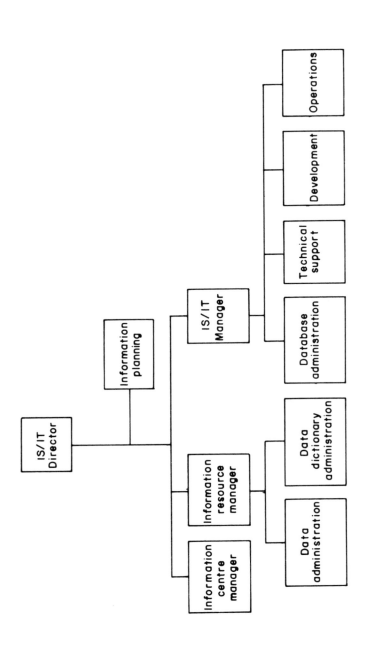

FIGURE 10.6 IS/IT organisation incorporating all IRM activities

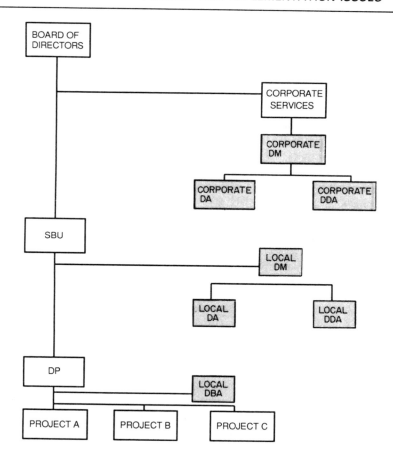

FIGURE 10.7 IRM at corporate and SBU levels

It is, of course, vital to market the benefits of managed information to the user community, and to deliver them, otherwise a natural disinclination to part with 'my' information may turn into outright lack of cooperation or even hostility. This is where top management commitment combined with well thoughtout and implemented policies are needed. Two-way trust is involved; users having faith in the integrity of the data, and data administrators trusting the users not to corrupt or misuse it.

Data Security

It is necessary to protect information from accidental or deliberate destruction, corruption or loss. This is an issue which is growing in importance since organisations are so dependent upon their information, and its exposure to risk is so great. Computer hackers are a growing breed of criminal.

Shared databases are prevalent and the number of terminals which can gain access to information continues to expand, as does the awareness of users. The risk of damage through physical failure or human intervention is also growing and must be analysed and contained as far as possible. The Data Protection Act in the UK and similar legislation in other countries puts an onus on organisations to protect private data.

Measures to protect information should be implemented where they are necessary and can be shown to be effective. Barriers can be designed and built into hardware and software, as can recovery procedures. These can be supplemented by audit and other security monitoring procedures.

Problems which may be Encountered during Implementation

Naturally there are problems associated with implementing IRM. One of the most difficult is in bridging the gap between 'top-down' defined databases and existing databases, and the resulting need to 'manage' the differences. Goodhue *et al.* (1988) noted that this was one of the main problems they observed in a study of 20 firms introducing IRM. Others are:

1. Time and cost. If broadly based IRM is being implemented, key people have to commit themselves. This level of commitment is difficult to obtain and to keep.
2. Systems developed while IRM is being implemented take longer and cost more, due to the inevitable learning curve and to increased up-front analysis effort. This is a problem for line managers who want quick results. It is also hard for IS managers who are resistant to allocating the extra effort.
3. New skills are needed, which are sometimes not easily acquired by existing staff.
4. Changes to business requirements may impact plans while information planning and implementation is underway.
5. Total implementation is very expensive. This level of expenditure will often be resisted if current systems are performing effectively, and IRM is not being implemented on the basis of developing new strategic systems to support business objectives.
6. Application packages can be difficult to absorb within IRM policies.
7. There may be difficulties in managing expectations. Some may view the process as a means of identifying applications portfolios, others a systems and data architecture, others creating database designs. These expectations may all be relevant, but they need to be pulled together under the business expectations of improving business performance over a long period through optimal exploitation of IS/IT.

The study was designed to examine experiences of companies embarking on strategic data planning for a variety of reasons. These findings serve to underline the importance of effective marketing to all parts of the organisation for it to succeed.

Business Benefits can Result from Improvements in Managing Information

Most of the organisations claimed that they had achieved direct business benefits from information planning and management. All had specific business goals they sought to attain.

- One claimed a 20% reduction in spares stock after introducing a common stock control spares system for 12 of its plants,
- Another cut resources needed for consolidation of financial reports by a factor of six. More importantly the figures were ready much sooner for the business to act upon.
- A third significantly reduced errors due to poor data handling, greatly increasing confidence in business data.
- Another set up an information base by extracting information from operational systems and then accessed it through a powerful query tool. It could then answer previously unanswerable questions which directly affect short-term critical decision making.

Lack of Data Standardisation is a Major Problem

The general conclusion was that it prevents or makes very difficult sharing of data across boundaries. The problems surface when there is a requirement to combine information from different functions or organisational groups. All companies claiming any success had tackled this issue if only for key data items.

Total Standardisation is not the Goal

Without exception all companies agreed that not only is it extremely difficult and time consuming, but that it does not make business sense to attempt to incorporate all the information used by a business.

Information Databases are the Main Product,
derived from the Conceptual Global Model

Information databases providing a standardised source of management information, usually drawn mainly from non-standardised applications and built quickly using fourth generation tools and relational databases were the most common and useful product of their efforts.

Resource Allocation must Balance Short- and Long-term Considerations

Investment decisions should apply sensible balance between short-term payoffs and long-term infrastructural constructions that aim to ensure greater standardisation of data.

Address Difficult Organisation Culture Issues

There are often conflicts to resolve in different parts of the organisation.

● Line management preference for short-term results and payback,
● Resentment from local areas that central information management removes some local autonomy,
● Potential opposition within the IS/IT culture to elevation of information management at the perceived expense of the rest of the function.

SUMMARY

Successful implementation of an information management strategy means achieving maximum contribution to the business over an extended period, at an acceptable cost and risk, and with the commitment of the business community at large. IRM is one of the principal mechanisms put into place to continuously aim for optimising this value.

This chapter has attempted to highlight the criteria that affect obtaining the right balance and also to address some practical issues of introducing new activities into the business both inside and outside the IS/IT function.

The whole of the information environment throughout an organisation cannot be treated in the same way, and it is useful to categorise it in an information portfolio, related to business needs and potential. The starting point for implementing IRM may be having identified high level information portfolios for each business unit, aligned to their respective application portfolios, and their business needs. The aim then is to bring information into the managed environment according to needs and priorities, and the risks associated with not managing it.

This entails

● focusing on *strategic* information which must be managed,
● evaluating the *factory* information in the current portfolio and determining how best to exploit its potential,
● maintaining a watchful eye on *high potential* information which may become strategic, but where structures and relationships are as yet hazy,
● perhaps choosing to ignore low potential, *support* information which does not warrant a high priority for being managed.

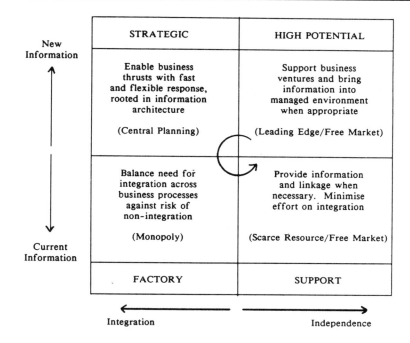

FIGURE 10.8 Information management strategies

Figure 10.8 illustrates the differing aims around the information portfolio. Managing the information portfolio over time, there is naturally an increase in the ability to integrate more information, and thus to build up the information assets of the business. A sensible balance must be struck between the cost of integration, especially where old systems are retained, and the overall cost to the business of not integrating them, and also between the freedom given to end-users to create and use information innovatively and the disciplines imposed within the managed environment.

REFERENCES

Appleton, D. S. (1987) 'Information asset management', *Datamation*, 1 Feb.
Butler Cox (1986) *Unlocking the Corporate Data Resource*, The Butler Cox Foundation Report Series, March.
Drucker, P. F. (1988) 'The coming of the new organisation', *Harvard Business Review*, Jan/Feb.
Goodhue, D. L., Quillard, J. A. and Rockart, J. F. (1988) 'Managing the data resource: a contingency perspective', *MIS Quarterly*, September.
Guimaraes, T. (1985) 'IRM revisited', *Datamation*, 1 March.

Henderson, J. C. and Treacy, M. E. (1986) 'Managing end-user computing for competitive advantage', *Sloan Management Review*, Winter.
Holloway, S. (1988) *Data Administration*, Gower Technical Press.
Martin, J. (1982) *Strategic Data Planning Methodologies*, Prentice-Hall International.
Rock-Evans, R. (1987) *Analysis Within the Systems Development Life-cycle* Pergamon Infotech.
Synnott, W. R. (1981) *Information Resource Management*, John Wiley.
Synnott, W. R. (1986) 'The building blocks of IRM architecture', Abstract from *Data Processing Digest*, June.
Watson, B. G. (1987) Extract from *Information Management in Competitive Success*, Pergamon Infotech.
Watson, B. G. and Omrani, D. (1988) *Information Resource Management*, DCE Information Management Consultancy.

Chapter 11

APPLICATION MANAGEMENT—
INVESTMENT, PRIORITY SETTING, DEVELOPMENT
AND SERVICING APPROACHES

INTRODUCTION

The applications portfolio which represents the most important element of the business IS strategy, contains a list of systems which have been identified as new developments or enhancements to existing systems. Before resources can be assigned and development begin, several other steps have to be taken. These are, justifying the investment in systems and technology, allocating priorities to individual developments across the complete portfolio, and determining how development work should be tackled. Each incorporates decision-making processes. Other aspects of application management relate to the development processes themselves.

The decision-making processes can all be aided by reference to application portfolio analysis which provides a straightforward, and powerful means of attributing the contents of the current and proposed portfolios into categories that relate to current and future business strategy. The case for adopting it as a core technique within strategic IS/IT planning was argued in Chapter 8, which also described the principles behind generic IS/IT management strategies (monopoly etc.) overlaid on to the portfolio. It provides useful insight into the policies to be adopted for application development and management. The composite matrix in Figure 8.1 illustrates many of the issues associated with determining and managing applications portfolios.

Once the portfolio has been justified and prioritised, and a suitable approach defined, then development can proceed. It may be user-only, or jointly undertaken by users and IS/IT. Project management, quality management, change control, configuration management, etc. are all applied in different ways, depending on the portfolio category and chosen development approach.

This chapter tackles some of the main issues relating to decision making and development.

- How to justify investment in application systems development, and the associated technology, using various ways of assessing benefits.
- How to assign priorities, taking into account economics, tangible and intangible business benefits, and logical factors of precedence.
- How to select the right development approach, and what tools are needed to support development.

It then describes the two main approaches—traditional development within a systems development life-cycle, and rapid systems building methods under a fourth generation environment. A further approach is also considered which combines some of the traditional steps with new ways of building systems.

INVESTMENT AND PRIORITY SETTING POLICIES

Investments in systems and technology compete with alternative investments, such as buildings, plant, equipment, R&D and advertising, for the organisation's funds. Whilst application software may for 'legal' reasons be written off as an expense item, it is in reality not a consumable item whose benefit accrues in the year it is purchased. It is an investment whose benefits accrue over time. Technology is normally treated as a capital item, to be offset over time against benefits which accrue from applications which use it. Projects involving IS/IT investments have traditionally been evaluated like 'capital projects', assuming a 'fixed cost' offset against net revenue over the 'life' of the application. This is not meant to be confusing, but is intended to show the rather odd status of IS/IT investments— the real 'asset' is the software, not the hardware. There is no simple answer to the question—on what basis should IS/IT investments be evaluated against other investments? However, it is important that some general rules are established within which applications and supporting technology requirements are evaluated. Otherwise any strategy will be distorted over time by inconsistent, even arbitrary, decision making.

If the organisation was able to develop at any one time all the applications demanded, inconsistent evaluation would not really matter. The overall return on IS/IT investment might be very poor but at least the worthwhile would get done as well as the worthless! However, in most cases not all demand can be satisfied and priorities must be set. If no consistent justification approach is followed, the more beneficial applications may well be deferred, allowing those that are worth less to proceed. Assuming that does not mean an opportunity completely forgone, which may occur with delay, the resources and funds invested have provided a poorer return than could have been achieved—hardly good management practice!

An obvious conclusion from the above is that the same principles and practice should govern the GO/NO GO decisions for individual applications *and* deciding priorities across applications competing for resources. The only additional factor, assuming that systems are not sequentially dependent, is the amount of resource consumed. The limiting factor is normally people in quantity or quality (particular skills) but the same logic applies whatever the limiting resource—priority setting should enable maximum return from the use of that resource.

The discussions below consider investment evaluation first and then priority setting, assuming not all applications can be achieved in parallel and skilled staff are the scarce resource. One inevitable product of IS/IT strategic planning as opposed to bottom-up, 'wish-list' based planning is that demand will increase for applications, making priority setting a serious issue, even if it is not already.

EVALUATING IS/IT INVESTMENTS

A 'technology' investment cannot strictly give a return on investment unless it replaces an older technology and carries out the same functions more efficiently. Most 'technology' investments are justified on the back of applications. Even if capacity on computers and networks has to be purchased in advance of the need, the justification should be based on systems that will use that capacity and the benefits they will provide. However, it is often difficult to associate all 'infrastructure' type investments with the subsequent benefits of using applications, even where sophisticated capital cost recovery accounting techniques are used. The arguments below will assume that reasonable cost allocations of shared resources can be arrived at—reasonable in the sense that

(a) unused capacity is not 'free'—there is at least an opportunity cost of using it for another application;
(b) each application need justify only the incremental capacity *it* requires, not the next capacity increment which has to be purchased;
(c) where the technology is dedicated to an application the full cost is attributed to the application.

Another point of evaluation logic which is peculiar perhaps to IS/IT investments is the way particular costs and benefits should be treated. Most accounting evaluation practices are conservative, expecting the worst and mistrusting the best! Raw IT costs have been reducing at 25% p.a. for some 25 years and this is difficult for accounting procedures to accept when evaluating systems with 5, 8 or 10-year lives. This changing reality of running costs of systems over time must be allowed for where shared resources are used. It is important to take a realistic (even marginal) view of the costs rather than a theoretical one.

On the other side of the coin quantifying the benefits of any system can be a difficult, even impossible task. In the book *Information Economics* Parker *et al.* (1988) assess in detail the ways in which information and systems benefits accrue and how they can be quantified to help in justifying investments. They consider three main types of application:

(a) *Substitutive*—machine power for people power—economics being the main driving force, to improve *efficiency*.
(b) *Complementary*—improving productivity and employee *effectiveness* by enabling work to be performed in new ways.
(c) *Innovative*—intended to obtain or sustain *competitive* edge by changing trading practice or creating new markets, etc.

They then identify the ways in which applications should be justified and define five basic techniques for evaluating benefits.

1. the traditional cost/benefit analysis;
2. the 'value linking', which estimates the improvement in business performance, not just savings made, e.g. more accurate billing of customers;
3. the 'value acceleration', which considers time dependency of benefits and costs in other departments of system improvements, e.g. being able to prepare invoices one day earlier;
4. the 'value restructuring' which considers the productivity resulting from organisational change and change of job roles;
5. the 'innovation evaluation' attempts to evaluate the value to the business of new business or new business practices levered from IS/IT.

Summarising the ideas, it is suggested that costs and benefits should be appraised in both business and IS/IT 'domains' in assessing any project. The above categories of benefit evaluation are suggested to be related to the application types below:

	Substitutive (efficiency)	Complementary (effectiveness)	Innovative (competitive)
(1) Cost/Benefit	✓	✓	✓
(2) Value linking	✓	✓	✓
(3) Value acceleration	✓	✓	✓
(4) Value restructuring		✓	✓
(5) Innovation evaluation			✓

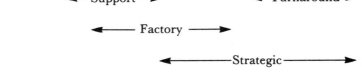

By analysing costs and benefits using these techniques the overall 'economics' of an application can be assessed. The ideas are certainly more creative in interpreting information's long-term value than traditional accounting views of systems investments.

Whilst it is important to quantify and express in financial terms as many of the costs and benefits as possible, it is not essential to convert all 'intangibles' to financial figures. It is simply not possible to express all the benefits of 'systems' in quantitative terms and it serves no useful purpose to develop spurious calculations to quantify the unquantifiable. If a new system will improve staff morale because at last the company has seen fit to invest in improving office functions and modernising the environment, how can that increase be financially expressed even after the event, let alone before it has happened?

What is more important is to use the appropriate basis for judgement of applications based on the role they are expected to fulfil in the business. The portfolio approach can offer help in making such judgements. The rationale for developing applications or investing funds and resources in each segment of the matrix is different and therefore the evaluation process should be different. The arguments used to justify a prototype expert system to model customer buying behaviour are not the same as those used to justify a rewrite of the general accounting system. Equally, response to a competitor's action and a decision to integrate applications via a database require different approaches to evaluation. The risks of failure in the various segments are different. This can be allowed for by asking for a higher predicted rate of return where the risk is higher, although this may in turn merely lead to creative accounting for the benefits!

The portfolio approach suggests that:

(a) quantified justification of applications is easier in the factory and support quadrants—where all aspects of the application will be better known or can be determined and risks are lower and the rate of change is slower;
(b) a singular approach to system justification will tend to produce one type of application to the exclusion of others. This argument is particularly strong where a scarce resource approach has been adopted and pure financial return on investment decides whether projects go ahead and also the priorities.

The generic IS/IT strategies and the way applications are to be managed by the organisation will also affect the way they are justified—whether they are applications integral to achieving business objectives or systems to make major local economies.

Figure 11.1 highlights some of the key points to be considered in the evaluation of applications in each segment.

Support Applications

The main argument for such systems is improving efficiency, which should be possible to quantify and convert into a financial argument for investment. Additional arguments may revolve around system and technology obsolescence and improving staff morale and these may be difficult to quantify. If the application development requires the use of scarce (central) resources, then in this segment, it is reasonable to expect potential benefits to be estimated *before* resources and costs are incurred to identify the most economic solution within the benefits achievable. Again, if the application is contending with others for the limited resource, then a support application must show a good economic return for the allocation of a scarce resource.

STRATEGIC	HIGH POTENTIAL
•Competitiveness and effectiveness •Critical success factors •Central planning HIGH RISK−FINANCIAL AND BUSINESS	•Proactive •Research and development •Leading edge or free market VERY HIGH RISK− MAINLY FINANCIAL
•Current effectiveness •Integration •Avoid disadvantage •Monopoly KNOWN RISK−FINANCIAL AND BUSINESS	•Efficiency •Scarce resource free market LOW RISK−MAINLY FINANCIAL
FACTORY	SUPPORT

£ Tangible/quantifiable/economic benefits

  Intangible/unquantifiable/business benefits

FIGURE 11.1

If, however, the project can be carried out within the user department's control then it is reasonable that, since the budget or funding is under local control, the GO/NO GO decision is made by local user management. The IS/IT investment is an alternative use of funds to other investments locally and is not competing with alternative use of scarce IS/IT resources. Hopefully user management will expect the case to be argued in predominantly financial terms, but if not that is their responsibility.

In summary, assuming a scarce resource strategy is being adopted 'centrally' for all support applications, then any allocation of that resource should be argued on economic, return on investment, grounds primarily. At the same time, some discretion can, without great risk, be left to local management via a free market strategy. The balance of scarce resource/free market in this segment will depend on how centralised or decentralised the organisation is overall.

Factory Applications

Whilst as far as possible all costs and benefits of a new development/redevelopment/ enhancement to a factory system should be converted to a financial evaluation this may not allow for all the arguments involved.

For support systems it was suggested that benefits should be estimated before any resource is allocated or costs determined. This is inappropriate for factory applications where financial benefits are not the only driving force, and also the most economic solution may not be the most effective. This is the area for strict 'feasibility study' to find the best solution from a range of alternatives, each with differing costs and benefits and risks.

The business success may be at risk if a system falls behind the business needs. It also might be worth spending more to achieve an integrated solution which meets a range of needs more effectively and upon which new strategic applications can be built. The relationship of the 'project' to other existing, proposed and potential systems must be included in the evaluation. Normally this will increase the cost and the 'intangible' benefits. Some of those benefits will be able to be related to critical success factors which by inference will, if achieved, lead to achievement of business objectives (and vice versa if they are not!). An argument often used here is 'what will happen to the business if we do not invest in improving factory systems' and therefore 'can we afford the risk of not doing it?'

The strategy that works best for factory systems is monopoly which implies a central control and vetting of all applications and enhancements. This enables a standard check-list of questions to be considered in the evaluation of any new project. Factors that are important (other than economic return) from either a business or IS/IT perspective can be allowed for and if necessary changed over time. The monopoly should also preclude solutions based on only economic expediency rather than business benefits, although it may mean a particular application may cost more in the short term.

In conclusion, it should be stressed that for factory systems the business unit management should be the final arbiter. It is their business which will suffer by lack of investment and they should (provided they can afford to pay) be allocated the necessary resource to meet such systems needs, for whatever reason they feel the case is justified.

Strategic Applications

The fact that an application is deemed strategic implies that it is seen as important, even essential, in achieving business objectives and strategies. Obviously, it is important to cost the investment and where possible put figures to the potential benefits, even if the latter are only orders of magnitude, not estimates suitable for a discounted cash flow calculation. However, the main reasons for proceeding are likely to remain 'intangible'—expressed as the Critical Success Factors that the application addresses.

The strategy most appropriate for this part of the matrix is central planning, whereby IS/IT opportunities and threats are being considered along with the business issues and strategies. Hence, an application will get the GO/NO GO decision based on whether it is relevant to the business objectives and strategy and likely to deliver benefits in those terms, not as a system in its own right. Whether this will actually happen is partly a question of luck (that the target does not move), partly of judgement (the quality of business acumen of senior managers), and partly good management of the application as and when it is developed.

The key issue is whether the management team, steering group or whatever body makes such decisions, is unified in endorsing the project and that the 'organisation' deems the investment worthwhile. The critical factor is then resourcing the task sufficient to achieve the objectives in the optimum timescale. This may need repeated senior management intervention to ensure both user and IS resources are made available. The budget for such investments and then financial control of actual expenditure should perhaps reside with the 'steering group' to ensure that progress and resourcing are centrally monitored as well as planned.

High Potential Applications

The very essence of high potential projects is that the benefits are unknown. The objective in part is to identify the benefits potentially available. It is the R&D segment of the matrix and should be justified on the same basis as any other R&D and preferably from a general R&D budget rather than IS/IT central funds. In practice where the money comes from, R&D budget or IS/IT or user budgets, is important but not critical. What does matter is not pouring money down the seemingly bottomless pit that R&D can become, if not properly monitored. The idea of 'product champions' to be responsible for such projects, given a budget against agreed general terms of reference, to deliver results or otherwise, is the most effective way of initiating and managing the 'high potential' stage in application life cycles. So whatever the source of the funds, once the project starts the 'champion' has control over the budget, and is accountable for its use.

The word *evaluation* is what the high potential box is really about—nothing should stay in it too long or have too much money spent on it. When initial allocations are used up, further sums have to be rejustified, not just allocated in the vague hope of eventual success.

This approach fits the leading edge and free market strategies that the box needs. However, it should be obvious that those responsible for ensuring that central planning works for strategic applications are well aware of what is being evaluated in the high potential segment, and by whom and to what purpose.

The above approaches to application justification in the various segments may lack the precision ideally required. But this is no more than is true of other aspects of research and development, advertising, reorganisation, building new plant or facilities, taking on new staff or training people.

IS/IT investments should be considered just as objectively and just as subjectively as other business investments. The portfolio approach allows the balance to vary according to the expected contribution required.

SETTING PRIORITIES FOR APPLICATIONS

As mentioned earlier, the mechanisms used to decide whether or not applications go ahead should also be used to set priorities across applications when all cannot be done in parallel. Some priorities are logical—project B cannot proceed before project A has built the database, etc.—but many more are independent of each other.

It is important to introduce some consistent, rational approach to priority setting if any strategy is to be implemented successfully. Short-term business pressures will change, projects will not proceed as planned, resources will not be available as expected, new opportunities and requirements will emerge. Each of these can change the priorities and unless a consistent rationale is employed, the short-term issues will override the strategy. In that short term, resources are limited and must be used to maximum effect. The main constraint is normally skilled IS labour, often in particular skill areas.

Based on the earlier discussion of application evaluation it should be seen that setting priorities across applications of a similar type, i.e. support or factory, etc. is not too difficult. Other than ranking them on similarly expressed benefits, the remaining parameter is to optimise the resource use. It might also be prudent to modify the final 'score' by consideration of the ability to succeed—the risk of each application—to ensure that not just high risk projects are tackled, resulting eventually in no achievement! Risk can either be allowed for as contingencies in cost and resources or by reducing the potential benefits or, in some cases, both!

Hence, three factors need to be included in the assessment of priorities:

- what is most important to do   —benefits
- what is capable of being done   —resources
- what is likely to succeed   —risks

Spadaro, in an article in *Datamation* (Spadaro, 1985) shows a matrix-based approach for assessing 'request factors against success factors' to identify a ranking for projects based on importance and risk of failure. The risk factors are classically those which can cause any project to go wrong (size, duration, experience of the technology, user availability and experience, etc).

Priorities need to be set in the short term to enable the best use of resources within the acquisition lead time for further resources, assuming these are actually obtainable.

Within the **support** segment setting priorities should not be too difficult—those with the greatest economic benefit that use the least resources should get the highest priority. This will encourage users to express benefits quantitatively and look for resource efficient solutions, such as packages, to obtain a priority. Support applications will tend to be low risk but relative risks may modify the priorities to ensure an overall return is guaranteed.

Within the **strategic** segment the basic rationale is equally clear. Those applications which will contribute most to achieving business objectives, and use least resource in the process, should go ahead first. To assess this, some form of simple decision matrix, such as that shown in Figure 11.2, can be useful in assessing the 'strategic contribution' or weighing of different projects. It produces a strategic 'score' or value for each application or project. It should be noticed that whilst 'critical success factors' cannot be weighted (by definition) the various business objectives can be given an order of preference to indicate relative business

PROJECT/SYSTEM CONTRIBUTION

	HIGH (3)	MEDIUM (2)	LOW (1)
HIGH (3)			

Objective 1:
  CSF1
  CSF2
Objective 2:
  CSF1
  CSF2
  CSF3			

MEDIUM (2)			

Objective 3:
  CSF1
  etc			

LOW (1)			
Objective 4: etc			
STRATEGIC CONTRIBUTION			
VALUE			

FIGURE 11.2 Strategic weighting (an approach)

priorities. Each application should be explained in terms of how, and therefore to what degree, it will help in achieving the various success factors.

Such a decision support tool should not be used mechanistically—a score of 25 is not necessarily better than 24, it means they are about equally important. Again, by dividing the 'score' by the man years of scarce resource required, the overall contribution can be maximised.

All applications, wherever they fall in the matrix, should be assessed against such a 'strategic weighting' table to help decide or confirm in which segment they belong. *High potential* applications should demonstrate some, if as yet unclear, relationship to objectives, whereas *Strategic* applications will be more obviously contributing. *Support* systems should show little strategic contribution, otherwise they are more important and *Factory* applications should relate to at least some CSFs.

Setting priorities amongst **factory** systems is more problematic than support or strategic, where the basic rationale is clearer. The arguments for (i.e. benefits of) factory systems will comprise basically:

- economic,
- critical success factors,
- risk to current business,
- infrastructure improvement.

Each of these issues must be given some form of relative weighting to decide an order of preference before looking at resource constraints.

In each case the cost/resources used by the project should be matched against its importance in each of the four categories to establish overall priorities. Economic benefits are straightforward and business objectives can be included via CSFs. The IS/IT view of 'infrastructure' implies implementing coherent architectures, increasing skills, improving the resilience or flexibility of systems, etc. Risk to current business could be assessed by describing 'what risks are run if the project does not go ahead'.

Applications scoring highly in all four categories are obviously higher in priority than those scoring highly in 1, 2 or 3 categories and those at each level in the ranking using less resources get priority. It is a subjective method but does allow for the strategic, financial, user and IS/IT perspectives to be included.

Buss, in an article in 1983 (Buss, 1983) makes an important observation concerning, as he says, the 'misconception' that 'a steering committee can decide the priorities'. In general he suggests that politics may interfere, that representation in discussion will be unbalanced and the only common ground will end up as economics! He says the best way to set priorities is to make them the product of a formal planning process at corporate or business unit level. The mechanisms to be employed can be agreed by a steering group but it should not be implemented as a meeting based process.

High potential applications are difficult to prioritise and will tend to be driven somewhat in the reverse of strategic applications—what resource is available to do it and then which application might best employ that resource? If, as is suggested earlier, high potential applications are 'individually' driven, normally a keen champion exists, it is the secondary resources that are the problem. Whilst it sounds wrong to suggest 'he who shouts the loudest', or 'has the most influence' will obtain priority in this segment, it may be the best way to allow priorities to be set because:

(a) the results will depend not just on the value of the idea, but also the force with which it is pursued;
(b) setting objective priorities on scanty evidence is not very reliable anyway.

If the idea potentially impacts many CSFs it clearly stands out from others and should be elevated above the general scramble for R&D type resources. In the discussion below high potential applications are not considered as being in competition for IS/IT funds, but are funded from R&D general budgets. But of course they may compete for certain key skills or resources.

The remaining task is to set priorities across the segments of the portfolio to decide how much resource to devote to the different types of applications. This is not simple since the rationale for investment in each is different, as shown above. However, the approach recommended for Factory applications can be extended out of the Factory domain. The problem is that strategic applications will score heavily on 'critical success factors' whereas support applications will score heavily on 'economics'. Management must decide the weighting they wish to attribute to each type of benefit and then rank the systems.

The relative weighting given each will depend on a number of factors a few of which are listed in Table 11.1. In general the greater trust the management have in their own judgement relative to the need to be reassured by figures, and

TABLE 11.1 Examples of effect on weighting of various factors: (high, medium, low)

Factor	Objectives/ CSFs	Business risks	Infra- structure	Economics
1. All types of investments have to be cost justified	L	L	L	H
2. Business is in weak position or in decline—short-term profitability	L	L	L	H
3. Business is growing rapidly and high growth market	H	H	M	L
4. Environment is very competitive	H	M	L	H
5. Need for redevelopment of old systems. Systems are out of date	M	M	H	L

the trust they have in the users and IS in developing effective systems, the greater the weighting placed on the CSFs etc., relative to financial aspects. In a way this is a sign of maturity of the organisation and how it plans and manages IS/IT. It also tends to reflect on the strength of the company within its industry. The stronger the position the less IS/IT investments are expected (like other investments) to prove an economic case in advance.

If the overall plan is developed and maintained in a priority sequence that reflects the ratio:

$$\frac{\text{Benefits to be achieved (adjusted for risk)}}{\text{Limiting resource consumed}}$$

then it helps both in short- and long-term planning decisions because:

(a) Resources can be reallocated where necessary from lower to higher priority applications on a rational basis, with the agreement of users.
(b) Appropriate resourcing levels for the future can be set, and action taken to obtain the right type of resources to meet the demands, expressed as a consensus view of the benefits available.

It is quite possible then to produce a 'planning system' which should keep the plans and resource utilisation up to date. It is important to 'report' the current plan to *all* involved to aid understanding of the reasons for the ranking of any particular users' project. Mystery or uncertainty are far more destructive of strategies than the discussion and reconciliation of real problems.

Again the above arguments may lack the precision ideally required for setting priorities. Much subjective judgement is inevitably involved, but rules for the various factors involved can be sensibly established, rather than each priority decision being effectively made on a different set of criteria.

In both the evaluation of projects and setting priorities, one aspect must not be ignored—'after the event'! Some form of review/audit (not a witch hunt!) must be carried out on a high percentage of projects to identify whether (a) they were carried out as well as possible and (b) whether the benefits claimed (and possibly different benefits) were achieved or not.

One of the factors that differentiates successful from less successful companies in their deployment of IS/IT, according to a very thorough survey (Brunel University/Kobler Unit of Imperial College, 1987) was the management resolve to evaluate IS/IT investments *before and after* they occurred.

There is no point in any sophisticated system of investment evaluation and priority setting unless the 'system' is examined in terms of whether or not it works!

DEVELOPMENT APPROACHES RELATED TO THE APPLICATIONS PORTFOLIO

It is evident from the preceding discussion about investment and priority setting policies that decisions about how to develop or acquire systems are not taken in isolation from other business issues, or solely on a technical basis, but are part of a wider process of evaluating IS/IT investments and assessing their priorities. These in turn consider resources, skills, timing considerations, risk, etc., and also the right choice of development approach to use. What is needed from an IT supply perspective is a cohesive and balanced framework for the development or acquisition of all types of systems, incorporating appropriate methods, tools and mechanisms, for their development, management and maintenance.

As stated earlier portfolio management principles are useful here, as they are for so many other aspects of IS/IT, in selecting appropriate development approaches and tools. In an organisation where applications are distributed around the portfolio model, then it is likely that a variety of development and project management approaches is also needed to be put to use by different groups of people in the organisation, delivering products built to suit their end use. Broadly applied selection criteria would indicate that the best solutions for the four portfolio categories are:

- Traditional systems development life-cycle methods for 'factory' systems,
- Relational database technology, embedded in a sophisticated fourth generation environment for 'strategic' systems.
- Rapid development user oriented tools for building 'high potential' systems,
- Packaged software products for 'support' systems,

The richness of the menu of available development approaches must reflect the diverse needs of the portfolio, tempered by any underlying constraints. These will include economic considerations, technical limitations, and availability and accessibility of suitable ingredients—organisational capability, skills and resources. With the benefit of an IS strategy, defining the business IS demand over several years, an organisation can plan and justify its long-term development infrastructure with considerably more certainty than if it was only aware of short-term needs. The resulting migration path needs to take into account the progressive implementation of new methods and tools, in parallel with increasing capability, as improving technology provides more satisfactory vehicles.

Selecting development approaches on the basis of the application portfolio matrix gives a good provisional decision, which may then have to be varied when other criteria are considered.

Strategic systems   These are vital to the future success of the business, and are part of its business strategy. They are usually linked to specific business initiatives, and often necessary to obtain competitive advantage. Traditional non-automated developed methods are not appropriate here, since speed and flexibility are essential, and effectiveness is more important than efficiency, especially when the goal is gaining and sustaining competitive advantage. They are best achieved through a close partnership between business users (preferably senior managers who understand the business needs) and very experienced IS/IT business analysts to ensure that the business needs are analysed and met in the most effective way. This is doubly important when the system has an external linkage, and is delivering benefits to both bodies. There is often a need to develop further increments along with extensions to the business initiatives, and it is vital that the logical analysis can be revisited easily and quickly. Typically the system is not automating an existing business process, but evolving or creating one.

The information content of the business product is often crucial in strategic systems, whether the information is part of the product itself, or provided or exchanged in order to boost delivered value or customer satisfaction. Easy access to relevant information is therefore very important, and often best served by relational technology, associated with a sophisticated data dictionary, based on a top-down model of the business. A scenario may serve to illustrate the point.

When contact is made between a company and one of its customers, which may be by telephone, face-to-face, or linked by a computer terminal, it is a great advantage if all the information about that customer and his dealings with the business can be made available at the point and time of contact. This might include a sales and maintenance history for several different types of products, location information, financial status, areas of interest which could prompt add-on selling, etc. Clearly it is also important to have access to pertinent internal information at the same time—stock availability, schedules for delivery or service, etc. Whether the purpose of the contact is to place an order, ask a question or make a complaint, the aim is to improve the value of the dialogue, to the satisfaction of the customer, and essentially gain competitive advantage. The customer must perceive that he is a 'known individual', even if this is engineered by the system having to extend its own version of human courtesy by displaying 'Hello, Bob Smith. What can we do for you today?' when the contact is made by terminal.

This scenario would entail accessing information about people/organisations, locations, products/services, money, scheduled work, stock, distribution, and probably more. In order to provide that breadth of information, the level of internal integration must be high, and the information probably based on a business-wide model, implemented in relational form.

As it demonstrates, strategic systems are often linked to primary operational systems, at the external interfaces of the business, exchanging information or sometimes delivering a service or product in their own right. Others may provide the interfaces to improve internal integration. Another category of strategic systems is the executive support variety, taking pertinent information right into the boardroom. This type of system needs to be developed quickly, and relies on gaining access to up-to-date information from internal sources or perhaps external databases. It is then usually packaged so as to deliver its message in a clear, almost dramatic fashion, sophisticated colour graphics being a favourite medium. There are a few good proprietary board-room system builders available, although several major companies have developed their own and claim very satisfactory response to them.

The best design for the majority of strategic systems is probably a well researched, analysed and structured core, encapsulating the essential business processes, surrounded by flexible user-driven modules. Fourth generation tools or, increasingly, CASE tools are appropriate development vehicles here, where the CASE set includes front-end planning capability to capture the results of strategic analysis and model business requirements, and back-end application generation capability. Prototyping can also be effective here in clarifying user needs. Relational databases containing the principal elements of the corporate database are frequently used in strategic systems, since they give the necessary flexibility in terms of viewing, manipulating and accessing information. Interconnectability rather than integration, may be another goal here, in order to assess the value of the strategic system, while protecting the installed base of factory and support systems.

High potential systems   These sit in the 'R&D' category, where new technology can be tried out to ascertain its potential for the organisation, or where partially formed user ideas can be prototyped. In this case it is advantageous to be able to explore the potential of an innovative business idea. The need is for independent, rapid, low-cost development, which can be abandoned without wasting massive resources, since risk is high, success far from certain and cost control essential.

The approach may use comprehensive application generator software suitable for producing prototypes, or when appropriate, knowledge-based technology, CAD, and advanced management support software. Speed and access to sophisticated development facilities are more important than detailed definition and efficiency. Integration and data management are rarely considered here, although may well form essential elements in any emerging target strategic or factory products following the R&D process. There is, of course, a danger that users become so enthusiastic about a prototype that it gets adopted along with all its drawbacks! Conversely, there is a danger that unless managed carefully, R&D developers forget the business need, and concentrate on the joys of technical experimentation.

Systems in this quadrant may be developed by a user or by a user and an IT professional jointly analysing and developing the application. They are often found under the wing of an Information Centre which can provide access to information, without jeopardising current systems, and can monitor the effectiveness of experimentation. These systems may start as single user PC developments, which prove themselves as worthy candidates for more widespread use, and thus have to be redeveloped with the broader production environment in mind.

Factory systems are critical to sustaining current business, and if they fail the business may suffer competitive disadvantage. They are generally the workhorse systems, and need to be well designed, efficient and robust, with a long cost-effective life. Since they often need to be integrated with other primary business process systems, they benefit from adhering to global data management standards, and from complying with an emerging long-term systems and data architecture. They can sometimes be met by well built packages, or bought in core software, but this often precludes them from effective integration, resource sharing, and data management, and this approach is only worth considering when development resources are not available and time is short. When developed in-house, they are usually produced using traditional project management and systems development life-cycle methods, increasingly automated with CASE and IPSE tools. Old systems which are showing the debilitating effects of age and years of maintenance could well be candidates for re-engineering or retrofitting.

Support systems are invariably found in organisations who have computerised applications, since they largely consist of the legally necessary financial systems, and payroll and personnel records systems. They have a value to the business, but are not critical to its success. If they need replacing or acquiring, the most appropriate solution is to buy in a sound standard package that meets the business requirements as closely as possible, and requires minimal maintenance and 'interference'. Very rarely can an organisation justify the allocation of valuable skills and resources to develop support systems for themselves.

The resources required to implement a package are frequently underestimated. Requirements still need to be carefully analysed and documented, and the search and evaluation process undertaken must be linked to the justification and prioritisation processes. Even if no tailoring of the package is necessary there are often interfaces to be built to existing systems, and there may be considerable work needed to acquire the system and tailor package parameters, undertake user awareness and training programmes, develop adequate testing material, and implement the system. An allowance may also be needed for vendor management relating to supply and service activities.

There is some overlap between quadrants but the principal development approaches, and some characteristics that epitomise them can be illustrated in another version of the portfolio matrix. See Figure 11.3.

Bytheway (1988), has developed a table (Figure 11.4) which relates systems development stages to application portfolio categories. It follows similar principles to those advocated here, except in its suggestion that packages are the appropriate solution to 'factory' systems, rather than in-house developments built to meet integration needs.

Applications are managed to move anti-clockwise around the quadrants, with the exception of high potential applications which may be abandoned if their

STRATEGIC	HIGH POTENTIAL
INFORMATION ENGINEERING CASE RELATIONAL TECHNOLOGY • close partnership user - IS/IT • modular • interconnectable • fast and flexible	PROTOTYPING END USER COMPUTING NEW TECHNOLOGY • independent • rapid development • low cost • iterative
SYSTEMS DEVELOPMENT LIFE- CYCLE CORPORATE DATA MANAGEMENT CASE / IPSE RE-ENGINEERING • well designed • efficient • robust • integrated	STANDARD PACKAGES • minimum intervention • minimum maintenance
FACTORY	SUPPORT

FIGURE 11.3 Development approaches and characteristics

potential is not proven. The rate of enhancement, degree of desirable integration, control and resourcing requirements, relating to the life-cycle of applications was covered in Chapter 8.

The Systems Factory

Taking an application portfolio management approach, an organisation is likely to have a portfolio with systems in most sectors. In this case, it needs to adopt appropriate development approaches, methods and tools and a means of identifying the correct one in each case.

A systems 'factory' could be expected to undertake a number of tasks in order to meet differing requirements. It may need to:

● Develop systems according to a full systems development life-cycle, perhaps

	HIGH POTENTIAL	STRATEGIC	FACTORY	SUPPORT
PROJECT DEFINITION	Loose and open Cost limits rather than firm objectives. User-led	Strong manager-led team Broad brief Strategic tools for the job	Technically-led team Tight definition of standards Meticulous project management	Use external services if possible Let the user manage the project
ANALYSIS OF REQUIREMENTS	Exploratory and informal Use prototyping to establish ideas	Creative and broad in scope Carefully document work Reviews	Contained but thorough Attention to interfaces Work to efficiency	Limit to essential needs and possibly to isolation of the system at hand
BUILD SYSTEM	Rapid and iterative Use peer reviews to identify weaknesses and firm ideas	Innovative but carefully planned and rapid Limited prototyping	Contract out or use packages Aim for efficiency	Avoid undue effort Contract out and assume packages
TEST SYSTEM	Informal	Well planned meticulous and biased to the end user's needs	Exhaustive, with a bias to the technical, and efficiency of the system	Assume it works? Otherwise minimum effort
HANDOVER	Crossed fingers and an expectation to re-work with user experience	With great care! Big Bang may be the only way Lots of education	With great care! Parallel run will probably be the best way	Plug in and run? Minimise effort and ensure user self-sufficiency

FIGURE 11.4 Systems development mapped on to the strategic grid

supported by advanced development tools. Systems must be high quality in order to ensure a long effective life, delivering sustained value at acceptable cost.

- Work closely with users in designing and developing systems, using high-level tools.
- Develop prototypes, where business strategy is still emerging or where the value of new technology needs to be explored.
- Provide advice and consultancy support to users developing their own systems. Users are now considerably more IT literate and confident. They are used to PC software and to getting systems to work quickly.
- Produce systems using complex techniques or special purpose tools, such as expert systems technology, process control technology, or advanced graphical tools.
- Use general purpose software packages to improve standard business techniques—spreadsheets, financial modelling packages, *ad hoc* enquiry and report generators.
- Select and supply packages bought in to meet a defined purpose.
- Upgrade, re-engineer or retrofit systems.

Tozer (1987) also uses a factory analogy, referring to an 'information factory'. In it he describes a 'clearing house' which allocates development approaches to candidate applications. The tasks of the clearing house are to:

- Assess all the information available about the nature of the required system and its users, thus defining its inherent characteristics.
- Take decisions based on these characteristics, e.g. system is 'throwaway' or 'built to last',
- Build a case for or against fourth generation tools,
- Analyse suitability for end-user development,
- Select appropriate class of tool.

Whilst he does not classify applications with reference to the application portfolio, the aim is the same—to select the right approach on rational grounds.

The collection of methods and hardware and software development tools used by systems and information engineers, may be considered as the production systems and plant of the 'systems factory' of the business; managed, planned and scheduled on the basis of decision criteria that indicate the most appropriate production route to take. This analogy was used in Chapter 10 in likening the activities associated with information management to an industrial plant's activities.

Methods might include structured analysis, design and programming techniques, prototyping, and fourth generation approaches. Many of these are automated and incorporated into sophisticated tools, a large number of which are now available. Some of the most advanced are the integrated or interfaced sets of CASE—computer-assisted software (or systems) engineering tools, which can drive the whole development cycle from planning to implementation of completed systems. They may include a planning front end driven by business needs, leading to an analysis tool, which drives a design tool, and finally, application generators, all of which may be linked into an IPSE (Integrated Project Support Environment).

Development tools for software and information 'engineers' would be selected from:

CASE and IPSE products
Fourth generation environment tools
Data dictionaries
Database management systems
Expert systems development tools
Graphics tools
Decision management software
CAD and other computer-assisted products

A rational balance must be struck between informal rapid development methods, and formal, highly disciplined methods, incorporating the detailed standards, quality assurance and tight project management of the traditional systems development life-cycle. Indeed there are already moves evident that are diluting the polarity between traditional and new approaches, offering more flexible approaches to development, combining some of the best characteristics of each in order to produce the best match with business needs. These are briefly considered later in the chapter. In effect, the aim is simply stated—the right approach, the right people, the right software and technology, and the right management style in every circumstance!

There will of course already be a number of systems in the existing portfolio, and some of them will be candidates for replacement or enhancement. In many organisations the budget for maintaining existing systems is up to 80% of the overall allocation for IS/IT development and maintenance work. Assuming that the system is shown to be making an essential contribution, there has to be a balance struck between whether to continue to maintain systems or whether to develop new ones. The decision will be dependent on:

● The value of the extra contribution that can be made by redeveloping the systems, versus the value being displaced.
● The cost of maintaining the systems for its expected lifetime, against the cost of replacement.
● Operating costs of both old and new systems.

Any system in the strategic quadrant will presumably have a potentially increased value. A factory system may warrant redevelopment based on improved efficiency and cost, but more likely as a stepping-stone to beneficial integration or other valuable support. A support system can only be justified for replacement if the cost of replacement can be shown to significantly lower the cost of maintaining or operating the system. Then packaged solutions should be considered. If packages are not suitable then re-engineering may be the best solution.

Sprague and McNurlin (1986), identify five options for systems replacement:

1. *Restructuring* to tidy up old inefficient systems. Software aids are available to perform this retrofitting function.
2. *Refurbishing*, adding valuable extensions to systems that are basically sound, using fourth generation tools if possible.
3. *Rejuvenating*, adding a fourth generation front end or back end to create new databases with significant value in their own right.
4. *Rewriting* using traditional or fourth generation approach.
5. *Replacing* with tailorable packages.

Any of these approaches may be impacted by the growth in software tools incorporated within CASE that can offer re-enginering or reverse engineering facilities.

The two main routes to building systems are now considered, the systems development life-cycle, and rapid development methods. A third route is also included in which the first two start to converge.

SYSTEMS DEVELOPMENT LIFE-CYCLE

A systems development life-cycle according to Bytheway, encompasses initial development, implementation, its use in the business and any changes that may need to be executed during its lifetime. His model also includes the management of resources (information, human, technical), and technical management (IT supply policies, servicing criteria, standards, etc.).

Rock-Evans view of the SDC (Rock-Evans, 1988a), incorporates a set of activities needed to develop and implement robust and efficient systems, typically, the organisation's factory systems. The cycle starts at strategic level, in effect overlapping much of the high level work done in strategic IS/IT planning, but perhaps focusing on a smaller business area. The strategy study will determine which parts of the business should be studied further, in order to define required information systems. Subsequent feasibility studies will define the scope of detailed systems studies and perhaps eliminate other parts.

A cut-down version of Rock-Evans's model of the components of the full SDLC is included at Figure 11.5. It omits all deliverables and activities associated with managing suppliers and resources, for simplicity. Strategy management in this

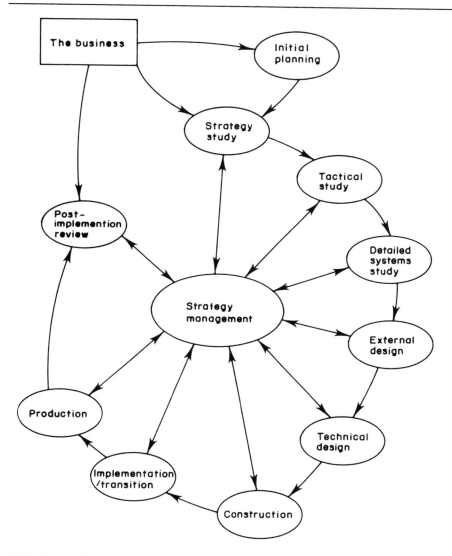

FIGURE 11.5 Systems development cycle

context refers to the management of data applications and hardware and software. It also refers to various organisational issues which are dealt with in Chapter 9, and to several systems management and administration matters. Of these, investment and prioritisation issues have been covered earlier in this chapter.

An SDLC will employ various methods, techniques, and tools (optionally), and will produce a number of deliverables. An integrated collection of these covering all or part of the SDLC is referred to as a *methodology*.

Most of the suppliers or consultants who deal with methodologies subscribe to the broad principles of information engineering, that is, developing top-down independent data and process models of the business, and using them to drive the development life-cycle. It may be useful at this point to define the other ingredients in the SDLC; IPSEs, deliverables, methods, techniques and tools.

An IPSE, according to Alvey is:

> A compatible set of specification, design, programming, building and testing tools *supporting* a development methodology that covers the entire life-cycle, together with management control tools and procedures, all using a coordinated and consistent project database.

Deliverables are required pieces of output at any point in the SDLC. These may be facts, flowcharts or programme documentation, etc.

A *method* is a proprietary or predefined way of undertaking an activity in the SDLC, for example, NIAM—Nijssen's 'Information Analysis Method', or, Gane and Sarsen—'Structured Systems Analysis—Tools and Techniques'. Some are multi-purpose. For example, information analysis can be applied at several levels—strategic, tactical, systems analysis, systems design.

Techniques are proven ways of undertaking activities in order to produce required sets of deliverables. They differ from methods in that ownership of the approach is not defined, although in many cases, their original author is acknowledged. A number of these have been described in the earlier part of this book as techniques within strategic IS planning, for example, value chain analysis, critical success factor analysis, application portfolio analysis. In the SDLC context these may include logical data structuring or data flow diagramming.

Tools are items of software that automate one or more activities, and retain their deliverables for subsequent revision, output or transfer to another stage in the cycle. Tools, which were available before 1987, supported early phases of the SDLC, usually analysis and design. These were the analyst work-benches, plus some project management tools. By June 1989, an estimated 600 products were available in the UK alone providing support for much larger proportions of the cycle, and including built in life-cycle management, although their use is still not widespread. As well as supporting the main life-cycle activities, some of these CASE tools also support prototyping, generation of database schema, re-use of components, expert systems, reverse engineering and other maintenance aids.

The most advanced CASE tools support large portions of the full cycle, although at the time of writing there are no tools that adequately cover the whole cycle. There are two main variants within the umbrella term CASE:

- 'Upper CASE'—including planning, analyst and designer workbench tools, sometimes called 'front-end' case.
- 'Lower CASE'—including application generators and active DBMSs—'back-end' case.

The degree of integration achievable with CASE products varies widely, ranging from manipulated interfaces between systems to virtually total integration in a very small number of true IPSEs. To give an indication of the magnitude of the task, it has been estimated that there are almost a quarter of a million separate tasks to automate within the full SDLC. To get a broad perspective on the range and capabilities of a very wide range of CASE tools, Rock-Evans (1988b) has produced a report which is an extremely comprehensive survey. In another book on the possible future of CASE, Holloway (1989) has compiled a table summarising the parts of the SDLC supported by some 15 tools. See Table 11.2.

There are a number of problems with software tools. As shown in the table, most products are far from complete in covering the full SDLC. They are, in general not 'user friendly', and frequently do not integrate the stages of the SDLC adequately, often relying on paper-based output. According to Rock-Evans, proprietary tools actually *automate* only 1% of the SDLC, although they *support* most of the main processes entailed.

In the future, it may be perfectly acceptable to have several workbench products working in the same environment, communicating through a common resource repository. It will then be a matter of strategic choice to implement an open Information Resource Dictionary Standard (IRDS) environment or to choose a closed proprietary one.

The benefits gained from CASE come in two main categories. There are the obvious productivity gains, although claims sometimes range from the merely extravagant to the entirely ridiculous! Certain improvements are bound to be achievable if only because the deliverables of analysis are more easily drawn with a mouse and screen than with template, pencil and paper, and much more productively amended. The real gains come from implementing CASE within a sound development methodology, and alongside effective information management, and where a good data dictionary or encyclopaedia is embedded within or accessed by the CASE tools. Substantial benefits may be derived from identifying reusable modules and having the ability to include these in other systems. If users are trained in the methodology, so that they can work independently or alongside analysts in capturing business details and understand and interpret the resultant models, then the ingredients are all there to create very good, high quality systems, with a long life expectancy, and far less risk of early degeneracy through excessive maintenance. Users so trained, can constructively challenge the system developer's views at a very early stage. In this environment, users' awareness can hardly fail to increase their commitment to the use of IT.

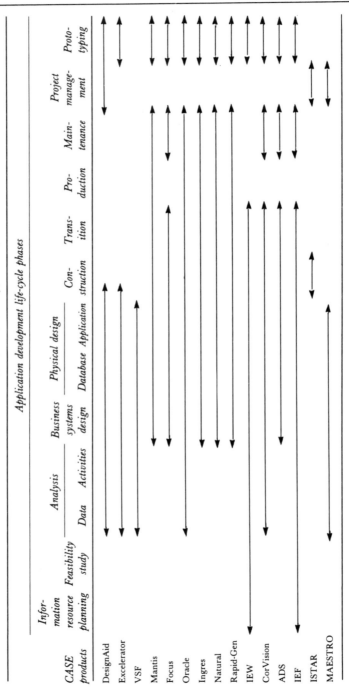

TABLE 11.2 (after Holloway, 1989)

Getting the most out of CASE depends on far more than selecting a good tool, or set of tools. Implementing them properly in the right environment for developing really robust cost-effective systems includes not only the right tools but also employing sound software development methods, effective project management procedures, appropriately focused data administration and (independent) database administration functions, and providing a satisfactory level of support and training for users and practitioners.

Inevitably the introduction of CASE and the accompanying practices/methods means a big commitment. Existing methods and standards may need review, enhancement or replacement.

RAPID DEVELOPMENT METHODS

These are a range of methods and tools that are primarily useful for generating high potential or strategic systems. Rapid development clearly necessitates use of a fourth generation environment tool (4GE), and may involve prototyping.

4GE Tools

There is no precise definition of a 4GE. They encompass a huge range of products covering everything from COBOL code generators to integrated CASE tools. They can be designed for use by inexperienced users or experienced IT professionals. Whilst they follow on from third generation tools, they do not represent a simple evolution from one to the other. For a start, they have changed from a procedural orientation involving stating the steps for *how* to produce the required result, to a form in which the desired result is described, and the tool performs the translation from the *what* to the *how*. Some of the more sophisticated allow the embedding of lower level languages within the 4G code. The productivity improvement expected from use of such tools is 10 to 1 or considerably better. Of course, if the tool is used only to write program code, then there is no productivity advantage in the very considerable remainder of the development cycle.

Speed of learning varies very considerably. Some 4GE tools can be taught to end-users in a few days, on the other hand it may be several months before most IT people have mastered the intricacies of getting the very best performance out of a complex tool.

4GEs are frequently seen as the salvation to the application backlog, whereby users can produce their own systems, and IT can devour the remainder of the backlog. Although this is indeed a major factor to consider, it should not be the primary reason for introducing 4GEs. They can earn their place on the basis of providing the correct approach in particular circumstances.

● When requirements change rapidly and speed and flexibility are the main characteristics needed.

- When prototyping is indicated.
- When end-users, either alone or with IS support, need to access information flexibly.
- When old systems need major upgrade.

It is imperative that their use is managed correctly. It must find the right balance between being slack enough to encourage use and creativity, and tight enough to guard against sloppy design. It is also important not to allow conflict to arise between users who love them and IS people who hate them. If the business benefits are not 'sold' well, the risk is that an unnecessary 'free market' may explode in user areas, and the opportunity may be lost for IS to demonstrate real business contribution by providing rapid development in response to immediate pressures.

The main components of 4GEs are described by Sprague and McNurlin (1986) in a book edited from papers in *EDP Analyser*:

- Database management system, often with quite sophisticated features, since a number of 4GEs have evolved from database technology.
- Data dictionary, ranging in sophistication from the very basic, allowing short descriptions of data elements, to the very rich allowing lengthy descriptions of data, activities, high level entities, plus associated characteristics, relationships etc.—indeed a complete IRDS.
- Tools to generate:

  —enquiries built up from some form of structured query language or prompted dialogue.
  —reports of varying complexity, sometimes standard formats, sometimes involving complicated data and format manipulation.
  —documents or letters using word processing capabilities, and perhaps involving mailing list management.
  —screens including menus, field location, and validation up to full screen-painting facilities.
  —graphics, such as graphs, pie charts, and other diagrams.

- Tools to aid analysis, such as data modelling and activity decomposition, together with diagramming capabilities.
- Productivity aids such as retrieving reusable code, storing and calling macros from a library.
- 'Housekeeping' facilities such as back-up and recovery, security and privacy capability, selection by Boolean or other criteria and sorting of retrieved records.
- Interfaces to other programming languages or to other DBMSs.

Some of the advantages and disadvantages of 4GEs are given below.

Advantages of using 4GEs

- Can experiment quickly, and so be creative in trying out capabilities of the elements in the software, for example the database structure.
- Self-documenting, so documentation can be concentrated on clearly describing the business requirement, and how to use the system.
- Easy and fast to create and manipulate data.

Disadvantages of using 4GEs

- Relatively slow, in terms of processing speed and response time, and often extravagant with use of core storage and data space. Often the intermediate output of a 4GE is a set of code that then has to be interpreted into COBOL for later compilation. Conversely this type of 4GE produces more efficient code in the long run than that produced by an applications generator that does not go through COBOL as an intermediary.
- It is often said that the greatest legacy from 4GEs has been many bad systems which were built quicker! The serious warning behind that, is that it is not advisable to let inexperienced technicians build 4G systems unless they have learnt how to analyse requirements.
- To get the best out of a 4GE, it is necessary to bear in mind design constraints so as to get the best performance out of them.

Prototyping

Prototyping is almost the exact opposite approach to development to that of the traditional third generation SDLC, where so much emphasis is placed on rigorous analysis and design. In contrast, it is employed with no attempt to fully define systems before construction and user testing begin. It depends on fast iterative development, with assumptions being tested out as development proceeds. These can relate to technical factors, or user's perceptions of business requirements. Initial systems are relatively inexpensive to build, although resource utilisation has to be managed to control the number of iterations, before a satisfactory conclusion is reached. It should not be treated as an excuse to abandon good analysis, design and documentation.

The ideal environment (Sprague and McNurlin, 1986) in which prototyping will succeed provides:

- a fast and flexible fourth generation tool, with good self-documentation of the evolving system,
- good access to corporate data,
- effective partnership between a suitably trained user with strong business knowledge who has a problem or an idea and an open mind, and an IT

professional who has experience with the tool and good knowledge of the information resources and their accessibility,

● good feedback channels and productive dialogue between user and IT person while the product is being built, so that ambiguities can be resolved as they arise, and unclear requirements clarified.

If a user is left alone to develop a prototype, there are dangers that must be avoided—IS/IT controls may be ignored (data integrity, adequate testing), operating costs of the finished system may be unacceptably high, etc.

If on the other hand the team is allowed to become too big, other problems arise. Trying to obtain consensus on requirements definition is one; or allowing too many requirements to be satisfied thus expanding the scope too far.

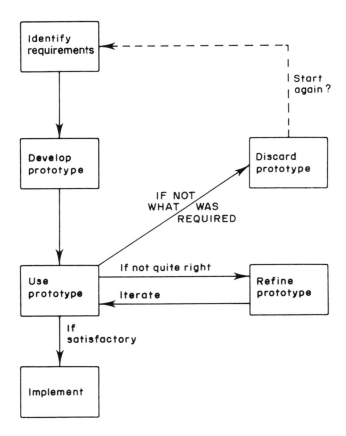

FIGURE 11.6 Steps in a simple prototyping process (Naumann and Jenkins, 1982)

The steps in developing a prototype are described by Nauman and Jenkins (1987). These are illustrated in Figure 11.6.

Prototyping is most suitable for:

High potential systems, where the technical feasibility needs an experimental approach or the business viability of an idea needs to be explored. This is using it in an R&D sense, where perhaps nine out of ten ideas are discarded.

Strategic systems, where the business requirement is clearly identified, and commitment obtained, but no detailed solution has been worked out. Systems may be developed in a series of increments, where each increment is created through prototyping, new functionality being added to the previously implemented version. Metpath, described in Chapter 3, could have developed its systems for doctors in this way, first the basic service to return analyses, then adding additional facilities that appealed to doctors, and finally adding some expert system capability to address more technical analyses.

Prototyping may also have a place in developing *Factory* systems, where users' requirements are known, but there is a value in using prototyping to obtain full clarification of ideas to be incorporated. Benefits may be obtained in two ways here:

- from eliminating errors at the analysis stage, and thus ensuring a more stable and robust design, very important for an operational system,
- from providing a development service to support joint design of systems which straddle internal functional interfaces, and multiple functions which place demands on the system.

A few further pointers are worth remembering with regard to a prototype:

- It is a live working system, and not just a simulated model, and so the prototype itself may become the actual production system, although this is unlikely with the first design.
- After building the initial prototype, it can be reprogrammed using traditional methods to the fully agreed design requirements, taking care that the target environment and prototyping environment are well matched.
- It is fast to build and easy to change and so appropriate in most cases where genuine urgency demands fast response, or swiftly changing conditions demand flexibility.
- It demands time and serious commitment from users, and these people can be fairly senior since by and large they are the 'owners' of business opportunities or problems.
- It demands management of resources, to guard against too many iterations and to apply appropriate configuration management.

HYBRID APPROACHES

Both basic approaches described above are prone to abuse. A structured approach, with or without tools, if used badly can prolong a project's timescale and cost—and worse, not deliver what the business needs. Rapid development tools and prototyping can also produce poor systems, if used incorrectly. In either case the key would seem to be ensuring that the user's needs are properly investigated, analysed and interpreted, and that the whole process is oriented to producing the correct response.

Improvements in the structured approach can perhaps be achieved by using prototyping methods to produce the detailed specification, at least for the user interface parts of the system. The principal benefit being in involving the user throughout this vital process. This close partnership also supports incremental development, which is likely to be valuable for strategic systems.

A beneficial effect on rapid building methods may be in adopting some of the standards of the traditional structured approach, for example covering back-up, recovery, audit and data integrity. See Figure 11.7.

Sprague and McNurlin recommend taking a hybrid approach, referring to 'mix and matching' at the clearing house stage. They also stress the pitfalls to be avoided:

● Analysis of problems must not be skimped.
● Users must not become attached to prototypes which are suitable for demonstrating facilities but not for operational use.
● Large fourth generation developments require very competent programmers.

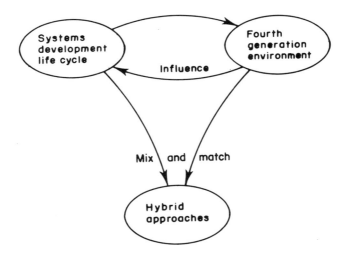

FIGURE 11.7 Hybrid approaches formed from combining SDLC and 4GE approaches

SUMMARY

Previous chapters have dealt with the response to determining the business IS needs by offering a practical way of categorising and managing the applications portfolio, aligning the IS/IT function with the business organisation, and managing its information resources. This chapter has considered some of the processes involved in managing applications. At first sight it might appear that these would be mainly IS/IT concerns, but the decisions that have to be resolved are essentially general management decisions. Business involvement in producing systems is also significant, and growing, as user roles in the systems development life-cycle are extended and users take on more development work using sophisticated fourth generation tools.

It is possible to focus on each category of the application portfolio, and take decisions on investment, priorities and development approach. These in turn will lead to developing the investment justification case, assigning priorities within each category, and, using a clearing house facility, selecting the appropriate development route to use.

This is inevitably an over-simplification. For instance, priorities still have to be assigned across the whole portfolio using some form of universally applied weighting factors. Also some systems 'demand' their place in the development plans on the basis of precedence or necessity to the infrastructure.

Development methods are evolving, and so too is the capability of tools to support development and upgrading of systems. An organisation that adopts application portfolio management principles, equips itself with a powerful set of methods and tools, and then filters demands through a clearing house, should feel confident that each development or redevelopment is being tackled in the most suitable way. In addition, there should be more confidence in the robustness of core systems, and in their improved longevity, thus making inroads into the enormous waste of resources currently expended on maintenance in holding together sick old systems.

REFERENCES

Brunel University/Kobler Unit of Imperial College (1987) A survey *The Strategic Use of IT Systems*.

Buss, M. D. J. (1983) 'How to rank computer projects', *Harvard Business Review* (Jan.-Feb.).

Bytheway, A. J. (1988) *Information Systems Development. Variations on a theme*, Cranfield School of Management.

Holloway, S. (1989) *Methodology Handbook for Information Managers*, Gower.

Naumann, J. D. and Jenkins, A. M. (1982) 'Prototyping: the new paradigm for systems development', *MIS Quarterly*, (Sept.).

Parker, M. M., Benson, R. J. with Trainor, H. E. (1988) *Information Economics*, Prentice-Hall.

Rock-Evans, R. (1988a) *Systems Development for the 1990's*, DCE Information Management Consultancy.

Rock-Evans, R. (1988b) 'CASE analyst workbenches: a detailed product evaluation', *Ovum Report*.

Spadaro, D. (1985) 'Project evaluation made simple', *Datamation* (1 Nov.).

Sprague, R. H. and McNurlin, B. C. (1986) *Information Systems Management in Practice*, Prentice-Hall.

Tozer, E. E. (1987) 'The information factory', in *Information Management in Competitive Success*, Pergamon Infotech.

Chapter 12
STRATEGIES FOR TECHNOLOGY MANAGEMENT

INTRODUCTION

Chapters 9, 10 and 11 have explored the issues concerning how to develop and manage the IS/IT strategies from the perspectives of organisation, information and application management. The fourth dimension of the strategy concerns the technology itself, which addresses the issues of the hardware and software environment within which the strategy and applications portfolio can be implemented.

In this context the term 'technology' will be considered as being the products or services consisting of hardware and software which can be bought 'off the shelf'. This covers the following:

1. Hardware—mainframes, midframes, PCs, workstations, printers, plotters, disk storage, tape storage, etc.
2. Systems software—operating systems, teleprocessing monitors, database management systems, language compilers and interpreters, etc.
3. Communications—hardware, software and services.
4. Productivity tools—application generators, 4GLs, CASE, IPSE, prototyping tools (which were discussed in Chapter 11).
5. Artificial intelligence—expert systems, knowledge based systems.
6. Office systems—including the associated basic software (word processing, electronic mail), etc.
7. Computer aided design and manufacturing systems.
8. Executive support systems—management information systems, executive information systems and decision support systems.
9. Packaged application software, both general purpose (e.g. spreadsheets) and application specific (e.g. payroll).

When developing strategy for each of these 'technology' areas it is first important to consider the management issues to be taken into account.

MANAGEMENT ISSUES

Some of the issues which must be addressed are as follows.

Centralise/Decentralise

When organisations initially use information technology it often starts simultaneously in several departments or locations. There then often follows a period of consolidation when, for economies of scale and for control there is a centralisation of technology. Subsequently, control of technology often develops as a tug-of-war between forces preferring centralisation or decentralisation. A number of factors will influence the appropriate balance that should be achieved between the two extreme pressures in the tug-of-war. The broader management issues were considered in Chapter 9 but a number have to be addressed more specifically with regard to technology. There is the straightforward question of economics. Would it be cheaper and more cost effective to have mainly central processing compared with decentralised processing?

Does the centralised processing organisation reflect the true management style of the enterprise? In a large, homogeneous or bureaucratic organisation it might be entirely appropriate to have centralised control of technology. But in a conglomerate type of organisation or one with diverse business operations then it is more appropriate to consider decentralising much of the control.

In previous chapters it has been pointed out that, to a large extent, the more innovative uses of technology do not derive from the centre but, more often, occur at the edges of the business where it interfaces with the real world. If more innovation in the use of systems and technology is required then a decentralised strategy would tend to encourage that innovation.

There is a continual battle for scarce resources within the information technology industry and it may be that decentralising the operations of the organisation in terms of technology may enable the organisation to tap a wider market for these scarce human resources. In reverse, specialist expertise may become spread too thinly to be effective and resources cannot be easily shared across the business if widely distributed and locally based. In a multinational organisation a further set of factors come into the equation. One has to consider the legal situation where some countries demand that data be processed within that country; there are the high costs of international telecommunications; there may be different time zones and quite often there is a cultural and political dimension as well.

Vendor Strategies for Sourcing the Technology

It is not always easy to define the requirements for a particular component of technology. For example, if an organisation wishes to replace its ageing general ledger system then, because the organisation is familiar with the requirements of the system and, because the systems have been installed in organisations for at least thirty years it is relatively easy to define precisely what is required from the system. It is then quite straightforward to survey the market and find an appropriate selection of general ledger packages which can be evaluated. If, on the other hand, an enterprise was looking for technology which could provide added value to a product and give a competitive advantage for the next three years then it would initially be quite difficult to define what the requirements of that technology were and then equally difficult to find sources for that particular technology.

It is important that the organisation develops 'business based' strategies for dealing with vendors, rather than leave the type of relationship to the discretion of the technical specifiers. The organisation will be dealing with multiple suppliers of more or less importance or criticality and of variable competence and reliability. It is therefore important that a consistent professional approach is taken to dealing with the procurement of IT products as with any other critical supply.

The level of support required from suppliers, contractors and from in-house resources differs widely between different types of technology and will depend on the criticality of the business applications using the technology. It is rarely necessary for the supplier of a general ledger, asset accounting or other 'support' application software package to be on call 24 hours a day. The number of problems which occur with the general ledger package will be relatively few and far between assuming it is an established and widely used package, and secondly the nature of the application means that an immediate response to a problem from the vendor is not always necessary. On the other hand, if a problem occurs with the control programs in a teller machine then it is very important that the supplier should be available immediately to resolve the problem. On the hardware front it is quite common that the type of support required for a PC is for the PC to be taken back to a service centre for it to be repaired, with maybe a two- to three-day turnaround. However, if any component on a mainframe or the network controller fails then it is generally expected that an immediate call out from the engineers is required, with a fix to be implemented within a matter of one or two hours.

Clearly, therefore when determining the requirements of the IT strategy it is sensible to discuss some aspects with vendors on whom its success will depend. It is not realistic to establish performance expectations which are not consistent with what the vendors can provide. Alternatively, only vendors who can satisfy certain stated policies of service support, interconnectability, etc. should be considered. Standards for certain areas of IT use can specify absolute technical policies to be adhered to, e.g. operating systems for micros (e.g. MSDOS) or workstations (e.g. Unix), or communications (OSI), etc.

Security and Privacy

These issues are becoming increasingly important with the widespread use of technology and some of the developments in the industry. There are a number of countries which have serious misgivings about the transfer of data across their national boundaries. This is due to a genuine fear that international information transfer could strengthen the multinational corporations' domination of their countries. Many countries are beginning to introduce data protection legislation concerning the rights of individuals. These are not standard from country to country and often impose quite strict regulations.

It used to be that, given the physical connection of modem to modem, with suitable data encryption it was quite reasonable to expect that data was going to be secure. It is now possible to record the number from which a call into a computer is being made, and hence identify potential security breaches. However, with the advent of satellite broadcasting systems and the use of cellular telephones it is very easy for anybody with equipment costing only $10 to be able to listen in to anybody else's telephone conversation or data transmission. Other types of coding and encryption are going to be required. Even worse, the ability of hackers to introduce 'viruses' into organisations' IT set-ups has become a major security issue, more difficult to detect and deal with than 'computer fraud'.

Capacity Planning and Disaster Recovery

There are some systems for which the capacity requirements of processing power, memory, storage and network requirements can be very precisely calculated and projected so that future capacity requirements can be clearly predicted. There are other types of systems where usage is less predictable and where the capacity requirements would fluctuate quite broadly due to, for example, seasonal changes, business cycles or daily buying patterns. If these are systems which are critically important to the business then there has to be sufficient capacity to deal with the peaks in demand. There are, however, other systems which are totally unpredictable in their nature. For example, if a market analyst is busily running some multivariate analysis on a large database then he may consume an enormous amount of resource for one or two days while looking at his models and then not use the system again for several months. In this case it would not be appropriate to have sufficient capacity for that unpredictable usage.

Managing these capacity issues and potential conflicts is considered in more detail later. A logical extension of capacity planning is contingency planning against a major failure of the technology—disaster recovery. Increasing dependence on computer systems has made organisations seriously concerned about the business problems which would occur if any of their main computer facilities were unavailable for usage due to some sort of disaster, such as flood, fire, or explosion, or even sabotage. The major question which has to be asked in each case is just how much back-up capacity should be provided. Obviously it is very important that an automatic teller machine network should be available within a matter of minutes of a disaster. But is it as important that the marketing information database system be available in that same timeframe? Clearly, there is a difference here and the operational systems that keep a bank running from day to day have to be supported by some sort of back-up centre, but the marketing information system or other systems which help to develop more competitive opportunities, are not quite as important in that disaster scenario. If the computer centre could be re-established elsewhere to full capacity within, say, one month, then it is probably not necessary to provide disaster recovery capability for all systems that are operated; only those which are of absolute necessity.

Future Technology and Research and Development

One of the most frequent comments made about IT strategy is 'we can't possibly produce a technology strategy when the technologies themselves change so quickly'. This statement is absolutely wrong. It is precisely because the technology is changing so quickly that organisations need some form of strategy rather than react to every change in technology. Strategy defines the general directions in which the organisation is going, in this case with respect to technology. It is against that sense of direction that developments in technology can be assessed. Short-term decisions can only be based on available and proven technologies. This book is specifically not concerned with predicting where information technology is going to be heading in the next thirty years.

A recent article 'IT and Tomorrow's Manager' (Applegate *et al.*, 1988) considers not only likely technology developments over the next thirty years, but also the implications for business and its management. It refers directly to a previous set of predictions in 1958 (Leavitt and Whisler, 1958) about 'Management in the 1980s' which did not really predict technology trends very well but forecast many of the business and management implications fairly accurately.

This does not mean that trying to anticipate technology trends over three to five years is not worthwhile. The key is to consider potential technology in the light of IS/IT in the industry and vendors and independent IT analysts can be used to identify application and economic trends which can be exploited ahead of competitors. In general, technology does not change as quickly or dramatically as the pundits would like! It is more incremental, and the products of fundamental IT component development can take several years to become significant in IT products in spite of predictions of the apparently immediate impact! Some never actually materialise in the general market place.

Whether the company wants to take technology risks in the pursuit of strategic advantage will determine how far back in the IT value chain it goes looking at technology development. Lyons, in the early 1950s, built its own computer from basic components, today Allied-Lyons no doubt buy many packages! Figure 12.1 attempts to show the development value chain and the risk to benefit relationship of going further back in the chain to pick up options easily and then add all the value within the firm to develop the application and even some parts of the required technology.

The emphasis that an organisation places on research and development in the information technology area reflects whether it wants to be leading edge, state of the art, the first to follow, or a follower. The more an organisation wishes to be leading edge then, of course, it follows that they must be investing heavily in research and development. However, even for those organisations that are prepared to invest heavily how are they going to maximise the return on that investment? It is impossible to monitor every new item of technology which appears on the market. It is clearly important for the research and development effort

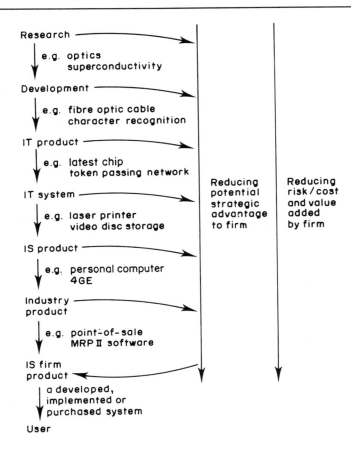

FIGURE 12.1   Strategic advantage and the IS/IT industry value chain. The greater the value added by the IT industry the less the advantage that can be obtained and sustained by the firm

to be focused in areas which are going to be of most benefit to the organisation. So it is important to draw some boundaries within which the research and development effort can operate. For example, for a large multinational company involved in trade, finance, marketing and production it is probably entirely appropriate to be researching electronic data interchange, expert systems and external market databases but these may not be particularly useful ways of spending money for a social services department of a local authority. On the other hand, the viability of technology for home shopping services for old or disabled people in run-down inner city areas, may well be of considerable value to an over-stretched social services department.

Having some coherent R&D approach to the assessment and evaluation of emerging and available technologies is one aspect of the technology strategy for the high potential segment of the application portfolio—through which much of the new technology should be introduced.

GUIDELINES FOR TECHNOLOGY STRATEGIES—BASED ON THE APPLICATION PORTFOLIO

A number of the management issues along with more specific IT issues can be addressed using the applications portfolio approach which has been a basic analytical technique used through the book. It can offer significant guidance on the best approaches to technology management based on the business value and criticality of systems, and hence the requirements of the supporting technology. The technology issues of high potential, strategic, factory and support systems differ significantly but the strategy should address all segments of the portfolio in complementary ways. Within the portfolio segments each application will have particular requirements which the technology must satisfy, and over time those requirements may change due to the changing role the application has in the business.

Each of the segments of the portfolio is considered in more detail below to determine the main features of the IT environment which are most appropriate. These environments can then become the guidelines or even policies for the management of the technology both in the IS central organisation and in user organisations. The composite of these environments then constitutes the overall IT strategy which can evolve as application demand changes and new and better technology options become available.

SUPPORT APPLICATIONS

Within this category are all of the applications which are important to the running and administration of the business but not absolutely critical for success.

Key Characteristics

There are two main characteristics which have a major impact on the technology strategy for these systems.

(a) **Low criticality** A way of judging whether the systems are critical or not is to consider what would happen if that system was not available to the organisation for a few seconds, or an hour, or a day, or for a week. By definition most administrative and other support systems are not critical because the organisation could survive for quite a long period without them being available.

(b) **General business applicability**   The other key characteristic of these particular systems is that they are often applications which are not only common to companies in the same industry but even common across industries. For example, general ledger systems are, within certain limitations, universal in the functionality which they provide and the data which they require. Similarly, personnel systems tend to have characteristics which make the personnel system in a financial institution very similar to that in a manufacturing institution and even a government department.

Alternatively, they perform a localised task specific to a particular department in the organisation, but often a task performed in a similar way in many other companies (such as company car fleet management).

These characteristics lead to a number of requirements for the types of technology best utilised, which fall in-line with the need to scarce resource or allow free market management strategies.

Software Packages

Because of the general nature of the applications there are typically many software packages available on the open market to carry out these applications. Therefore, it should be incumbent on both the user and the MIS organisation to look primarily to the implementation of packaged software to satisfy these requirements. Even if the 'databases' in the packages are not ideally suited to the organisation's information architecture, integration of data is often less critical than the ability to transfer data. Meeting the task requirement in the overall most efficient way is essential to success and therefore packages should not be ruled out just because they cannot be integrated. The user needs are paramount in the final choice, but the IS veto of certain options must be allowed if they cannot provide support for the required technical environment. Otherwise overhead cost build-up will offset the direct efficiency benefits. Equally, it is best to adopt a low risk or conservative approach—only selecting packages with a well established base of customers, rather than be the first user of a new package, however good its apparent features. A package selection checklist can easily be drawn up to help users define requirements and decide on options.

Complexity

Although many support systems provide relatively simple local task orientated solutions to specific problems, others, especially those systems which were among the first to be computerised in any organisation, often have become very complex, or have many interfaces with other systems. However, because these systems have been in existence for a long time the complexity of the functions and interactions should be understood. The application systems which can be bought off the shelf as packages will contain, usually, the full range of functions to be expected from the application. It is quite unusual for additional functionality to support user requirements needing to be added into the packages before implementation. In fact, 'modifying a package' is a route to problems and high costs. Compromising some needs to the facilities of the package is usually feasible and, since the application is not critical, often desirable.

Skills

As this type of system is an ideal candidate for an application package it is not usually necessary to have particularly high levels of technical skills for implementation. Neither is it requisite that a considerable business analytical skill is available because the functionality required by the business is likely to be found within the package. However, there are particular skills required which are associated with the problems of implementation of packages. It is necessary to be able to identify those aspects of the business which the package would not support and which require either additional functions around the package, modification of related systems or modification to existing business practices. This may require considerable care by the system implementors, both technicians and users to ensure that these aspects are not overlooked, and hence benefits forgone or costs increased.

Capacity

The capacity usage of most support applications is generally quite predictable. There will be peaks and troughs but these can be predicted in terms of resource requirements. However, given the low criticality of these systems their 'scheduled' use of capacity may be disrupted by demands of more important applications. Therefore, some contingency planning should be in place which enables alternative action to be taken and which specifies how long the reduced priority can be tolerated before real business problems will arise. For disaster/recovery planning these systems will have a low priority and plans to 'get by without them' should be considered.

Any additional capacity costs incurred because of the application should be clearly identified as part of the application justification.

Risk

This is the area where proven technology is the order of the day. In this type of system no undue technical risk should be introduced in development of or changes to systems. The particular software/hardware may be new to the organisation but it must not be new to the supplier! The only consideration at the other extreme is to avoid obsolescence of the technology used which will, in due course, lead to higher costs.

Disinvestment

These systems, because they are not critical to success, are candidates for disinvestment. There may well be good arguments for subcontracting this kind of system operation to a third party. In Britain, for example, there are a number of third party suppliers of payroll systems, either to run in-house or on a bureau. Because of the constantly changing tax legislation this particular type of application becomes very expensive for an organisation to maintain, and outside suppliers provide the benefits of economies of scale provided the package is extensively used. Problems can occur if other users migrate away leaving remaining users with an increasing bill to pay. Other systems in this support area could equally be contracted out to third party vendors. The use of facility management services is particularly relevant here, especially if the system is using up resources which are needed on more important applications and in addition the organisation needs to develop different skills.

Summary of Implications

Overall the technology strategy for this category of system will be characterised by low-risk approaches and localised planning. Strict criteria concerning returns on investment ought to be used to control activity, risk and expenditure. In the event that the in-house supplier of the system is not cost effective, or would need to develop new skills especially for one system, then consideration should be given to individual businesses going outside to the free market for the provision of that particular service or application. The user is then accountable for the quality of development and implementation, but should have an understanding of these issues to ensure effective management. Decentralisation or centralisation here is normally a matter of economics or if that is unclear then user preference. If that preference is for decentralisation then the user management must clearly understand for what they are responsible and accountable.

A way of enabling considerable support systems activity, without draining away valuable technical resources, is to channel the development and operational services through an 'end-user support' facility or 'information centre'. A limited resource can provide the necessary technical guidance on many simultaneous projects, identify implications due to data or systems relationships and commission add-on functions to packages. This enables the essentially decentralised activity to be co-ordinated, consistent relationships with vendors to be sustained and user experience to be shared across the organisation.

The information centre can perform many more pro-active roles, including training, and should enable the user systems selection and acquisition process to be as risk free as possible. To this end it can provide users with information about proven technology from which they can select in the knowledge that it will be fully supported. The 'list' can show four levels of status:

- proven and supported,
- under evaluation and likely available date,
- not centrally supported but exists in the company,
- becoming obsolete—support to be withdrawn at a future date.

This obviously applies to distributed hardware, operating software and packages but can also apply to central mainframe facilities to which users have direct access.

Some of the key aspects of technology strategies in the support box are summarised in Figure 12.2.

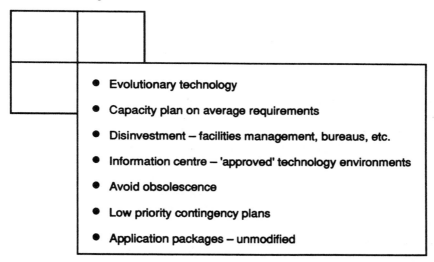

FIGURE 12.2 Support applications: technology strategies

FACTORY SYSTEMS

These applications are absolutely vital for the on-going running of the business. They may, for instance, be the order entry, stock control, purchasing systems and customer database of the organisation and would include the ATM systems for banks and the reservation systems for airlines. It is impossible for the organisation to conduct its business if it is without these systems for any length of time; even a few seconds could lose the company business and extended or repeated failure could well threaten the very existence of the enterprise. Complete failure is not the only concern. If a system is not achieving business requirements accurately or efficiently it may cause problems in other related factory systems, due to delays to other processes, lack of confidence and even breakdown of key information flows. A re-ordering system that cannot respond adequately to changing customer buying patterns may leave shelves empty or warehouses full of unwanted goods.

Again, a number of key requirements of these systems affect the IT strategy options.

Application Packages

The factory applications of the enterprise will tend to be specific to its particular industry and even the particular way the firm conducts its business, and whilst packages may be available, there will be fewer than for the support systems and they will tend to be more industry specific. For example, there are only a few systems available for retail banking, for point-of-sale in retailing, for hotel reservations, or manufacturing requirements planning, etc. Since integration is a key issue in factory systems the data structures and functions provided by the package should be consistent with the information and application architecture defined by the strategy. If they are not the package should be rejected. Alternatively, a particular core package, e.g. a manufacturing resource planning package, may be used to provide that core architecture and other, probably smaller, applications may be designed to integrate with the package architecture. Therefore, it is important to understand which primary process is most critical to success. Often bringing in a package is the best way of achieving integration of application requirements amongst various departments who otherwise would attempt to satisfy their own needs without regard to the effects on others. 'Making the package work' can often override localised objectives, although if badly managed it could become a target for every department to engineer its failure! Unlike support type packages, however, a 'factory' package will probably need considerable IS professional support to ensure integration and effective operation are achieved. Whilst user functionality is the prime reason for package selection the IT strategy should specify the technical checklist to be satisfied before a package is adopted.

Functional Complexity

Factory applications will tend to be functionally complex, have integrated interfaces and dependencies and will need to satisfy requirements with minimum compromise of the user's main needs. Even where a package is selected, it may have to be customised in spite of the risks involved—and this will require a thorough technical understanding of how the package works as well as what it does. For example, there are two main suppliers of airline reservations systems in the world but each airline which has purchased one of these packages has extensively customised it so that it looks, to the agent or the individual making a booking, as though it is specific to that airline. Whether a system is developed or a package modified, an accurate specification of what it does and how it does it will have to be established. A structured logical model of the system must be developed to enable the application to be accurately engineered. That model, documented or simulated via software engineering tools, plus supporting data dictionaries, etc. must be maintained and updated whenever the system changes. Strict change control procedures must be introduced to prevent errors being introduced which may only manifest themselves in downstream systems.

Skills

Because this type of system will require on-going modification in order to avoid falling behind the business needs, they will need a high level of technical support skills to be available both for emergency action and changes. If a package is used it can produce considerable difficulties to the organisation when new releases of the underlying application package need to be implemented, i.e. changes may have to be made even if the business does not require them. Due to the complexity and criticality of these systems it is important that knowledge of the system is not allowed to decay in periods of low rates of change and control procedures should not be overridden for expediency. For many of these systems a dedicated support team is required after implementation, consisting of both users and IS professionals. It is important to develop skills related to the specific system, not just employ generalists to correct and amend the system when available. Releases of new versions of the system moved into operation must be carefully controlled and checked after introduction.

Capacity

In this area system performance and availability are usually critical. This implies the need for back-up and duplication of substantial amounts of data and systems software by way of test systems and previous releases which can be brought up quickly when problems arise. A 'hot restart' process is essential to minimise downtime and all critical components, both hardware and software, should be duplicated. Hardware and data duplication may be shared with other applications. Capacity planning should be based on peak loadings, rather than risk degradation. The capacity needed could be made available by the specified down-grading of the service provided to support applications. In every case specific service agreements should be established with the users, IS department and vendors and continuously monitored for compliance. Computer or network or even technical resource capacity should not become a constraint to the system achieving its performance targets or the business will suffer.

All factory systems should be able to be recovered and quickly restarted in the case of a disaster which implies off-site back-up of all systems data, code and documentation as well as hardware and operating software. An alternative resource needs to be available either inside the company or provided by the vendor or shared with other companies. Disasters must also be simulated from time to time to ensure the recovery procedures can be carried out!

Risk

These systems are critical to the running of the organisation and, to reduce risk of failure they are required to be kept as stable as possible. Not only must changes to these systems and underlying technology be well tested, checked and quality assured before being implemented, the need for any change must be justified before it is allowed to go ahead. There has to be considerable discipline exercised by users, developers and operations staff in order to assure continued running of the application. The risks are of two types: the system fails in some way and the direct aspect of the business it deals with is affected to the immediate disadvantage of the organisation; or the system fails and affects other systems, and hence other areas of the business. Often the IS/IT people are in the best position to identify the latter case and therefore can stop the users from making a change that will have an effect elsewhere.

One way of reducing unnecessary risks is to avoid technology innovation in the factory systems area. For instance, using new CASE-based software engineering tools for the first time on a critical factory system development is risky. Try them out first somewhere else. Installing a new computer which the organisation (or worse still, the vendor!) has little experience of using in a critical operational environment, has obvious inherent risks. Some factory systems that started as strategic may bring with them new technology. A decision has to be made whether to provide full support for that technology or re-implement the system on safer technology. This will depend on a number of factors:

- the overall economics of supporting the application,
- the skills available,
- whether the application can run on other technology,
- how much integration with other applications is required,
- vendor performance in meeting service obligations, etc.

A conscious decision must be made, the system must not be allowed to drift into a new mode of use where its innovative nature is less important than the efficiency, reliability or effectiveness with which it achieves the requirements. Some re-implementation is almost essential across the boundary to reduce the long-term support costs for what will inevitably be a much changed system, not designed to minimize the cost and ease of long-term maintenance, i.e. to reduce the resource required to keep the system satisfying user needs.

Many an organisation has introduced unnecessary business risks by replacing its core hardware and operating software on which the factory systems have been built. This also often involves changing the primary vendor. This major decision often becomes the so-called 'strategy' and in fact in many instances this becomes the only strategy since few resources remain to do anything other than convert the systems. If done badly many years may elapse before the functionality of the systems can be improved and in the meantime they can fall well behind the business needs. The technology strategy effectively constrains the application strategy severely. It is a high-risk strategy to be adopted only in certain circumstances:

● major functionality improvements required cannot be met by the existing environment,
● significant long-term cost savings can be assured to offset the high conversion cost,
● application effectiveness can be improved by developing a more integrated or robust infrastructure which can deliver better long-term options, which are more advantageous than short-term functionality enhancements.

The general rule should be steady increments in technology which enable the organisation to develop its technical infrastructure in a controlled way. Even major hardware, operating software or networking upgrades will create short-term application risks and may slow-up developments. Some risks will have to be taken but the implications of technology change on application performance, effectiveness and development plans must be accurately assessed and contingency measures developed to deal with any potential failure.

Some of the key issues are summarised in Figure 12.3.

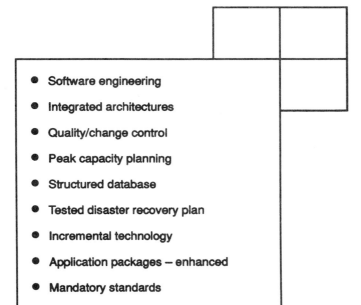

● Software engineering

● Integrated architectures

● Quality/change control

● Peak capacity planning

● Structured database

● Tested disaster recovery plan

● Incremental technology

● Application packages – enhanced

● Mandatory standards

● Careful technology selection (IS/IT veto)

FIGURE 12.3 Factory applications: technology strategies

STRATEGIC SYSTEMS

Strategic systems are those which should enable the enterprise to gain some form of business advantage and/or achieve its business objectives. In the process this is likely to mean a change in the way it conducts or controls the business. The advantages may not last long and the system may need continuous enhancement to gain further advantage. Incremental development is often the key to success.

Many of the technology management issues associated with factory systems also relate to strategic systems, but additional issues need to be considered. The major differences are due to the need to take business risks and to the uniqueness of the application which is implied if advantage is to be gained or a specific objective achieved.

Software Packages

It is unlikely that there will be any software packages available for this type of application. It is difficult to envisage how significant advantage will accrue from a generally available piece of software, unless the business adds considerable value to the package, e.g. by considerable enhancement, a new use of the package, or by changing business practice in an innovative way. Even then the process converts the package to a *unique application* of the package and as such must be supported as if it were tailor-made. Alternatively, a short-lived advantage could occur from being the first user of a new package—but success could be very quickly and easily copied. Sustained advantage comes from the uniqueness of the application which others cannot easily replicate or improve on.

There are a few circumstances where an application is deemed strategic to the business and a package could fit the requirement: if the organisation is trying to catch up with competitors or a strategic objective is major cost reduction, or the business is being severely rationalised, all of which are situations where 'preventing disadvantage' is really the target of the strategic system.

Functional Complexity and Skills

These systems are likely to be complex or will become complex as functions are incrementally added. For example, developing a marketing database from external and internal data, or a 'just-in-time' manufacturing system are innovative and quite complex in business and technical terms. They require considerable business and IS skills for their development and implementation and both are not entirely within the control of the organisation to effect.

They are also required to be developed quickly and the application may have to be 'generated' many times as it is changed. Ideally the system should be piloted or prototyped before embarking on the full system project. Speed, flexibility and complexity all lead to problems of controlling the development and then achieving effective maintenance. New technical and management skills may have to be developed. Continuity in terms of systems team members will be critical to keeping that knowledge in an environment which will not encourage accurate documentation or the best in quality control process. Those standards should not be ignored, but business expediency will have to overrule technical idealism in many cases. The risk is that problems will occur later which cannot be easily rectified.

It is vital that the business users fully understand what the system does and as far as possible how it does it. As these systems are taking the enterprise into new areas there will often be a need for new business process or operational skills as well as technology skills. For example, in the use of databases for marketing then advanced statistical analysis techniques would be required. A customer ordering system could require new ways of dealing with customers, e.g. tele selling. In the area of computer-integrated manufacturing there will be significant changes in the type of machine tools required and in the methods of production control. User management must ensure that these business skills are developed.

Data Sources and Dependence on Other Systems

Strategic systems frequently use data from various existing underlying source systems. The data in the strategic application will often need to be vertically integrated with the underlying systems and may take data from outside sources as well. An example of the need to integrate data comes from the financial institutions where relatively few banks are able to offer comprehensive cash management facilities to the customer. The difficulty lies in taking data from all the underlying different product systems, which are account orientated, linking all the accounts together by individual customer and then managing the customers' accounts accordingly. The underlying product systems have evolved in a piecemeal fashion with relatively little control or thought towards the total view of, or relationship with the customer. This is often the case unless the underlying factory (and even support) systems have been developed or redeveloped to use common integrated data architectures.

Equally, these systems may rely on interfaces with existing factory systems to follow through the processing of data to achieve the full business potential. For example, car and hotel reservations facilities are built on top of the existing airline reservation systems, as are new products being offered through automatic teller machines, such as cash deposits, bill payment and financial transfer transactions. For these to be successful there is a need for a very solid and firm architecture to the underlying system. If these underlying systems are in any way weak, then building new strategic applications on top will inevitably expose those weaknesses and could well cause the new strategic systems to collapse. Few organisations have developed successful strategic systems without first having established coherent and stable application and data architectures for factory systems.

Capacity and Disaster Recovery

In direct contrast to the 'support' and 'factory' applications, the capacity requirements for 'strategic' applications are often very hard to determine. For example, in a marketing database the data requirements could be immense but the pattern of usage would probably be quite irregular. If a new information access or ordering facility is being provided for a customer, despite all the market research which should be undertaken before its release, the actual pattern of take-up by the customers will never be certain. It could be that demand is immediately very high or it could take a long time to develop. This uncertainty must be allowed for in the capacity plan for the use of the application.

The effects of capacity are twofold. First, if the application is designed to attract more customers or to give a competitive advantage via better handling of transactions, then there has to be sufficient capacity to cater for any pattern of uptake and the means identified for meeting the expected total demand. It would not be appropriate for a new facility to be offered through a terminal to the customer population only for them to find that the system is unavailable due to the capacity constraint or that there are no effective recovery arrangements when failure occurs. However, the system is likely to suffer more breakdown due to its inherent instability than a well engineered factory system. In failing it could bring down other applications or even a whole computer resource. The need for continuing enhancement often under time pressure will inevitably increase the risk of failure. It is therefore reasonable to isolate the application from others it might adversely affect even if this means it cannot take capacity from less important systems when it needs it. This may imply dedicated capacity which may have to be increased rapidly to satisfy demand. Therefore a technology should be chosen that can easily or rapidly be incrementally added to or upgraded.

When eventually the capacity needs are clearer and patterns of use become more predictable the application will be better able to share capacity with other systems. Particularly where applications use networks it is often better to start by using a Value Added Network Service (VANS) provider where capacity is paid for as demand develops. Later it may be more effective to use the organisation's own network.

Risk

Projects in this category are clearly high risk. This is due to the direct relationship between risk and potential benefits, and the risks involved here are both business and technical due to the high degree of business value adding the enterprise needs to achieve in a short time. The risk is compounded by the fact that the enterprise may be entering into new areas for the application of technology, combined with relatively significant changes in business practice and even organisational relationships. The key risk, however, is not achieving the expected advantage or the business objective. Since that is the case, the business manager responsible for the system must decide which risks to take, based on best advice from the technical experts. As has been said before, introducing any unnecessary technical risk, however exciting the prospect of new technology, is inappropriate, unless it is the only way to achieve the requirements in the time available. The risk should be expressed in terms of potential business impact.

Implications for the Technology Strategy

1. Strategic applications are often developed due to needs of the business which are driven by its industry environment. This implies that the prevailing IT direction of the industry may well have to be incorporated in the strategy, especially if the applications are linking the organisation to that external environment. For example, design process changes may force the organisation to a limited choice of CAD systems. It is very likely therefore that new technology will have to be introduced as part of a strategic system. Some retailing organisations tried to develop 'patent' networks with suppliers only to find the industry has generally adopted the use of incompatible value added data services, leaving major conversion costs to the early investors.

   The conclusion is that not only is the external business environment likely to drive strategic applications, but the choice of technology will often also be driven by external factors. Therefore an awareness of technology trends in the industry is important if advantage is not potentially to turn to disadvantage quite quickly.

2. It is obviously important to develop these applications quickly, since the window of opportunity may be short-lived or uncertain. It will, therefore, certainly be argued by the business managers that it is better to develop the systems without applying the full 'factory' rigour of documentation, methodologies and standards—especially if adherence could extend the development time, and hence perhaps miss the business opportunity. The potential implications of this approach should be understood and some appropriate, if not ideal, development control process put in place.

   This need would also argue for the use of application generators where the initial analysis and design can be performed using automated tools which would then produce code which, while not particularly efficient, will at least be very quickly developed and enable changes to be identified and implemented rapidly. The benefits will come from both rapid, iterative design *and* rapid generation of the code and perhaps two types of generator will be needed.

   As these systems will frequently require input from a number of underlying systems and aim to provide flexible facilities for analysing and using the data in different ways, there is a strong argument for the using of relational rather than structured databases.

The speed of developing the application is considerably more important than its efficiency of operation. Eventually these applications would probably turn into regular 'factory' applications, when they may need to be reimplemented in order to make them more efficient in their operation. Even while they are still strategic, some elements of the system can be reimplemented in more efficient code, to meet required performance criteria.

3. Due to the nature of these systems they will more effectively be developed by a small dedicated project team focusing on delivering business functionality rather than subcontract any aspect of the project to people whose time is shared with other applications. The team will have to consist of members who have between them high technical ability and considerable business knowledge and expertise.

Some key aspects are summarised in Figure 12.4.

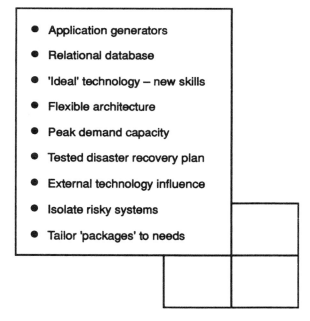

FIGURE 12.4 Strategic applications: technology strategies

HIGH POTENTIAL (TURNAROUND) APPLICATIONS

Unlike the other three segments these applications will never really exist in business terms if managed properly. The R&D nature of this segment has already been emphasised. An application should stay in this part of the box for a limited period until its future is clearer—the evaluation of its potential is complete. It can either turn into a major strategic opportunity, produce a valuable enhancement to existing strategic or factory systems, become a more efficient means of carrying out a support activity or have no value at all!

Many strategic systems started life as pilots or prototypes in this segment, but many essentially support uses of IT also started with high hopes in much the same way. The whole concept of the high potential segment is innovation, either with new technology or a new use of technology as far as the organisation is concerned. One major danger is that successful 'prototypes' are allowed to drift into becoming unsuccessful systems and also produce an expensive technology support problem.

Many aspects of this area will be considered below in discussion concerning the identification of future technologies and introducing technological change. However, some issues are worth highlighting in the context of the relationship with other parts of the portfolio.

As has been said before these R&D type activities should be separated from mainstream systems, to enable them to be evaluated on their merits. The main objective is to evaluate the *business* potential of applying any technology, but in some cases the potential may not only be where the initial use of a new technology is tried. This may mean splitting the prototyping objectives into those which are application specific and those which are of more general interest. This would be the case for instance in the first use of an expert system or new communications technology. Even if an initial attempt fails the technology should not be totally rejected. Equally the potential of the technology should not be explored in abstract without some application in mind. This is a recipe for pouring money down the drain! Clear terms of reference or objectives should be established at the start, but they may need to be consciously (and overtly) modified as knowledge is acquired.

One great danger is to give the evaluation of new technology solely to technologists! They often have preconceived prejudices or develop an enthusiasm for the technology without any focus on its business value. A business 'product champion' is the best approach to its management, supported by appropriate technical skills.

Often the organisation will have to acquire or develop new technological skills to develop the applications and support the process of evaluation. Some may have to be acquired through the vendor or outside experts. The key to success will be the knowledge transfer that should occur during the evaluation phase. The organisation should avoid future dependency on technical skills only available outside. If this proves the case, then the new technology should probably be rejected unless the business case for its deployment is overwhelming. Even then the development of a suitably capable internal resource must be pursued urgently.

Whilst high potential applications need to be evaluated in association with a particular technology, it may be that more than one option exists for evaluation. It can be advisable to carry out parallel, competing R&D projects focused on one business application, especially if the potential benefits appear very high, speed is of the essence and/or competitors are carrying out similar evaluations. However, in this case the eventual decision criteria must be clearly spelled out or the process will only leave more uncertainty at the end than there was at the start.

Whatever the success of the evaluation, the application should not proceed without a further review of the technology options and implications. It may be that only support type benefits, mainly economic, are available in which case the potential of better known technologies to meet the bulk of requirements should be considered. If the result is an 'add-on' to a factory system, such as new hand-held data collection equipment, then the functional needs should be clearly established and other feasible technologies in the market place should be re-evaluated. This is especially true if other, perhaps less innovative but more reliable existing, vendors are close to launching a more compatible product to the existing environment. If the outcome is clearly very strategic the need for speedy development will naturally inhibit the desire to stop and evaluate alternatives. However, as the development proceeds, other available technology solutions should be monitored with a view to later change if necessary.

Even if the R&D is a failure, it may be only due to the poor current economics of the idea or the poor performance of the technology, in which case a 'back burner' strategy should be adopted. Should the economics change or the technology become more appropriate, a further evaluation should be considered.

It is also worth remembering that a valid product of early R&D is to recommend a differently focused or different scale of evaluation to be undertaken—a second prototyping stage. Before any new technology 'leaves' the high potential segment any risks and requirements should be fully understood and then dealt with in proportion to the business contribution expected, by elimination or improving the management process.

Lastly, it should always be borne in mind that the risks of not doing some R&D are in business terms often greater than the risks of getting it wrong or spending too much money. The technology base of the business could quickly deteriorate and its systems possibilities will be strictly limited by an outdated set of technologies and skills.

Some of the key high potential issues are summarised in Figure 12.5.

MANAGING TECHNOLOGICAL DEVELOPMENT

Technology change will occur at a rate outside the control of the organisation. The management skill is to intercept that changing pattern of technology availability and use in the company's industry and then manage technology change within the organisation to achieve the maximum benefit.

A number of views of how that can be done have been put forward from which some technology management strategies can be devised.

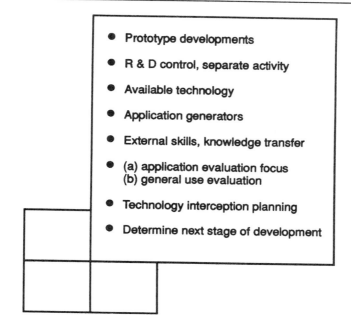

- Prototype developments

- R & D control, separate activity

- Available technology

- Application generators

- External skills, knowledge transfer

- (a) application evaluation focus
  (b) general use evaluation

- Technology interception planning

- Determine next stage of development

FIGURE 12.5 High potential applications: technology strategies

Looking from an industry perspective a new technology, such as LANS, portable terminals will follow a relative standard path in their deployment in any particular industry. The following description is primarily derived from the terms used in a report by Arthur D. Little Inc. (1981).

Stage 1—the technology is not in use in the industry but is under development by suppliers (such technologies are described as 'emerging')
Stage 2—technology leaders in the industry will implement trial applications often in partnership with the vendor ('pacing technology')
Stage 3—technology leaders implement major systems incorporating the technology ('key technology')
Stage 4—the technology becomes widely used in the industry ('base technology')

This is a useful classification—emerging, pacing, key and base—for describing the status of a technology in an industry. That does not mean the status will be the same across industries. Point of sales systems, while well established in grocery retailing are only just being implemented in builders' merchants. CAD systems are at different stages of maturity in different industries. This implies that monitoring technology development in other, probably related, industries can be very useful.

The window of opportunity to gain major advantage from utilising new technology is in stages 2 and 3, during which other organisations still have much to learn, although their cost of following could well be less. With success in one or two firms the vendors will be quick to sell the technology to others in the industry. It is important that the senior management is kept informed about its position in this development scenario *vis-à-vis* its main competitors.

There is clearly a relationship with the strategic grid, even if the technology types also clearly overlap the segments (see Figure 12.6). Figure 12.6 also suggests overall strategies to be adopted against each of the technology types.

1. *Emerging*   Monitoring of vendors' developments and the early stages of the use of the technology within the industry, or outside it, is important. Even if no action is taken implications should be drawn and 'trigger-points' for more intense action decided.
2. *Pacing*   If the organisation's overall posture is to be a technology leader, then it should invest via a prototype or R&D evaluation in any technology that appears to offer benefits. A technology follower on the other hand would wait, but should monitor others' experiments and also open up a dialogue with potential vendors. It will be the general management attitude to these pacing technologies which will determine its overall technology strategic

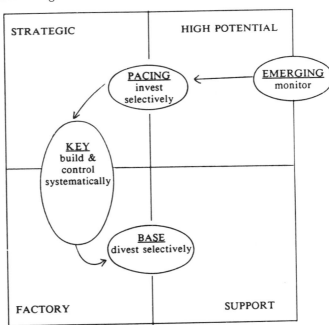

FIGURE 12.6 Technology maturity/life cycle in relation to the application portfolio

approach. This should normally reflect its attitude to all technology, not just IS/IT.

Some technologies, such as office technologies and LANS, are industry non-specific, which means a wider view than the industry should be taken. In the early 1980s the Aalsmeer Flower Auction led its industry through auction clock technology. A competitor introduced videotext to the industry, a technology Aalsmeer had ignored but which had been adopted in other international commodity-type trading.

This 'pacing' strategic choice will probably be reflected in the number of different vendors the company uses—the greater the leadership sought, the greater the number. The choice of major vendors is a strategic procurement decision not a tactical technical one. Often a particular pacing technology will be provided by a limited number of vendors initially.

3. *Key* These form the main operational technologies of the company and its competitors and the company that fails to master their use will fall behind. There will undoubtedly be a number of vendors offering broadly similar and (no doubt claimed) compatible products. Restricting the number of vendors, unless the compatability is truly seamless, is often the wisest course even if optimum functionality is sacrificed.

4. *Base* Well established, even ageing technologies do need to be managed positively, not just allowed to continue to be used—they may inhibit further technology development and/or freeze the skills in the past. A strategy for selective divestment of the obsolescent or incompatible technologies must be established. Undue consumption of scarce skilled resources could be a prime reason for divestment. Again, monitoring the discontinuation of technology use in the industry or elsewhere is advisable to anticipate and avoid problems. It is often more difficult to get rid of a much loved, if inadequate technology than to bring in a new one!

These approaches to overall technology management are entirely consistent with the application driven requirements described earlier in the chapter.

MANAGING THE INTRODUCTION OF NEW TECHNOLOGIES

Often the introduction of new technology to the organisation fails either in the short or long term due to mismanagement. Office automation, CAD, local area networks, personal computers, hand-held terminals, expert systems and other technologies have all in many companies been mis-employed, under-exploited or become an expensive white elephant—ornamental rather than useful.

McKenney and McFarlan (1982) propose a way of managing the assimilation of new technology into an organisation. Research by Raho *et al.* (1987) has generally verified the usefulness of the model in ensuring successful introduction and then diffusion through the organisation.

The model has essentially four major phases, separated by decision points at which mismanagement can occur. (See Figure 12.7.)

The different phases can be summarised as follows:

1. *Identification and initial investment* The emphasis is on learning about the technology and how it can be applied. Often the 'learning' results in more of a consideration of the technology's shortcomings and problems, so that longer-term potential is not understood. Lack of management attention to the evaluation leaves the decision making in the hands of technical people (who may reject the technology due to its imperfections), or keen users (who are focused on a limited aspect of its potential use). Stagnation or failure

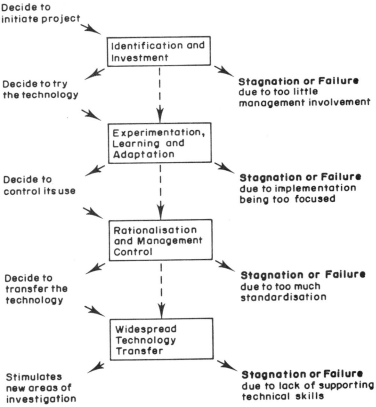

FIGURE 12.7 *Phases of assimilation of technology in organisations (reprinted by permission of* Harvard Business Review. *An exhibit from 'The information archipelago—maps and bridges', by J. L. McKenney and F. W. McFarlan (September–October 1982). Copyright © 1982 by the President and Fellows of Harvard College; all rights reserved)*

then occurs, rather than a clear decision on how to proceed or reject the technology. For instance, this has commonly occurred with evaluations of office automation products, where all the features may not be ideal but then all the features may not be required. Equally, CAD may merely become a drawing tool rather than a design aid linked to engineering and new product development and introduction.

2. *Experimentation, learning and adaptation*   Gaining the users' awareness of what the technology can do and developing the essential technical skills to support applications are the main objectives of this piloting phase. There are two main dangers at this stage. The chosen pilot area may be too focused on a specific problem of no general business relevance and the experience gained is of very limited value to the organisation. Alternatively, too many parallel pilots are attempted due to user demand, no coherent development plan is established and applications drift into widespread use without the necessary management control or technical support. Often then the vendors of the technology are effectively driving the future strategy.

It is important that this stage is carried out relatively quickly to avoid missing opportunities and causing other potential users to become frustrated. At the same time the lessons that are being learned must be recorded and analysed to identify how to proceed further. This is particularly important since the adaptation of the original concept of the use of the technology may well steer the pilot project in directions which are more or less generally useful. Few pilot uses of technology produce the exact results expected, and often more is learned from what is not achieved than what is.

One key aspect of this stage is to identify the economic implications of using and supporting the technology on the larger scale.

3. *Rationalisation and management control*   The main objective is to develop necessary skills and control the rate of release of the technology to avoid unnecessary risks in its more general application, or excessive expenditure with little real return. The purpose is to allow the technology to be incorporated in new systems developments where it is appropriate. The emphasis is on a short-term (1–2 years) plan to ensure the technology is effectively supported and used efficiently based on its now understood requirements and facilities. Further experimentation is to be discouraged until its implementation can be properly supported.

The management controls will focus on justification of its use, rationalising and containing the technical support costs, establishing control of procurement and verification that its use is achieving the benefits projected.

The main danger is that the controls are too restrictive and the pace of development slows to a halt, and hence knowledge and experience gained in stage 2 decays. The technical skills will reside in certain individuals who may well, in frustration, even leave the organisation—they are likely to be valued by other companies. Users may in the process return to stages 1 and 2 based on a different set of parameters for evaluating the same technology, resulting later in stage 3 issues being raised once more. Equally, no control will lead to the need perhaps for more draconian measures later. The introduction of PCs into many organisations suffered from either over-control or too lax management at this stage of their exploitation.

4. *Widespread technology transfer*   Having gained all the necessary expertise in using and managing the particular technology, it can be made generally available for incorporation in a wide variety of applications. This may include, for instance, allowing users to directly use 4GL tools to develop some applications rather than just use them in the IS department. Controls need to be in place, offering strong guidance on when, where and how best to deploy the technology. Resources need to be well organised to respond to the demand for support efficiently and also to plan for the further development of the technology, as part of the longer-term strategy.

Often the greatest problem is under-resourcing the support, such that the resource is used up in only meeting short-term requirements. The longer-term development hence suffers and again stagnation occurs. This is particularly true if all the expertise is in one user department, not in some centralised resource which can facilitate developments in other parts of the organisation. A user department becomes the only repository of knowledge and is by default having to provide a service to others. This is commonly the case with office systems, expert systems and certain PC software packages where the primary pilot site retains critical expertise. The organisation must establish a centre of competence independent of a main user. A user group forum can also be established to exchange knowledge and develop future requirements, which can be planned by the central resource.

In summary, it is clear that any new technology introduced into the organisation will go through a number of stages of assimilation, the management of which will effect its eventual deployment, and hence benefits to the organisation. The model reviewed above enables a proactive approach to the management of technology change. It is important to establish such a coherent process since it is likely that a number of new technologies will be introduced simultaneously. Each needs to be managed successfully and all need to be managed coherently. Otherwise IT strategic planning and supporting resource development will become a matter primarily of post-implementation rationalisation and control to avoid expensive duplication, repeated failure or resources being too thinly spread.

TECHNOLOGY STRATEGIES IN A MULTI-BUSINESS UNIT ORGANISATION

Throughout the book there has been a focus on achieving a coherent IS/IT strategy for a business unit, because each business unit should seek to maximise the benefits from its information, systems and technology, and it is most feasible to achieve that coherence at a business unit level. However, most corporations consist of a number of businesses and there is a need to consider the strategic management of technology across the businesses to obtain the maximum *corporate and business unit* benefits.

This corporate dimension has been considered under various earlier headings which in each case conclude that a number of factors will drive the degree of beneficial central co-ordination and control over and above the business units. The main factors affecting the technology strategy can be summarised as:

(a) *Business driven factors* include the following:

- degree of inter-company trading,
- similarity of products and business processes,
- coherence of markets served, and channels of distribution used, and main suppliers,
- similarity in scale of operation,
- industry maturity and competitive situation of units,
- geography, especially in international companies,
- how corporate management exercises its control over the units' business strategies and activities,
- the rate of business and organisational change

(b) *IS/IT supply-driven factors* which include:

- the economics of processing and procurement,
- availability of skills and human resources,
- availability of technologies and vendor services in different countries and areas,
- the existing IS/IT investments in the different units.

Often, however, these 'logical' factors can become obscured by organisational and political factors due to the way the business units have been developed or acquired and/or the degree of real trust that exists between the corporate centre and the units. This desire for conformity or independence often manifests itself more emotionally over the control of IT than many other business issues, especially in companies which grow by acquisition, where IT environments often pre-date the organisational relationships. Based on the above factors there appears to be a structured way of addressing these issues which is consistent with discussion earlier of achieving application, information and organisational coherence and synergy to the degree required by the business relationships. It is important that the degree of IT conformity or divergence reflects the business, organisational and cultural characteristics of the organisation, not the preferences of IT specialists or it will fail in the long term to deliver corporate benefit.

How much the corporation should direct the technology architecture and the selection process cannot be prescribed but there is perhaps an escalating scale of corporate intervention that can be considered. At the lowest level this can provide benefit even if the organisation is a conglomerate, buying and selling businesses and operating in many industries with companies of varying sizes and differing business situations. At the highest level the benefits will be far greater in a corporation which has a number of companies in the same overall industry.

Level 1

Centralisation of technology control will be mainly an economic issue to exploit corporate buying power with suppliers and ensure that resources are not unnecessarily duplicated. This will have most effect at the 'commodity' end of technology—in data communications, processing power and basic operational software plus the related technical skills to support the IT operations. Even if the companies have different application requirements, establishing a target environment based on supply economics can enable selection decisions in each unit to consider a preferred set of options. These will not be mandatory, but will be expected to be adopted, unless the local economics are poor, perhaps due to the unit's size, or application needs cannot be adequately satisfied. Some centralised resources and skills will then be available to support the companies' implementation and operation of the main hardware, operating systems and networks, and even application packages. This can make the preferred solutions more attractive to the units, providing the charge out of costs from the centre is equitable. The central resource can also act as the main point of contact with suppliers to ensure the corporation obtains the best value from group purchasing, and monitor centrally the vendor performance against agreed service levels as and when problems arise anywhere in the corporation.

In most, even diverse, organisations telecommunications management is centralised to provide the necessary skills, manage the capacity, deal with major vendors and ensure costs are not unnecessarily incurred.

Level 2

If the corporation has a number of businesses operating in different industries, but of a limited number of types (e.g. several manufacturing businesses plus some distribution and/or service companies) there may be opportunities for further benefits at the corporate level or at a subgroup level, over and above those mentioned at level 1. For instance, manufacturing companies may all need some form of Manufacturing Resource Planning (MRPII) system or each subgroup has similar supply chains or trades in similar ways. There is probably some similarity in the type of applications required and data used, and therefore benefits will exist if application software knowledge and even resources are shared between the units. This will add weight to the need for consistency of basic operating environments, otherwise the benefit of application knowledge will be reduced by the need to support diverse implementations on different manufacturers' hardware and operating systems, and deal with a large variety of suppliers. The benefits are not purely economic, although obviously the ability to replicate business benefits is a financial gain. The benefits also accrue by enabling companies of perhaps different sizes and in different states of maturity to develop applications ahead of their own local ability to develop the necessary skills. Similar applications may even be run centrally and hence be able to be upgraded as the hardware and software base changes with less cost and disruption to the units.

The potential downside is that the units do not develop their own business application and technical expertise to move beyond using IT for essentially support and factory applications. Too much centralisation of IT control can lead to reduced innovation at a unit level, and if there is no central or group level management IS/IT business steering mechanism, merely satisfying the 'lowest common denominator' of needs can stifle overall and local progress.

Level 3

Where companies are in the same industry and/or trade with one another and/or deal with a similar customer or supplier base, there is obviously greater benefit available from strong co-ordination of technology management at a corporate level. Not only are there economic and application supply-side benefits but also significant benefits from sharing data, and from its proficient and consistent processing throughout the company and in systems linking the company to its trading partners. Here it is worth ensuring that the technology environments are consistent to the level of data management software, communications standards and some application software, even if to any one unit company the 'overhead' may appear uneconomic. The benefits of strong central direction and hence support in terms of skills and resources may again be negated if innovation is stifled. A corporate mechanism to deal with strategic and high potential areas of development must be in place. Equally, the corporation may need to fund part of the cost of technology in the units to encourage conformance to the target architectures.

There is obviously a strong central role in defining the core information architecture as well as the core technology architecture, from which appropriate selection can be made to implement the application architecture for the unit which, as discussed in Chapter 9, should still originate from the units. This implies that the units may have to compromise some requirements and the consequences of such compromise must be understood. The compromise may not always be worthwhile—meaning that the corporate architecture must evolve and develop with the needs and not become a force for business stagnation due to the limited options it allows.

This three-level approach obviously is somewhat simplistic but is an attempt to reflect in technology management terms the likely business and corporate cultures which will prevail across the spectrum from a 'financial conglomerate' to a highly focused and organically developing company. Essentially it suggests an increasing need for central co-ordination across business units to gain benefits at economic, application and information resource management levels in the appropriate circumstances. The progression follows a rationale from the support via the factory to the strategic/high potential quadrants of the matrix in terms of increasing potential gain from central co-ordination of technology strategy in order to gain the business benefits both corporately *and* in each part of the business. It reflects also the types of strategy required at a corporate level in addition to local generic strategies and the need to increase the technology co-ordination of 'base', 'key', 'pacing' and 'emerging' technologies described earlier, in relation to the increasing business benefits they may provide at each of the three levels.

The more business strategic co-ordination expected the more IT strategy needs a centrally planned component, whereas the more the units are expected to deliver purely a financial contribution to the corporation, the greater the emphasis on free market choice and the economics of supply management (scarce resource or monopoly control). Again, at the three different levels the organisation in total will be more or less vulnerable in terms of the impact of IS/IT on its component firms. At the highest level the corporation must be fully aware of IS/IT developments in the industry on which it depends for success and direct activity accordingly. At the lowest level, in diverse industries this is more difficult to achieve central planning, but also the risk to the corporation of failure in any one business environment is less.

SUMMARY

This chapter has attempted to describe strategies for managing technology in line with previous strategic approaches to resourcing, information and applications. As such it has dealt with issues which need to be managed, driven by the application of technology rather than by the specific problems of deploying certain types of technology. The issues tend to be similar across technologies and have to be considered as part of the overall strategic IS/IT management process and understood by those who are not intimately familiar with any particular technology. Technology strategy should never become the exclusive domain of technologists, although obviously their input to the general management process is very valuable and must be able to be incorporated effectively.

Three points are worth reiterating in summary.

1. The theme of the technology strategy should always reflect how it can be deployed to add value in the business. Business future success will occur because today's technology is well used and managed. No sensible organisation will assume that future technology will resolve current problems in due course—it is more likely to exacerbate them.

2. The organisation must be aware of how technology is being deployed and for what purpose by others in the industry, and even in other industries. The influence of what others, customers, suppliers and competitors are doing and the technology they are using, will become a significant factor in determining strategic technology options in the future, especially for firms that cannot easily adopt a leading role in their environment. A responsive 'following' strategy can be very successful but it requires an accurate monitoring of developments elsewhere. Even then there is a considerable organisational learning process to manage.

3. It is in the technology that an organisation is vulnerable to undue outside pressure from IT suppliers whose interests will not always coincide with those of the business. That is only to be expected, but it means the organisation must adopt a coherent procurement approach as it would with any other set of critical suppliers. As such it should also exploit the knowledge of those vendors, who are also supplying many other organisations, even some in the same industry. Almost every IT vendor will claim to be providing 'business solutions'. It is important to find out how effective those 'solutions' are elsewhere and in particular how they are affecting the industry. The organisation would be unwise to rely exclusively on its own judgement of particular technologies without a broader understanding of the business context in which they are being deployed. Many companies ignore this and are led up many blind alleys. Establishing mutually respectful business partnerships with a number of key IT suppliers can be very important, provided the management of the business remains in the driving seat!

REFERENCES

Applegate, L. M., Cash, J. I. and Mills, D. Q. (1988) 'Information technology and tomorrow's manager', *Harvard Business Review* (Nov./Dec.).

Arthur D. Little Inc. (1981) 'Strategic management of technology', Report to European Management Forum.

Leavitt, H. J. and Whisler, T. L. (1958) 'Management in the 1980s', *Harvard Business Review* (Nov./Dec.).

McKenney, J. L. and McFarlan, F. W. (1982) 'The information archipelago—maps and bridges', *Harvard Business Review* (Sept./Oct.).

Raho, L. E., Belohlar, J. A. and Fieldler, K. D. (1987) 'Assimilating new technology into the organisation: an assessment of McFarlan and McKenney's model', *MIS Quarterly* (March).

Chapter 13

STRATEGIC PLANNING FOR INFORMATION SYSTEMS—QUO VADIS?

INTRODUCTION

Information systems planning has to some extent been carried out since computers arrived on the business scene in the 1950s. However, 'doing' has normally taken precedence over planning, except where critical resources had to be developed or obtained. Planning IS/IT in many organisations was seen as an unnecessary indulgence. Despite this, management has generally come to realise that making such large risky investments as information systems, based on an ever-developing technology requires planning. Business performance gains of all types can be improved further by better planning, provided that the planning is linked in a coherent way to business development.

This book has explored the means by which those planning and management processes can be brought together to produce strategic IS/IT plans and the means to achieve them. It has considered the overall business and management processes required and how various techniques can be adopted in analysis and formulation of strategies. Some of the most valuable models and approaches are summarised in this chapter. It has also considered and offered insight into the aspects of business and IS/IT management that have to be successfully addressed if an appropriate strategy is to be converted to business success. Again, some of the key issues are reprised in this chapter.

In terms of strategic IS/IT planning the story is only just beginning. Whatever processes are being successfully developed and adopted today have to be considered against the backdrop of an erratic evolution of IS/IT in most businesses, the prevailing business pressures faced by organisations and the opportunities and constraints presented by the technology and our understanding of how to use it. All of these will change over time and hence the IS/IT strategic planning and management approaches will evolve and develop as these factors change and as experience accumulates of how best to define and execute strategic IS/IT plans. Carrying out IS/IT strategic studies has been a popular initiation process for many organisations, but as has been said IS/IT strategic planning is an ongoing process not an event, and repeated studies do not offer a smooth path to success.

Comparing the development of IS/IT strategic planning to the development of business strategic planning offers some insight. Tools and techniques of business strategy are continuing to develop and processes are changing—especially to devolve to and involve more of the business expertise spread throughout the organisation. At the current stage of IS/IT development, organisations have to think overtly about IS/IT strategy and for all the suggestion of integration with business planning, it still demands some specialist knowledge to facilitate the process. It will be a long time before it becomes intuitively included in day-to-day strategic thinking. This *was* the case with many aspects of business strategic management, which is perhaps seen now as being more of a practical part of management and less of an esoteric, mystical exercise. IS/IT strategic planning must evolve to become such a natural part of business management practice.

Why? Because as discussed later in this chapter, the future scenarios for IS/IT strategy will involve changing the inherent trading structures of industries and the rationale behind business activities, organisation structures and how people will work. Some of these future areas with potentially significant impact on the integration of IS/IT business strategy are examined below. Like many aspects of business these effects will not announce their presence with a dramatic entry. They will increase in importance slowly but inexorably, and at the same time the constraints to achieving the potential offered will evolve.

RÉSUMÉ OF SOME KEY IDEAS

It is unrealistic to attempt to summarise all the contents of the twelve preceding chapters. However, there are some basic ideas or models which are core concepts in any approach to IS/IT strategic planning. First and foremost is its relationship with corporate and business strategic planning. Two earlier models (see Figures 1.7 and 3.5) have been combined in Figure 13.1 to show three key relationships:

(a) the need to incorporate an understanding of the potential impact of IS/IT on the industry, the corporation and its component businesses;
(b) the best level at which IS/IT strategies can be developed within the corporate umbrella—i.e. at strategic business unit level, with allowance for corporate information requirements plus a process of consolidation to gain potential synergy from business applications;
(c) the differentiation between managing the demand for IS applications to establish needs and priorities to be satisfied by the supply (or IT) strategy. Whether or not *an* IT strategy, or several IT strategies, will be required depends on the similarity or otherwise of the businesses: their competitive situations and strategies, any business interrelationships, common processes, suppliers or customers and organisational structures.

Achieving the appropriate impact is obviously a difficult process due to the need to react to changing circumstances plus the need to plan ahead to supply the applications and supporting coherent infrastructures.

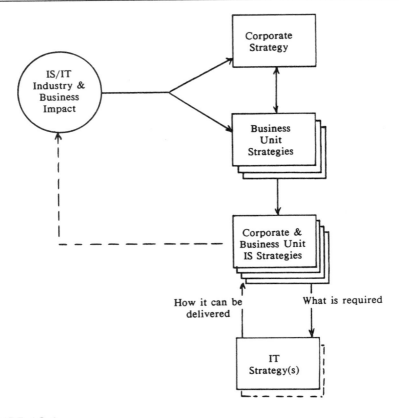

FIGURE 13.1

In order to enable the ongoing IS/IT strategic planning process to allow for evolving circumstances, a number of inputs have to be continually reviewed. These have been classified as:

- external business environment,
- internal business environment,
- external IS/IT environment,
- internal IS/IT environment.

The importance and implications of each have been discussed. The eventual manifestation of all of these is the application portfolio required or possessed at any point in time by the business. That portfolio of applications and its supporting IT strategies will be contributing more or less appropriately to the business in relation to its environment and will be required to evolve over time to contribute more. This implies that applications should be managed according to their value or contribution to the business. The IS, IT and management 'strategies' described are a means to an end—the 'end' being an appropriate application portfolio at each stage of business and IS/IT development. A model of that portfolio, based on the idea originated by McFarlan *et al.* of considering applications as high potential, strategic, factory and support has been a central concept of the book, upon which many aspects of the strategy depend.

Creating the applications portfolio and then developing it further as the business and the systems change over time, implies a process of planning that can interpret the effects of each of the four key inputs continuously. Although an initial strategic IS planning project may be used to realign the planning of IS/IT closer to business planning, the process so established must be capable of rapid and partial reuse to interpret changes in any of the inputs without the need for another extended project. This implies a framework or structure for interpretation in IS application terms of the changes in the environment. The framework is effectively the 'logical' steps in the planning process whereby techniques can be adopted and applied in a coherent way. Following discussion in Chapters 5 and 6 of the various techniques—derived equally from IS/IT and business planning approaches—such a framework is described in Chapter 7. That framework is reproduced in Figure 13.2. It reflects the three main components of the process of developing a strategy:

(a) a thorough understanding of where the organisation is—*a situation appraisal*—and the strengths and weaknesses of that position;
(b) a means of *analysing* where IS/IT applications are needed to meet known business requirements;
(c) a way of *creating* ideas for future investment in IS/IT to make a more valuable contribution in the expected environment.

The process must ensure that a common understanding is reached by all the relevant managers of the business and the IS/IT providers. Then, as anything changes the implications can be re-interpreted and understood by all.

Whilst the application portfolio represents the moving target for the business, the means of achieving it need to be expressed in more detail in terms of the development and operation of systems, the provision of resources and technology and the organisational approach required. The four major components of IS/IT strategies which all have to be managed effectively and co-ordinated by the overall strategy are each considered in more detail in the latter part of the book. These components:

● organisation and resourcing,
● information,
● applications,
● technology,

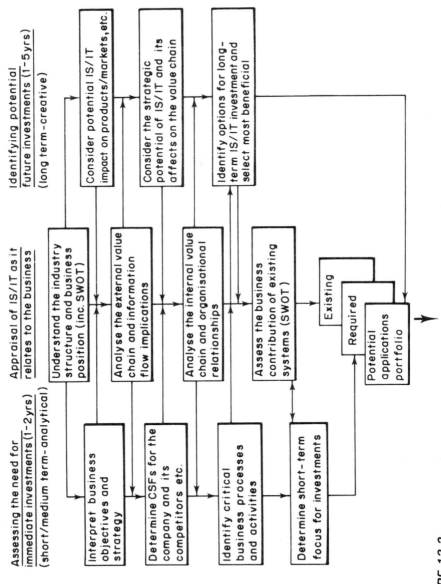

FIGURE 13.2

are each considered within the overall concepts of the portfolio. High level, 'generic', IS/IT strategies were described in Chapter 8, which provide the guiding management principles which lead to pertinent practical processes for managing each of the areas above, once more in proportion to the existing or intended contribution to the business.

These ideas provide approaches to managing all segments of the portfolio, and the relationships between the applications in the different segments which, when compared with other business portfolios, require:

(a) allowance for the evolving/changing contribution over time—the application's business life-cycle;
(b) the re-investment of resources into future applications to capitalise on achievement;
(c) the appropriate deployment of resources and delegation of authority in decision making.

Without doubt, the most important and hence challenging area of the portfolio for business management is the **strategic** box. What strategic information systems in general terms are is described in Chapter 1 and the new management challenges involved in these applications were outlined. Strategic applications involve changing the way business is conducted, either externally or internally, and consequently require an amount of involvement by senior management not traditionally expected and not easily made possible. The concept of 'centrally planning' such applications is not easy to bring about unless senior management commitment and time is overtly made available and mechanisms established to:

(a) convert direction through plans to successful implementation;
(b) be able to continually interpret business objectives and IS/IT potential impact;
(c) ensure all other aspects of IS/IT are being managed effectively without requiring senior management involvement on matters of lesser importance.

Whilst this requires an organisational approach to the provisioning of IS/IT, no current way of doing this seems to provide the appropriate co-ordinating mechanisms in all dimensions. A 'steering group' is suggested by both research and also the 'common sense' concluded by most companies. Figure 13.3 reproduces the steering structure seen earlier in Chapter 9 to propose that such a balanced and tiered structure must be established either organisationally or by an overlay to that organisation. The structure relates the development of strategy to its execution and the ongoing reconciliation of demand and supply and can enable effective co-ordination of applications across related parts of the business.

The overall processes of developing and executing a strategic approach are depicted in a slightly different way in Figure 13.4 to show the conversion and consolidation stages and the need to reflect the business world in the eventual

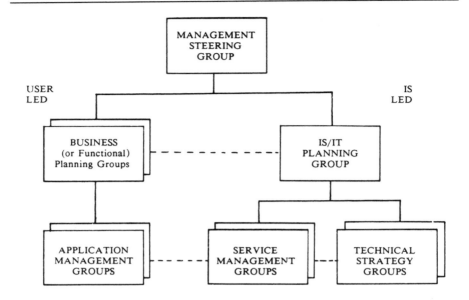

FIGURE 13.3 Steering organisation for IS/IT strategy. The same groupings are required to develop and implement the strategy—a coalition of the users, management and IS/IT professionals

implementation of appropriate systems. The 'steering' mechanism described is aimed at ensuring that can happen in a multidimensional business even when IS/IT cannot be structured in an ideal fashion to meet the unique demands of each business *and* the best infrastructure and most economic means of supply.

Any eventual IS/IT strategy will be the result of many compromises. The issues which affect where and how those compromises should be made will change due to external business factors as well as internal IS/IT factors and the process of strategic management must recognise the need for change and make it happen effectively. As organisations become more dependent on IS/IT for business success and development the compromises will be made less and less because of supply-side issues, although the problem of compromising the long-term plans to satisfy short-term business issues will remain. The decisions are business decisions and the strategy will be at least the basis of understanding the implications as well as guidance for the best trade-off. In the long term the supply-side issues will become less of an economic factor, the value achievable from the best business fit of systems will be better understood and perhaps even possible to quantify.

The steering mechanism is also intended to achieve another critical success factor in IS/IT strategic management—ownership and therefore commitment to the strategy. 'Having' a strategy is not enough, it must be 'owned' and 'believed in'. Strategies can be acquired by a number of routes. How the strategy is

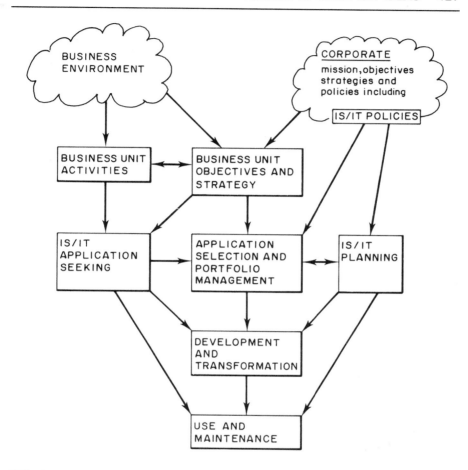

FIGURE 13.4

developed will determine the ownership. Even if senior management sponsor the strategic approach, if it is dominantly produced by IS/IT specialists or even worse, outside consultants, it will not be owned by the business line managers. Development of and agreement to the strategies by all parties in the coalition— users, IS and senior management—is a prerequisite for successful implementation. It is impossible to implement a strategy that key parties do not understand or believe in. It is difficult to understand and believe in something that is developed by others, especially others from outside the business.

Most IS/IT strategies developed to date have only been partially successful. Some have been a waste of time and a few no doubt have caused more problems than they resolved! Organisational ownership is one factor which clearly distinguishes failures from successes.

A recent survey (Brunel University/Kobler Unit of Imperial College, 1987) highlighted a number of other factors which differentiate companies where IS/IT can be seen to be an integral part of the business strategy from those where IS/IT makes a marginal contribution, even in the same industry.

TABLE 13.1

'Successful' Companies	*'Less Successful' Companies*
(A) *Use of IS/IT—main emphases*	
(a) *As a business weapon*	
● response to customers	
● improve delivery times	
● improve company image	● improve company image
● after sales service	
● improve product quality	● reduce product price
(b) *As a managerial tool*	
● faster/better communication	
● data accuracy	
● faster business planning cycle/more responsive	
● decision support	● decision support
	● reduction in staff costs
	● control staff activities
(B) *Management of IS/IT*	
● better informed on IS/IT development and use of IS/IT by competitors	● not interested, leave it to DP people
● use multiple suppliers	● do not shop around for solutions
● learn from mistakes	● repeat mistakes!
● have IS/IT policies linked to business policies	
● set 'two-year' plans and budgets for IS/IT investment and use steering committees to set priorities based on the strategy	● Finance Director sets budget and spend is by DP based on user requests. Priorities not clearly defined
● frame corporate strategies in terms of customers/products/services	● frame strategies in terms of £
● top management informed about IS/IT performance—projects appraised before development and after completion	
● separate resources for current operations from future developments	
● high spend on education and training of all management and IS staff	

Some key points from that survey are shown in Table 13.1 under two basic headings:

(a) How the companies use IS/IT.
(b) How they manage IS/IT.

The messages are reasonably clear and support the overall rationale of this book. Two general conclusions were drawn

(a) There is no correlation between IS/IT spend and business success.
(b) There is good correlation between what IS/IT is used for and how it is managed, and business success.

One could argue that a well run, successful business will also manage IS/IT well and vice versa.

THE FUTURE DEVELOPMENT OF IS/IT STRATEGIC PLANNING

In Chapter 1 a three-era model for the evolution of IS/IT in business was described. The realisation that a business-based IS/IT strategy was important could be said to have dawned at the same time as the strategic information systems era in the 1980s. The increasing complexity of having three objectives—efficiency, effectiveness and competitiveness—plus the greater significance of IS/IT in achieving business success, drove the need for more strategic approaches to planning and management. However, the IS/IT strategy cannot only consider the strategic subset of the applications and their implications since they do not exist in isolation either from the business or other systems or use of resources. Hence the strategy has to deal with the whole portfolio and its evolution in both demand and supply.

The processes of IS/IT strategic planning described in this book are therefore principally the result of the latest era of information systems. To determine the approaches for the future therefore, it would help if the nature of the '4th era' could be understood early and new approaches developed. These may then either supplement what has been described here or potentially replace it. Predicting the nature of the 4th era is not easy but some of the themes may be easier to identify. Two in particular seem worth exploring further.

ORGANISATIONAL DEVELOPMENT BASED ON IS/IT

Drucker's suggestion that information and systems will be the key factor in organisation design is embodied in a quote from his article (Drucker, 1988) already mentioned.

> We are entering a period of change—*a shift* from the command and control organisation, *to the information-based organisation*—the organisation of knowledge specialists . . . it is the management challenge of the future!

This implies that businesses and organisations may be built around information structures rather than IS being used to make a business or organisation structure work more effectively. There already are examples of businesses which have been devised and developed purely on the ability of IS/IT to enable new ways of doing business. Argos, the showroom retailer, is such a business. They have provided a service to customers based on information about products (like mail-order) but with the ability to make the item available instantly, without holding any significant stock of their own. 'Comp-u-card' is a similar business concept. Where the business is new, organising the functions and people around the systems is easier than converting an existing business to that approach. Whether the IS/IT potential can become the key driving force behind the business strategy and structure of all types of organisation is doubtful but many more companies will become primarily service based and most services are both knowledge and information intensive. Service industries represent the highest growth sector of the economy.

It could therefore be argued that 'organisational design' rather than 'organisational fit' will be a key consideration in IS/IT strategy. Strategies for dealing with the organisational relationships, job and people changes implied will become more important. In Chapter 3 'human impact policies' were mentioned as one of the products of strategy, but have not really been discussed in more depth. Basic policies regarding how pay and job descriptions associated with systems implementations will be dealt with are often outlined in strategies but more far-reaching implications on organisation structuring and job roles are rarely mentioned. This book has mainly considered how a business strategy can be either enhanced or in some cases be formulated on the potential offered by IS/IT. It appears that many companies are now asking questions like 'In what aspects of our business can IS/IT help us achieve our goals?' rather than 'What is the bottom line on this project?' This book shows how these new questions can be addressed and then translated into achievement. IS/IT impact on the *business* is perhaps beginning to be assessed in a coherent way.

But how many companies ask questions such as 'Before we re-organise what effect will it have on the use of our information resource?' let alone 'Could we re-organise to exploit our information resources?' Many reorganisations of activities and individuals have destroyed information structures, meant IS/IT investments are prematurely obsolete or simply decay into uselessness. Others complain that reorganisation is less feasible because of constraints imposed by systems (or even technology). That complaint is at least a realisation that IS/IT and the organisation are interrelated. The traditional response has been to attempt to produce 'organisational independent (data driven)' systems. This is extremely expensive and very difficult when the business is also changing. Inevitably, it limits IS/IT investments to the lowest common denominator of general requirements to reduce its effect as a constraint! Obviously IS/IT use can be made more responsive to organisational and personnel changes by better design. However, in the future management should consider how it can develop the organisation to exploit IS/IT before making the changes. This will require a far better understanding of the impact of IS/IT on organisational relationships, job roles, use of knowledge, etc. which in time will provide new techniques of analysis to add to the strategic tool-kit.

Charles Handy (1989) in his book *The Age of Unreason* opens up the whole subject of what will future organisations consist of and how will they be 'structured', if at all! Like others he suggests that 'intellectual capital' will become the critical strategic resource of many organisations in achieving advantages. The technology employed in coherent systems of information gathering, retrieval and use will be the key to releasing this new capital. He suggests that IT will change what people do, where and how they do it and the organisations they do it for or in! IT, combined with social changes, changing population balances and economic consequences will mean that organisations will have to use information systems better if they are to remain effective in obtaining and keeping highly skilled staff. However, as he says 'technology is neutral—we can use it to enrich our lives or let them lose all meaning'.

Both Handy and Drucker suggest how organisation structures will change, becoming flatter, more federal and flexible, even to quote Handy 'Shamrock shaped'—a three-leafed structure comprising a management or professional critical core of people, a largely subcontracted set of specialist skilled resources and a flexible, part-time distributed low skilled workforce, all linked through systems to carry out and control, allocate and plan the work to be done. The point is made that in 1989 it is cheaper to dictate a letter to a typist in Taiwan from an office in London than get a secretary in London to type it!

Undoubtedly we are only at the start of the process of understanding and taking appropriate advantage from the potential IS/IT offers for organisational change and development. It will require a major change in management thinking (plus some new tools or techniques of analysis perhaps) before the full implications are realised. However, again to quote Handy 'it is the changes in the way our work is organised which will make the biggest differences to the way we will live'. And IS/IT will be one of the most significant causes of such changes.

INDUSTRY DEVELOPMENT BASED ON IS/IT

The other potential '4th era' is the result of extensive development of the currently embryonic electronic trading systems. Many of the 'strategic information systems' examples quoted in this book and elsewhere involve either systems to link organisations in an industry together or develop new types of product or service. Electronic Data Interchange (EDI) and Value Added Data Services (VADS) have become the subject of considerable interest not only for companies but also for governments. Many reports have been written to consider the potential implications of the use of inter-company information systems and the technological infrastructure to support them. The Department of Trade and Industry Report

'The Economic Effects of Value Added and Data Services' (DTI, 1987) concluded in 1987 that:

(a) Key limiting factors for wider exploitation were

- customer resistance to changing conventional business practice and scepticism about the benefits;
- a failure to achieve the critical mass of sufficient firms in the business sector;
- lack of data standards.

(b) The effects so far on industries are variable as are the reasons for investment, e.g.:

- in motor and retailing industries the main objective is cost reduction in dealing with suppliers;
- in financial services new products and services can be launched more effectively;
- in travel better, faster service can lead to a significant competitive edge.

The report overall suggests that whilst some economies from EDI/VADS use are beginning to be seen, only a few companies and fewer industries are adopting electronic trading as part of the business strategy.

Many others who have studied what companies are doing in terms of EDI based applications conclude that

(a) 'EDI' is more than a technical development to extend data exchange across companies;
(b) it changes the relationships between trading partners;
(c) it usually requires consequent internal reorganisation of the company and its systems to achieve the benefits;
(d) the key issues to be addressed are business and management, not technological;
(e) the 'EDI' approach is at a very early stage of development—perhaps comparable with the arrival of 'computers' as a business tool.

Robinson and Stanton (1987) propose a developmental model of the increasing opportunities presented by EDI and how the management of the organisation must become increasingly involved in the process of decision making to enable opportunities to be exploited. They identify four main types of potential benefit:

(a) *Process automation*—e.g. exchange of invoices, etc.
(b) *Boundary extension*—integrating the processes carried out by the trading

partner with the company and probably changing the way those processes are carried out internally;

(c) *Service enhancement*—providing more or difficult types of information to trading partners to help partners develop their business;

(d) *Product innovation*—providing something which the customer requires based on information or a processing service he will pay for.

At each stage the inter-company relationship becomes more mutually dependent. For each stage of development the understanding of the issues and establishing the strategy for exploitation becomes more of a subject for senior management. Eventually the whole nature of the business, how it trades with others, the activities it performs and hence how it is organised may well change significantly.

A number of these views can be brought together to show that over time EDI will facilitate major new aspects of business relationships, although progress in different industries will vary due to a number of factors. EDI-based trading systems can essentially occur at four levels of increasing complexity and interdependence.

Level 1—Transaction Passing Systems—normally batched and sent via a network carrier (VADS) to customers or suppliers for processing in due course.

Level 2—Enquiry or Information Exchange—allowing a customer or supplier to enquire directly on data held on the company's computer systems.

Level 3—Transaction driven interactive systems where an 'online' transaction triggers action and a response on the supplier/customer system based on processing the transaction.

Level 4—Interactive processing systems where several steps in processing can be carried out interactively on both supplier and customer system using and updating information from both parties.

Obviously each stage requires greater co-operation to agree data standards and information meanings, processing specification, even systems design, as well as other obvious aspects such as security. This implies increasing trust between organisations and a realisation of the growing mutual interdependence. Given that an organisation deals wtih many suppliers and customers, many of whom trade with its competitors, this will make any move beyond Level 2 very difficult. Existing VADS only really offer the capability for Levels 1 and 2—further stages require significant changes in trading practice within industries (Level 3) and also changes inside organisations (Level 4).

In Chapter 6 a number of examples of successful EDI-based systems were discussed and techniques for identifying the implications based around the concept of value chain analysis were considered. The essence was to understand how information flows in the industry and the primary activities of the business could be better organised to the advantage of the enterprise, and also trading partners. Taking the longer-term view, no organisation dealing with many suppliers and customers, each of whom is a part of a complex chain (maybe linking to other industries), can decide how it can exploit EDI in isolation from other parties. Obviously the more dominant a company is in an industry the greater pressure it will be able to exert on others to conform to what it wants to do.

This can be seen by the effects major UK retailers such as Marks & Spencer, Sainsburys and B&Q are having on the way EDI-based systems are having to be adopted by clothing, grocery and DIY suppliers. Equally, Thomson's Holidays have established standards for the use of EDI-based systems for dealing not only with the travel agents, but also with the holiday component suppliers (airlines, hotels, etc.). Car manufacturers such as Ford are establishing logistics and design system standards with their component suppliers. Similarly, in aerospace the major companies are setting the pace which their suppliers must follow.

It can be summarised by saying that through the 1980s the major companies in many industries are determining the EDI systems strategy and therefore aspects of the business strategy of other companies in their industry. This may continue in the future but at some stage it is likely that strategies for exploiting EDI-based systems for the whole industry will have to be developed. This has already been attempted in some industries such as chemicals, where within Europe an EDI messaging standard has been established. In most cases it has tended to uncover the potential problems of devising such systems in international markets rather than conclude the ideal way ahead. These potential issues and problems are highlighted in an article 'The Coming Chaos in Paperless Trading' (Evans, 1989). These include:

- the implementation of the EDI FACT standard within and across industries;
- implementing EDI requires no new technology, but does need a change in business process and practice and therefore a management approach to its use;
- competitiveness between VADS suppliers leads to incompatible solutions;
- security fears of competitors using the same network;
- a great shortage of skills to develop/implement EDI-based systems.

Successful networks in Europe include those in airline and insurance industries where international data standards and information conventions have long existed. Other industries have never developed standards sufficiently precise for the use of EDI to be easily implemented.

As electronic trading between organisations develops so will 'electronic markets' through which buyers can select products and services from a range of sellers, via a value added network service. Examples already exist from TELCOT (the electronic Texas Cotton market) to Comp-U-Card (selling consumer-durables). Many such examples are quoted in an article by Malone *et al.* (1989) who also argue that electronic markets will make fundamental changes to how some firms conduct their business. They believe firms will move away from vertical integration within the value chain and towards specialisation in one process within the value chain. Trading exchanges between the firms in the chain will become much more efficient, reducing the potential economic advantages of the firm taking over a number of processes in the chain.

The obvious general conclusion from this is that in the future many key aspects of an enterprise's IS/IT strategy will be outside its direct control. Its IS/IT strategy will not only have to link with its business strategy, but also with the IS/IT and even business strategies of its trading partners and even competitors.

IMPLICATIONS FOR IS/IT STRATEGIC PLANNING IN THE '4th ERA'

IS/IT will obviously become an increasingly important factor in how well organisations achieve their goals, especially in competitive environments. The two main concepts of this 4th era, organisation and industry development, will in time affect all organisations in public and private sectors. Figure 13.5 attempts to show this in the context of the previous three-era model, by extending the model to include the ideas considered above.

The future will almost certainly involve using inter-company trading systems, initially perhaps for efficiency gains, but later to change relationships between firms and processes in the industry value chain. This perhaps in conjunction with the changing organisation and job structuring options partly enabled by IS/IT will make information and systems a more important consideration in developing the organisation. Both of these moves, plus the ability to develop new products and services and hence the nature of the industry, will lead from firms changing the conduct of their business, to the structure and relationships in and between industries being fundamentally altered. This is already happening. The third, or strategic era will probably 'explode' into three (or perhaps more) parallel but related threads in IS/IT strategic development.

Meiklejohn, in an article in *Management Today* (Meiklejohn, 1989), emphasises the interrelationship of these threads and the significant implications for management. He discusses how companies that do not simultaneously look at the role of IS/IT in the business environment and trading relationships *and* to change of the organisational structure to exploit IS/IT will become rapidly less competitive. Managing such a transformation to a more information driven business and organisation will be a major challenge for the executives of the 1990s, and a challenge most are not currently knowledgeable enough to address coherently.

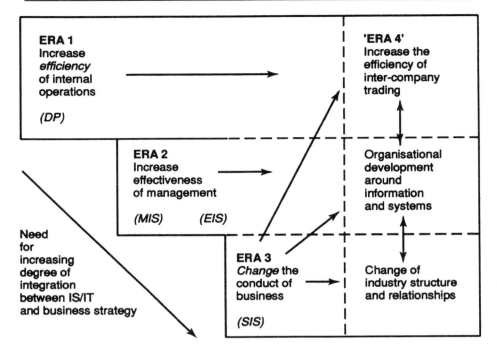

FIGURE 13.5

Some of the implications of this for IS/IT strategic planning would seem to be:

1. The relationship between the business strategy and the components of IS/IT strategies will become more complex but more appropriate. Historically the IT part of the IS/IT strategy has dominated the process, probably because IT management initiated 'strategies' in most cases. This book has shown how an IS strategy should drive the IT strategy and how *information* planning and management is a key part of that strategy. However, information needs should drive the application strategy and influence the technical options required. It is too simplistic to say 'information strategy should precede systems strategy should precede technology strategy'—they are interdependent and in a real world the applications will often be developed before the value of the information base obtained is understood. However, more of the strategic planning effort will have to be devoted to developing the information resource within the context of the industry. This is both from the viewpoint of operational data and information exchange and exploiting the data resource *vis-à-vis* competitors in the market place at all levels within the organisation.

This implies, of course, involvement in establishing data standards within and across industries and implementing those standards for internal as well as external purposes. Overall the means of devising an *information strategy* and hence a robust and usable information architecture will have to be improved and the process must more easily involve senior and line management. Perhaps the concept of the application portfolio should be extended to produce an information portfolio, both of which should be used together in defining the strategies for how the technology, data and resource should be managed. Perhaps the model to be used should be that shown in Figure 13.6, indicating a corporately driven information portfolio approach linking into the more 'local' application and information portfolios of the business units.

2. The availability of skills and resources at all levels of IS/IT planning and implementation will be scarce. At the lower levels new skills for the new types of applications and technologies will have to be developed by organisations and purchased in the market place. More significantly managers of business functions will have to become more aware of the potential beneficial changes from developing the business and the organisation around its information resources and systems. This can be partly achieved by using outside consulting skills but the management must become more educated in identifying, planning and implementing those changes.

In dealing with the more global implications at an industry or even inter-industry level, the organisation and its top management must actively discover what their suppliers, customers and competitors are using IS/IT for and deduce the implications for their company. In general companies employ consultants today to help identify 'what should our IS/IT strategy be?' Almost inevitably this produces a strong focus on internal issues. In future the external skills required should be perhaps more to understand what is happening in the world outside. Undoubtedly more specialist industry-based IS/IT strategy skills are being developed by consultancies. Using such generally available, if expensive, knowledge may help the organisation avoid disadvantage but to gain advantage the management need to develop a unique understanding of how IS/IT can enhance *its* business strategies. As a consequence the organisation must be capable of developing its own IS/IT strategy and implementing it at least in the critical areas where advantage is sought.

Irrespective of the means used to develop an IS/IT strategy, a strategic management mechanism must be established to carry out and update the strategy in line with the business direction. That implies senior management must continuously update themselves on the state of IS/IT in the industry and the appropriateness of the firm's existing systems, plans and resources. They will inevitably, if reluctantly, have to be actively involved in defining application and information architectures, rather than be merely specifiers or clients for systems projects. To do this they will have to acquire some new knowledge

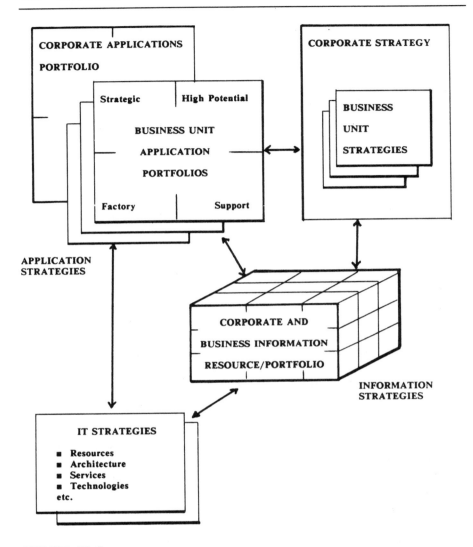

FIGURE 13.6

and skills, as would be expected in any other field of business management where change will produce a potentially significant impact.

3. Some points above could be seen as simplistic repetition of points made about senior management and IS/IT over the last 20 years! 'Involvement, commitment, etc.' of senior management has been preached by almost everyone. The problem has been, what should they do and how can they do it? Until recently the sum total of practical involvement seemed to be to convert

objectives into Critical Success Factors and hence establish some information needs and perhaps priorities for systems investment. Other than that, the tools and techniques available for thinking strategically about IS/IT have been low level application based methods, unsuitable for obtaining a clear vision of what has to be done. This book has brought together these IS/IT based techniques with derivations of business strategy techniques such as portfolio and value chain analysis. These are more meaningful to executive management, but in spite of the framework defined in this book they remain largely a kit of tools and techniques rather than a totally comprehensive and assured means of identifying the ideal strategy, to meet every set of circumstances.

Business strategic planning has evolved from specialist tools to a management process, which accommodates many aspects of strategic analysis and management practice yet still requires creativity and good judgement. The same improvements can and will be made to the process of developing IS/IT strategies, to reduce the uncertainty involved, but perhaps never make it a certain science!

At the lower levels of application management, more assured engineering based approaches, and greater automation plus faster implementation can make each application satisfy specific requirements more effectively and economically. Even where this fails the application can be changed more easily! Quality and productivity can be improved together and even a degree of flexibility can be built in! By modelling and prototyping, the system requirements can be refined and feasibility evaluated and even tested to avoid meeting the wrong needs, the wrong way! Some of these lessons and even the software ideas can be translated into the strategic planning process. Currently many CASE tools are being adapted to help support strategic planning studies, the data collection, analysis and documentation especially.

What appears to be needed, and indeed may be feasible in due course, is to use IS/IT itself to simulate the business in its environment to enable analysis and even creative ideas to be tested and then to comprehensively document the output as an IS/IT strategy (capable of 'automatic' update if any parameter in the simulation changes). The techniques included in the modelling and simulation would probably derive from both the business and IS/IT techniques currently in use or more sophisticated combinations developed for the purpose. All of value chain analysis, critical success factors, organisational modelling, entity analysis and functional decomposition could ostensibly be brought together in a modelling or simulation process. The term *'enterprise modelling'* might be appropriately coined to describe the process of simulating the organisation in its environment, to establish not only information and systems strategies but also better business practices and organisation structures. Such a model would be a significant aid to strategic planning and could be both logically and physically developed using today's technology. It would still only represent one view of the business which is more than a set of simulated activities, financial ratios, resources, customers and products, etc. It has a culture, values, beliefs and is run and populated by people whose eccentricities and talent will never be able to be simulated in any model.

Research into enterprise modelling to establish the ideal and realisable information, systems and even business strategies has been pursued rather tentatively in the past. Such research could now produce the means of developing more effective IS/IT strategies in the future, especially if the enterprise modelling approach could become easily used by the business managers. The development of IS/IT strategy cannot be automated but it could be made a lot easier using sophisticated technology which brings together and enhances the tools and techniques of analysis described in this book. Such research may well reveal the means of developing IS/IT strategies in the next decade.

SUMMARY

What will happen in the future is obviously conjecture. What happened in the past is obviously history! Henry Ford said 'History is Bunk!' and maybe that is relevant to IS/IT strategic planning! Perhaps fortunately there is little history of IS/IT strategic planning to go on, but there has built up a significant history of IS/IT activity, even in 30 years, and much of it has definitely the status of 'bunk!' The process of strategic planning for information systems is new and rapidly evolving as experience, both good and bad, is obtained. Already the extended, expensive strategic study is deemed worthless, yet it only really started a few years ago. This book has described what seems to be possible, indeed feasible and practical as we enter the 1990s, and for the next few years the messages will be relevant to most organisations attempting to tackle the problem. *But* if you consider how the Boston Square of cash cows, etc. attracted the attention of management for the first time 25 years ago to the ways of devising business strategies, and then that the application portfolio grid has only in the late 1980s achieved a similar usefulness in IS/IT strategy, it is easy to see how far there is to go before IS/IT strategic planning becomes as well researched and developed as say marketing or financial planning.

This book is one of very few that address the issues of strategic information systems planning. It will need to be updated as the theory and practice develop. We are at the start of an era—IS/IT strategies are becoming very important to organisations. Therefore the means of developing such a strategy and managing it to success are also important. Few of even the best managed organisations have good IS/IT strategies. Everyone is still learning, and there is, no doubt, much to learn. But remember the art of *Strategic Planning for Information Systems* is very much the art of the possible.

REFERENCES

A survey by Brunel University/Kobler Unit of Imperial College (1987) *The Strategic Use of IT Systems*.

Drucker, P. F. (1988) 'The coming of the new organisation', *Harvard Business Review* (January–February).

Handy, C. (1989) *The Age of Unreason*, Business Books Ltd.

DTI (1987) The Vanguard Initiative report for the Department of Trade & Industry *The Economic Effects of Value Added Data Services*, Her Majesty's Stationery Office.

Robinson, D. G. and Stanton, S. A. (1987) 'Exploit EDI before EDI exploits you', *The Executives Journal* (Spring).

Evans, R. (1989) 'The coming chaos in paperless trading', *International Management* (January).

Malone, T. W., Yates, J. and Benjamin, R. I. (1989) 'The logic of electronic markets', *Harvard Business Review* (May–June).

Meiklejohn, I. (1989) 'New forms for a new age', *Management Today* (May).

INDEX